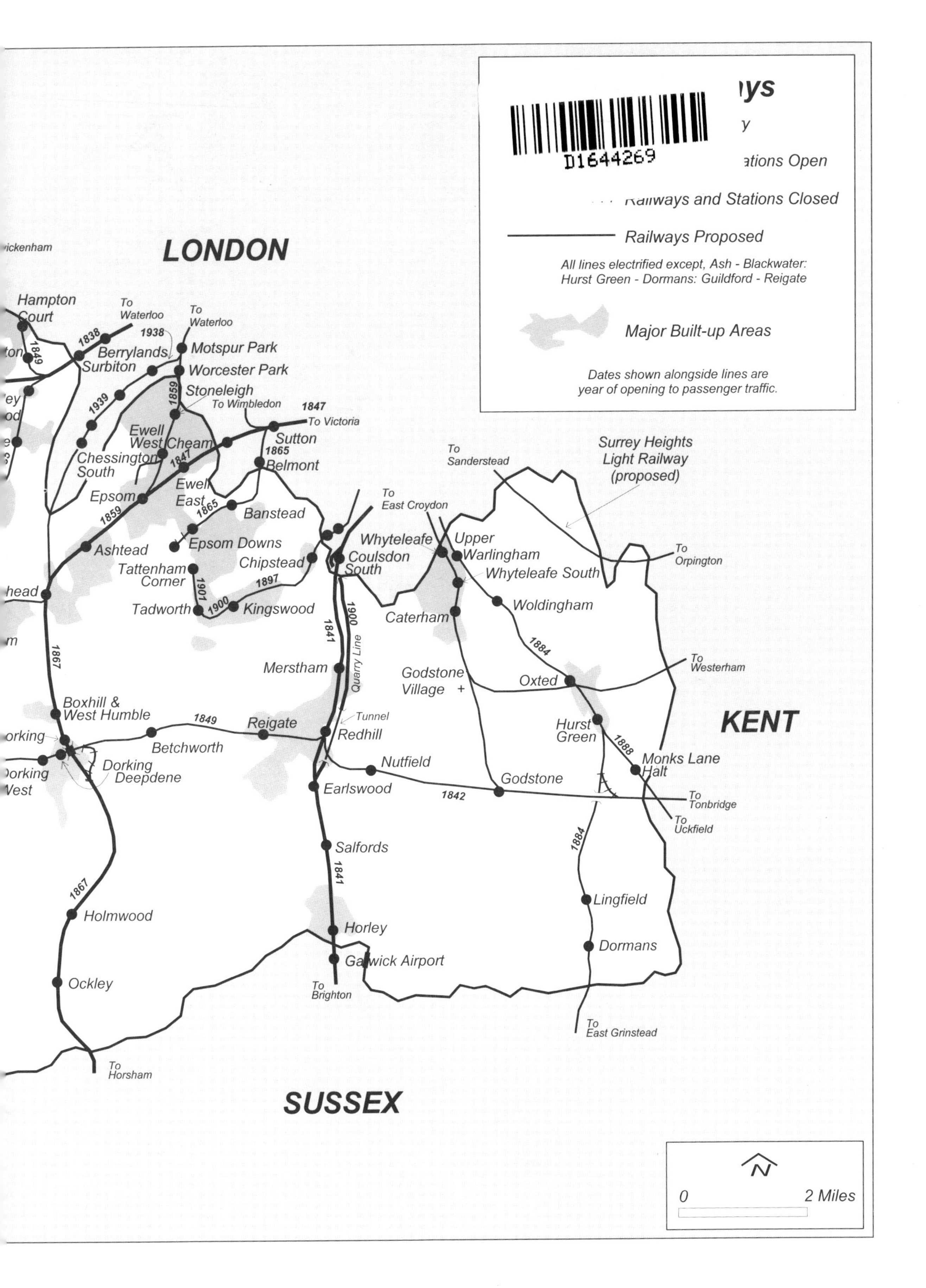

D1644269
Railways and Stations Closed
Railways Proposed
All lines electrified except, Ash - Blackwater: Hurst Green - Dormans: Guildford - Reigate
Major Built-up Areas
Dates shown alongside lines are year of opening to passenger traffic.
LONDON
KENT
SUSSEX
Hampton Court
To Waterloo
To Waterloo
1838
1938
1849
Berrylands
Surbiton
Motspur Park
Worcester Park
Stoneleigh
1939
1859
To Wimbledon
1847
To Victoria
Ewell West
Cheam
Sutton
1865
Chessington South
1847
Belmont
Epsom
Ewell East
1865
Banstead
1859
Epsom Downs
Ashtead
Tattenham Corner
Chipstead
1901
1897
Tadworth
1900
Kingswood
To East Croydon
Whyteleafe
Upper Warlingham
Coulsdon South
Whyteleafe South
Woldingham
Caterham
To Sanderstead
Surrey Heights Light Railway (proposed)
To Orpington
1900
1841
Quarry Line
Merstham
1867
1884
Godstone Village
Oxted
To Westerham
Boxhill & West Humble
1849
Reigate
Tunnel
Redhill
Hurst Green
Betchworth
Dorking Deepdene
Nutfield
1888
Monks Lane Halt
Godstone
Earlswood
1842
To Tonbridge
To Uckfield
Salfords
1884
1841
1867
Holmwood
Lingfield
Horley
Dormans
Gatwick Airport
Ockley
To Brighton
To East Grinstead
To Horsham
N
0
2 Miles

The Railway In SURREY

Alan A Jackson

TRANSPORT
Atlantic
PUBLISHERS

Published by Atlantic Transport Publishers
Trevithick House, West End, Penryn, Cornwall TR10 8HE

ISBN 0 906899 90 7

Design by Richard Joy, Paris
Reproduction & Printing by The Amadeus Press,
Huddersfield, West Yorkshire

All uncredited pictures are from the author's collection; it has not proved possible to establish correct attribution for these from information available on the reverse of the image or otherwise.

British Cataloguing in Publication Data
A catalogue record for this book is available from the British Library

Contents

ABBREVIATIONS

nb: Surnames other than those shown here which are cited as sources in the main part of the book refer to works included in the bibliography.

Bevan	*Tourists' Guide to Surrey*, G Phillips Bevan, 1887
ch	chains (see 'Dates and Distances' below)
CM&GIR	Croydon, Merstham & Godstone Iron Railway
Faulkner & Williams	Faulkner, J.N, and Williams, R.A, *The LSWR in the Twentieth Century*, 1988
GWR	Great Western Railway
L&BR	London & Brighton Railway
L&SWR	London & South Western Railway
LB&SCR	London Brighton & South Coast Railway
LCC	London County Council
m	miles
NRA	National Rifle Association
RG&RR	Reading, Guildford & Reigate Railway
SCC	Surrey County Council
SCC/HT	Surrey County Council Highways & Transportation Department *Rail Line Improvements in Surrey* Report, 1995
Scott	Scott,The Rev. W.J, 'London Outer Suburban Services', *Railway & Travel Monthly*, 1910-11
SE&CR	South Eastern & Chatham Railways Joint Managing Committee .
SER	South Eastern Railway
Thorne	*Handbook to the Environs of London*, James Thorne,1876
TPO	Travelling Post Office
Williams I/II	Williams, R.A, *The London & South Western Railway* Vols I and II, 1968, 1973

DATES & DISTANCES

Opening dates given are the first day on which public service was operated or facilities were available for public use; as far as possible, the closure dates given are the last full day on which public services were operated.

Most distances are as stated in official publications, ie in Imperial Measure (80 chains = 8 furlongs = 1,760 yards = one mile = 1.61 km),

THE RAILWAY IN SURREY

Author's Preface

This work is intended as a tribute to Surrey's railways, used intensively by the author during 40 years residence in the county, first at Ashtead and latterly at Dorking, in houses never beyond the welcome sight and sound of trains. It was written at a time when Surrey's railways seemed about to complete a full cycle. Here, as elsewhere, they began as small or medium-sized private companies, soon to form up into three large ones which, in 1923, merged into the Southern Railway, one of only four major private companies covering the whole of Great Britain. This so-called 'grouping' lasted only until 1948, when the county's network became part of an integrated nation-wide system under public ownership and under that, a single network was sensibly formed to manage the passenger services in London and the South East. As the book was being written, political dogma, under the banner of 'market forces', was imposing a convoluted and costly process of 'privatised' fragmentation amidst a sea of controversy. What public benefit might result from this seems questionable but at least the lawyers will be richly-rewarded, just as they were before 1923. Complications, confusion and blame-passing certainly abound: Surrey now has no less than five train operating companies and behind them, a numerous supporting cast: Railtrack, Rail Regulator, OFRAF, Freight operator, ROSCOs et al.

But it is not with management structures and organisation (or even very much with locomotives and rolling stock or train services) that we are concerned here. Rather it is with the way the county's rail system developed, its subsequent modernisation, and (sometimes simultaneous) retrenchment; and above all, with the interaction between the railway and Surrey's fabric, life and evolution since the first line was opened in 1838.

For the purposes of this book, Surrey is the administrative county which emerged from the local government reorganisation of 1974. In the interests of logic and cohesion there is some trespassing over the boundary into adjacent areas, including the enclaves of Sunningdale, Poyle and Colnbrook recently given to Berkshire. Certain railways crossing the boundary with Greater London - the Epsom Downs, Tattenham Corner, Hampton Court, Shapperton and West Drayton-Staines branches, receive less thorough attention than the other Surrey lines becauuse they feature in another book*, in which railway and social history have been interwoven in a similar way.

To avoid tedious overloading of the main text, data which merits inclusion for reference purposes has been assembled in six Appendices. Here readers unfamiliar with the old private railway companies will find the 'family tree' underlying names and initials now familiar only to a dwindling band of cognoscenti.

Dr Edwin Course of the University of Southampton and the late John Faulkner, President and Librarian of the Railway Club, friends of many years standing, kindly read early drafts and made valuable suggestions. Thanks are also due to George Burnett, Head of Passenger Transport Services, Surrey County Council Highways & Transportation Department for commenting on Chapter 10 and to his staff for supplying statistics of passenger traffic; to

*_London's Local Railways,_ (Second Edition 1999).

Above *'Farnham: The 9.01' From the 1966 painting by John Verney* (reproduced by kind permission of Lady Verney)

Stephen Fortescue, for information on the Bookham area; to N E C (Ted) Molyneaux for help with military history; to Paul W. Sowan for assistance with the history and location of the extractive industries and their railways; to G A Jacobs for checking the appendix on signalling modernisation and supplying additional material; to J B Horne for comments on rail-served public utility undertakings; to David A Ruddom for elucidation on aspects of bus history; to Gordon W Green and Andrew Neale of the Industrial Railway Society for assistance with this aspect; and to Hugh Compton for answering questions on navigable waterway facilities. Lady Verney graciously agreed to reproduct ion of her husband's 1966 picture of Farnham station, *The Nine-One*, which so vividly and wittily portrays an important aspect of the theme.

ALAN A JACKSON
Dorking, March 1998

On the Opening of the Railroad to Dorking

Sure old Time's runnning on with a step passing fast
For the railroad to Dorking is open at last
And where nought save green pastures and cornfields were found
Now the Train casts its Smoke, Fire and Cinders around.

Yes the Railroad is come! In our quiet old Town
People run to and fro, looking out for 'the Down'
And the Rustics all gaping with wonder are still
As the 'Four Twenty-Five' rises over the Hill!

Oh, how changed from the time when with trappings so fair
BROAD's grey team rattled through the clear summer air
And himself on the coach-box so trim and so neat
Cracked his whip as they cheerily dashed up the street.

Surely changings and shiftings on all sides we view
For the times are all changed and we change with them too
Where our sires were content to arrive there in four
We complain if we don't get to Town in an hour.

And now that our Railroad has opened so true
May it do all the good we hope it would do
May it further our pleasure, our trade, our renown,
Be of use to our Gentry, our Tradesmen, OUR TOWN.

W H HART (1849)

CHAPTER ONE

The Fortunate County

Owing to its vicinity to the metropolis, no county in England is better off for travelling facilities than is Surrey. The London and South Western, London Brighton and South Coast, London, Chatham and Dover and the South Eastern, supply almost every village with a railway, and frequently with two.

-Tourists' Guide to Surrey (Bevan), 1887

Although the last part of this statement was always an exaggeration, it is certainly true that Surrey is very well-endowed with railways. And, uniquely among British counties, it retains almost all the lines and stations it ever had, most of them in heavy daily use. Of an all-time maximum of almost 100 public passenger stations, a mere dozen or so have been closed without replacement*, whilst only three railways of significant length have been completely closed.

Since details of these abandonments will be given later, it will suffice here to note briefly that Ash Junction to Farnham Junction via Tongham, 3 3/4 miles, was closed to passengers in 1937, to freight in 1960; that Guildford (Peasmarsh Junction) to the Surrey border at Baynards via Cranleigh, just over 9 1/2 miles, was closed to public freight traffic in 1962, to passengers in 1965; and that Colnbrook to Staines, 3 1/4 miles, was closed to passengers in 1965 and to all traffic in 1981. This adds up to only 16 1/2 miles, but a tiny fraction of the county's railway route mileage.

Reasons for Surrey's happy immunity from rail closures are not hard to find. Proximity to London has for long supplied its rail operators with a healthy and demanding passenger business, both commuter and off peak. And in recent years we have seen a growing public awareness of the value of the railway as a fast and environmentally-friendly alternative to journeys on the increasingly-congested and polluted motor roads around London. Driving into inner London from Surrey has become more unpleasant and tedious with each year that passes as the 'sheer weight of traffic', to use a laboured media term, grows ever heavier. In an age of unrestricted and thoughtless over-use of the private motor car, which may now be ending, it is significant that the train services offered to Surrey's towns and many smaller settlements remain far superior to those at most places of comparable size outside the south-east.

In its first sixty years or so, as elsewhere in Britain, the railway in Surrey did much to influence the mobility of the population and dilute local customs and dialects; it speeded up the transmission of news and mail, created a degree of uniformity in building styles and required local time to be replaced by Greenwich Mean Time. These and other general changes to the national social and intellectual fabric which followed the spread of the railway system have been admirably described and discussed by Professor Jack Simmons.** Here we shall concentrate on what the railway did in one small but very important part of south east England, which it soon made into an extension of the metropolis, albeit an often pleasantly scenic one.

London's influence on Surrey does of course predate the railway but its arrival mightily accelerated the process. Since the middle of the 19th century,

* *See Appendix I*

** *In his* The Railway in Town and Country 1830-1914 *(1986) and* The Victorian Railway, *(1991)*

Above *Refreshment and rest for the weary traveller:* The Star & Garter Hotel, *strategically placed at the end of the Approach to Dorking station, LB&SCR, displaying an impressive range of shrubs in about 1905. The omnibus connecting the station with the town and the SER station has been drawn forward for the photographer* Commercial postcard.

the association of the railway with the development of the county as the home for many of those making their money in the capital city has been strong. There was also a reverse flow, once significant, but now much less so. Surrey was long known as 'London's playground' and here again the railway greatly advanced an existing trend. For around a hundred years or more, before the spread of car ownership to all but the most disadvantaged levels of society, it provided cheap and convenient access for Londoners to the Surrey countryside, at first for short or extended holidays and later for day trips devoted to rambling, racegoing and other recreational pursuits.

When considering the question of London's influence, it is interesting to note that railway companies serving Surrey, in particular the L&SWR, successfully kept the London local companies at bay, resisting all attempts to invade their territory beyond the continuously built-up area. Later in the book we shall see how the Metropolitan District Railway's expansionist ideas were frustrated by the construction of the L&SWR's New Guildford line. There is also some evidence to suggest that the L&SWR's fear that the Central London tube railway might somehow manage to tap its lucrative Thames Valley residential traffic played a part in its 1912 decision to electrify suburban services. And in the 1920s, the SR sought to gain some control over any proposals to project the Morden tube further into Surrey.

For many years Surrey's rail traffics fell into two categories of almost equal importance in terms of revenue. The principal arteries have always carried passengers and freight in transit between points outside the county, e.g. between London and Brighton or London and Hampshire and Wessex, and more recently, between Gatwick Airport and a variety of traffic centres as well as London. Secondly there is the traffic starting and/or ending journeys within the county boundary, our main concern here. Although in this group commuting remains important, the variety and weight of other passenger train traffic was under severe attack by road transport from the early 1920s. Churns of 'railway milk', originating on Surrey farms and moving to London daily had vanished from station platforms by around 1930. After the 1970s, passenger trains no longer carried London daily newspapers to Surrey stations ; the evening papers were the last - we recall the vans waiting at Ashtead in the 1960s for the bundles to be thrown out on to the platform from the guard's van. Carriage of letter and parcels mail to and from Surrey stations by passenger train ceased in the 1980s, leaving only a small amount of parcels business. Towards the end, mailbags were often stacked up in locked compartments of passenger trains, their peculiar smell lingering to intrigue commuters' noses next morning. We shall see later that as early as the 1880s an assessment of relative costs had led the Post Office to transfer back to road transport some non-urgent parcels traffic through Surrey.

With regard to the passengers themselves, it should be said that until the 1910s, the business was largely confined to the upper and middle classes; Surrey's manual workers, particularly farm hands, were rarely seen on the railway especially if based some distance from a station. Turner notes that before the opening of the New Guildford line in 1885, a wagonette working a daily run from Horsley to the 1867 station at Leatherhead, charged a fare of two shillings each way, or seven shillings if engaged to meet a particular train. This was not the sort of expenditure to be considered lightly by a farm labourer receiving rather less that twenty shillings a week.

As elsewhere, the railway brought new and better- paid jobs to the Surrey countryside. A newly-opened rural station might require a shift staff of as many as 15 men and most such stations soon attracted a 'railway hotel' for the accommodation and sustenance of casual travellers, as well as generating a steady business for a new breed of cab and wagonette operators. Even today, many Surrey stations retain their public houses and in their approaches cabs still wait for business.

Although movement of freight has never been an important feature on the county's railways the pace of Surrey's 19th and early 20th century industrial development and its long history of residential growth would have been severely checked had railway accommodation been non existent or less generous. There is in some evidence, for example the location of the Joseph Billing printing works and Dennis Brothers motor works alongside the railway at Guildford, that the presence of good railway facilities encouraged the establishment of new industries in the old Surrey towns. Whilst rail's role in distributing solid fuels for industrial and domestic needs for a hundred years or more must not be overlooked, it was road transport which was the principal engine of modern industrial development in the county, a feature which owed much to early 20th century technological progress and the demands of the two World Wars. Perhaps the strongest railway influence in the growth of industry in the county was to be seen in the servicing of the extractive enterprises along the North Downs, but even this had vanished by the beginning of the 1960s. Indeed such was the encroachment of road transport on railway business in the immediate post World War 2 era that most station freight yards had disappeared by the mid 1960s and although freight trains were still running through the county and train load business was coming in from elsewhere, the mid 1980s saw Surrey entirely without public rail freight depots.

From early in the early Victorian era, Surrey's railways nurtured some highly specialised activities. One was the development of the nation's modern defences, which geopolitics caused to be largely concentrated in the south east. Following the establishment in the middle of the 19th century of the important permanent army base at Aldershot, just across the border in Hampshire, and the subsequent related spread of military occupation over the heathlands of West Surrey, movement of troops, military equipment and supplies became a major task for rail, a business well-practised and honed to a high state of efficiency in peacetime which contributed to a smooth mobilisation in 1914. And, as indicated in G T Chesney's mythical *Battle of Dorking* (1871), had invasion by a mainland European power taken place, as was long feared from around 1860, Surrey's railways would have had a prominent role to play. In

World War 2, their contribution to the successful withdrawal from France, to the subsequent preparations for meeting a German invasion, and to the mounting of the victorious assault on mainland Europe was of prime importance.

Surrey's proximity to both Windsor Castle and Buckingham Palace and the royal occupation of Claremont from 1816 to 1914 meant that its railways were much involved in the sustenance, amusement, comfort and mortal departure of royalty. Transport of royal personages to and from Portsmouth, Aldershot and Osborne House in the Isle of Wight, trips to the races and to ceremonial occasions was for many years almost a routine. Royal journeys on Surrey's railways continued into modern times: on more than one occasion in World War 2, an overnight sojourn in a siding at Horsley station gave King George VI's sleeping car some refuge from the noise and danger of German air attacks when travelling between London and Portsmouth . Stations on the main line from London Waterloo were lined with waving arms when his grandson's honeymoon train passed by during the afternoon of 29 July 1981 ; and the Queen still uses the railway to reach the Derby on Epsom Downs as well as making journeys through Surrey on other occasions, increasingly in recent years on scheduled passenger trains.

It was in mid-Surrey, on 2 February 1901, as the funeral train approached Dorking from Gosport at around 75 mph, that Queen Victoria's coffin almost tumbled from its bier, causing the attendants some anxiety. During her lifetime, the Queen Empress preferred her trains to proceed at a sedate pace but at the start of her last journey, ten minutes had been lost and the driver had been told to try for a punctual arrival in London, where the new King Edward VII was waiting . He did better than that, drawing into London Victoria two minutes early, greatly impressing the German Emperor, who was a passenger on the funeral train. As we shall see later, coffins carried on Surrey's railways were not restricted to royal remains; the county housed a great rail-served cemetery, regularly supplied with custom by special funeral trains steaming down from London.

Many artists, writers and other well known personalities were attracted to Surrey's fine scenery by the ready accessibility from the metropolis afforded by the railway. We shall see later how from the 1860s, the south western sector of the county was for the same reason much favoured for the country homes of wealthy and influential tycoons and professional men.

When the poet and novelist George Meredith moved to Flint Cottage, below Box Hill in 1867, he was no doubt influenced by its proximity to the LB&SCR station which was opened nearby that year. Thirty years later, the young George Bernard Shaw was regularly visiting Dorking by rail to be with his future wife, writing to Ellen Terry about her as his train, 'joggle - joggled' its way through the Surrey night. For the honeymoon in 1898, he took a house at Hindhead and was often to be seen at Haslemere station. Indeed Shaw got to know the Portsmouth line well, since two other houses were later rented in the same area and in 1900 he moved for a while to St Catherine's, Guildford, after losing patience at having to set aside up to three hours for the door-to-door journey from his Hindhead houses to a London appointment. Train service improvements on this line came much too late for him; by 1904 he had finally settled in Hertfordshire. Other litterateurs and artists attracted to south west Surrey by the railway facilities in the late Victorian and Edwardian years included Alfred, Lord Tennyson, whose house, Aldworth, was completed in 1868 just over the Sussex border. Tennyson, with his long hair, black coat and hat, was a readily-recognisable figure on the platforms at Haslemere for almost 30 years until his death in October 1892. His coffin was borne on a decorated wagonette to that station, whence it was carried by a special train for the funeral at Westminster Abbey. Sir Arthur Conan Doyle, a later arrival, attracted to the newly-fashionable Hindhead, sometimes deserted the railway at Haslemere for the infant and often unreliable motorcar. The novelist George Eliot (Mary Ann Evans) came by train to Haslemere in 1871 to complete *Middlemarch*, afterwards spending much time on the railway house- hunting in Surrey until eventually purchasing 'The Heights' at Witley, in 1876.

From his frequent trips over the years 1868-97 between his rooms at Oxford and his sisters' villa on Castle Hill, Guildford, the Rev. Charles L Dodgson (Lewis Carroll), became well acquainted with the Reading, Guildford & Reigate and other lines in Surrey. His many journeys to and from Guildford may well have inspired the well-known piece about Alice in the train (*Through The Looking-Glass and What Alice Found* (1872)) which perhaps suggests he nursed a suppressed anxiety of being on the railway without a ticket. Little girls encountered on Surrey trains and stations were certainly entranced by his conversation and personality, so much so that some recalled these chance meetings in later life. One entered his compartment at Woking with her sister and escort in April 1892 on her first visit to the London Zoo. Fifty years afterwards she recalled (to Dodgson's nephew) 'the railway journey with the delightful stranger whose face and gentle way of speaking I remember perfectly, (and which) is as vivid as though it happened yesterday'. His diaries and letters contain a number of references to his railway journeys in Surrey including a meeting on Guildford station on 9 June 1890 with Mrs Liddell, Alice's mother, who had 'come over to look at houses (to take for the summer)' and a return by train from Dorking after walking there from Guildford via Albury.

The convenience of access afforded to the fine scenery below the scarp of the North Downs by the new railway between Guildford and Redhill quickly attracted such residents as the versatile Sir Henry Cole (1808-82), writer, designer and civil servant, inventor of the adhesive postage stamp and publisher of the first Christmas card. Soon after his appointment as Director of what is now the Victoria & Albert Museum in 1853 Cole rented Seaforth Cot tage in the picturesque village of Shere, travelling to and from Gomshall station daily.

A passage in his 1910 novel *Howard's End* suggests that E M Forster, who lived at Weybridge from 1904 until 1925, had formed a favourable impression of the railway company which served that town:

> *'That smoke we saw cannot have been Margaret's train?'*
> *'I can assure you it was - the London & South Western sets great store by its punctuality.'*

A decade or so earlier, Jerome K Jerome had been less complimentary. In Chapter 5 of his 1889 book *Three Men in a Boat*, he used the uncertainties attending a railway expedition into Surrey from the then muddle of Waterloo as a rich source of humour. As we shall see later, another author well familiar with the county's railways was H G Wells, who lived at Woking for a few years and then for a while at Worcester Park, using both places as backgrounds for novels.

The young Winston Churchill was a frequent visitor to Deepdene, Dorking, the home of his uncle's widow, the Duchess of Marlborough, always travelling down by train from London. In Chapter 6 of his *My Early Life* (1930), he relates how in 1895 he was invited to a dinner party at Deepdene at which the future King Edward VII was to be present. Increasingly concerned that he should have chosen an earlier train, Churchill began to change into evening dress 'much to the concern of the gentleman who shared my carriage'. Hurried up the hill from Dorking station in a brougham driven by anxious servants, Winston found Edward and the rest of the dinner party still waiting in the drawing room, 20 minutes after dinner was due to be served, the superstitious Prince having point blank refused to sit down with 13 at table or to accept any rearrangement of the furniture. Churchill made a grovelling apology, drawing a royal rebuke.

Although railways were cut through some of the county's finest scenery, the only attention given to their effect on the environment came from the restrictions imposed by some landowners, notably the fastidious catalogue of requirements set out for the line between Leatherhead and Dorking by the owner of Norbury Park, which will be referred to later. Only wealth and influence could affect the path of a new railway, as in the southward diversion of the Reading, Guildford & Reigate to avoid the Albury Park of Percy, Lord Lovaine and the property of Henry Drummond Esq, MP. Apart from appeasement of such private interests, promoters did not have to face any general adverse reaction to the visual impact of the railway upon the rural landscape of Surrey, a landscape already much altered by the hand of man. As elsewhere, once the initial scars had healed, the narrow swathe of steel tracks and ballast, half hidden in cuttings or modestly exposed on low and well-greened embankments, blended into its immediate surroundings, almost becoming part of them. Today's noisy motorways, so greedy of space and abundant with ugly concrete, are much more obtrusive and seem likely to remain so. In 1865 the writer of *Murray's Hand-Book Surrey, Hampshire & Isle of Wight*

Above *Croydon, Merstham & Godstone Iron Railway plate rails and stone blocks mounted as a display in Merstham High Street: 24 June 1994.* Alan A Jackson

appears almost to welcome the newcomer as he surveys the scene from the North Downs above Reigate. Discerning the lines from Redhill to Brighton, Redhill to Dorking, and Three Bridges to East Grinstead, he comments benignly on; '....the wreaths of white smoke that float above the deep foliage of the Weald marking the progress of the trains across the old country of the Iguanodon and the Plesiosaurus'.

So dense was the railnet established by 1901 that only a few small communities in the less populous outer edges of the county found themselves more than two miles from a station. Yet, hopelessly uneconomic as they would have been, optimists, as we shall see, brought forward schemes to fill even these modest voids with steel rails. Since 1838, in all these ways, and in a few others, minor and curious, the railway in varying degree, has stamped its image on the fabric and life of Surrey and influenced the pace and form of change across the county. Much of this will be examined in detail in later chapters but we begin with a survey of how the network was built up, going on to look at subsequent changes in the infrastructure.

Surrey's First Railway

To those unfamiliar with railway history, it may come as a surprise to learn that the first railway to enter Surrey was intended solely for freight. The Croydon, Merstham & Godstone Iron Railway was authorised by an Act of 17 May 1803 to run from Pitlake Meadow, Croydon (the south end of the present Tamworth Road) to Reigate, with a branch from Merstham to Godstone Green. Although a second Act of 3 July 1806 sanctioned additional capital, the railway never reached either of its two proposed southern termini. When opened on 24 July 1805, it extended from Pitlake Meadow through Purley, Coulsdon and Hooley, then, approaching Merstham village, turned south east, following the route of the projected line to Godstone Green. This final section served Merstham lime works and the associated chalk pits, terminating at the firestone quarries just east of Quarry Dean Farm.[1]

In practice, although an independent concern, the CM&G was effectively a southern extension of the Surrey Iron Railway, which had been opened between Wandsworth and Pitlake Meadow, Croydon in 1803 and was similar in character, possessing no rolling stock of its own, requiring users to provide their own wagons and haulage animals and extracting tolls on a per ton per mile basis.

The 8½-mile fenced double line consisted of L-section cast iron rails, 3ft (0.91m) long, laid with the horizontal flanges outwards and supported by square stone blocks resting in gravel ballast. The rails were secured to the stone blocks by spikes driven into oak trenails. Measuring over the outer faces of the vertical rail flanges of surviving trackwork, modern researchers have established the gauge as 4ft 2in. (1.27 metres). The wagon wheels had no flanges and were kept in position by the vertical section of the rails.

No documents survive to indicate the nature of the traffic carried but it may be surmised that southbound it was mainly coal for lime-burning at Merstham and London horse manure for Surrey farms. Northbound it seems likely to have been predominantly firestone, chalk, lime and fullers earth. It has been suggested by Sowan[2] that after the opening of the Croydon Canal in 1809, stone traffic was moved Londonwards from Croydon by that means (a transhipment wharf had been provided at Pitlake).

Trials for a wager proved that a single horse could haul 12 loaded wagons, a total weight of just over 38 tons, over six miles in lh 49min, almost four miles an hour and it was established that a single animal could haul up to just over 55 tons. These demonstrations were held on the generally descending gradients of the northbound track. One problem which emerged was that the type of wagon used proved too heavy for the rails when fully loaded, causing the narrow wheel treads to wear deep grooves in the cast iron. By 1826. a strengthened design of rail was in use in an attempt to reduce this damage. All the wagons appear to have been of similar design, perhaps originating from the same source. Of about 80 cu. ft. capacity, they proved inconvenient for the carriage of large pieces of freight such as lengths of timber. This difficulty, along with the necessity of transhipment to road or water transport to access most final destinations was regarded by contemporary investigators as a limitation on the line's ability to attract a wide spectrum of traffic.[3]

Another railway, the London & Brighton, was responsible for closing this not particularly successful enterprise. Requiring to make use of two short sections of the CM&GIR alignment south of Coulsdon for its main line, the L&BR secured power in its Act of 15 July 1837 to purchase the CM&GIR outright. This was exercised.[4]

Bayliss carefully notes the few remains of the CM&GIR now visible in Surrey. In 1951 a reconstructed length of track using plate rails recovered from in and around the Merstham lime works was mounted on original stone sleepers and placed on public display outside the Jolliffe Arms at the top of Merstham Hill; the plates were later removed by thieves. Another display was subsequently erected in Merstham Village Gardens (Merstham High Street) with plates and stone blocks from the Godstone underground firestone quarries, at least some of which almost certainly saw their first use on the CM&GIR. Neither of these reconstructions was related to the actual course of the line.

Notes

(1) This account is largely based on the descriptions of the route and history in Lee, Charles E, *Early Railways in Surrey...*, 1944, Townsend, Charles E C, *Further Notes on Early Railways in Surrey*, 1950, and Bayliss, Derek A, *Retracing the First Public Railway*, 1981. The southern (Surrey) end of the CM&GIR is closely examined by

Sowan, Paul W, in 'The Southern Terminus of the Croydon, Merstham & Godstone Railway', *Journal of The Railway & Canal Historical Society*, XXVII, 6, 159-167 (1982).

(2) Sowan, Paul W, 'Firestone and Hearthstone Mines in the Upper Greensand of East Surrey', *Proc, Geologists' Association,* 86(4), 571-91, (1976).

(3) Oeynhausen, C von, and Dechen, H von, *Railways in England, 1826 and 1827,* (a translation of the descriptive section of the report published in Berlin, 1829), *Transactions of the Newcomen Society,* vol 29, 1-12 (1958).

(4) Preamble of the Croydon, Merstham & Godstone Iron Railway Act of 1 July 1839 (2 & 3 Vic c 52) dissolving the Company.

CHAPTER TWO

Development of the Network - Main Lines

Four major or trunk railways traverse Surrey. Moving around the map in an anti-clockwise direction, these are: the London to Southampton, Salisbury and Exeter line, through Weybridge and Woking, crossing the county from east to west from a point between Surbiton and Esher until entering Hampshire just east of Farnborough; the Portsmouth Direct line, branching from this just west of Woking and leaving the county at Haslemere; the Mid Sussex Line, formerly the London, Brighton & South Coast Railway's main line from London to Portsmouth, passing through Epsom, Leatherhead and Dorking and entering Sussex north of Horsham; and lastly the Brighton line, entering the county just south of Coulsdon, and leaving it between Horley and Gatwick.

London to Southampton & The West

This well-engineered railway, with gradients and curves benignly-adjusted for steam-hauled expresses, was to become the principal main line of the former London & South Western Railway. Projected as the London & Southampton Railway, it was the first passenger railway in Surrey, opened from London (Nine Elms) to Woking Common (now Woking) on 21 May 1838, with intermediate stations at Ditton Marsh (now Esher), Walton and Weybridge. It was the L&S which gave Queen Victoria her first experience of the railway in use: when on an outing from her home at Claremont in 1837, she saw the construction works, where a steam engine was hauling trucks over the contractor's track, she declared it 'a curious thing indeed'. Throughout her life she was to make much use of the railway in Surrey and elsewhere but never lost her dislike of speed and was always unduly nervous of disaster, just as today many are uneasy whilst airborne.

At Woking, where the station stood isolated amid heathland (a Railway Hotel kept it company from 1840), much of the traffic handled initially was moving to and from the as yet railwayless towns to the south. For another seven years there was an almost continuous procession of horse-drawn coaches, carriages and flies over the narrow muddy road to Guildford and beyond.

On 24 September 1838, public rail services were extended into Hampshire, to a temporary terminus 38 miles from London, at Shapley Heath (now Winchfield). Basingstoke was reached on 10 June 1839 and through services between London and Southampton began on 11 May 1840. The London terminus became Waterloo when that station was opened on 11 July 1848. Four further stations (now Brookwood, West Byfleet, Byfleet & New Haw and Hersham), were added between 1864 and 1936, principally to cater for residential growth but, as we shall see in chapter 7, the first originally had a rather special role. To meet the increasing traffic load, the double track through Surrey was widened to four lines over a period of some 20 years up to 1904, work which entailed a substantial amount of station reconstruction and provision of non-conflicting

Above *Seventeen miles from Waterloo: the original London & Southampton Railway station at Walton on Thames in about 1880. Some eight uniformed railway staff are posing on the Up platform, including the stationmaster* Surrey County Libraries.

layouts at Pirbright Junction (30 June 1901) and Byfleet Junction (19 April 1903). Subsequently the Hampton Court Junctions were also improved, as mentioned below. From 20 December 1908 there were some fifty miles of four-track line all the way from London Waterloo to Worting Junction in Hampshire, the point where the Southampton and Salisbury lines part company.[1]

Rebuilding of Esher station with four tracks, completed on 1 April 1888, included royal waiting rooms on both local line plat forms for the benefit of the Duchess of Albany, daughter in law of Queen Victoria, who lived at nearby Claremont. Architecturally, the new work here was exceedingly dull and plain, bearing an affinity to contemporary construction at West Byfleet. Provision made at Esher for the Sandown Park race traffic will be mentioned later.

At Walton on Thames, four tracks were available through the station from 25 April 1893 , a central island for the Through roads replacing the old Up platform. Unprepossessing new buildings were provided on the Up local line in April 1888, but the former Down (now Down local) platform remained unchanged. Sidings laid at Oatlands in 1898 were used as a refuge for delayed freight trains or to store empty carriage stock.

The additional Up line installed at Weybridge station in July 1890 took over the existing Down alignment; the Down platform then became an island with a new Down line laid beyond it. Further work, completed in 1904, involved construction of a new entrance building and cab approach on the Up side; a wide covered footbridge led to the refurbished Up platform, with its Chertsey line bay and then to a new platform serving the Down Local line . This station was not regarded as of sufficient importance to justify platforms on the central Through roads.

Above *The original London & Southampton Railway station at Weybridge, looking towards London, about 1885. The road level entrance building on the left still survives but in non-railway use.*

Tite's 1838 entrance building, with its round-arched windows, rising high from rail to road level, survives today out of railway use. It became successively a post office, the Shanty Cafe and the Buffers Restaurant.

Its birth assisted by some local subsidies, what is now West Byfleet was opened as Byfleet & Woodham on 1 December 1887. Built in a very plain style, it had at first just two side platforms but with the widening to four tracks in April 1903, the Down platform became an island serving the Down Through and Down Local roads, an odd arrangement which persists today.

Woking's two-platform station, with its simple and square two-storey building on the Down side underwent some reconstruction when the line to Guildford opened in 1845 but much of the original was to last until 1888 when major alterations were made, including provision of a small ticket office on the north (Up) side, although the main building with its entrance on the south side was to survive until 1937. After the opening of the Guildford and Portsmouth line, traffic here much increased and the place became something of a bottleneck. An additional Up Through line was added between the Junction and East boxes in 1879, with new sidings, a Down Local Line and Down bay platform following at the country end in July 1884. The final L&SWR layout for Woking included an Up bay and a central island platform on the Down Through line; since the southern face also served the Down Local this line now had a platform each side. A somewhat unusual feature of this work was the extension of the canopy on the island platform to cover both the southernmost track and platform.

Freight traffic through Woking grew sufficiently to justify a marshalling yard, completed in August 1893 on the Up side at the Junction and serviced by a new 81-lever Junction box. The small locomotive shed east of the station on the south side of the line, which had received a 50ft diameter turntable in the

Above *Woking station, looking to London about 1905. A Down stopping train waits in the Down Loop platform, headed by L&SWR class T1 0-4-4T no. 70, built in 1889* Commercial postcard.

1880s was downgraded to become a sub shed to the new Guildford loco depot in 1889. By 1896 it had ceased to function even in that reduced role.

To coincide with the opening of the branch to Bisley in 1890, Brookwood received a single storey red brick building on the Up side, where some residential development had begun. A new bay, at the country end of the Up platform accommodated the branch train. Widening through this station was finished in November 1903, entailing replacement of the old Down platform by a new one, 576ft long, with a handsome single storey, canopied building for waiting rooms and lavatories. This platform, which served the new Down Local line, was linked by a subway to extended buildings on the Up side, These now boasted three sets of Flemish-gabled first floor rooms, one at one end of the 1890 structure, two at the other. No platforms were provided on the centre pair of Through lines.

Widening the main line entailed a major engineering job between Pirbright Junction and the county boundary. This involved stopping-up the aqueduct carrying the Basingstoke Canal over the railway whilst building two new tunnels by cut-and-cover. The work was completed in time to allow the canal to be reopened on 1 December 1902.

Around the turn of the century, additional traffic also required building of intermediate signal boxes at Mole, between Esher and Walton, at Oatlands between Walton and Weybridge, at Maybury between West Byfleet and Woking and at Goldsworth Cutting between Woking Junction and Brookwood.

Finally, working at Hampton Court Junction was greatly eased by the provision of a dive-under for the Up New Guildford Line trains from 21 October 1908 and a flyover for the Hampton Court branch Down trains from 4 July 1915.

A serious omission in this list of improvements , especially given the level of traffic which would be built up after electrification, was elimination of the Portsmouth line's flat junction at Woking.

Through Surrey to Brighton and Dover

Over on the east side of the county, a second major line, between London and Brighton, was finished in 1841. North of Redhill, between 1842 and 1868 , this also carried all the South Eastern Railway's main line traffic between London and the Channel ports of Folkestone and Dover. Sharing of this section came about because a parliamentary committee had proposed the SER (which had begun a shorter line to Dover from Purley through Riddlesdown in 1837) should use the same route into London as the London & Brighton Railway to avoid wasteful competition. This option was therefore included in the latter's Act of 1837. The cash savings involved appealed to the SER, then in severe financial difficulties, though in the longer term it was to find the resulting indirect main line into Kent highly disadvantageous.

In Surrey the most impressive engineering works were those necessary to cut a path through the North Downs south of Coulsdon. At the north end, a cutting over 100ft deep, with side slopes at an angle of four to one led to the straight 1 mile 253 yd Merstham Tunnel. To reassure timid passengers (there were at first no lights in the carriages), the tunnel sides were whitewashed and the central portion illuminated by gas jets supplied from a small works about 3/4 mile from the south end. This did not last long and after some modifications, the gas pipes were used by track workers to whistle warnings of approaching trains to each other. Many hundreds of tons of soil excavated to form the tunnel and cuttings was moved south to make embankments through Redhill and across the boggy clay near Earlswood Common.

The 28 1/2 mile section between Croydon Junction (later Norwood Junction) and Haywards Heath was opened on 12 July 1841 and the line reached Brighton on 21 September. Stations were provided in Surrey at Merstham (in Battlebridge Lane and not opened until 1 December 1841), Red-Hill & Reigate Road (on the south side of Hooley Lane) and Horley. Merstham , with side platforms and Through roads in the centre, was provided to remove any opposition from Lord Monson, occupant of Gatton Park, to the west of the line, and therefore sited to suit him rather than the villagers. Red-Hill was a very modest structure, its main purpose to serve Reigate, two miles west. At this time the railway here was in more or less open country.

Horley, named after a small village to the west of the line, was sited about 300 yd north of the present station. As it was approximately halfway to Brighton, on level ground, it was chosen as the site for the railway workshops and 20 acres were purchased, although in the event not used for that purpose; some of the unwanted land became a cattle market. A freight yard was laid out on the west side but the goods shed here was not ready until November 1842. A pair of Through roads without platforms ran through the centre of the passenger station and there were level crossings at each end of the platforms. Horley was reconstructed in 1882-83, when David Mocatta's pretty Tudor style building on the Up side gave way to something much more utilitarian which butted on to the large goods shed. A more drastic rebuilding took place in connection with the main line widening in 1905. The two level crossings were then abolished and the well-built new station, sited just under 1/4 mile south of the old, had platforms on all four tracks. Elaborate approach roads, supported on arches of engineering brick, were erected over the line from each side , coming from two directions on the Down side, A quietly dignified single storey Domestic Revival entrance building, containing a lofty ticket hall was erected above the platforms on the south side of the new overline bridge.

Following the statutory imposition of route-sharing, it was arranged that the section between Coulsdon and Redhill would be purchased by the SER once that company started to work its main line eastwards from Redhill to Tonbridge, That section was opened on 26 May 1842 but although SER trains used the section north of Redhill from this date, the company did not secure control over its purchase until July 1844. Each company ran without tolls over the other's lines from Redhill into London.

At Redhill, the SER erected a 'temporary station' near Redstone Hill, just south of the present

Top Right *Horley station, LB&SCR as reconstructed in 1882-83, looking to London in 1886; the site was just under a quarter mile north of the present station.*

Right *The handsome 1905 rebuilding of Horley station for the widening of the Brighton main line, looking to London. The entrance block, on a new road approach eliminating the former level crossing, is seen at centre left, straddling the second pair of tracks. Almost everyone in this picture of about 1906/7 seems to be aware of the activities of the photographer* Commercial postcard.

Above *Redhill, SER as rebuilt in 1858, looking towards London in 1865. The hazardous cast iron pillars are prominent; they were to remain in place for some 30 years after this picture was taken.*

platforms. Passengers passing to and fro between here and the Brighton station found the transfer irritating and often uncomfortable. Disputes arising between the London & Brighton Railway and the SER over the location for interchanging traffic, the former favouring Merstham and the SER expressing a desire for a single Redhill station just north of the junction, had led to the nonsense of providing two separate stations. The will of the SER eventually prevailed and much to the relief of the harassed passengers, a station for the use of both companies, sited north of the junction, replaced the dispiriting duo in April 1844. The new facility, on the SER-owned line, and therefore its sole property, had two through roads in the centre, with side plat forms on loops for stopping trains. To maintain confusion among passengers, it was at first known as Reigate since that was the nearest place of any consequence. There was initially virtually no shelter for passengers waiting on the platforms and no footbridge to cross the lines until 1846. A small gas works was erected to supply illumination.

A substantial rebuilding of the shoddy 1844 premises at Redhill was undertaken in 1858. Canopies erected along each platform extended out over the adjacent track, supported by rows of cast iron pillars placed between the Through and Local roads. These obstacles, which formed almost the only feature of any architectural interest, proved a very dangerous hazard to enginemen and others leaning out of trains, causing several nasty casualties. However it was not until a Pullman car conductor had been killed in 1895 that they were removed and the roofing reconstructed with canopies of conventional design. The 1858 alterations included new buildings on the Down side, together with a bay, and the Up platform was rearranged as an island, the station now having to accommodate trains to and from the Reading line. From this time, the name Red Hill Junction came into use. The word 'Junction' was not dropped until the 1920s, by which time the town's name had become one word.

Since the LB&SCR ran more trains through Redhill than the SER, there was ample scope for friction, especially as all Up Tonbridge and Down Reading SER workings had to move across the Brighton line. LB&SCR dissatisfaction with the arrangements continued even after many SER

Above *Merstham, looking to Redhill in 1905. the platforms are in process of reconstruction, , preliminary to the rebuilding of the station. This postcard was published to exploit public interest in the murder of the 22 year old Miss Mary Money, whose body was thrown from a Down train in Merstham Tunnel on 24 September 1905 after a struggle with a man. The assault was seen by a signalman but the murderer's identity was never established* Commercial postcard.

trains were diverted via Sevenoaks in 1868, the bad feeling persisting until the end of the 19th century, when, as we shall see, a somewhat drastic solution was applied.

Merstham and Redhill to the Kent border

Before turning to subsequent developements at Redhill and points south, something should be said about the SER main line in Surrey.

Once it had obtained possession of the Redhill-Coulsdon section, the SER resolved that Merstham's wooden station was more nuisance than it was worth, summarily closing it in September 1843. This provoked a legal action by the Gatton Park parties, a move which obliged the company to build a replacement. Sited further north and much closer to the village, the second station was opened on 4 October 1844. Since not much money was spent on it, improvements were to be made in 1860 and in 1878. Following a stipulation by Lord Hylton when selling land for a new goods yard at Merstham in 1903, the passenger station was completely rebuilt in 1905-06 with a single storey Up side main block handsomely fashioned in the Domestic Revival style.

East of Redhill, the SER at first provided only one station in Surrey. Although called Godstone, it was almost 3 miles south of that village:

> *...a ridiculous station, put down in the middle of a country road, bearing a name to which it has no right whatever, and serving simply as a trap to catch unwary travellers.*

So wrote Louis J Jennings in 1876 of a place where, hungry, cold and tired, he had been obliged to wait three hours for the next train. True there was an inn, but he found that 'a cheerless hole' full of 'drunken tramps'.

Above *Godstone, as rebuilt in 1914-15 by the SE&CR, photographed in about 1969. The blank wall at ground level, with its circular recesses added as if by an afterthought, spoils what might otherwise have been a pleasing frontage.*

In 1914, the 1842 station was rebuilt as a two-storey structure with a hipped pantiled roof and gables at each end. Unfortunately the overall effect was marred by a bodged elevation on the road side.

Godstone became a railhead for sea-borne coal distribution over a wide rural area. The fuel came in via the Medway Navigation and the railway from Tonbridge to Heasman's Wharf at Godstone, where the original coal staging remained in use until the 1950s.

Rather more than a mile to the east, at Crowhurst Lane End, where Tandridge Lane passes under the railway, a public freight siding opened with the line and survived until the 1960s. A similar facility was subsequently added at Mid-Street (now South Nutfield). Within Surrey , the only major engineering work on this east-west line was the 1,326 yd Bletchingley Tunnel, east of Godstone station. Construction through waterlogged and faulted weald clay containing detached sandstone rock proved a hazardous and difficult task for the engineer Frederick Walter Simms (1803-65) and his team of navvies. The labourers were housed in a camp at the western end of the tunnel, south of the line. Simms was so pleased with himself at the success achieved at Bletchingley that he used it as the basis of what was to become a standard work, *Practical Tunnelling...*, a book which ran to four editions between 1844 and 1896.

A second passenger and freight station in Surrey was added at the beginning of 1884 between Redhill and Godstone, replacing the Mid-Street public siding. Called Nutfield, it was about a mile south of that village. The pleasant building, in the Domestic Revival style with its timber-framed brickwork, steep-sloping tiled roof and matching signal box, formed for many years one of the most architecturally pleasing wayside stations in the county.

Redhill to Horley 1868-1923

We now return to developments at Redhill and along the Brighton main line in Surrey up to 1923. Redhill's strategic location on the railway system was belatedly recognised by the Post Office in 1884, when a mail sorting office was established near the easternmost (Down) plat form. This was designed as a forwarding centre for the area bounded by London, Reading, Brighton and Dover. As will be not iced in chapter 4, it grew in importance over the years, justifying extension and improvements in the 1930s and again in the 1960s.

In August 1868 a station was opened at Earlswood, between Redhill and Horley, in what was already a southern suburb of the rapidly-expanding new town of Redhill. Another source of traffic here was the 1855 Royal Earlswood Institution on the east side of the line. With the widening of the main line, Earlswood station was handsomely rebuilt in 1905; its platforms, on all four tracks, were serviced by a very pleasing two-storey Domestic Revival building on the Up side.

To assist transport of munitions workers, a crudely-built halt was provided at Salfords, south of Earlswood, from 8 October 1915. Its two platforms on the Slow Lines were linked by a lattice girder footbridge which also gave access to the Monotype Works east of the line. As will be explained later, this halt was classified as private for some years.

Like the L&SWR main line, the Brighton route saw a steady increase in traffic, met by widening to four tracks. The first of these works in Surrey was an additional Up Relief line, opened between Gatwick and Horley in October 1892. Much more costly, but justified by the desire for higher running speeds and improved punctuality on the Brighton main line, was a new stationless 6 7/8 mile double track between Earlswood and Coulsdon, avoiding Redhill. Opened to freight traffic early in November 1899 and to passenger trains on 1 April 1900, this by- pass became known as the 'Quarry Line' [3]. South of Coulsdon, it ran west of the SER, crossing over it at Hooley before entering the 1 mile 353 yard Merstham Tunnel (later known as Quarry Tunnel). Continuing to the east of the old line, it passed through a second tunnel and covered ways (648 yards) on the eastern outskirts of Redhill before rejoining the 1841 line just north of Earlswood station. Since construction involved opening out the existing cutting sides south of Coulsdon and boring two tunnels, the Quarry Line was expensive to build but the LB&SCR's satisfaction at owning the whole of its route to Brighton and at achieving im-

Below *Neglected and boarded up when this picture was taken about 1969, the attractive Domestic Revival station building erected at Nutfield in 1883-4 was well-deserving of careful restoration. It was later demolished by BR.*

Above *Earlswood, looking to London in 1909, as rebuilt in 1905 for the widening of the Brighton main line. The Up and Down Fast line platforms on the right were demolished in 1984 and the subway access blocked up* Commercial postcard.

munity from the delays arising across the flat junctions at Redhill was no doubt substantial. So far as Surrey was concerned, operation of the main line was further improved when four tracks, designated (east to west) Down Fast, Up Fast, Down Slow, Up Slow, became available between Horley and Earlswood in 1905, and from Horley over the county border to Three Bridges in 1907.

Also helping to speed up working were intermediate signal boxes opened at Earlswood Common (between Redhill and Horley) about 1865 and on the new Quarry Line at Star Lane, Quarry, and Worsted Green. Holmethorpe Siding Box, between Merstham station and Redhill, was added in 1900 and Earlswood Common was replaced by the new Salford box in 1907.

Before leaving the LB&SCR main line, mention should be made of an event which illustrates that the railways did not always have everything their own way, even at the height of their hegemony. Although mail between London and Brighton was carried from the opening of the line in 1841, the Post Office decided in the 1880s that the overnight parcels traffic, which was less time sensitive than letters, might at some advantage to cost be moved back to two-horsed road vans. Horses were changed at Horley, where the Down and Up vans met at 00.55 nightly. Apart from a brief trial of steam-engined vans in 1896, this reversion to horse road transport continued until June 1905 when it was replaced with motor vans. These, carrying 2½ tons, passed at Redhill, where they were fed by another new motor van service operating out of Dorking.

With Difficulty to Portsmouth

The naval base of Portsmouth, a third major objective for railways crossing Surrey, was to engender fierce rivalry between the L&SWR and the

Above *LB&SCR Class I3 4-4-2T no.21 (built 1907) on a Victoria-Brighton via Quarry Line express south of Coulsdon in 1908 or 1909. The original SER line to Redhill is at the right.*

LB&SCR, with the SER playing a minor role in the wings. On 5 May 1845, a track was completed over the six miles from Woking Junction to Guildford, where the station was sited just west of the river Wey. This line had been promoted by the Guildford Junction Railway, whose directors perversely chose to adopt a novel form of railway consisting of square-section, chemically-hardened wooden rails carrying trains with flangeless support wheels kept on course by angled guide wheels. Invented by William Prosser, this system was claimed to produce great economies in construction, partly because it allowed use of very sharp curves. However the L&SWR, frightened by a proposal to reach Portsmouth through an area it regarded as its private preserve, moved in to take over the Guildford Junction, building the line in conventional manner after arranging for Prosser to be sent into limbo with suitable financial compensation.

Guildford's station with its main building, of two storeys on the Down side facing the town, was unremarkable and very soon enlarged. Doubling from Woking was completed by the contractor Thomas Brassey in July 1847. By then Guildford had an island platform on the Up or west side serving a third running line. This westernmost track and the two main roads were protected from the elements by glazed ridge roofs and there was a wooden footbridge at the London end. Further enlargement had taken place by the end of the 1860s, with a second very mean and narrow island platform on the west side, separated from its fellow by only one track. Whilst the twin overall roofs at least suggested to the traveller that what the platform name boards boldly called 'Guildford Junction' was after all something more than a simple wayside station, the generous use of cheap timber construction and crude design work produced premises which were unworthy of the town and were soon to acquire a shabby and shoddy air.

The doubling from Woking to Guildford was soon followed by a logical extension to Godalming, where the terminus in Bridge Road was dealing with public traffic from 15 October 1849. Sir William

Tite designed the two-storey building which although severely plain, conveyed an elegance and dignity typical of his skilful hand.

Immediately south of Guildford station, the extension passed through two short tunnels, the northernmost (938 yd) through chalk, and so named, the second, St Catherine's, (132 yd) through sand. This sainted bore proved troublesome, disgracing itself by collapsing on no less than three occasions. In June 1876 the northern mouth of Chalk Tunnel also fell in, after which the affected area was opened out to make room for a steam locomotive depot, reducing the length of the bore to 845yd.

After the arrival of the L&SWR at Godalming, almost another ten years passed before the problem of providing a more direct link between London and Portsmouth was resolved. Eventually the matter was forced to a head by the Portsmouth interest combining with Brassey to push forward the completion in May 1858 of a cheaply-engineered 32-mile single track, known as The Portsmouth Railway, between Godalming and Havant, in the expectation that one of the larger companies would take it over. At first it was thought the Portsmouth Railway trains would approach London via the SER's Reading-Redhill route and to this end, work was started on a south to east spur, Peasmarsh and Shalford, the embankment then made surviving today. Nervous about upsetting either the LB&SCR or the L&SWR, the SER refused consent to a junction at Shalford, or to a lease of the Portsmouth, causing the works to be left unfinished.

Navvies constructing the Portsmouth Railway exhibited the general rowdiness of their breed. Over indulgence in alcoholic refreshment frequently followed receipt of pay on Saturday nights, with consequent disturbance to the peace of small country communities. At Haslemere in July 1855, the townlet's total police resources of two men were brutally attacked and overwhelmed in an incident which resulted in the death of Inspector William Donaldson, the first Surrey policeman to be killed on duty.

Brassey's new railway through south west Surrey lay unused for over seven months. Foreseeing the

Below *Godalming's second station, with its elegant Tite station house, looking to London in 1906* Commercial postcard.

Above *Farncombe L&SWR, looking to London in about 1902 from the level crossing with Farncombe Street. If the ubiquitous motor traffic and modernisation of the signalling and level crossing equipment are disregarded, this scene is recognisable today.* Commercial postcard.

risk of an SER change of mind or a LB&SCR grab at the Portsmouth line, Waterloo finally agreed in August 1858 to take a lease , making a connection with the new line in a cutting 25 chains north of the 1849 Godalming terminus. Trains ran to Haslemere and beyond from 1 January 1859, but the birth of the railway was not easy. Upset by the prospect of a L&SWR monopoly on this, the shortest Portsmouth route, the LB&SCR at first physically prevented the necessary access to the joint station at Portsmouth, in what some railway historians have romanticised as the 'Battle of Havant'. This action temporarily caused the L&SWR services via Godalming to be terminated short of the Havant junction. A fares war ensued until the antipathy was resolved by an agreement to eliminate competition from 8 August 1859. Through trains from London to Portsmouth via Godalming operated from that day.

The new main line gave Godalming a second station, in Mill Lane, nearer the centre, yet prettily sited below the park of Westbrook Place. Thought to be the work of Tite, the attractive range of buildings on the Down side was dominated by a stone-faced three-storey station house, its steep barge-boarded gable reflected in the angle of a single storey lean-to on its south flank and by another gable on the northernmost single storey block. Here, as at Haslemere, Guildford and Esher, the business at the town's inns and other licensed houses from passenger and commercial traffic along the Portsmouth Road fell away sharply. To meet the needs of a new kind of 'passing trade' , an existing house near the new station was converted to become the Railway Tavern. And as in Farnham, a new road had to be made through the built-up area to link town and station.

At Milford, the next station down the line, the main buildings were on the Up side, a Tudor cottage style house of two-storeys and steeply-sloping roof, parallel to the line. An adjacent single-storey booking office and entrance block was flat-roofed, with a recessed central section. The other two Surrey stations, Witley and Haslemere, were again in a different style; a two storey red-brick Italianate station house containing the ticket hall on the ground floor, flanked on each side by hipped lean-to pavilions. This design was repeated on the Hampshire section of the line at Liphook and Rowland's Castle and as we shall see, also appeared at Ewell.

South of Godalming, the minimum-cost, contour- following engineering of Locke & Errington produced steep and curving gradients up to the Haslemere summit. In theory the undulating pro-

Above *The rebuilt Guildford station, east side, looking to London, in 1909. Note the locomotive inspection pit between the running lines at the south end of platform 2, now awaiting discovery by puzzled 22nd century archaeologists* Commercial postcard.

file of the line lowered the cost of construction, the extra expense of working up the gradients offset by the saving in running over the downhill sections, these also compensating for the loss of speed in climbing. In practice, the long stretches of 1 in 80 up brought steam locomotives down to a canter and overall speeds were generally low. E C Matthews, in his 1911 book *The Highlands of South-West Surrey*, notes how 'From Witley the panting of the engine bears witness to the steepness of the gradient through some very lovely scenery'. This remains a very pleasing line for the sensitive traveller, especially if a forward view can be secured, and most of all in bleak weather when Nature seems to challenge the train's progress, although, with electric traction, the profile now offers no impediment to speed.

At Godalming the 1849 terminal remained in use for passenger traffic as Godalming (Old) until 30 April 1897, after which it was replaced by Farncombe, a new station on the main line serving a burgeoning northern suburb, by then embraced by the town. Since Farncombe had no freight yard, the old terminal continued to handle that traffic until January 1969. Dignified and comfortable, Farncombe's buildings were a gesture to what was largely a prosperous middle class clientele. On the Up side, a seven-bay single-storey block was flanked at each end by two-storey gabled pavilions and on the Down platform, reached by a covered and glazed footbridge, there was a matching smaller building; all the windows and doors and decorative features were in a vaguely Tudor style.

For the protection of the Portsmouth interest, the 1859 amalgamation legislation had included provision for a minimum train service and a requirement that the Portsmouth Railway should be doubled once receipts reached a stated level. In Surrey this work was completed between Godalming and Witley in 1875, to Haslemere in October 1876 and to the county boundary and beyond on 1 January 1877.

Worplesdon station, between Guildford and Woking and 1½ miles from the village of that name, was added on 1 March 1883. This had a substantial house for the stationmaster on the Up side, with a

Above *Guildford locomotive depot and the entrance to Chalk Tunnel, looking to Godalming. Over 20 locomotives are 'on shed' on this Sunday evening in August 1953* Pamlin Prints.

tall Flemish style gable, a design to be repeated at Brookwood in 1903. Abutting on to the house was a low entrance block with a barrel-roofed dormer window. As we shall see later, it has proved difficult to generate much business here.

Pressures of growing traffic and new services led to further rebuilding at Guildford, where the station was not only shoddy but in places dangerous. This work included an additional island platform on the Up side, widening of the former westernmost island, a bay at the London end of the original Down platform for the New Guildford Line trains and a rather dull row of Domestic style entrance and office buildings on the east or Down side, facing the town. Many of these improvements were completed in November 1887 but further works and widening of the layout followed in 1898. Even then, Guildford remained a confusing station for the passenger, its platform arrangements seeming almost deliberately designed to produce what is nowadays termed a stressful environment. Platform 1 was a Down side bay hidden away at the London end of no. 2; platforms 3 & 4, 5 & 6 and 7 & 8 formed three islands, the latter pair separated from its neighbour by only one track, so that trains would arrive at or depart from not one platform but platforms 6 <u>and</u> 7. To add to the confusion, railway geography caused London-bound L&SWR and SER trains to leave in opposite directions. Small wonder then that notices were exhibited to advise the bewildered:

DO NOT GET INTO ANY TRAIN
WITHOUT ASKING THE OFFICIALS[4]

As part of the 1887 reconstruction, the locomotive depot was reprovided, the new one cleverly squeezed into the restricted site between the country end of the station and the shortened Chalk Tunnel. Slightly enlarged in 1896, this depot, which in its final form had 18 tracks radiating from a turntable, replaced the original two-road shed north of the station as well as the small facility at Woking. For a consideration, it

Above *The original L&SWR station at Epsom (on the site of the present station), looking to London about 1870. Note the very low platform height and the slotted post signal.*

also housed LB&SCR engines rendered homeless after the little Bramley shed was blown down in an 1882 gale. Due to the somewhat restricted nature of the site , engines had to coal at a stage opposite platform 8. Following its closure on 9 July 1967, the site of the loco shed was eventually sold for construction of a multi- storey car park; this was finished in 1988 and like its predecessor no thing of beauty, even if its poisonous fumes were less visible.

Despite the statutory imposition of a minimum service, the L&SWR always treated Woking-Guildford-Portsmouth as very much a second-order main line; its speeds and frequencies never matched those on Southampton and West of England services. This blight lingered on under Southern management until the 1937 electrification brought about a revolutionary improvement on both counts, with very satisfactory results for passenger revenues.

The Mid Sussex Line

Always rather unsatisfactory in its wandering, indirect route, and now no longer a main line, the Mid-Sussex came together in somewhat piecemeal fashion, to some extent owing its existence to frontier rivalry between the L&SWR and LB&SCR. Here too the Portsmouth business was in contention. From an early stage, both the L&SWR and the London & Croydon Railway (subsequently the LB&SCR) showed interest in reaching Epsom and Leatherhead, whilst the Portsmouth promoters were active in advancing schemes to approach London through these towns.

First in the field was the London & Croydon, with its Epsom extension from what is now West Croydon. This line was opened on 10 May 1847 by the newly-formed London, Brighton & South Coast Railway and terminated on the north side of Epsom's Upper High Street . There was another station in Surrey at Ewell, sited half a mile east of that village on the Cheam Road. What is believed to be the original single storey building, of distinctly plain aspect, survives on the Up side, rendered and pebble-dashed in recent years. A footbridge and platform canopies were not considered essential until almost 50 years after opening. The goods yard was also on this side. Although freight workings ceased in 1960, the well-built shed now serves other purposes.

An independent local company secured parliamentary sanction for an Epsom & Leatherhead Railway in 1856; its 3m 54ch single track was to run from the LB&SCR station at Epsom via Ashtead to a terminus on the east side of Kingston Road, Leatherhead, on the northern outskirts of that town. The directors of this company then projected a larger scheme, for a Wimbledon & Dorking Railway, which they hoped would be taken up by either the LB&SCR or the L&SWR, then in contention in the area; eventually the latter was persuaded to build and work a double line as far as Epsom and also to lease the single track Epsom & Leatherhead, which was opened on 1 February 1859. At first, passengers for London had to make their own way between a temporary station at Epsom and the LB&SCR terminus but on the following 4 April, the 5¾ mile line, linking Epsom with the main L&SWR system at the point where Raynes Park station is now, came into operation, giving Leatherhead and Ashtead their first through services to London. This new line, with its initial seven trains each way daily, also brought Ewell a second station, at the western edge of the village, as well as securing for the L&SWR a share in the lucrative race and pleasure traffic to Epsom. Behind the bald facts just related, lies a fair measure of railway politics arising from the border rivalries of the two main line companies and their anxiety to reach Portsmouth[5]. Finally, after agreement had been reached between the L&SWR and the LB&SCR, the two stations in Epsom were linked on 8 August 1859 and LB&SCR trains (six each way daily) began to work through from London Bridge to Leatherhead, the Epsom & Leatherhead becoming a jointly-worked line (also jointly-owned from 1865).

With one exception, the stations on these new lines offered little architectural interest, At Ewell, the L&SWR provided a pleasant Italianate Station

Below *Station Road and the LB&SCR station at Epsom (right) in about 1905 looking to the town centre. Parts of the Down side building seen here survive but the cab yard is now occupied by lock-up shops* Commercial postcard.

Above *Ashtead L&SWR and LB&SCR, looking towards London about 1905. The platforms are still lit by paraffin lamps but an estate agent's office and domestic coal merchants have already established themselves in the station yard (now a commuter car park). The L&SWR train for Waterloo is composed of at least eight, possibly ten 4-wheel coaches and the stationmaster's sons keep the photographer under close observation.*

house with symmetrically-placed narrow arched windows, flanked by lean-to single storey pavilions with hipped roofs. Bearing a close similarity to the contemporary Witley, Liss and Rowland's Castle, on the Portsmouth Railway. and perhaps owing something to Tite, this building, sited on the Down side, incorporated a ticket office and waiting hall on its ground floor. To accommodate a stationmaster with a large family posted here in the early 1890s, additional domestic space was provided by demolishing the northern lean-to wing and repeating the gabled block in its place. Unfortunately matching did not extend to the fenestration, which included a large oriel window upstairs on the road side. The building is now listed Grade II.

Initially, traffic at Ewell justified only one freight siding with a loading dock at the London end, on the Down side, but by 1895 a goods shed had been added close to the London end of the Down platform and there was also a new siding parallel with the Down line which was long enough to serve the flour mills on the banks of the Hogsmill River.

At Epsom the 1859 Joint L&SWR and LB&SCR station was a very crude affair with side platforms and a double line junction at the London end. A simple wooden building with gabled roof and canopy on the platform side was eventually completed on the Down side to accommodate waiting rooms and the usual amenities . This survived until the 1929 rebuilding mentioned in Chapter 4. Around 1890 multi-gabled wooden canopies decorated in vernacular style were added over both platforms to give shelter to the increasing number of passengers. About the same time the layout was altered: a loop was laid behind the Up platform converting it to an island and two centre roads were inserted; LB&SCR trains to and from the Sutton line then ran through, no longer having access to the platforms. The cramped two-road L&SWR goods

yard was on the Down side at the country end, where there was also a short loading dock, mainly used for horse boxes.

The 1847 station in Upper High Street appears to have been rebuilt by the LB&SCR around the 1870s and this second structure, on the Down side, hidden behind some shops, can still be seen from the railway at the time of writing. Set back from the road to allow a cab forecourt, it followed the design used for many contemporary LB&SCR small town stations : a single storey in brick, with projecting gabled pavilions at each end punctuated by pairs of narrow arched windows. A recessed central section, housing the main entrance hall, was reached by a flight of three steps from the road, protected by a canopy connecting the end pavilions. Inside, the platforms were staggered, the Up one nearer to London. At the London end, on the Down side,

Above *Charles H Driver's ornate 1867 Up side building at Leatherhead, now listed Grade II, together with its near-twin on the Down side. When this photograph was taken in July 1968 the stationmaster's house was still occupied.*

there was a signal box and a goods shed , and on the Up side, a small two-road locomotive depot. This last was closed in 1929 but the signal box, renamed Epsom East Goods in 1931, survived until 1967.

At Ashtead, trains initially stopped only by request at a platform with minimal facilities on the south side of the single line . Here, with no great pressure of traffic for many years, the station buildings and layout evolved gradually, When the railway between Epsom and Leatherhead was doubled in 1866-67, a short platform was provided on the Up

Above *In contrast with the LB&SCR premises slightly to the north and just visible in the right centre background of this c. 1906 picture, the L&SWR Leatherhead station was plain and unremarkable* Commercial postcard.

side at Ashtead and at its London end, in 1874 a narrow two storey, gable-ended station house was erected, its starkly plain exterior relieved only by finialled barge-boards. In 1885 a modest single storey brick station building was added on the Down side by the L&SWR . This accommodated a booking office, entrance hall, waiting room and a staff room, The opposite platform then received a small wooden canopied structure sheltering a waiting room and men's urinals (and later, a W H Smith bookstall for the commuters). Sidings for excursion traffic and a freight yard (on the Down side) appeared around this time, To operate the rather more complex layout now in place , a signal box of standard L&SWR design with hipped roof, brick base and large, small-paned, sliding windows was erected about halfway along the Up platform.

It has not so far proved possible to discover any illustrations or information about the 1859 terminus at Barnett Wood, Leatherhead, which appears to have been a simple affair, possibly of wooden construction, with a single platform on the east side. Its small brick-built locomotive shed on the same side, out of railway use from 1877, did however survive until 1988, when demolition was allowed by planning officers apparently ignorant of its historical importance.

The sharing of the Epsom-Leatherhead line arose from an accord of July 1859 which accepted that beyond Leatherhead, the LB&SCR might eventually go on to Dorking and the L&SWR to Guildford. In preparation for its southward thrust, the LB&SCR opened a new station in Leatherhead on 4 March 1867. This was half a mile south of the original terminus which closed the previous evening. Charles H Driver's building, on the Up side, now listed Grade II, was a handsomely superior and fancifully embellished example of the typical LB&SCR, 'pavilions with linking recessed centre block' plan, the London end dominated by a two-storey stationmaster's house sporting a low turret with a her-

Above *'West Humble for Box Hill' to quote the large nameboard, looking to Dorking soon after the opening of the line in 1867. The full ornamental splendour demanded by Thomas Grissell in return for allowing the railway through his land is seen in all its pristine glory.*

ringbone brick frieze. A matching brick built structure on the Down Side, reached by a narrow subway under the line, received its own road approach and boasted a doorway with a fine pillared portal of foliated capitals, a feature repeated on the Up side at the stationmaster's front door. The prettily valanced platform canopies were supported by slender decorated iron columns until 1969, when, neglected beyond repair, they were replaced with utilitarian metal girders and corrugated plastic.

Quite how the unremarkable little town of Leatherhead earned such special treatment is not clear: perhaps it was thought that Grissell, to be mentioned in a moment, might be bought off by it; or maybe it was just a question of the LB&SCR showing the L&SWR which company had the class.

Contemporaneous with the new Brighton station at Leatherhead was the doubling of the line from Epsom to Leatherhead and the construction of a separate L&SWR station just south of Driver's exercise in exuberance. The South Western's dreary premises, entirely devoid of architectural pretensions, were on a spur line immediately to the west of the LB&SCR , aligned for the proposed extension towards Guildford. Each of the two companies pretended the other did not exist; passengers unwise enough to attempt interchange found themselves out in the street.

Shortly after all this activity, on 11 March 1867, the LB&SCR line to Dorking through the Mole Gap in the North Downs was opened to public traffic. This extension proved to be an expensive venture, since it crossed the edge of Norbury Park, the territory of Thomas Grissell, lately High Sheriff of Surrey and a retired railway contractor, a man wise in the ways in which crafty landowners could extract favourable treatment from railway promoters. Grissell set out to obtain the best possible deal for the LB&SCR's intrusion, laying down rigorous stipulations to minimise environmental damage and secure maximum benefit. He required a highly ornamental station building at Westhumble to massage his sense of importance and meet his personal convenience. Here, at less than a mile from Dorking station, Grissell and those that came after him at Norbury Park were given the right to stop any train. He also insisted upon ornamentation at the mouth of the 524-yd Mickleham tunnel through the chalk spur in the Park and on the three viaducts over the meandering river Mole. Every possible measure had to be taken by the surveyors and engineer to render the railway as inconspicuous as possible from his windows[6].

Charles H Driver happily provided his most extravagant design for Grissell's station. In the French chateau style, with steeply-gabled, pattern-tiled roofs, pompous porte-cochère, pyramidical, crested turret, and hammerbeam roof in the entrance hall, Westhumble no doubt inflated Grissell's ego throughout his few remaining years. Today, like Leatherhead, it is a listed building, Grade II, and trains still call.

Below *At Dorking, Charles Driver was more subdued with his architectural flourishes. His 1867 Up side building, seen here in 1962, allowed to fall into advanced decay, was replaced in 1982 by commercial offices with some railway accommodation on the ground floor. The narrow subway between the platforms is now the only relic of the original station.*

Driver was also let loose on designs for Dorking station[7], but here, in the shadow of Box Hill, his work was more muted, with few decorative touches, since savings had to be found after the prodigality to the north. There was however some pretty ironwork beneath the platform canopies, of which an example survives to be admired in the town's museum. Thanks to its more direct route to London, the new Dorking station soon became the principal one for the town, although for sound engineering reasons it was sited at what is still the northern edge of the built up area.

A further extension, from Dorking to Horsham, with intermediate stations at Holmwood and Ockley and another at Warnham in Sussex was opened on 1 May 1867. This had been promoted by an independent company, the Horsham, Dorking & Leatherhead Railway, mainly local landowners, their spokesman John Labouchere of Broome Hall, Holmwood, father of Henry, the famous journalist and politician. The expectation was that the LB&SCR would work the completed line and as funding problems had arisen the 1862 Act restricted the powers to the Dorking-Horsham section. Parliament insisted a connection be made with the SER at Dorking, a move which raised the threat of SER intervention and caused the LB&SCR, already authorised to build the four mile link between Leatherhead and Dorking, to intervene. In 1864 the Brighton company secured legislation which allowed it to absorb the small local concern.

Above *LB&SCR B2 4-4-0 'Telford' (built 1897) on a Victoria-Portsmouth line train just south of Dorking station about 1905. The connecting single line to the SER Reading- Redhill line can just be discerned above the roofs of the train*
Courtesy Bluebell Railway Archive.

To conform to requirements in the 1862 Act, a 21-chain connecting link was made to the SER's Redhill-Reading line at Dorking, some 150yd east of that company's Box Hill station (now Dorking Deepdene). Although the LB&SCR had no wish to operate services over it, it was no doubt realised that parliament saw its potential value as a direct connection between between Aldershot and the Sussex coast should invasion threaten. Some race trains between Hastings and Epsom worked over it, reversing at the SER station, but, never used on a regular basis, it was severed around 1900, the residual track serving as a siding for the LB&SCR. All remaining trackwork here was removed by the SR in 1926 but as we shall see later, the connection was briefly restored for strategic reasons in World War 2.

Immediately south of Dorking station there was a reverse curve on a rising gradient, an awkward hazard for southbound steam trains, especially if they had stopped at Dorking, but the only alternative would have been a long and costly tunnel through the greensand ridge, which even then would not have allowed a station to be sited any useful distance nearer the town centre. As it was, the short (385 yd) Betchworth Tunnel proved troublesome enough, with sand falls during construction and a serious collapse on 27 July 1887 just after a train had passed through. This fissure filled the bore with sand, closing the line for over seven months whilst rebuilding proceeded[8].

The brick-built stations south of Dorking, both given freight yards on the Down side, lacked architectural interest. Holmwood's roadside building, housing waiting, luggage and ladies' rooms and ticket office, sat on the bridge astride the railway, a single-storey structure with little gabled projec-

Above *Everything stops for the photographer at Ockley station around mid-day on a summer morning in 1922. LB&SCR 0-4-2T 297, 'Bonchurch' (built 1877) heads a Dorking-Horsham service and a junior porter proudly displays a new bicycle. Even before the days of widespread car ownership, this station, sited roughly halfway between the then small Weald villages of Ockley and Capel, never exactly bustled with traffic* Commercial postcard.

tions at each end, a canopy protecting the entrance from the roadway. Passengers passed through the waiting and ticket hall to a covered footbridge leading to both platforms. A stationmaster's house, in even plainer style, with stuccoed elevations stood next to it on the east side. Handsome and workmanlike wooden waiting shelters, with pitched roofs were subsequently provided on each platform. At Ockley, the main building was on the Down side. This had gabled projections at each end, the southern one of two storeys. There was a glazed canopy over the road approach entrance and the stationmaster's house abutted at the south end. A pair of railway staff cottages was placed at right angles to the line just south of this house, the three habitations and the adjacent brick works forming a tiny snug community in an otherwise remote spot. The Up platform also later gained a waiting shelter similar to those at Holmwood. Just within the Ockley parish boundary, but in fact closer to Capel village, this station suffered some vacillation in namings (Appendix I).

To provide extra line capacity, intermediate signal boxes were subsequently opened: at Lodge Farm, south of Betchworth Tunnel in 1877; at Mickleham at the Swanworth Lane crossing in 1891 (painted green all over in deference to the aesthetic sensibilities of those looking down from Norbury Park); at Ashtead Woods in 1898; at Epsom Common in 1899; and at Tilehurst Lane between Dorking and Lodge Farm in 1908 . Another intermediate box at Cuddington Cutting, just south of Worcester Park station, was installed for Epsom race days remaining in this infrequent use until December 1924.

Although difficult to work at speed with steam locomotives owing to its curvature and short but steep inclines, the Mid-Sussex served for many years as the LB&SCR's main line from London to Portsmouth and Bognor. Its main line character lingered, enhanced by the 1938 electrification, until its through fast trains were diverted to serve the needs of Gatwick Airport in 1978/84. As we shall see later, with the removal of inter-company rivalry following the formation of the SR in 1923, its station provision was rationalised.

Notes

(1) A detailed chronology of the widening of the L&SWR main line is given in Faulkner & Williams, pp 64-5

(2) Jennings, Louis J *Field Paths And Green Lanes,* 1877

(3) This name, at first unofficial but later adopted, derives from the chalk, building stone and hearthstone quarries around Quarry Dean at the south end of the line's Merstham Tunnel.

(4) In a letter to *The Times*, 31 July 1935, Lord Farrer referred to this notice as 'recently removed'.

(5) Davies, H J, 'The Epsom & Leatherhead Railway 1856-59', *Proceedings, Leatherhead & District Local History Society*, vol 5, 6 (1993) and Jackson, Alan A, 'Racing to Residential: The Wimbledon and Epsom Line', *Railway World,* July, 1980.

(6) A full list of Grissell's stipulations is given by Turner, John Howard, in *The London Brighton & South Coast Railway, II: Establishment and Growth*, 1978.

(7) For a fuller account of the Dorking station and approaches, see Jackson, Alan A, *Dorking's Railways*, 1988.

(8) Ackworth, W M, *The Railways of England*, 5th edition, 1900.

CHAPTER THREE

Development of the Network-Links and Branches

To Chertsey and Virginia Water

Surrey's first subsidiary line was a branch from the Southampton Railway at Weybridge to a temporary terminus in the ancient little town of Chertsey. With an intermediate station at Addlestone and opened on 14 February 1848, this was a relic of a frustrated proposal to connect the L&SWR with the London & Birmingham Railway. An 1847 Act for a western extension of the Windsor, Staines & South Western Railway as far as Wokingham authorised a Chertsey branch and parliament required the L&SWR abandon its proposed extension from Chertsey to Egham. But this 1847 scheme fell victim to the financial depression which followed the boom years of the Railway Mania and Chertsey was to remain a terminus for nearly 20 years.

Eventually, in its 1864 Act, the L&SWR obtained powers for a 2½ mile extension north from Chertsey to Virginia Water on the Staines-Wokingham line mentioned below. This connection was opened on 1 October 1866, the works involving the construction of a new station at Chertsey, resited on the opposite (north west) side of the Guildford Road. On the town side of the line, the station building, almost the twin of that at Netley, Hampshire completed earlier in the same year, was a substantial two-storey brick Italianate villa with hipped and slated roof, carved eaves brackets and brick quoins, and semi- circular arched openings at ground level. A goods shed, cattle pens and sidings occupied the site of the 1848 terminus, all east of the running lines. A two-road locomotive shed erected on the west side survived until 1937.

Addlestone station, half a mile east of the village centre, was immediately north of the level crossing over what became Station Road. Its building, on the east side is mid Victorian in style, a dignified but unremarkable twin-gabled slate-roofed single storey structure with decorative courses of red brick marked by arched openings. Although lacking their original and pretty valancing, the long canopies over both platforms, which on the east side appear to have been extended at a later date beyond the station building, miraculously escaped maintenance economy drives of the 1970s and 1980s.

A curve enabling trains to run directly from Virginia Water and Chertsey into Woking (Addlestone Junction-Byfleet Junction) was available from 10 August 1885 but carried no regular service until 4 July 1887. After 30 January 1916 when wartime constraints caused withdrawal of the Woking to Windsor service, this curve saw only a few advertised workings and none at all after July 1921. At the other end of the Chertsey line, a single track

Top Right *Addlestone's well-sheltered platforms offer a fair sprinkling of passengers for a train arriving from Virginia Water in about 1905 but to add to the animation, four uniformed staff have been inveigled to pose for the camera* Commercial postcard.

Right *A tank engine running bunker first brings a Waterloo train into Staines, L&SWR in about 1904. The footbridge and the station house on the Up side still survive, but the Down side buildings were replaced by the SR* Commercial postcard.

curve towards Wokingham, provided with the Virginia Water- Chertsey link, was relaid, doubled and resignalled in December 1898. Carrying no regular passenger services, it saw most use on Ascot Race Days . Both curves will be mentioned again later in the light of more recent developments and proposals.

The Windsor & Reading Lines

Another early arrival in north Surrey, the Windsor, Staines & South Western, took the form of a western extension of the 1846 Clapham Junction-Richmond line. This company's line was leased to the L&SWR, which took it over completely in 1850. It reached Datchet, just across the Thames from Windsor, on 22 August 1848, with intermediate stations in present-day Surrey at Ashford and Staines. Until the L&SWR was shamed into providing a proper station for the 1857 visit of the Prince Consort to open the Welsh Charities School, Ashford's facilities were decidedly primitive. Even then, although adequate, the buildings were plain and unprepossessing. Staines received better treatment, with a substantial two-storey station house similar to that at Chertsey in its proportions and recessed central bay but devoid of decorative features. This, like that at Chertsey, survives today.

Access to Windsor along the north-western outskirts of the Home Park was obtained by the railway offering a handsome sum towards the 'essential improvements' of the royal estate, a pet project of the Prince Consort for which parliament had refused funds. Public service over this section started on 1 December 1849. West of Staines, the railway reached Ascot on 4 June 1856, with stations at Egham and Sunningdale, all three with rather plain two-storey houses, twin-gabled with a ground floor bay window on the Up platform side. At Wokingham, attained on 9 July 1856, junction was made with the Reading, Guildford & Reigate Railway. Virginia Water station, which had the standard house on the Up side, was also opened on that day. As we have already noticed, proposed access to Chertsey and Woking had to be postponed. This new line was the property of the euphonically- titled Staines, Wokingham & Woking Junction Railway. Worked by the L&SWR, it was purchased by that company in 1878.

For many years, traffic west of Staines proved to be disappointingly thin, the train services being tailored accordingly. It was not until after World War 2 that this became a very busy line, which by the 1980s had commuter flows in both directions following major residential and industrial developments in south east Berkshire.

There were few improvements to the line's infrastructure up to 1914. Following a collision in 1899, a siding loop to hold the Chertsey line trains was added at Virginia Water, where the platform layout followed the 'V' of the converging lines. On the Windsor branch, a new curve was laid at Staines to allow trains to run direct from Windsor to Woking or to Reading and beyond. Opened on 1 July 1884, its trains required another station in Staines. This timber- built structure, placed on the embankment high above the north side of Staines High Street, came into use on the same day. At first the curve carried a regular Windsor-Egham service, extended to Woking from 1 May 1889, but by 1911 this had been reduced to four trains each way daily. An easy target for wartime economies, it was completely withdrawn after 30 January 1916, Staines High Street closing with it. After 1919, when it was demolished, little or no indication of this wooden station's existence remained but the western curve at Staines was put to further use between July 1921 and July 1930 for a Windsor-Chertsey-Waterloo service. Staines became a busy freight centre and major new works at the main station, including road vehicle loading docks, a second freight yard and Up and Down freight loops came into use in March 1904. As noted in Appendix IV, the signalling here was modernised at the same time.

By Rail to Hampton Court

By the late 1840s the old royal palace at Hampton Court had become a major public attraction with almost 180,000 sightseers arriving each year. With potential traffic growth in mind, the L&SWR promoted a lm 52ch branch from a point on the main line just west of what is now Surbiton station to a

terminus in East Molesey, opposite the Palace at the south end of the road bridge over the Thames. Described in the contemporary *Illustrated London News* report as 'a holiday railway', this line, which ran mostly on an 18ft high embankment, was opened to public traffic on 1 February 1849. It would seem there was a problem with the stability of the embankment, since a letter published in *The Times* twelve days later revealed that the published timetable had been abandoned because horse traction had replaced steam locomotives.

Sir William Tite designed the Hampton Court railway buildings in a suitably 'Tudor' style. The passenger station was given a two-storey building in deep red brick with stone dressings, its central portion recessed between wings decorated with Flemish gables and even the humble locomotive shed on the east side was dignified by a steeply pitched roof, with buttressed walls below. Never one of his best works, Tite's station house suffered sadly from unsympathetic alterations in 1896 and again in 1933. New locomotive facilities (without the turntable originally provided) were erected about 1895 at the Summer Road level crossing in the south-west corner of the station area, when Tite's engine house building became a goods shed. After the 1916 electrification of the passenger services, to be mentioned later, the 1895 locomotive depot saw little use. Another short-lived facility was the extension around 1890 of a track on the east side of the goods yard to serve a riverside wharf.

Above *The Tudoresque buildings of Hampton Court station and a later extension in much more utilitarian style, as seen from the roadway about 1905* Commercial postcard.

In the early years the terminus was served by a single long platform and a shorter one behind it which extended a little way south of the station building. In 1899, in response to traffic growth, the platforms were lengthened and a third inserted to the south of the station building, on the west side. Shortly after this, four berthing sidings were added on the east side south of the River Ember. As we shall see later, the increasing tide of tourists and pleasure-seekers was by this time swollen at certain times of the year by racegoers bound for meetings at Hurst Park. The additional capacity provided by the new works just mentioned also proved useful for accommodating excursion trains which were run to Hampton Court from many departure points, often quite distant. Pleasure traffic was also encouraged by the issue of circular tour tickets which covered a train journey from London to Hampton Court station, a river steamer trip thence to Windsor and return to London by rail via Staines.

Thames Ditton, another river resort, was served by a station added to the branch in November 1851. Here the stationmaster's house and a second brick building with staff and passenger facilities, both of unassuming appearance, were set into the embankment on the Up side. As there was no freight yard, coal and building materials for the subsequent residential development around the station had always to be carted from Hampton Court.

Leisure traffic remained the principal business for many years but some villa building was begun at East Molesey and in nearby Kent Town in the 1860s, that at Thames Ditton following towards the end of the Victorian era. Substantial suburban growth in the catchment areas of the two stations had however to await the late 1920s and the 1930s.

The Reading, Guildford & Reigate Railway

Promoted as an independent concern under the leadership of the Guildford banker Frederick Mangles, the Reading, Guildford & Reigate Railway[1] was a potentially useful cross country link between several main lines and the Channel ports. From its opening it was worked by the SER, taking that company's trains well west of its original system, deep into L&SWR territory and even penetrating that of the GWR. After leasing the new line from 15 March 1850, the SER purchased it from March 1852, a move much criticised by its restive shareholders.

Public train services began at the eastern end, over the eight miles between Redhill and Dorking (the present Dorking West station) on 4 July 1849. This section, built by George Wythes, a local contractor, replaced the intended SER branch from Redhill to Dorking and had intermediate stations at Reigate Town and Betchworth. A 'platform' at Box Hill (the present Dorking Deepdene), was available from February 1851. At Pixham, just east of Dorking, the River Mole was spanned by a graceful viaduct of five brick arches, forming the principal engineering feature of this section. Just west of this, a three arch skew bridge allowed for the proposed Direct London & Portsmouth Railway (authorised in 1846 and 1847 as a single line from Epsom with atmospheric traction but never in fact started) to pass beneath before climbing up to attain the alignment taken up by the RG&RR in Dorking.

Also opened on 4 July 1849 were a further 16 miles between Reading and Farnborough, together with a single line north to east curve to the L&SWR main line, all this built by William Jackson. The curve at Farnborough was used to bring locomotives and rolling stock on to this northern section but subsequently saw no regular use and was severed at the L&SWR end about 1870, the remainder serving as a siding. During World War 2 some clearance work was undertaken to allow rapid restoration of a double track connection at the eastern end should this become a strategic necessity. This did not prove necessary and the curve was removed around 1950.

Charles Henfrey built the Dorking-Shalford section which had an intermediate station named Chilworth & Albury. There were also short 'temporary platforms' to test public demand at Gomshall and at Shere Heath. Public service between Shalford and Redhill started on 20 August 1849 but Shere Heath platform, deemed unsuccessful, was removed in 1850 and as a consequence in 1852 Gomshall became Gomshall & Shere and subsequently received a permanent station building erected on the Up or north side by the SER . This time-lag showed in the architectural style since it was of a somewhat severe Italianate appearance

Top Right *As it passes below Box Hill, the Reading, Guildford and Reigate Railway moulds well into this attractive area of Surrey countryside. At the left in this photograph of about 1906, is the viaduct over the River Mole, which powered Castle Mill, seen in the bottom right hand cor ner. In 1846, George Dudeney, tenant of the Mill, assured the parliamentary committee considering the railway bill that he would use the new line to bring red wheat from Reading to mix with the local white wheat.*

Right *The extended station house on the Down side of Dorking SER station (now Dorking West), looking to Guildford from the end of the staggered Up platform in 1968. The signal box has already been boarded up out of use and the Victorian station building, with its pretty* cottage orné *features, and its SR signage, was to be demolished in the following year. The under-line subway survives at what is now an unstaffed halt* British Rail.

NG TOWN

Above *Box Hill, SER, now Dorking Deepdene, looking towards Redhill and showing the wooden structures added by the S ER in the early 1880s, still in place in 1968. This station is at the end of a long descent into the Mole Valley which presented some difficulties to drivers of heavy steam trains* British Rail.

compared with the earlier buildings at Reigate, Betchworth, Dorking, Chilworth and Shalford, which were in *cottage orné*, mock timbered or tile hung and decoratively barge- boarded, blending in well with the splendid backdrop provided by the North Downs. A feature of the Dorking-Shalford section destined to generate much noisy difficulty to westbound steam trains, was the long climb at 1 in 100 and 1 in 96 out of the Mole valley at Pixham to a summit just east of Gomshall station.

Hoping to acquire extra business at Guildford, the L&SWR had agreed to share with the RG&RR the Ash and Guildford section of its new branch from Guildford to Alton. This double track line, which climbed out of Guildford at 1 in 100, curving sharply west and running parallel to but north of the Hog's Back, was ready in August 1849, enabling the RG&RR to operate trains between Reading and Guildford from 20 August. On the RG&RR section between Farnborough and Ash Junction, the SER services called at an intermediate station named Ash, where a station house with Italianate roof lines and vaguely Continental air was later built by the SER on the Up (north) side.

Delayed by the Guildford tunnel collapse mentioned in chapter 2, the final piece of the Reading-Redhill line, between Guildford and Shalford, was opened on 15 October 1849[2], the same day as the L&SWR extension from Guildford to Godalming. In return for offering running powers over its lines, the L&SWR was entitled to 35 per cent of the SER's receipts on the relevant sections but some ill feeling was generated when in September 1851 the SER cheekily set up a free horse bus service for its passengers between Shalford and Guildford to reduce this financial obligation. For a time the unprincipled SER management even worked a connecting horse bus between their station at Ash and Farnham in an attempt to snatch some L&SWR traffic. Desperate

Above *Shalford, looking to Redhill on 20 February 1965. Some oil traffic is evident in the goods yard* Alan A Jackson.

to secure custom, the SER also undercut L&SWR fares to London, causing that company to protest in May 1850; this initiated skirmishing which continued until a fares agreement was finally reached eight years later.

Although the line was now open throughout from Reading to Redhill, the start of freight traffic was delayed by a shortage of funds for completion of sidings and related buildings. Freight trains eventually began to roll in September 1850 but the goods sheds at Gomshall and Betchworth were not available until 1851 and that at Ash not until 1856. Again in a desperate fight to gain custom, the SER began to undercut L&SWR freight rates. At Dorking, where Thomas Cubitt was building himself a great country mansion on top of the North Downs, he paid for a private siding on the Up side to bring in materials. When his Denbies house was finished and the SER had brought the Prince Consort to see it and plant a tree on the estate, the Dorking siding, with cattle pens and an eight-ton crane, continued to serve the great estate. As we shall see in chapter 8, private sidings were also added later to service the several extraction industries established along the North Downs between Gomshall and Redhill.

At first travelling conditions for the common people able to afford only the cheapest class of ticket were very primitive, though an account in the *Sussex Express* of 2 August 1851 does indicate that their uniformed brothers were not without compassion for their plight in severe weather:

> *We feel great pleasure in recording the very laudable conduct on the part of the officials on the South Eastern Railway.... as the train was proceeding along the line on Monday last, a thunderstorm was pending and upon the train nearing Gomshall the rain began to fall in torrents. The moment the train got up to the station, the passengers in the third class carriages which were uncovered, were informed that they might get into the second*

class carriages during the storm which offer, as a matter of course, was most thankfully accepted.

In the same issue of the same newspaper SER excursion traffic over the line in connection with the Great Exhibition in Hyde Park was noticed and a suggestion made which, as we shall see in chapter 7, was eventually adopted:

On Monday last a monster train came through here, which almost reached from Dorking station to Box Hill station. As allurements are constantly held out to the country people to visit London, we think it would be but fair for the Company to show some sympathy towards the poor Londoners and to give them a cheap trip now and then to visit Dorking for the benefit of a little fresh air; they can be well accommodated here, and would no doubt be gratified by the unequalled scenery of the place.

As elsewhere, the opening of the Reading to Redhill line damaged the profitability of road passenger services. On 10 October 1849. three months after the arrival of the SER service at Dorking, *The Times* advertised an auction in the City of London of:

FOURTEEN superior, good-sized, seasoned HORSES, with their harness, the genuine property of Mr James Hay, which have been working a pair-horse coach from Dorking to London and are to be sold in consequence of the opening of the Reading, Guildford & Reigate Railway.

Boldly imaginative in conception, this cross-country line was to prove a financial disappointment for many years, hampered as it was by the lack of a good physical link to the GWR at Reading and poor facilities there. The awkwardness of running in and out of Redhill and crossing the main Brighton line on the level for journeys to and from the Channel ports was perhaps less important but nevertheless a factor in damaging prospects for fully developing the through traffic potential. This railway stood or fell by its performance as a through route; intermediate business, with no towns in its monopoly territory other than the sleepy hollows of Dorking and Reigate, was bound to be poor. Small wonder that the SER directors were castigated for hauling the RG&RR on board. Even after a suitable junction was provided at Reading in 1858-59 and the terminal facilities there were enhanced, traffic remained unsatisfactory.

Under SER management, improvements and additions to facilities were few: the station buildings at Dorking and Betchworth were enlarged sympathetically to accommodate stationmasters with large families; second platforms were added at Reigate and elsewhere; platforms were extended and in some cases footbridges and subways appeared, to stop the dangerous practice of passengers crossing the line on the level, although this came only after lengthy agitation and constant appeals to the Board of Trade. New traffics eventually arrived after the construction of the Army base at Aldershot (where what is now North Camp station was opened in 1858) and also from the excavation and quarrying of minerals between Gomshall and Redhill. Consideration of these aspects will be found in chapters 7 and 8.

After 1858, with the minor exception of Westcott Rifle Range Halt (opened only as required for military firing parties from November 1916 and demolished after a fire in 1928 when it was already out use), no further stations were provided on the Surrey section of the line. Dorking and Reigate provided a moderate amount of general passenger traffic, supplemented from around 1860 by a slowly increasing trickle of London commuters but at Dorking passenger business was seriously diminished following opening of the more direct LB&SCR line through Leatherhead in 1867. In response to this competition, the SER introduced a few speeded-up workings between Dorking or Gomshall and London Bridge, with corresponding return trains in the evenings. In the early 1880s , seeing a need to add some increase in status in view of its proximity to the LB&SCR station, the SER erected a wooden building containing a ticket office and waiting rooms on the Up platform at Box Hill (now Dorking Deepdene). A resident stationmaster was also installed and by the early 1900s there was a hoarding visible from the roadway which advertised the availability of trains to the

company's four major central London stations.

By the late 1880s traffic was at last showing some signs of growth, enough indeed to stimulate some minor works. In 1887 an intermediate signal box called Westcott was installed to break up the long block section between Dorking and Gomshall, easing the problems of working the long climb on the Down line. A second intermediate box at Brookgate Crossing between Gomshall and Chilworth, along with further signalling refinements were put in place in 1891-2. Through cross-country services between Birkenhead, Birmingham and Dover via Reading and Redhill which had been tried with disappointing results in 1863-68 were revived with more success in 1897, working on a daily basis over improved junctions at Reading. Known to the staff as the 'Contis' these trains ran until the early 1960s except in war years. When through coaches from Manchester and Birmingham to Folkestone and Dover were arranged with the GCR and GWR in 1904 and Midland Railway through coaches from Bradford to Deal were agreed the following year , the SE&CR decided to strengthen some of the bridges between Reading and Redhill.

Above *Farnham station looking to Guildford in about 1868 (the disc signal was removed in 1871). The station house on the Up side still survives, as does the level crossing. The siting demonstrates the lack of importance given to road traffic in the early days of railways; when the longer electric trains arrived here in 1937, the rear of Down trains stood on the level crossing when they were stopped in the station, causing much irritation to motorists.*

The line's function as a link between many important provincial centres and mainland Europe avoiding London assumed great value in both world wars, when, as we shall see later, it had to respond to heavy military demands. With the completion of the Channel Tunnel it may yet show its full potential as a transport artery, but this will first require heavy expenditure on layout improvements at Guildford and Redhill. Meanwhile, in addition to a modest local passenger business it earns useful revenue carrying air passengers between Gatwick Airport and traffic centres outside London and within Surrey, gathers some

Above *Ash Green station, L&SWR, looking to Farnham on 20 February 1965. The station house survives as a private residence* Alan A. Jackson.

through traffic to and from the former Great Western main line at Reading. But its former daily postal trains (between Dover and Manchester and Tonbridge and Glasgow) ceased in 1996 following the opening of the Post Office road/rail hub at Willesden.

The Guildford - Alton Branch Line

We have already noted the opening of the first double track section of the L&SWR Guildford- Alton branch as far as Ash Junction on 20 August 1849 and its use by the SER on behalf of the RG&RR. It was on the following 8 October that this line was extended to Farnham as a single track, through a station called Ash (later Ash Green), just west of Ash Junction, with a small and very plain station house on the Up side. The building still exists, converted to a private residence whose unusual entrance at first floor level no doubt excites curiosity in those unaware of its original purpose. A public freight siding was provided at Tongham, lm12ch beyond Ash. Passenger trains called here from October 1856 to meet the need for access to the new military base at Aldershot, some two miles to the north. The permanent passenger station subsequently built at Tongham's overline road bridge featured a station house extending up from the Down platform to road level. Farnham had a severe-looking, very plain-faced station house on the Up side with a stone cornice at first floor level and was entered by a short flight of steps protected by a canopy.

Alton, just over the Hampshire border, was connected to Farnham by a single line from 28 July 1852. Double tracking of this final section did not take place until June 1901, by which time military requirements in the area were assuming increasing importance. With the doubling, new signal boxes were opened at either end of Farnham station.

Above *Wanborough, looking to Reading, c.1905. The postman on the Down platform is transferring mail between the post office on the station and the guard's van of the train* Commercial postcard.

Doubling between Ash Green and Farnham, completed in June 1884, is less easy to explain; there had been no heavy increase in the line's freight load and after the opening of the Farnham-Aldershot- Ash (SER) connection and the introduction of through services between Aldershot and Guildford via Ash (SER) in 1882, passenger business at Tongham and Ash Green stations was falling away, as was the traffic between Farnham and Guildford by this older line. The decline in revenue over the Farnham-Ash Junction line was belatedly recognised on 1 December 1926 by classifying the two intermediate stations as unstaffed halts and closing the freight facility at Ash Green. In February 1930 to further reduce costs, the SR singled the line between Ash Junction and Farnham Junction[3]. Although hopelessly uneconomic, the Ash Junction-Farnham passenger service was allowed to linger on until July 1937, when a new regular interval service between Ascot, Aldershot and Guildford with Farnham connections at Aldershot provided an excuse for what was to be the first passenger line closure in Surrey. During World War 2, the single line between Farnham Junction and Tongham was used for wagon storage and late in 1954 it was dismantled. The electric key-token system of single line working introduced in 1932[4] was taken out at the same time and thenceforward the Tongham - Ash Junction section was worked as a siding. Latterly demand justified only two trains a week and the predominant traffic was to and from the Aldershot Gas Works as noted in chapter 8. This continued until the late 1950s when the works ceased production and after that, until the end of 1960 when the line was completely closed, the only activity was an occasional load of sugar beet at Tongham in season.

In September 1891, a new passenger and freight station was opened in the long stretch between Ash (SER) and Guildford. Named Wanborough, this was situated in the parish of Normandy about halfway between these two small communities, Here the main building, a plain single storey red

Above *The original station at Caterham with its forest of chimneys, elaborate porch and steeply-inclined roof, looking towards London. This photograph appears to have been taken immediately before its demolition for the 1899/1900 rebuilding; enamel signs on the platform fencing have already been taken down. Some Eton-collared boys are admiring a steam traction engine in the goods yard.*

brick structure, was on the Down side abutting on to a two storey house for the stationmaster and his family. This had barge-boarded gables and on the side facing the road approach, tile hanging which extended from the eaves to the ground. The only building on the Up platform was a canopied wooden shelter. When the 1939 electrification made a footbridge necessary, the SR added a crude concrete structure to further contribute to the muddle of building materials and styles. An unusual feature for Surrey was the post and telegraph office at this station' which the 1933 *Post Office Guide* shows as open for business for twelve hours daily, from 08.00, except Sundays. Drew states that both the station and post office were the result of pressure exercised by Sir Algernon West, tenant of Wanborough Manor, one time secretary to W E Gladstone and chairman of the Board of Inland Revenue. For many years traffic was very light but by the 1930s this once isolated station had attracted its very own little cluster of housing.

Rails along the Caterham Valley

A 4½ mile single line, connecting what is now Purley station to the then small Downland village of Caterham was opened on 5 August 1856 with an intermediate station in Surrey called Warlingham (now Whyteleafe South). Climbing up this steep sided valley, the railway ran close to the main road, terminating below the village. At first there was no other building nearby apart from a small

Above *At the bottom of the hill up to the original settlement, Caterham station (right) as rebuilt in 1899/1900 to handle the traffic from the suburban development stimulated by the railway in this steep-sided Surrey valley. The Railway Hotel (left) was rebuilt in 1902. This photograph dates from about 1903/1904.*

hotel but within a few years, a new townlet named Caterham Valley, had begun to appear around the railway station.

This line was promoted and initially worked by the splendidly independent Caterham Railway Company undertaking which found itself suffering the disadvantages of having to operate within SER territory whilst dependent on a main line junction station controlled by the SER's rival, the LB&SCR. The resulting conflict of interests, which ensured that every hindrance was placed in the small company's path, with its passengers receiving hostile treatment especially as regards main line connections, is lovingly documented in Spence's book[5]. Eventually the opportunity arose for negotiation on a quid pro quo basis between the two main line companies, resulting in the SER purchasing the Caterham Company in 1859 for less than half its initial capital. Even then, as LB&SCR officials were slow to change their attitude, some harassment of Caterham passengers continued for several years.

Optimism must have been strong in the minds of the original promoters since there were rather less than 500 people living in Caterham and but two or three firestone workings offering any prospect for freight traffic (a 1 1/2 mile southward extension to serve the latter was proposed but never built). However despite the inauspicious start, as will be elaborated in chapter 6 this line was to be remarkably successful in encouraging residential development along this once pretty valley.

Showing some consideration for the impact of the railway on the attractive scenery of the area traversed, the Caterham Valley promoters erected buildings in what was then called the Old English Domestic style, nowadays better known as *cottage orné*. Their architect, Richard Whittall, produced

Above *Whyteleafe station, just inside the border of present-day Surrey, seen here under construction in September 1899, looking towards Caterham.*

designs which featured tall, steeply-gabled, pattern-tiled roofs with half-timbering on the upper storey above quoined walls of masonry rubble. His roofs sprouted high finials and tall chimneys and entrance porches were all but overwhelmed by peaky gables. Whittall's attempt at trying to resurrect the past was seen at its most exuberant at Caterham, where the result was certainly eye-catching. The building here stood in the centre of the station area, approached by a carriage drive which descended steeply from what is now Station Avenue. There was only one short passenger platform, on the east side, and a small freight yard to the west. At what is now Whyteleafe South, Whittall's station house was on the west side of the line, offering sparse shelter for passengers and without a goods yard. Some years later the SER added a Down platform carrying a single storey building of studied plainness together with a sash-windowed, weather- boarded signal box for the level crossing. Although it is no longer in Surrey, brief mention may be made of Kenley (called Coulsdon until December 1856), where the Whittall station house was placed east of the line . This station later received a three-road freight yard on the same side.

By the end of the 19th century, with little improvement made in the first 40 years and traffic showing signs of strong growth, the SER decided on some substantial new works including doubling of the track throughout. In the Surrey section a third station was added, at Whyteleafe. This had a two-road freight yard and whilst its passenger building was no more than the usual SER weather- boarded shed, the generous canopies of equal length over both platforms were perhaps some sort of recognition of the importance of the Valley's growing residential traffic. An unroofed lattice girder foot-bridge connected the two sides.

This major upgrading of the branch, all completed in January 1900, also included total rebuilding of the terminus at Caterham with a wide island platform much longer than the old and generously canopied. The freight yard was enlarged and given a new goods shed and a locomotive turntable was provided on the west side. Whittall's pixie cottage and its approach road disappeared, to be replaced by a single-storey block placed across the end of the line, fronting what is now Station Avenue and connected to the plat form by covered sloping footway. In brick under a hipped slate roof, with a substantial canopy over its entrance, the new building was given little decorative treatment but in appearance was solid and dignified, instantly recognisable as a railway station.

By the Thames Valley Railway to Shepperton

Shepperton, then in Middlesex, was the terminus of the mostly single line Thames Valley Railway, running 6 1/2 miles west from Thames Valley Junction near Strawberry Hill[6]. W S Lindsay, one time lord of the manor of Shepperton and the company's chairman, was moved to promote the line by the problems he had in reaching London in winter after the collapse of the two central arches of the Walton bridge over the Thames. As was not unusual with such independent promotions at the time he arranged the proposed line as bait for more than one large company, including a connection with the GWR near Brentford as well as one with the L&SWR near Twickenham. Early in 1862 the GWR's terms for working the Thames Valley were rejected as unacceptable and that part of the scheme was abandoned but there was one no doubt intended outcome : nervous of the possibility of the GWR entering its territory, the L&SWR had moved quickly into agreement to work the new line. Aird & Son then accepted the construction contract, taking up the largest share holding. Built with a single line, but with earthworks and bridges to accommodate double track, the branch saw its first public services on 1 November 1864, the L&SWR trains taking about an hour to reach Waterloo via Twickenham. There was one intermediate station in present day Surrey, at Sunbury and both this and Shepperton had freight yards. The double track was eventually provided between Fulwell and Sunbury from 17 July 1878 and onwards to Shepperton from the following 9 December, an improvement largely stimulated by the opening of a race course at Kempton Park with rail facilities which will be described in chapter 7.

All the stations had two-storey houses of standard design in a distinctive and pleasing Italianate villa style characterised by a yellowish brick, pedimented gables, dentilled cornices at the eaves, and windows formed by groups of three narrow lights,

Below *Sunbury, looking to Shepperton, 3 March 1962. The private siding to the Millboard works is seen at the right and the somewhat inactive public goods yard at the left. The large building beyond the end of the war-damaged Up platform, the sub-station erected for the 1916 electrification, originally housed two 1,250 kW rotary converters*
J N Faulkner.

each rounded into an arch at the top. Since an extension across the Thames to link up with the Chertsey line south of Addlestone had been proposed, Shepperton was laid out as a through station with two side platforms. In October 1864 John Aird had offered to finance and build this further section but whilst the Thames Valley board were in full support of this scheme, the L&SWR, still fearing the Thames Valley could be taken over by the GWR and upgraded as a thrust into its territory, firmly opposed it. The L&SWR bought out the small company in January 1867, but had to continue to demonstrate its opposition for another twenty years or so in the face of attempts by local interests to keep the extension a live issue.

In retrospect it would seem short-sighted for the L&SWR to have so obstinately opposed the extension across the Thames beyond Shepperton since at the very least it would have provided a useful diversionary route and relief for the main line. And with the extensive residential developments around Woking and Byfleet since World War 2, it would have offered an alternative for journeys to workplaces at Shepperton and elsewhere along the line now made by car. As a dead-end line, the Thames Valley never came to very much, traversing as it did unpromising territory for development of rail traffics to and from Kingston or Twickenham and London. Even in modern times, with electric services, loadings have never been very substantial.

The Epsom Downs Branch

Completed in May 1865 and primarily designed to serve the famous Derby race course, the 4m 10ch branch to Epsom Downs climbed steeply up from Sutton. Independently promoted as the Banstead & Epsom Downs Railway Company, it was purchased by the LB&SCR in 1864.

The bleakly situated terminus, which eventually acquired as many as nine uncovered plat forms, was located at the extreme north east corner of Epsom Downs where until the 1920s there was little or no population, the place only coming to life on the few race days each year. Indeed. so sparse was the ordinary traffic that for many years the trains did not venture beyond Banstead station after early evening. Nor was business much more lively at Banstead, where, for sixty years or so the station was in a somewhat solitary spot almost a mile north west of the old village it was supposed to serve.

Architecturally the stations had no merit. At

Below *The building across the end of the Epsom Downs branch, 8 March 1969. The whole of the extensive area occupied by this station and approaches is now covered by a housing estate* Alan A Jackson.

Above *Cranleigh station, looking towards Horsham about 1905; only one passenger seems likely to board the Guildford train which is entering; the other figures visible are railway staff. Everything seen here is now covered by a shopping complex and its access roads* Commercial postcard.

Epsom Downs a range of single-storey stuccoed brick buildings and a two storey house were placed across the end of the tracks. Platforms here were built for crowd handling, broad and lengthy but in view of the sporadic nature of the business, no shelter was provided from the elements other than a small covered area immediately behind the ticket hall. Banstead's single storey building was on the west side of the bridge carrying Banstead Road over the line, with a very plain looking double- fronted house for the stationmaster immediately to the south. A freight yard subsequently built on the Down side west of the station was supplemented by two sidings for loading chalk, one here and another on the Up side east of the road bridge, this traffic fading away in the 1920s. With electrification of the passenger services and new commuter housing sprouting up all around, the SR refurbished the entrance building, reglazing the windows in steel frames, reconstructing the interior and placing a canopy over the doorway from the road. At the same time the stairways down to the plat forms were rebuilt and there was some enlargement of the original structure over the tracks. At rail level, platform canopies were extended on a steel girder framework to twice their original length, affording adequate shelter for the growing crowds of commuters. All this was finished by the end of 1936, when houses were still being erected in the area. Subsequent changes on the branch and its role in carrying race traffic will be mentioned later.

Guildford to Horsham: Surrey's Sole Sacrifice to Beeching

The Horsham & Guildford Direct Railway, a 15m 48ch single line, with passenger and freight stations in Surrey at Bramley, Cranleigh and Baynards, came into public service on 2 October 1865[7]. Leaving the L&SWR at Peasmarsh Junction,

Above *Bramley & Wonersh, LB&SCR, looking to Horsham about 1903. This company showed great consideration for its passengers when providing station accommodation - note the windscreen at the north end of the Up platform* Commercial postcard.

1 3/4 miles south of Guildford, it joined the LB&SCR Mid-Sussex line at Stammerham Junction, 2m 18ch southwest of Horsham. After contributing to the cost of construction, the LB&SCR had purchased the promoting company in 1864 and faced with the threat of legislation to secure separate access into Guildford, the L&SWR had conceded running powers into its station.

Regular passenger services, at first a mere four each way daily, were worked between Guildford and Horsham but the new line also offered a convenient route for through special trains to south coast resorts. These not only included Sunday School outings from the south western suburbs and the Thames valley but excursions from more distant parts, such as the Midlands cities and towns.

Although Cranleigh and Bramley were already fair sized communities, Baynards, the tiniest of hamlets, owed its station to the need to appease Lord Thurlow, owner of Baynards Park, which the railway wanted to cross. Since it was at the approximate halfway point, this isolated spot received a passing loop, signal box and two platforms. It was not until 1876 that Bramley gained similar provision and another four years after that before Cranleigh was so enlarged. With these extra passing places it became possible by the early 1880s to operate up to seven trains each way daily though Sunday services never exceeded three each way.

Bramley and Cranleigh stations had simple and quite plain buildings of similar design with a two-storey house for the stationmaster abutting on to modest single-storey passenger and staff accommodation. Cranleigh did eventually acquire a covered footbridge, an indication of an increase or expected increase in high revenue traffic, but at Bramley and Baynards passengers were left to walk round over the level crossings . At Baynards, the neat brick buildings on each platform included canopies of arched section and on the Up side there was a small staff cottage and a goods shed.

After the line had been open for some years, some of its regular and more articulate users based at Cranleigh and Bramley considered the LB&SCR was paying more attention to making good connections with its own services at Horsham rather than into and out of the more direct London trains at Guildford. As related in chapter 9, several unsuccessful attempts were made to remedy this situation by advocating a railway from Cranleigh through Ewhurst to join the LB&SCR in the Dorking area. This discontent was still rumbling in 1908 when a motor bus service was proposed between Cranleigh and Guildford in the hope of stimulating some reaction from the LB&SCR.

Despite this agitation and some significant residential growth at Bramley and Cranleigh, right through to the 1960s virtually nothing was done to improve the sparse and slow passenger service. Reductions made in World War 2 lasted long after the return of peace and by the 1960s, with population growth continuing in the Surrey section, at eight each way on weekdays and four on Sundays, the service was much as it had been in the Victorian era. By this time those without cars were turning to the more frequent competing buses.

Freight traffic was mostly inwards coal and agricultural requirements, movement of cattle to the markets at Guildford and Horsham, processed timber from a Cranleigh firm and bricks from a works at Baynards. Once in place, the railway soon rendered the parallel Wey & Arun Canal unprofitable, reducing its receipts and tonnage by around half in the first year of its operation although final closure of the waterway was deferred until 1871-72. As Appendix III shows, the line sprouted five sets of private sidings on its Surrey section and these were supplemented by a public goods facility at Stonebridge near the Wey & Arun wharf of that name. As noted in chapter 8, the Baynards brickworks just north of the station on the west side of the line became a chemical works which was receiving wagon loads of sulphur right up to the final closure of the railway.

This cross country link was selected as Surrey's single contribution to the great pile of branch and secondary lines sacrificed on the Marples/Beeching altar. Put to investigating the simple fiscal receipts and expenditure, the accountants recommended the death sentence. As a preliminary, Sunday trains and all excursion workings were withdrawn in 1962, then in June 1965, without any experiments with more economical working methods, the passenger and freight services ceased.

Since then, after repairing collapsed bridges, the respective local authorities have converted much of the trackbed to a waymarked footpath and bridleway known as the 'Downs Link'. At Bramley the station postbox and platforms survive but Cranleigh's station site, close to the main street offered commercial possibilities and was in due course sold off and covered with a remarkably ugly shopping development. Only at Baynards does the railway site remain almost unaltered with all its buildings intact and well maintained but this sympathetic restoration is not accessible to the public.

The wisdom of the 1962-65 decisions may be questioned. Cranleigh's population had continued to expand and the 1991 census showed that the built- up area contained around 11,000 residents, forming the largest settlement in Surrey without railway facilities. Heavy strains were being thrown on local roads and by the mid 1990s consideration was being given by the local authorities to construction of a light rail system which would make use of the old trackbed northwards towards Guildford.

Brookwood-Aldershot-Farnham and the Aldershot-Ash Curve

With the construction and subsequent expansion of the Aldershot military base pressures built up from the early 1860s for better railway accommodation to serve it and eventually, fearing that others might intervene, the L&SWR was moved to promote its own scheme. From 2 May 1870 a double track came into public use from Pirbright Junction (on the main line west of Brookwood) to a station in Aldershot new town just inside the Hampshire

Above *Ash Vale's lofty station building on the Down side, photographed on 23 November 1974 just before it underwent a major reconstruction* Alan A Jackson.

border. Beyond here, the new railway continued as a single track back into Surrey, joining the existing branch serving Farnham. East of Aldershot there was a station called North Camp and Ash Vale (now Ash Vale). Sited on a high embankment, this had a tall three-storey station house in buff-coloured brick, which rose from the approach road on the Down side up to rail level. The existing single track between the new Farnham Junction and Farnham station was doubled with the opening of the new line but the Farnham Junction-Aldershot section remained single until 10 March 1875.

With the opening of the line, an L&SWR curve was built to connect Aldershot with the SER line at Aldershot Junction South, situated immediately north of that company's Ash station . On 1 May 1879, following an agreement on reciprocal running powers, SER trains began to work over this curve into a new bay at Aldershot L&SWR station. Ash (SER) was altered to provide Up and Down bays for what became a push-pull shuttle in and out of Aldershot L&SWR, the locomotives housed in a small new shed at Ash. For its part, on 1 October 1882, the L&SWR started a direct Guildford-Ash (SER)-Aldershot service. With these improvements in place the Army base at Aldershot had direct rail links to London and to Portsmouth both for special trains carrying troops and equipment and for individual journey by public services.

Further improvements over these lines were introduced by the Southern Railway between the wars. From July 1937 there was a regular interval steam push-pull service between Ascot, Camberley, Aldershot and Guildford and this was replaced by electric trains from 1 January 1939.

Ash Vale-Bagshot-Ascot

From the 1860s onwards a whole clutch of schemes came forward to fill the railway void that existed in north west Surrey between the London

Above *Frimley, looking to Aldershot in about 1905. The presence of passenger coaches and no less than three locomotives in the goods yard beyond the end of the platform suggests that the photograph was taken on the busiest of the Ascot Race Days.* Commercial postcard.

& Southampton and the Virginia Water-Wokingham lines. Most of these proposals aimed at meeting royal and military favour and convenience by offering direct access between the GWR at Windsor, Ascot, the new Army Staff College at Camberley (then known as Cambridge Town) and Aldershot. Only one made some progress. This was the independently promoted Sunningdale & Cambridge Town Railway which secured the support of the military authorities and was authorised in 1864. A year later, an extension through Frimley to join the SER at Blackwater, giving access to Aldershot, also gained parliamentary approval. Alas after some construction work had started in 1864 the little company fell victim to the financial panic of 1866, leaving as its memorial some completed earthworks between Frimley Road, York Town and Crawley Ridge, on the eastern edge of Camberley.

All these schemes greatly worried the L&SWR, which eventually secured its position in 1873 by obtaining sanction for a railway from the main line just east of Farnborough through Camberley to Ascot, with stations at Frimley, Camberley & York Town, and Bagshot. The 1873 Act also included a 2m 19ch extension at the southern end to join the Pirbright Junction-Aldershot-Farnham line just east of what is now Ash Vale station. When construction of these lines started, use was made of the aborted work at Camberley just mentioned. Initially there was only a single track from Ascot to Frimley Junction although a double line was provided on the east curve from Frimley Junction to the main line at Sturt Lane Junction. A corresponding west curve towards Farnborough was also authorised though this seems not to have been completed until later. It was first regularly used from 1 June 1901, by a daily Waterloo-Ascot-Basingstoke train, this reduced to Saturdays only after October 1908, ceasing altogether in December 1914. This western curve carried another advertised service, between Ascot and Winchfield, from 17 July 1933 to 4 July 1937. After that, it continued to be useful for special workings, notably Ascot race trains and will be mentioned again later.

Passenger services between Ascot and Frimley were started on 18 March 1878 followed by freight on 1 April. There were six passenger workings daily each way between Woking and Ascot via Sturt Lane Junction but single line working initially made travel to and from London miserably slow. A Bagshot - Waterloo journey for example could take anything from lh19min to 2h. Between Frimley station and Frimley Junction the line was doubled in June 1879 and double track was available all the way to Ascot from 11 June 1893.

Frimley, Camberley and Bagshot stations showed a distinct similarity in appearance and plan. All three had neat and workmanlike single-storey buildings comprising a short central block containing the entrance hall and ticket office, this flanked by gabled barge-boarded pavilions. Attractive decorative features were incorporated in the brickwork and clover leaf ventilation openings were placed in the gable ends. Smaller brick buildings in matching style with pitched and slated roofs stood on the opposite platforms. Platform canopies were of generous dimensions.

From 2 June 1879 the strategic layout along Surrey's western borderlands and military districts was completed with the opening of the section south from Frimley Junction to join the existing line on the London side of Ash Vale station. Only a single track was provided but since the land was cheap, enough was taken for future doubling and bridge construction allowed for this, though it has never been done. initially trains ran between Frimley, Aldershot and Farnham. With these railways in place, the royal family and household and the military establishment no doubt took comfort from the thought that Aldershot military base, the Royal Military Academy, the Army Staff College, Ascot Race Course and Windsor Castle were at last all most conveniently and directly linked by rail without a penny of royal or government money having been spent.

Below *Construction of the New Guildford line by Messrs. Lucas & Aird in 1883, looking from the Portsmouth Direct line north of Guildford station towards the viaduct over the River Wey and London Road station.*

The 'New Guildford' and Effingham-Leatherhead lines[8]

The 1880s saw the last major bout of railway construction in Surrey, filling some of the few remaining voids. One of the latter was the countryside between the Wimbledon-Dorking and Woking-Guildford lines, which contained no towns and few villages of any size but was brought to notice by an 1881 bill. This optimistically and cheekily sought powers for a 25-mile Guildford, Kingston & London Railway extending from the Metropolitan District Railway at Putney Bridge to Kingston on Thames then striking out into this area. The promoting committee was bolstered with such prominent and influential Surrey personalities as the Lord Lieutenant of the county , Lord Lovelace of Horsley Towers; the Earl of Onslow of Clandon Park; and Lord Foley of Ruxley Lodge, Claygate. All three held land in the area to be served and the prospects of lucrative sales for residential development once a railway had opened up the area were perhaps passing across their minds. Civic interest was apparent in the presence on the committee of the mayors of Kingston and Guildford, no doubt hoping that if the L&SWR services to their boroughs were subjected to some competition (or the threat of it) that would be no bad thing.

Whilst Guildford was the main objective, branches to Ashtead and Bookham were thrown in and for good measure, running powers were sought through Guildford to bring the company's trains on to the LB&SCR Cranleigh and Horsham line. There was even a proposed spur to join the Guildford-Reading line north of Guildford station, passing over the L&SWR. Whilst it had no hope of raising the necessary capital on its own, the Metropolitan District Railway in the person of its chairman, James Staats Forbes, was very active behind the scenes giving tacit support and advice

Below *Construction of the Leatherhead-Effingham Junction line, 1883. Erection of the five-arch viaduct over the River Mole is just being started. In the background is the ornamented bridge carrying the LB&SCR Dorking line over the river. The L&SWR carriages in the background are standing on the spur beyond that company's Leatherhead station.*

and standing ready with offers to work the line.

This ambitious proposal, the last and strongest of several schemes for this part of Surrey, understandably aroused much interest at the time, not least in the offices and boardroom at Waterloo station. Faced with the prospect of a deep and wounding invasion of its territory , the L&SWR was jerked into a vigorous reaction. After negotiations with the promoters, a compromise was reached whereby it was agreed the L&SWR would build its own lines to fill the void south west of Surbiton. Writing about this area in *The South Western Gazette*, Sam Fay perceptively noted 'It is a beautiful country which certainly in time will become a favourite residential district for City men'.

To tap this potential spring of First Class commuters, the L&SWR undertook to build a 16 1/2 mile double track from Hampton Court Junction (lm 25ch south west of Surbiton) to Guildford, much of it using the route chosen by the 1881 promoters. Their proposed single line branch from Downside to Bookham was however replaced by a 4 1/2 m link from what was to become Effingham Junction to Leatherhead, passing north of the Bookhams and realising the 1859 proposal mentioned in chapter 2. The 1881 scheme's connections allowing through running from Surbiton to Ashtead and Leatherhead via Oxshott and from Guildford to Leatherhead and Ashtead via Cobham were omitted in favour of a simple west to east curve at Bookham which would allow direct services between Surbiton and Leatherhead, the one part of the L&SWR proposals which was never completed since it was in part to be rendered unnecessary by provision of an interchange station at Effingham Junction.

Otherwise the L&SWR did not stint in its investment in the new lines, which were opened to the public on 2 February 1885. They were adorned with handsome red brick stations of more or less standard appearance, with hipped and tiled roofs and ornamented chimney caps, In each case a two-storey house for the stationmaster abutted on to a single storey range of passenger and staff accommodation, which was well canopied on the platform side. All windows had square panes in the

Below *Horsley station, looking to Guildford, soon after its opening in 1885; six railway staff are in view including the guard and driver of the train. The leisurely attitudes of the latter suggest this is a train which has terminated here and will shortly return to Waterloo.*

Above *Bookham station about 1885, looking to Guildford. The Leatherhead train is headed by L&SWR 4-4-2T class 415 no.492.*

upper sash and the openings were finished with segmented brick arches. A characteristic feature was a bulky lavatory annexe crowned by a somewhat dominant ventilator, All the bricks and tiles used came from local sources, The names chosen were Claygate, Oxshott & Fairmile, Cobham, Horsley, Clandon, London Road (Guildford) and Bookham. Cobham, Horsley, Clandon and Bookham were all somewhat distant from the places they were supposed to serve.

Arthur George, Earl of Onslow and William, Earl of Lovelace, owners of 11,761 and 10,214 Surrey acres respectively at the time these railways were built, received goodly sums from selling their land to the L&SWR whilst retaining their 'sporting rights' over it at seeming risk to human life and limb, not to mention delay to the train services whilst fur and feather were chased over the tracks. Turner relates that the land sold for Horsley station and the railway line through his estate brought Lovelace a profit of almost £8,000 at 1883 values, whilst Onslow received the then enormous sum of just under £52,000 for lands required by the company in the Guildford area. Lovelace's lawyers secured construction of a 'private siding and enclosed coal depot' for his exclusive use. They also legally bound the railway to repair all gates opening on to the Lovelace estate; to keep fences, ditches and water courses in good order, and to plant and 'for ever keep planted' with firs, larch and spruce, 'in close and compact order, so as to present a neat, ornamental and copse-like appearance' all lineside land through the Lovelace acres.

Public freight yards were provided at Claygate (London end, Down side), Oxshott (country end, Up side), Cobham (Up side, country end), Bookham (country end, Down side), Horsley (Down side, parallel with the passenger station), Clandon (London end, Down side) and London Road (country end, Down side). Supplementing these was a public freight siding on the Down side at Merrow, 1m 28ch on the Guildford side of Clandon. Merrow was served by a signalbox on the Up side until a ground frame replaced it in 1932. This siding was accessible from the Burpham-Merrow road (Merrow Lane)

EFFINGHAM JUNCTION
RIARY

and led to another for the exclusive use of the Earl of Onslow, for which he paid a ten percent rent on its construction cost.

Effingham Junction station, sometimes referred to as a halt, was added in July 1888. Built mostly in wood, with a tiny ticket office perched on the east side of the road bridge over the line, it was very much the poor relation as regards amenities and building standards and had no freight facilities.

Although the greater part of the traffic handled was always local, what soon became known as the 'New Guildford Line' (a term which remains current) was to prove a useful diversionary route for traffic to and from points beyond Guildford and it is still so used at the time of writing. From around 1890 the line carried some fast Portsmouth trains, which secured an uninterrupted non-stop run after provision of refuge sidings for freight trains at Claygate and Horsley in 1897 and at Clandon and London Road in the following year. The 'New Guildford' also found favour with at least one guide book writer . In the *Homeland Handbook, Haslemere & Hindhead* for 1913, Joseph E Morris enthused:

> *Those who travel to Guildford by this latter route gain a better conception of the beauties of rural Surrey, for the countryside is everywhere beautiful with alternate coppice, pasture and ploughland. In spring the woods that lie thickly along the line are yellow with innumerable primroses...*

One wonders what words Morris would choose to describe a car journey along the parallel A3 dual carriageway motor road or the nearby M25 were he alive today.

Above *Claygate, Down side, on 20 June 1981. The lavish ventilation of the gentlemen's lavatories was a prominent feature of the architecture of the New Line stations* Alan A Jackson.

Top Left *Effingham Junction station, looking to Guildford, c.1910. Whilst the stationmaster (?) appears to be standing to attention for the photographer, the attitudes struck by the men at the platform edge give no clue as to what they are about. The shoddy wooden buildings are in marked contrast to the solidly-constructed and generous accommodation at the other stations on this line* Commercial postcard.

Left *The spectacular viaduct which carries the Oxted line over Riddlesdown Quarry on the Surrey/London border. A spotless LB&SCR Atlantic heads a six coach Up train in about 1914* Wentworth S Gray.

Above *Lingfield just completed, in May 1884, shortly after opening for public service, looking towards London. A top-hatted gentleman (the stationmaster) poses proudly with two uniformed staff. The facilities here had subsequently to be extended to accommodate the heavy traffic handled on race days.*

Top Right *Upper Warlingham looking south in 1884, its year of opening, when the nameboard read simply 'Warlingham'. The SER's cheap and cheerful clapboard bungalow style is well portrayed.*

Right *Oxted, looking south about the time of the line's opening in 1884. Almost all, if not all in this photograph appear to be railway staff and the public service may not yet have begun.*

The Oxted Lines

East Surrey's share of the final burst of 19th century railway building was a line from South Croydon to Oxted and East Grinstead and also one running out of this at Hurst Green Junction (lm 10ch south of Oxted) to Edenbridge and Ashurst Junction near Tunbridge Wells. The Oxted and East Grinstead was opened on 10 March 1884 and the second line reached Edenbridge on 2 January 1888. Between Oxted and East Grinstead, a 26ch connection known as the Crowhurst spur, first used by public services on 1 August 1884, allowed trains to reach the SER's Redhill-Tonbridge line. Between South Croydon, Oxted and Crowhurst Junction North box (at the Crowhurst spur) ownership and working was shared by the LB&SCR and SER under the management of the Croydon, Oxted & East Grinstead Railways Joint Committee; all else was LB&SCR property.

During construction by the contractor Joseph Firbank, use was made of the earthworks constructed in 1865-67 by Messrs Waring for the Surrey & Sussex Junction Railway, which was planned to connect Croydon to Oxted and Groombridge (for Tunbridge Wells). This earlier scheme had been launched with strong backing from the LB&SCR which saw it as a way of blocking off a threatened SER invasion of its perceived territory . The Surrey & Sussex was taken over by the LB&SCR in 1869, but was quickly abandoned by its new owners, who decided they had spent far too much money on a railway unlikely to pay its

Above *Dormans station entrance building, seen here in the 1920s, has not changed much over the years* Commercial postcard.

way and one no longer justified as a blocking line following new agreements with its neighbour, the SER. Before this in 1866, cheaper Belgian navvy labour had been brought in to construct the section between South Croydon and Oxted (including work on the Riddlesdown and Oxted tunnels) but these unfortunates had suffered attacks from rioting British navvies as well as seeing their numbers severely depleted by accidents, smallpox and cholera. After the LB&SCR had extricated itself, nature took over the half-built works, whose presence served as an irritant for the SER, still nursing the worry that this line might be revived by the LB&SCR and used as launching pad for a direct railway from London to Hastings. In the event diplomacy triumphed. An agreement concluded between the two companies in 1878-79 allowed for sharing operation and revenue from a substantial part of new lines in the area, as outlined above. In the authorising LB&SCR Act which covered this new construction, the preamble talked of reviving the powers vested in the company in 1869 and the ten miles or so from Croydon to Oxted was described as 'practically identical' to the 1865 line.

Stations in Surrey at the time of opening were located at Upper Warlingham, Oxted, Lingfield and Dormans, all except the last with public freight yards. Dormans did however eventually get a single siding on the Up side to bring in coal for the adjacent Homes of St Barnabas and also, between the country end of the station and the Cooks Pond viaduct, a private siding for the Dormans Park Estate, of which more later. The architecture presented sharp contrasts: the SER contributed its characteristic cheap and not especially cheerful weather-boarded timber-framed and sash-windowed single storey sheds for the stations at Upper Warlingham and Oxted. In more recent times, BR attempted to lengthen their lives by applying a pebble-dash rendering to the weather boarding. At Lingfield and Dormans, however, the LB&SCR, which in general tended to go for higher standards of passenger accommodation, did rather better.

Above *The viaducts on the Croydon, Oxted and East Grinstead were of an elegant standard pattern. This view of c 1904 shows the one just south of Oxted station carrying an SECR train* Commercial postcard.

Lingfield's Up side received the usual LB&SCR wayside station design of the period, one which combined a two storey house for the stationmaster, a single storey entrance building and gabled pavilion for the public accommodation and offices , the range closed off at the country end with a men's lavatory block. Valanced canopies were provided for the full length of these buildings on the platform side. The Down platform, reached by a covered footbridge, had canopies of matching design and length and another gentlemanly convenience (ladies were given facilities discreetly placed within their own waiting room on the Up platform). At Dormans, the main buildings were on the Down side and above the cutting. Here the standard stationmaster's residence adjoined a smaller single storey entrance and ticket office block through which passengers reached covered stairs and a roofed footbridge connecting the platforms, which were generously and prettily canopied. At both stations the brickwork and chimneys displayed tasteful decorative touches. The LB&SCR's Saxby & Farmer brick signal boxes also appeared elegantly solid and dignified in contrast to the shoddy looking clap-boarded sash-windowed affairs favoured by the SER.

These new lines involved much heavy engineering work, particularly for the crossing of the North Downs between Sanderstead and Oxted, which became one of the finest scenic routes out of London. Entering Surrey, the tracks shared the narrowing Caterham valley with the Godstone Road and the Caterham branch line, running high on a ledge on the eastern side. Just beyond Warlingham station the tracks swerved south east into a side valley crossing a four-arch brick viaduct above the Woldingham Road. Just under two miles south of Upper Warlingham station the summit was attained and almost at once the tracks entered the lm 506 yard Oxted or Woldingham tunnel. A start on this had been made by the Surrey & Sussex

Above *Woldingham, looking to London, about 1904, an interesting mix of LB&SCR nameboard and signalling and SER architecture*
Commercial postcard.

Junction contractor in 1866-67 and there were seven construction shafts at approximately 200yd intervals. During construction springs were encountered at the base of the chalk stratum and it was probably the flow from these which triggered the serious roof collapse which occurred in June 1917 and another in May 1919. These incidents caused the line to be temporarily closed and further interruptions to traffic occurred when the tunnel was rebuilt in 1920-21. Today water continues to drain out of the southern portal. Another engineering work of note on the Surrey section is the handsome 150 yard viaduct with its three maln wrought iron lattice girder spans supported on brick piers which carries the line across the valley of the infant river Eden between Oxted station and the 550 yard Limpsfield tunnel.

As explained in chapter 6, Oxted rewarded the railway with vigorous middle class residential growth. A gas works was opened in 1885 in Station Road East, close to the east side of the line at the country end of the station, requiring its own siding accommodation which was enlarged in 1892 and again in 1902. Until it ceased production in June 1933 this works proved a useful source of traffic, needing some 2,000 tons of railborne coal a year by the late 1910s. One customer was the railway itself which converted its lighting from oil to gas in 1892 and remained a loyal user for the next 75 years or so. In 1899 Oxted station received another public freight siding and in the same year a waiting room was added on the Down platform. More improvements followed in 1894-96 including a new signal box; two further sidings and a goods shed were added in 1902-03. The facilities used by the large lime works north of the station and provision at Lingfield for race traffic, along with subsequent improvements at Oxted station will receive mention in later chapters.

Another of the SER's weather-boarded sheds was provided for Marden Park station, opened on 1 July 1885. Now known as Woldingham, this was situated in the attractive undulating countryside

between Upper Warlingham and Oxted tunnel, where a local landowner, intent on high class residential development, had not only donated a suitable plot for the railway facilities but also contributed an eighth of the building costs. Following a modest start on construction of up-market houses, sidings were added here in 1892 to bring in building materials and domestic fuels.

Further passenger accommodation appeared in the summer of 1907 when a LB&SCR steam rail motor service was introduced between Oxted and Groombridge. These trains called at all stations and new wooden halts at Hurst Green (lm 10ch south of Oxted) and Monks Lane (just inside the Kent border). Always very poorly patronised, the latter was closed a few days after the beginning of World War 2 but as we shall see later, Hurst Green eventually did rather better. Additional signal boxes, mainly used for dealing with the increased activity generated by Lingfield race traffic, came into service in 1908 between Hurst Green Junction and Crowhurst Junction North (Hurst Green Intermediate) and between Crowhurst Junction North and Lingfield Station (Lingfield Intermediate).

Above *The caption of this c. 1907 postcard reads 'Hurst Green Motor Halt'. On the bridge above, a small boy is held up to see the latest in rail trainsport. The present Hurst Green station is sited just on the other side of the bridge* Commercial postcard

North of Lingfield, the Crowhurst spur carried no regular service from May 1955 but saw some occasional use for emergency diversions and special workings until finally closed in October 1965.

By GWR to Staines

Surrey is not a county one usually associates with the Great Western Railway but a fragment of that company's proud empire did cross over its modern boundary. The southern end of a 6 1/2 mile single line promoted by the Staines & West Drayton Railway reached Colnbrook on 9 August 1884 and

BRITISH RAILWAYS
STAINES WEST
436
GUILDFORD
KYY 512

Above *Everything well finished and spacious, as one expects from the GWR; Colnbrook, looking to Staines about 1908* Commercial postcard.

Top Left *Staines West, the station which was Mr Finch's house, seen in July 1955 with the front door wide open to allow passengers to reach the platform in what was his garden* Alan A Jackson.

Left *A train in Mr Finch's back garden, awaiting passengers for Colnbrook and West Drayton and the halts between on 18 July 1955* Alan A Jackson.

Staines on 2 November 1885. Worked from the opening day by the GWR, this independent undertaking did not become part of that company's system until 1 July 1900.

It had been intended to form a junction with the L&SWR at Staines but when that company held back from joint working with the GWR, a site for a terminus in the town had to be found. With an eye to economy, the small company settled upon a house and garden owned by CW Finch of Finch & Rickman's Mustard Mills which offered the possibility of easy conversion. Its entrance hall became a booking hall, a canopy erected over the back yard formed a small concourse and the spacious back garden accommodated a single platform, a platform line and an engine run-round road. Nearby, a suitable plot was found for a freight yard and goods shed.

Freight facilities were also provided at Colnbrook, which became a passing place when the extension to Staines was opened. Colnbrook's station building, on the Down platform, in the GWR brick-built style of its period, had end gables of vaguely Flemish appearance. In the middle of the Up platform there was a small canopied brick-built waiting shelter and passengers crossed the line on the level. The stationmaster and his family were accommodated in an elegant house with Flemish gables which was sited at right angles to the railway on the northwest side of the level crossing over the old London to Bath road. This station remained quite busy until well after World War 2. In the late 1950s, for example, it was handling some 15,000 passengers a year and 30,000 tons of freight.

TADWORTH STATION

AMPTONS

Over the years simple single-platform halts were added: in 1892 at Runemede Range (later Yeoveney), to serve new rifle ranges for the Volunteers (later the Territorial Army); in 1927 at Poyle to serve the Explosives Works and Stanwell Moor village; and as late as 1954 at Poyle Estate, only 65 ch north of Poyle , for a new factoring and warehousing development. None of these offered much comfort for waiting passengers: the first had but a wooden bench in the open air. Poyle boasted a crude wooden shelter and Poyle Estate a skeletal bus stop type canopy supported on concrete posts. Until its closure in May 1962, 'due to the cost of repair', Yeoveney remained a rare example of a conditional stopping place in the London area, where trains were halted by hand signal or after dark, by pulling a rope to raise a lamp up a post to bring its glow into the view of the driver whilst he still had time to brake. This once idyllic and very solitary spot is now submerged under the stink and roar of the M25 motorway.

Freight working south of Colnbrook ended in 1953 when all business was transferred to the Southern Region yard at Staines. After the 1965 Beeching Report had proposed the branch for closure, the passenger service between West Drayton and Staines (WR), latterly increased and partly worked by former GWR diesel cars, ran for the last time on 27 March 1965. But although Colnbrook lost its public freight facility in January 1966, oil traffic to a private siding there continued until 1982, resuming for a further short period from 1 March 1990, when rail tankers carried aviation fuel for Heathrow Airport from Ripple Lane yard at Barking to a siding just north of the Bath Road level crossing. Colnbrook's station buildings and signal box were demolished on January 1979 and very soon afterwards the manually-worked gates were replaced by a locally-monitored automatic open crossing.

Top Left *Suburban symmetry and solidity at Tadworth, in about 1903* Commercial postcard.

Left *Kingswood station, looking to Purley, on a summer afternoon in the early 1920s. A freight train is backing into the yard behind the platform but there is no other sign of life.*

This work was necessary because the line south of Colnbrook was at that time again in use, following conversion of the old GWR yard at Staines to a heating oil depot for Cory/Shell. These trains, originating at Ripple Lane, ran from October 1964 until 16 January 1981. Two days later a new connection was opened from the Cory/Shell depot into the Staines-Windsor line, enabling the former GWR line south of Poyle to be abandoned to facilitate the M25 motorway construction works. The first oil train to use the new connection ran on 30 January 1981 and the Staines West oil depot remained rail served until 24 June 1991. Even so the line is asleep rather than dead, since much of its route remains available for future use and it has featured in planning for possible new railways serving London Airport (Heathrow).

Through the Chipstead Valley to Epsom Downs

As the 19th century drew to a close, independent backers with an eye on profits from residential development obtained parliamentary powers for a 8m 25ch line from Purley to Tattenham Corner via the Chipstead Valley. The SER agreed to work the new railway, absorbing the promoting companies in 1899[9].

The first section to be opened, on 2 November 1897, was a single track between Purley and Kingswood & Burgh Heath with an intermediate station and passing loop at Chipstead & Banstead Downs. This was extended westwards to Tadworth & Walton on the Hill on 1 July 1900 through two very short tunnels (Kingswood, 310yd and Hoppity, 37yd) and a deep northward-curving cutting beyond. Doubling was completed as far as Kingswood on 2 July 1900 and to Tadworth in the following November. The final stretch northward to a terminus almost on the race course at Tattenham Corner was opened on 4 June 1901 in time for Derby week and as we shall see in chapter 7, facilities for handling the race course traffic were generously provided.

Except at Tattenham Corner, where there were

some very large specimens of the SER clap-boarded wooden sheds described at the time of opening as 'temporary', all the stations were substantial and attractive structures in Domestic style eminently suited for the quality residential areas they were intended to serve. At Chipstead the main building was on the Up side. Tall and handsome chimneys were set in its tiled and gabled roof from which three first floor dormer windows which peeped out over the platform canopy. A wooden porte cochere decorated the entrance from the approach road. At the London end of the Down platform there was a single goods and coal siding. In later years this was requisitioned to provide stabling for the standby locomotive for royal trains on race days.

As the station nearest to Kingswood Warren, the residence of the line's principal promoter, Cosmo Bonsor, Kingswood was quite the finest of the trio. The drive to the Bonsor mansion ran through an arch in the overline road bridge into a roadway behind the Down plat form. The three storey house on the Up side welcomed passengers with a wide arched entrance and the flat roofed canopy over the Up platform, which soon acquired a set of wooden railings, was accessible from first floor French doors. This arrangement suggests some use for al fresco activities, though examination of the quite extensive photographic coverage available gives no indication of what these might have been. Kingswood's two-road freight yard was on the Up side, with one track extending into the station approach.

Though handsome enough, Tadworth's main building was much smaller than the other two, no more than a single storey block along the north side of the three-arch brick road bridge over the line. A central entrance led to a ticket hall illuminated by an arched window in the gable and there were arched openings at each end above the covered slopes down to the platforms . A five-road freight yard with a cattle pen was provided on the Up side at the north end.

From 1902 the use of the line beyond Tadworth was restricted to race days passenger trains, horse box trains and special services for children's treats and pleasure seekers in the summer months. With regard to the latter, an interesting note against Tattenham Corner station in the July 1910 *ABC Railway Guide* warns: 'Trains only run when there are a sufficient number of passengers', arousing speculation as to what was regarded as a sufficient number and who made the decision. From September 1914 until the end of World War 1, the terminal section was under military control. After that, until regular daily services were inaugurated with electrification in 1928, it was again restricted to race traffic and occasional summer special workings.

Notes

(1) For an annotated reproduction of the Reading, Guildford & Reigate Railway Company's minute book, prefaced by an informative introduction, see Course, Edwin, *Minutes of the Board of Directors of the Reading, Guildford & Reigate Railway*, 1987. On the line, see also Kidner, R W, *The Reading to Tonbridge line*, 1974 and for the section through Dorking, Jackson, Alan A, *Dorking's Railways*, 1988.

(2) The Board of Trade imposed a temporary closure from 22-24 April 1849

(3) SR Traffic Committee Minute, 25 July 1929

(4) SR Traffic & Continental Committee Minute, 17 March 1932

(5) Spence, Jeoffry, *The Caterham Railway: The Story of a Feud-and its Aftermath*, 1952

(6) For further details of the early history of the Shepperton branch, see Heselton, Kenneth Y, *Sunbury and the Thames Valley Railway*, 1974

(7) For further details of the Guildford to Horsham line see Vallance, H A, 'The Horsham-Guildford Line. Southern Region', *The Railway Magazine*, September 1950, Sillince, David, 'The Horsham & Guildford Direct', *The Railway Magazine*, March and April 1966, and Hood, H R, *The Horsham-Guildford Direct Railway*, 1975.

(8) For a full account of the New Guildford line

and earlier proposals for the area see Faulkner, J N, 'To Guildford via Cobham', *The Railway Magazine*, September 1959. On the Guildford, Kingston & London Railway, and its fate see Wilson, B G, 'The Railway Development of Wimbledon', *The Railway World* March 1961.

(9) For a full account of the Epsom Downs Extension and Chipstead Valley Railway schemes which preceded the opening of the Purley-Tattenham Corner line, see Jackson, Alan A, 'Rails to Tattenham Corner', *The Railway Magazine*, June 1975.

CHAPTER FOUR

Electrification, Modernisation and Retrenchment

Southern Electric Surrey

The first electric trains to operate in Surrey[1] were introduced by the L&SWR. A network of 47 route miles was proposed and agreed by the directors in 1912, the main objective to recover traffic lost to electric tramcars and meet threatened projection of Central London tube railway services into the Thames Valley. Good progress had been made up to the summer of 1914, when the outbreak of war caused major delays. After the opening of the initial services in 1915-1916 a halt had to be called to further work. Electric trains operated the Shepperton branch services from 30 January 1916 and those on the Hampton Court branch from 18 June. On 20 November 1916, electric services were extended to Claygate half-hourly, Mondays to Saturdays. From there, passengers for stations to Guildford changed into hourly steam auto trains. As yet a mere stripling amongst London's suburbs, Claygate was hardly deserving of such treatment; the idea was rather to reduce the number of steam workings penetrating the newly-electrified area. However, second thoughts prevailed and from 1 June 1919, the Claygate electrics were withdrawn to provide more stock for the increasingly busier rush hours on the other suburban lines closer to central London.

Conductor rails were used, supplying 600 volts dc to multiple-unit trains converted from steam-hauled compartment stock. Three of the berthing roads at Hampton Court were electrified and sidings were electrified at Shepperton. The electrics ran through the day, seven days a week, at the same minutes past each hour; the Shepperton service was at 30 minute intervals, the Hampton Court every 20 minutes. Although journey times were reduced, the major benefit was the saving in costly steam mileage by a frequent, reliable and clean service which soon generated new traffic, much of it outside the peak hours.

Under the banner *Southern Electric*,[2] the Southern Railway greatly extended electric passenger services. Adopting the L&SWR precedents, the SR standardised on conductor rail current collection, using a dc traction supply, and, as on the first L&SWR services, all the new SR electric trains ran at fixed intervals throughout the day, often with extra workings at the peak periods, always offering a much more intensive and generally faster service than the steam trains they replaced.

Surrey's first section of the Southern Electric came into operation on 12 July 1925, running over the lines from Raynes Park to Epsom and Dorking North; Leatherhead to Guildford; and Surbiton to Effingham Junction, the latter restoring the Claygate section suspended by the L&SWR in

Top Right *A L&SWR electric train, set E 38, at Thames Ditton in 1916.*

Right *Although ex-L&SWR 0-4-2 527E (built 1887) heading an Up local service dominates this Guildford picture, it also shows the bunting erected to celebrate the arrival of the town's first electric rail services (via the New Guildford line) in July 1925; an electric set stands in platform 1* 'F. Moore'.

E38
H
MAPLE & Co
BEDSTEADS
NATIONAL
ENGINES

227
527

SOUTHERN RAILWAY
EPSOM
EPSOM

1919. A seven-road car shed for electric trains was erected on the Down side at the country end of Effingham Junction station, where a new signal box was provided. Electric trains serving Effingham Junction via Bookham used the former L&SWR station at Leatherhead until 9 July 1927 when it was closed; from the following day, all passenger trains were handled at the former LB&SCR Station and those to and from Effingham Junction, worked over a new connecting spur south of that station. One electrified road was retained in the old L&SWR station for berthing. Freight traffic was concentrated in the former L&SWR yard at Leatherhead. At Guildford a new bay plat form was built on the east side at the London end for the terminating electrics. Dorking also received an electrified terminal bay at the back of its Down platform and two additional car sidings on the east side, bringing the total to six.

The success of these new electric services was marked by a steady growth in house building in the area served, particularly in those districts nearest to London, a subject we shall examine in detail later, noting how new stations were opened to serve such developments. An era of privilege for the New Guildford line began on 1 December 1925, when its electric services were diverted over the Through roads to run non-stop between Waterloo and Surbiton, a move which undoubtedly enhanced the attraction of this route in the eyes of house-hunting commuters.

Further rationalisation was achieved at Epsom. where the former L&SWR freight yard was closed from 2 January 1928, all traffic being transferred to the old LB&SCR depot. On the site of the L&SWR premises,there appeared a workmanlike new station with two 650ft island platforms and four tracks. This had two sidings alongside the platform on the Down side for horse boxes and vans and berthing roads for electric trains either side of the running lines at the country end. A manual 60-1ever frame straddling the central pair of tracks at the country end of the platforms controlled the new layout, replacing the former East and West boxes from 24 February 1929. Most of the new work was ready on Sunday 3 March 1929, the first day of regular electric services between Victoria and London Bridge and Dorking North/Effingham Junction. Trains ceased to call at the old LB&SCR Epsom Town station after the previous evening. An increase in vehicular traffic over the level crossing at Ashtead, arising from housebuilding on the north side of the line made it desirable to move the signalman to a position overlooking the gates. With typical SR financial prudence, this was achieved from 18 November 1930 by closing the L&SWR platform box and moving the redundant Carshalton Beeches signal cabin to the required position.

Electric working to Tadworth and over the Caterham branch began on 25 March 1928, Tattenham Corner station and the Epsom Downs branch following on 17 June. At Epsom Downs, where six of the nine platforms were electrified, a signing-on point for drivers was established. Overnight and in the slack hours, electric stock was berthed and cleaned in all but two of the platforms, a practice which was to continue until 1972. Simplification of the layout at Tattenham Corner at the time of electrification will be described in chapter 7.

Epsom Downs and Banstead further benefited on 4 May 1930 when electric trains started to work to Victoria via West Croydon, a useful cross-country link which may well have persuaded people with workplaces in Croydon to consider the many new houses then beginning to appear south of the railway between Banstead and Epsom Downs. Passengers using the Caterham and Tattenham Corner branches, accustomed to a service to Charing Cross and Cannon Street at all times, were however not well pleased to find that to reduce delays caused by crossing over the layout outside London Bridge station, their new

Top Left *In 1929 a new station was provided at Epsom by the SR to replace those of the former LB&SCR and L&SWR, on the site of the latter. In this view, looking towards Dorking, the new signal-box straddling the centre tracks is almost complete and work on the signalling and the two island platforms is well advanced, though the gable roofing of the old station's Up platform remains in place for a little longer* Alfred Percival & Co.

Left *The exterior of the 1929 station at Epsom looking west from Waterloo Road in about 1931* Commercial postcard.

electric services were to terminate at London Bridge (Low Level) at peak times. This move probably had little effect on the pace of housing development in the areas concerned, although new purchasers commuting to town would have taken it into account when making their decision to buy, so it seems likely most of those choosing to live in this area had workplaces in the City rather than in Westminster or Holborn.

On 5 July 1930 the west curve at Staines was closed for regular passenger traffic. From the following day, electric services began between Windsor, Staines and London (Waterloo), half hourly off peak and twenty minutes in the rush hours.

A new stage in the modernisation of the Southern Railway was inaugurated on 17 July 1932 with the start of electric working over the Brighton main line to Redhill, Reigate and Three Bridges, just into Sussex, via Merstham . The 'Quarry Line' was also electrified but no regular electric workings ran over it until 1 January 1933. Also on 17 July 1932, Salford Halt (now Salfords) came into regular public use and Earlswood was opened on Sundays for the first time. Three-aspect automatic and semi-automatic colour light signalling was included in this scheme, the first stage of electrification between London and Brighton.

Included in the Brighton electrification scheme was the 1932-33 rebuilding of Redhill station. This provided a new main entrance and ticket hall on the Up side, facing the town centre and connected to a new 16ft wide subway serving all platforms and equipped with baggage lifts. Redhill had become an important point for handling mail traffic and improved and enlarged accommodation for this purpose was authorised by the SR Engineering Committee at the end of 1930. Three years later, Redhill Station Sorting Office was enlarged by the General Post Office. Additional facilities for handling Post Office parcels were approved by the SR Traffic & Continental Committee in October 1935 and further expenditure for Post Office purposes was sanctioned three years later. This was still not enough and more work was sanctioned in 1938. These improvements provided a new Down bay for mail vans at the London end of the Down platform with a two-way conveyor belt connected to the adjacent Sorting Office to assist rapid loading and unloading of mailbags. Bags from Up trains were fed to the sorters by a chute.

Redhill had already undergone a layout rearrangement in the 1920s which allowed trains from the Tonbridge line to work into any one of the three platforms or on to the central Through roads. Track changes in 1932 made it possible to start Down trains from Redhill and for Up main line trains and Up trains from the Reigate direction to be coupled together in the Up platform roads. No.3 signal box was then closed, all signals being controlled from Nos. 1 & 2.

Despite these changes, Redhill remained (and still remains) unsatisfactory to work. It is not only impossible to run off the Through Lines towards Reading but more importantly, through working from the east via Tonbridge to Reading and over the main lines beyond there, avoiding London, is not feasible without tedious reversals involving platform occupation. These defects were a particular headache for operators during World War 2, when the junction was deluged with traffic. Completion of a flyover, largely on railway-owned land, offers no serious practical difficulties and detailed plans have been drawn up more than once. It seems likely that pressures from growth of Channel Tunnel freight traffic between points west and north of London may cause such a direct connection to be built before many more years have passed.

Another of the 1932 improvements was to provide sidings for berthing electric sets at the London end of Reigate station on the Down side. Train services were further enhanced when the main line was electrified through to Brighton and West Worthing on 1 January 1933. Outside the rush hours, when there were extra services, Redhill and Horley then received hourly fast trains to and from Victoria and London Bridge respectively and two trains an hour in addition served the Surrey stations at Merstham, Redhill, Reigate, Earlswood, Salfords and Horley. Financing of the 1932-33 schemes was facilitated by a 1928 government decision to repeal the passenger duty paid by the railway companies for over eighty years on the understanding that its capitalised value would be spent on improvement works.

Improvements carried out on the former L&SWR main line in 1936-37 were designed to ease operation of the increasingly busy north east Surrey electric services working over it from the

Above *The all-Pullman electric 'Brighton Belle' (set 3053) on a Down service traversing the Quarry Line at Merstham in about 1950* British Rail.

Hampton Court, New Guildford and Epsom/-Dorking/Effingham Junction lines as well as preparing the way for main line electrification. A flyover was constructed on the London side of Wimbledon station to carry the Up Local over the Up and Down Through lines, along with the necessary rearrangement of tracks from there into London. These new works came into service from 17 May 1936. Colour light signalling, controlled from new boxes at Surbiton and Waterloo was in operation between Malden and Hampton Court Junction from 28 June 1936 and between Waterloo and Vauxhall from the following 18 October. From 5 July 1936 these improvements enabled trains between Waterloo and Dorking/ Effingham Junction via Epsom to run fast between Waterloo and Wimbledon on weekdays (and between Waterloo and Motspur Park in rush hours).

Apart from the remission of passenger duty mentioned above, the SR had until this time managed to finance electrification from its own resources but a major programme carried through right across Surrey into Hampshire and Berkshire in 1937-39 could not have been sustained without recourse to a new government unemployment relief scheme. Sanctioned by the Railways (Agreement) Act of 2 August 1935, this allowed the railway companies to obtain Treasury Guaranteed 15-year Loans from the Railway Finance Corporation at the very favourable rate of 2.5 percent.

Full electric working between Staines and Weybridge was in place from 3 January 1937. At this time, a 1935 proposal for a station at Egham Hythe, between Egham and Staines, was reconsidered in view of the inconvenient road access to Staines station but the matter was again deferred [3].

Following completion on 27 June 1937 of multiple-aspect track-circuited colour light signalling between Guildford and Woking, controlled from Guildford Yard and South boxes and a new power box with all-electric frame at Woking, full electric services between Waterloo and Portsmouth via Woking and Guildford and between Waterloo and

Alton via Woking, Aldershot and Farnham began on 4 July 1937. The new Woking box, with miniature levers and a building in the Southern's 'marine' style replaced three mechanical boxes. Two-aspect colour light signals were in operation at Haslemere (with intermediate colour light signals between there and Witley) from 18 July. These new services, with their much improved frequency and speed, soon built up impressive increases in traffic, notably between Woking and Haslemere, encouraging expansion of upmarket commuter settlement which produced many First Class tickets. The basic service on weekdays provided three trains an hour on the Portsmouth line and two on the Alton, one of the three Portsmouths calling at Guildford (35min) and Haslemere (55min) only. Many of the Portsmouth fasts had restaurant cars and there were extra trains in peak hours, including an 08.15 commuter service from Haslemere, with restaurant car, which reached Waterloo in 49 min. Aldershot was now only 52 minutes from Waterloo in peak hours, 61 at other times. This excellent service was heavily used by personnel of the armed services in World War 2 as well as by civilians seeking refuge from bombing in the remoter parts of Surrey. For many years, punctuality was impeccable. A resident of Worplesdon wrote to *The Times* in 1957 relating how the Up and Down fast 12-car trains leaving Portsmouth at 20 minutes past each hour and Waterloo at 10 minutes before each hour regularly passed each other in the same 220yd stretch flanking a field below his garden. Appearing without fail at 25 min past each hour through the day, every day, they were to him 'a parlour trick which always impresses doubting visitors'.[4]

Associated with the Portsmouth/Alton electrification was a long overdue rebuilding at Woking carried out in 1936-39 by Trollope & Colls. This gave the station 820ft platforms on all four tracks with all buildings reprovided in red brick and cream tiles exhibiting the restrained Modern Style favoured by the SR staff architect, J Robb Scott. The main entrance and ticket hall remained on the

Below *Southern Railway 'Moderne' style; Woking station Down side as rebuilt in 1938-39. The road coach connection to London Airport Heathrow is standing in the forecourt at the left of this January 1992 picture* Alan A Jackson.

south side, facing away from the town centre and opening on to the Down Local platform. The new central island platform (nos.3 & 4) serving the Up and Down Through Lines, was reached over a wide covered footbridge sited towards the London end of the station. There were bays at the London end of the Up Slow platform (removed in May 1968) and at both ends of the Down Slow platform (the one at the London end, not on a running line, was removed in March 1992).

Other works in this 1937 scheme included extension of platforms at Guildford and Haslemere to 820ft to take the 12-car trains. Haslemere's 1859 station received lengthened canopies and new buildings whilst its Up platform was converted to an island to enable stopping services t o be held on a loop as expresses passed. At Farnham, platforms were extended to 520ft, the waiting rooms refurbished and electric light installed instead of gas. Additional carriage sidings were provided at Chertsey, Woking and Guildford.

In 1938, under the title 'Portsmouth No.2 electrification', it was the turn of the Mid Sussex line between Dorking and Horsham, with its services to Bognor and to Portsmouth via Chichester. Some electric workings were operated from 22 May but the full timetable was begun on Sunday, 3 July. Colour light signalling had been installed from Mickleham Crossing, north of Boxhill station, to Holmwood, all controlled from a new box at Dorking, operational from 15 March. This contained a 44-lever conventional mechanical frame but outlying points were power-controlled. In red brick, with a flat concrete roof and curved fenestrated corners for the cabin section, this structure gave the old-fashioned town of Dorking its first and only example of the Modern Style of architecture. Although the station buildings here were not altered, platforms were extended to take 12-car sets and the Down bay was converted to a Down Loop. The Down line was arranged to allow for terminating trains and could also be used as an Up Loop. With electrification, Dorking gained an hourly service of buffet car trains to and from London (Victoria) in 37 min., whilst the half hourly Waterloo service was extended south, one train terminating at Holmwood, the other at Horsham; the hourly train to and from London Bridge was also extended to Horsham. This gave Dorking its best ever service , with four trains an hour through the day, one of them semi-fast and the relatively remote station at Holmwood three electric trains an hour, a wildly generous gesture no doubt designed to encourage building development, a rash of optimism soon to be frustrated by events.

These extensions of electric conductor rail working through rural areas upset the hunting devotees , long used to trespassing on railway property with impunity when Mr Fox tried to escape across or along the tracks. Fears that horses and dogs might sustain injury from the live rails (there was of course less concern for the fox) were soon shown to be not entirely ill-founded, though the reality differed slightly from the prognosis. At Ockley in 1938 and again the following year, foxes running for their lives were, as so often before, pursued across the railway by hounds. Although many of the dogs received a shock from the live rail, this did them no great harm, but their instinctive reaction was to turn angrily to bite their 'attacker' with wet mouths, and this action usually proved fatal[5]. Subsequently the railway was treated with more respect by the fox chasers.

The first day of 1939 saw a full service of electric trains working between Virginia Water and Reading (Waterloo-Reading) between Ascot and Ash Vale; and also over the Aldershot-Ash Curve (Ascot-Aldershot-Guildford). The Local roads along the main line were electrified west of Pirbright Junction to allow peak hours electric trains to run between Woking and Ascot via Frimley and live rail was laid between Frimley Junction and Sturt Lane Junction West as a precaution against over-runs. The west curves at Staines and Virginia Water were electrified, for use as required. This north-west Surrey electrification increased the train service over the lines concerned by as much as 85 per cent over the steam train provision. Notable features were that for the first time all trains over the Camberley line ran through to and from Waterloo and that Staines now had fast trains which reached Waterloo in 26-28 min. with similarly fast return workings. Many stations on these lines had their platforms extended to 540ft. At Ash, the Up bay was electrified and a new waiting room, protected by an extended canopy, was provided at the Guildford end of the Down platform. Although the international situation and subse-

Above *Dorking North (now Dorking) station with the signal box and track and platform changes associated with the 1938 Mid-Sussex electrification. Looking to Horsham, 5 August 1979. The carriage sidings have subsequently been removed and the station buildings have been replaced*
Alan A Jackson.

quent out break of war caused plans for the rebuilding of Virginia Water and Sunningdale stations to be set aside, the freight yard at the former was rearranged and enlarged.

By January 1939 the greater part of Surrey's rail network had been electrified. The exceptions were:

- a short section of the main line west of Sturt Lane Junction;
- the Reading-Tonbridge line between Ash and North Camp; between Shalford Junction and Reigate; and between Redhill and the eastern border of the county;
- the Guildford-Horsham line between Peasmarsh Junction and Baynards;
- the Uckfield and East Grinstead lines through Woldingham and Oxted;
- and the GWR line from Colnbrook to Staines.

At this time steam locomotives were also continuing to haul freight trains on all lines.

Other Changes 1923-39

Apart from the electrification works mentioned most other new provision between the wars in Surrey was relatively minor. In a period which saw vigorous residential expansion, a feature we shall look at in detail later, house builders or landowners were prepared to offer financial or other inducements for new stations in the expanding commuter zone around London.

The first example appeared between what is now West Byfleet and Weybridge at the bridge over Oyster Lane, where there were already two L&SWR staff houses. Opened in July 1927, this

Above *Byfleet and New Haw (opened as 'West Weybridge'). The SR Up side building of 1927, photographed on 26 August 1994* Alan A Jackson.

station was somewhat perversely called West Weybridge, although there is no such place and the adjacent signal box had always been known as Byfleet Junction. Even the SR's official residential guidebook was confused, reviewing the area served under its Byfleet heading. However it was not until June 1961 that the name became Byfleet and New Haw, a sensible solution since the site is more or less equidistant from these two communities. J Robb Scott and his assistant architects at Waterloo produced an elegant solution for the always difficult problem of an embankment site. The main block, built into the north side, was interesting in that its square-paned steel windows, mock-timbering and multi-coloured bricks reflected the appearance of much of the best contemporary suburban housing. At the arched entrance from the road approach, the company's initials were included in the ironwork, a feature which survives, despite subsequent organisational changes. At rail level, there were side platforms serving the Up and Down Local lines, the latter reached by a subway through the embankment. Although land and some finance were provided by the developers of the adjacent Wey Manor Estate[6], the use of the new station was not confined to the residents of this area, since it was also conveniently close to the aircraft factory on the Brooklands estate.

Despite some contributions received from house-builders, far less money was spent at another new station on a similar site erected between Esher and Walton and opened in 1936. Hersham was a steel-framed timber structure, with wooden stairs under corrugated asbestos roofing set against the embankment either side of the bridge over Molesey Road. As at Byfleet, the platforms served only the Local lines but here no subway or footbridge was provided to connect them.

Two other new stations benefiting from subsidies offered by interested parties were those erected at Hinchley Wood, between Surbiton and Claygate in 1930 and at Stoneleigh, between Worcester Park and Ewell West, in 1932. In both cases, costs were kept to minimum by providing island platforms between the Up and Down lines and placing the ticket office on the platform, a plan which eliminated the need for any other buildings whilst allowing the station to be staffed by one man. No architectural treatment was attempted, the civil engineers having sole charge of design and, as at the other two 'builders' stations', there were no goods yards.

A 1929 request for a station at Queens Road, midway between Walton and Weybridge was refused. This was within a largely built up area not likely to produce any contributions from developers. New traffic would have been little if anything above that merely transferring from the existing stations.

At Staines, the decaying Down side passenger accommodation was replaced in 1930. A simple and pleasing red brick building under a tiled, gable-end roof was provided, incorporating a wide entrance on the south side, where there was some new housing development. Always with an eye to economy, the Southern left the rest of this Victorian station well alone, including its substantial lattice girder footbridge.

Finance from the public purse brought a useful improvement to the approaches to Hampton Court station, where in 1933 the road layout was altered in connection with the completion of a new bridge over the Thames. This swept away the awkward access to the station from Creek Road by a narrow bridge over the River Mole, the new Hampton Court Way coming alongside the main entrance.

Little money was spent in Surrey by the SR on schemes unconnected with electrified services. At Redhill, the former SER loco depot, opened around 1855 and situated between the Tonbridge and Brighton lines had housed 23 locos in 1898, when it was also responsible for small sub-sheds at Kingswood, Caterham and Shalford, the first two about to be replaced by a new shed at Purley. Complete reprovision at Redhill, including a three-road shed, 65ft turntable and coaling stage, was authorised by the SR Engineering Committee in 1924. The turntable and stage were completed in 1928 but little if anything else was done at this location, which in the SR era was handling around 70 engines daily.

Elsewhere, thoughts were directed to economy . At Betchworth, where there had once been two signal boxes, the survivor, by the level crossing, was closed in 1934 to be replaced by a signal frame in the station house which could be manned by a porter-signalman who would also sell and collect tickets. Godalming saw some simplification around the time of the 1937 electrification: both crossovers in the station area were removed along with the road vehicle loading dock and shunting neck on the Down side. Subsequently, on 13 August 1939, the level crossing with Mill Lane at the country end of the station was abolished together with its accompanying signal box.

Modernising Surrey's Railways

During the 1940s the county's railways underwent no major changes other than those related to the war effort and national defence as described in chapter 7. Indeed there was little further development of the system until the 1960s. That decade saw the use of steam locomotives for parcels and freight and for passenger services over the unelectrified lines giving way to diesel- electric locomotives and railcars.

From 6 January 1964, diesel-electric multiple units, first introduced there in 1962, assumed charge of all passenger services on the Oxted-East Grinstead/Uckfield lines, bringing to an end all regular steam working into Victoria and London Bridge stations. It is a revealing reflection of the nature of the traffic in this area at the time that the new diesel sets perpetuated the long tradition of First Class accommodation on what was essentially a commuter service.

Although the Southern Railway had planned electrification of these services in the period immediately before World War 2, no work had been started. It has been suggested there was some influential local feeling against electrification on the grounds that it would generate an increased population. which would in turn produce a fall in property values - Woldingham and Oxted did not want to become mirror images of Stoneleigh and Tolworth. Whatever the truth of the matter, electric working into this area, which had received a considerable amount of quality middle class housing since the Edwardian years. was long deferred.

Above *Hurst Green station, opened in June 1961. This photo shows the exterior of the Up side, in April 1962, looking towards Oxted* Alan A. Jackson.

Then from around the middle of the 1950s. a demographic change occurred. Small private houses began to appear in quantity beyond the London Green Belt which then ended at the southern side of Oxted. Much of this new property was taken up by London commuters.

This population growth was especially vigorous at East Grinstead, which practically doubled in size, at Edenbrldge, and around Hurst Green, where in 1961 the traffic increase was such as to cause the Southern Region of BR to close the old halt and replace it with a station on the London side of the Hurstlands Lane bridge over the line. The single storey structure, in red brick with pitched roofs, was sited on the Up side, where a new road approach was made. It included an asymmetrical booking hall and entrance block, given prominence by a modest amount of additional height and width and a tiled and canopied elevation on the road side. On the 12-car length platform a back-tilted canopy ran the full length of the buildlng. Although somewhat utilitarian in aspect. with poor detailing (a pre-1914 style clock and SR-type lamp fittings), the new station, which incorporated the Area Manager's office, demonstrated the best aspects of a rather low period for architectural style and was certainly far superior to what was soon to follow at equally busy stations elsewhere. It was originally intended to divide the East Grinstead and Uckfield portions of trains at the new station and the building included the necessary train crew accommodation. This proposal was then discarded, with the result that when the trains were divided, the second portion was imprisoned at Oxted until the first had cleared the junction at Hurst Green.

For over 20 years after diesel services were introduced, the Oxted lines saw no other major changes, apart from a simplification of the once lavish layout at Oxted after the withdrawal of freight workings in 1969. This left just the two bay roads, one stabling siding and the redundant goods shed on the Up side.

Eventually the capital for electrifying as far as East Grinstead was somehow found and the new service started on 5 October 1987 [7]. With the electrification, the decrepit SER wooden buildings at Oxted were replaced by pleasing brick single storey neo-vernacular structures under pitched roofs, the principal block, containing the ticket hall, ticket office, waiting room, parcels office, staff accommodation, bookstall and lavatories, on the Up side as before. On the opposite platform, the 1990 canopied waiting accomodation was in matching style and the connecting subway was refurbished with patterns of broken coloured glazed tiles to discourage the mindless efforts of graffiti artists.

The stabling siding on the Up side was electrified. Signalling was also modernised in July 1987, with a new box at Oxted controlling all signals between Oxted and East Grinstead and in the following year, the whole of the Uckfield line as well. This resignalling included the first use of solid state interlocking south of the Thames. As the remaining diesel units reach the end of their economic life in the early 2000s, it seems likely that the Uckfield service will then be electrified as well since this will simplify operation.

On the Reading-Redhill-Tonbridge line, steam locomotives disappeared entirely from regular services from 4 January 1965 (some workings had been displaced earlier). At first operation was by diesel-electric units providing a regular hourly service, calling at all stations except Winnersh and Earley, each unit scheduled to work around 500 miles a day. To cope with the heavy mail traffic from the Redhill Sorting Centre, three compartments at the non-driving end of each driving trailer in these units were brought into the van space. These trains presented an odd profile since they consisted of one standard width driving trailer added to two ex-Hastings line restricted loading gauge cars, and they soon became known - even in some official documents - as 'Tadpoles'. Staff were removed from all stations from November 1967 following the introduction of conductor-guards selling and inspecting tickets on board the

Below *Electric services to Oxted and East Grinstead; set 3165 on a London Victoria service enters Woldingham on 'Electrification Gala day', 26 September 1987* Alan A. Jackson.

'Tadpoles'. Western Region diesel-mechanical railcars, also operating on a pay-train basis, took over most services between Reading and Tonbridge on 14 April 1979, and all of them from May 1981.

These measures saved the line from the fate written into the 1963 Beeching Report, which had envisaged complete closure of all intermediate stations except electrified Reigate, with the line kept open solely for postal and other through traffics. Between Shalford and Reigate the installation of track circuit block working and conversion of level crossings to automatic or remote control in 1980-83 secured further economies which helped to ensure the survival of this important cross-country link. A consequence of the modernisation of level crossing arrangements was the demolition of all but one[8] of the little single-storey crossing keepers' cottages erected in 1849 between Shalford and Reigate. Some of these had no piped water supply and until the end, water was brought in cans daily by trains specially stopped for the purpose.

At Redhill, the loco depot was re-roofed by BR in the 1950s when there was still an allocation of 34 engines. Dieselisation followed shortly afterwards and closure came in 1965. The three-road shed was however not demolished until 1971 and even after that diesel locos continued to be berthed in the yard.

In 1967, the short section of the former L&SWR main line between Sturt Lane Junction and the county's western boundary was fitted with conductor rails to power the new electric services between Waterloo, Southampton and Bournemouth introduced on 10 July. Electric working between Pirbright Junction and Sturt Lane Junction had ceased following withdrawal of the Woking-Ascot service from 7 September 1964, at which date the Sturt Lane Junction-Frimley Junction curve was closed.

Apart from station reconstruction, to be mentioned later, other improvements to Surrey's rail infrastructure from the early 1960s onwards were largely confined to replacing the remaining semaphore signals with colour lights and modernising and concentrating control of signalling. By the early 1990s, the traditional signal box with its mechanical lever frame had all but disappeared from the county. Details of this process are given in Appendix IV. Level crossing modernisation on the Guildford-Redhill line has already been mentioned

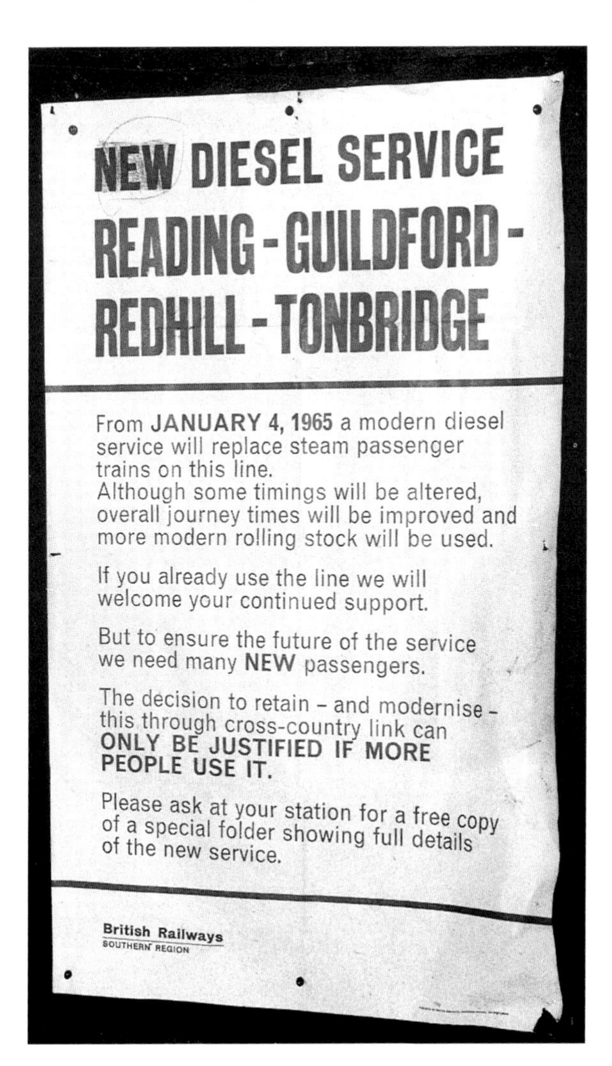

Above *The Reading-Redhill-Tonbridge service is dieselised; a 'use it or lose it' notice at Reigate on 2 January 1965* Alan A Jackson.

and this policy was pursued elsewhere; from the early 1970s, gated level crossings were replaced with lifting barriers, often remotely controlled from distant signal panels through television monitors. Lightly-used crossings were where possible converted to unsupervised foot crossings.

Rationalisation of rolling stock operations produced some minor works, as at Staines where four new berthing roads were provided from 29 April 1974 on the site of the Up side freight yard, replacing sidings at Windsor, Chertsey and Hounslow.

A spectacular addition to Surrey's railway infrastructure in this period was required for a new motor road and as such was fully financed by the Exchequer. The M25 was to cross beneath the Weybridge-Virginia Water railway at a skew angle of 28 degrees, requiring a bridge of 110 metres. During construction, the railway tracks were diverted round the site, allowing work to proceed without interrupting the train service. Completed early in 1979, the structure was one of the first examples of an all-concrete cable-stayed railway bridge. Its unusual appearance, dominated by the twin concrete cable towers makes Lyne bridge one of the very few architectural features to enliven the dreary vistas offered to those who use this road.

Rolling stock modernisation began in 1980 on the Shepperton and Hampton Court branches and the Waterloo-Epsom-Effingham Junction services. The slam- door suburban stock with its mix of open saloons and six-aside compartments was replaced by new sliding-door trains which featured train doors (allowing communication from one car to the next) and had open saloons throughout. Their wide sliding doors were closed from a panel in the guard's compartment but were openable by passenger-operated door control buttons from the interior and exterior after the operation of a remote release.

Station Reconstruction

Apart from platform lengthening to accommodate longer trains for the Gatwick Airport services at Merstham and Redhill in 1958 and between Surbiton and Woking (exclusive) in 1963-4 for 12-car commuter trains, little or nothing was done to improve stations in Surrey in the first two post war decades. By the mid- 1960s, reconstruction to meet modern requirements and reduce the heavy maintenance costs of decaying Victorian structures had become urgent. Hard pressed Southern Region managers, required to secure the utmost economies under the Beeching regime, siezed upon the seemingly cheap if not cheerful CLASP[9] factory-made building units which had been used for some signal boxes since 1964. Sunbury was the first Surrey recipient of this unappealing treatment in 1966 followed by Ashtead (1969), Sunningdale (1972), Virginia Water (1972-73) and West Byfleet (1972). Of the demolished buildings, none were of any architectural interest except Sunbury. The CLASP structures replacing them were essentially single storey boxes, steel framed and clad in precast concrete panels, plate glass and neoprene. With flat roofs, narrow slit windows just below the roof line, flimsy doors vulnerable to vandalism and mean little platform-side canopies crudely supported on squared timber posts, they looked cheap and nasty. Matching flat-roofed timber framed structures were designed to complement CLASP on the opposite platform . Even as CLASP buildings were being introduced, the BR Southern Region architect was describing them in rather apologetic terms as lacking the 'striking monumentality of some other new railway buildings...modest in size and unpretentious in design...even a little clinical.'[10] A less-committed party might have used stronger words then, and certainly later, as the effects of ageing and ill-treatment became all too apparent on their unsubstantial forms. CLASP's effect on the image of the railway was distinctively negative and as so often, low initial costs proved a poor investment in the longer run.

When West Byfleet's 1887 station buildings were taken down in 1972 it was no loss in architectural terms but the replacement on the Up platform was equally unprepossessing - a CLASP block with crude timber-posted canopies either side. The old subway under the line was retained but the platforms were also connected by a new concrete footbridge. In 1981, on the Down side, a 12,500 sq ft office block was completed on former railway land.

Ash Vale station was totally renewed in 1974-76. All existing buildings were demolished, a long job which involved shoring up the embankment. The main structure, on the Up side, was finished externally in blue brindle rustic facing bricks but the platform buildings were timber- framed with white panels, of the rather unappealing type developed to supplement the CLASP buildings. One flight of steps led down to the refurbished subway connecting the two platforms where there was a new glass-fronted ticket office. A section of the old L&SWR canopies went to embellish the East Somerset Railway at Cranmore.

Development of railway land for commercial

Above *The ugly 'CLASP' prefabricated building on the Up platform at West Byfleet; looking towards London on 26 August 1994* Alan A. Jackson.

purposes, already noticed at West Byfleet, was to become a useful means of obtaining capital for station reconstruction from the mid 1970s, rescuing the railway from the architectural bathos of CLASP. An early example of such development gains was seen at Camberley in 1976-77, where the forecourt area on the north side was given over to an ugly and boxy 14,000 sq ft 3-storey block of offices and showrooms. This incorporated a new station entrance under part of its first floor, leading into a separate glass-walled, flat roofed structure housing the ticket office, staff rooms, a shop and a waiting area. Crude waiting shelters were added to both platforms but the curious Victorian arched footbridge, with its separate portions for rail passengers and pedestrians avoiding the level crossing was left untouched.

Following a property deal, Driver's attractive 1867 building at Dorking, neglected beyond affordable restoration, was replaced in August 1982 by a flat-roofed red-bricked slab of commercial offices. Part of the ground floor was given over to the railway's requirements, including a spacious ticket and waiting hall. Designed by Gordon Lavington in association with the BR Southern Region architects, the new building had sufficient bulk to give it a measure of dignity although it lacked the symmetry and elegance of its predecessor. After another four years or so, the remaining LB&SCR buildings on the Down side were replaced by a flat roofed steel and glass building which contained waiting and staff rooms as well as sheltering the stairs down to the refurbished subway. Here, as elsewhere, social and transport changes had already seen the conversion of the freight yard and the station master's house and garden to provide space for the accommodation of dead motor cars patiently awaiting evening resurrection by their rail-borne owners.

Egham's old station, demolished in 1972, narrowly escaped CLASP. Reconstruction here was eventually completed in 1985, its scope enhanced by development gains from an associated three-

Network
Welcome to Esher
Life
P

Network
Epsom Downs
C151 BKL

Above *A single track and a narrow platform now suffice for the cut-back end of the Epsom Downs branch. Looking to Sutton from the buffer stops on 18 January 1990* Alan A Jackson.

Top Left *A station designed for the motor car age; the rebuilt Down side at Esher, 26 August 1994* AlanA Jackson.

Left *The re-sited Epsom Downs terminus (right) built to blend in with the housing estate which now occupies the extensive site of the old terminus and its yard. The columns supporting the canopy are from the Victorian building. 18 January 1990* Alan A Jackson.

storey office block in the old station yard.

At Esher and at Walton on Thames the disused central island platforms were stripped of their buildings in 1966 and a year later the 1838 structure still surviving on the Down platform at Walton was demolished. Esher benefited from a major rebuilding in 1987-88 when a single-storey, flat-roofed red brick and glass entrance and ticket office block was erected on the Down Side at the London end, replacing the old facilities on the west side of Station Road. Standing above a new road approach, the new station building was reached by a slope and steps also embellished with red brickwork. A timber footbridge replaced the former subway .

Railway land on the Down side at Sunbury was sold for commercial office development which produced an office block as part of that side of the station in 1989.

After the 1904 building on the Up side at Weybridge had been destroyed by fire in January 1987 a pleasing new block on the same site, containing entrance, ticket office and staff rooms was completed for opening in October 1990. Nearby Byfleet & New Haw underwent extensive refurbishment in 1990-91 but substitution of the original platform canopies with crude steel shelters glazed with polystyrene inevitably diminished the architectural impact of the handsome 1927 elevations at rail level.

An imaginative property deal brought an interesting change to the outer end of the Epsom Downs branch. Concentration of race traffic at the more conveniently-sited Tattenham Corner station had long rendered the spacious layout at Epsom Downs redundant, even if it had proved useful for berthing electric stock outside the peak. The whole area was sold, together with a section of the approach line, to developers who transformed it into a housing estate of closely-packed detached villas all but filling their small plots. As part of the deal, at the amputated end of the railway, 347yd nearer Banstead station, Messrs Charles Church provided a new platform for the single track and at right angles to the end of it , a station building which, from the road, might have been mistaken for another of the surrounding houses but for a valanced canopy at first floor level supported by posts rescued from the old terminus. This strange little doll's house of a station, where the hourly arrival and departure of an electric train amidst the tranquillity of a middle class suburban cul-de-sac assumes an almost dream like quality, came into use from 13 February 1989.

Yet another property deal secured the rebuilding of Shepperton in 1988. Here the replacement was an awkward angular exercise in the Post-Modern style, its gable end meant to recall the lines of the pretty Italianate building it replaced. Office space was taken by the transport publishers Ian Allan, formerly housed here across the end of the line. A single storey pavilion abutting on to the new office block housed a generously-glazed ticket hall and waiting area. Alas, allegedly because of poor connections with other rail services to the Surrey towns in which they dwell, only one member of Ian Allan's Shepperton staff, and he only occasionally, was said to use the railway.[11]

After some planning arguments with the local authority, a much-needed total rebuilding was undertaken at Guildford in 1988-89, financed by profits from sale of railway land for commercial development. Away went the leaking canopies and the already half-demolished range of assorted Victorian buildings on the east side, whose appearance had so long been a disgrace to the town. In their place there appeared a spacious and lofty pavilion housing the ticket hall, enquiry and travel centre, ticket office windows, and commercial units. Set back from a wide approach, the new entrance building offered a scale and dignity appropriate to the main station for the county's cathedral and university town. Bright and clean but more controversial were the new platform areas with their ungainly steelwork and box-like enclosures. Visual display units on each platform and a departure indicator in the main hall effectively banished the old confusion. The only parts of the old station to survive were the 1935 footbridge linking all platforms to a small entrance and ticket office in Guildford Park Road on the west side and the Victorian subway between the platforms. Both were refurbished but their continued existence, a memorial to penny-pinching, degraded the overall impact. Since this station is now sited in the centre of a pedestrian-unfriendly road traffic maelstrom, a useful adjunct is the frequent bus service, free to rail ticket holders, introduced in 1992 to afford a convenient link to the town centre, bus station and university.

1989 also saw the Victorian buildings at Frimley thoroughly refurbished with a new ticket office and 1,500 sq ft of space reserved for commercial letting. Welcome assistance from the local authority enabled the approaches to be given some landscaping.

Reconstruction at Redhill, completed in 1990, included a new street level building on the west side replacing the 1930s brick structure. In the Post-Modern 'glasshouse' style, the replacement featured a semi-circular entrance and ticket hall under an overhanging flat roof, flanked on each side by low glass-fronted blocks containing shops. At around the same time, platforms 1 and 2 received a narrow glass-walled building housing a combined waiting room and refreshment counter. The mail-handling facilities here, mentioned earlier, were further enhanced in 1965-66. A new sorting office was built against the Down side of the station, served by a. chain conveyor which transported mailbags to and from the platforms on a new bridge over the tracks. Redhill was however to lose its importance as a mail handling centre with the opening of the new Willesden postal rail hub' in 1996.

By the 1990s, the utilitarian wartime and early post-war provision at Upper Halliford had deteriorated into one of the most unpleasant stations on Network Southeast. Here the sadly-neglected structures, plastered with the frenzied scribblings

of the graffiti fraternity, were replaced by a new ticket office block on the Down platform in Neo-Vernacular style, complemented by an arched waiting shelter on the opposite side. These facilities, completed in 1991, were afforded some protection by closed circuit television surveillance. A 1994 rebuilding at Tattenham Corner, following an accident, will be noticed in chapter 7.

Track changes associated with a major resignalling scheme of 1997-8 included provision at Woking of a single track, 12-car length bay platform between the fast lines at the London end of the station to accommodate terminating trains.

New Train Services

For a long time after nationalisation, Surrey saw few innovative train services, the timetables of the old Southern Railway seeming set in tablets of stone. A notable example of fresh thought was Thameslink, which exploited the reopened Metropolitan Widened Lines and Farringdon-Blackfriars connection. A Bedford-Kings Cross-City-Gatwick Airport-Brighton service with a Surrey stop at Redhill, introduced on 16 May 1988, proved extremely successful. Much less so were the Guildford-Epsom-Luton workings started on 29 May 1990, these failing to build up viable loadings south of the Thames, mainly because passengers were deterred by their sluggish meandering through South London's congested tracks. Withdrawal ensued in 1994.

Above *Facing the town centre, but somewhat cut off from it by an unpleasant maelstrom of fast road traffic, the Down side main entrance of the rebuilt station at Guildford, is seen here on22 August 1995* AlanA Jackson.

Described as an experiment, alternate Staines - Chertsey - Weybridge trains were in May 1986 diverted over the north to west curve at Byfleet to terminate at Woking, with London connections made at Byfleet & New Haw instead of Weybridge. Subsequently this hourly working was extended at both ends, to Waterloo via Hounslow, and to

Guildford. Starved of publicity and not given adequate time to establish itself in the public perception, it was not well-patronised and was withdrawn as an economy in 1992. This left the curve and flyunder at Byfleet with just one passenger train daily each way . Running between Staines and Woking, this 'ghost train' was simply a device to avoid formal closure procedures for the curve.

Electrification of the Tonbridge-Redhill line for Channel Tunnel freight traffic via London (Willesden) inspired through hourly services from Maidstone West to Gatwick and Three Bridges, reversing at Redhill, introduced on 29 May 1994. A year later another new regular service was added, between Tunbridge Wells and London Victoria via Tonbridge, Redhill and East Croydon .

The huge increase in use of air passenger transport since the early 1950s had its effect on Surrey's railways, and, as we shall see in chapter 10, this seems likely to continue in the future. After experiments in 1964 with through rail/taxi bookings to and from Heathrow Airport via Woking station, a road coach connection between Woking (Down side) and the airport was started on 6 December 1965 . A similar coach link between Woking and Gatwick Airport was introduced in 1973 with seven services each way daily. By the early 1990s, the Heathrow link was operating hourly seven days a week, covering the road journey in 35 minutes but the Gatwick connection proved less popular and did not survive the provision of alternative rail services to that airport from Reading via Guildford mentioned in the next paragraph.

Dorking was adversely affected by the growth in traffic to and from Gatwick Airport which, along with burgeoning business generated by Crawley New Town and office and shopping developments at East Croydon, caused BR to seek to maximise loadings by diverting the Mid Sussex line Victoria-Bognor fast electric services via Gatwick Airport. From May 1978 the all-day fasts were re-routed, the remaining peak hour and Saturday workings following suit in May 1984. However, the increasing attention given to Gatwick Airport as a source of rail business was not all bad news for Dorking. From 12 May 1980 a fast hourly 'Train to Plane' diesel car service had been started between Reading and Gatwick Airport, calling only at North Camp, Guildford and Redhill. From May 1986, after some local pressure had been exerted, a stop was inserted at Deepdene (now Dorking Deepdene). Worked by new Turbo diesel sets since 1993, these trains were by the first part of 1994 already producing a traffic increase, by as much as 46 per cent at North Camp alone. They provided the basic service between Reading, Guildford , Dorking and Redhill from the mid 1990s, supplemented by a few local workings.

Another innovation in this period was the introduction in May 1995 of an hourly semi-fast weekday service between Horsham and London (Waterloo) in 54 min, stopping only at Dorking , Leatherhead, Ashtead, Epsom, Wimbledon and Clapham Junction. This gave a 23-25 min timing between London and Epsom, 37-39 minutes to Dorking, the best for a very long time on a service never noted for fast running.

Retrenchment

Served daily by steam-hauled 'pick-up' freight trains, the small freight yards that had once existed at almost all Surrey stations, as elsewhere on the rail system, were all closed in the first three decades after World War 2. Briefly checked by wartime and immediate post war exigencies, the impact of motor transport competition was to rise to new heights in the 1950s, making heavy inroads into such business as these small yards retained — mostly inwards movement of domestic fuels and builders' supplies. Solid fuels traffic, initially rationalised by concentration at a small number of rail depots, was very soon to fade away rapidly as houses were converted to oil or gas central heating. As the list at Appendix II shows, the process of freight yard closure had begun before the Beeching era but then accelerated fiercely. At busy commuter stations, the resulting release of land provided space for passengers' car parks, bringing back at least some of the lost revenue. Indeed the pressure for car space was such that at Effingham Junction, where there had been no freight yard, four railway houses and their gardens were razed to provide the necessary space. Peebles notes that at Claygate, on the same line, the clearance of the yard in 1971 allowed an expansion of parking spaces from 150 to 255, although the new total capacity proved in practice to exceed demand. Elsewhere, as at Horsley, Bagshot, Epsom and Holmwood, the land occupied by freight yards was used for small housing estates, some at least of the new occupants becoming rail commuters. Occasionally as at Wanborough, the old coal wharves remained in use, served by road transport.

From the late 1950s there was much pruning of the once very frequent electric passenger services in the county, an often delayed response to the fall in patronage outside peak hours which had followed the rapid spread of car ownership, particularly apparent in Surrey, from the end of the 1950s[12]. This caused mass desertion of the railway for journeys to shopping and recreational centres. Less important, but contributing to the decline, was the entry of television into virtually every household at about the same time, effectively banishing much of the train travel previously undertaken by those still without cars to reach cinemas, theatres and many spectator sports. In such circumstances the Southern Electric policy of providing a frequent service all day, every day, came under threat. Intervals were increased in off peak periods and, beginning in September 1964, some stations were closed completely on Sundays. At the same time Sunday frequencies were reduced to hourly on the Tattenham Corner and Windsor branches, between Woking and Alton, between Staines and Weybridge, and between Ascot and Reading/Guildford. Some Sunday station closures seen as too harsh were subsequently reversed.

One line was particularly affected by cuts in service frequency from 1958 onwards until what had been a double track, electrified main line descended into a moribund state which raised doubts as to its survival. Between Dorking and Horsham there had once been three passenger trains each way every hour, including one fast, and four each way between Holmwood and Dorking, but by 1967 this had dropped to an hourly service and two years later, off peak trains ceased to call at the intermediate stations , from which all staff were withdrawn. From 1986 there was no off peak service at all south of Dorking. Much too late, efforts were made to regain passengers. From October 1987 off peak service was restored and by 1995 there were again two trains an hour, Monday to Saturday, between London and Horsham via Dorking, though one did not call at the intermediate stations and the service ceased early in the evening. Despite this improvement, and a considerable growth in population in Holmwood's catchment area, loadings remained very light, even at peak periods. One factor operating here as elsewhere in Surrey was that with the spread of car ownership, those using the railway no longer needed their local station, preferring to drive often quite long distances to reach stations with faster and more frequent services, a tactic which could sometimes be frustrated by car parking problems.

Dispersal of central London workplaces to the suburbs or further afield, teleworking, flexible working hours, changing patterns of work in an era of developing electronic technology and then, from 1991-92, economic depression, drastically thinned out the once very busy and concentrated peak hour flows between 07.30 and 09.00 and 17.00 and 19.00 as well as diminishing the daily totals. As a result, the intensity of morning and evening business services was much reduced in the late 1980s and early 1990s. Peak hour Saturday workings, no longer needed with the virtual disappearance of Saturday morning attendance in London offices, finally vanished in May 1970. Another aspect of retrenchment was to open some stations only for part of the day, on weekdays only. At Longcross, from 11 May 1992, calls were confined to weekday peak hours. This station now also enjoys the distinction of being the only one in Surrey with a daily service which has no public road access.

Erosion of the regular interval and once frequent all-day, seven day electric services first introduced in 1916 by the L&SWR and much expanded as the Southern Electric grew between the wars also continued into the 1990s: weekday late evening services on the Hampton Court and Windsor branches and over the New Guildford line were reduced to hourly from 4 October 1993; from the same date, all Monday to Friday off-peak workings between Ascot and Aldershot were reduced to hourly. Adjustments were also made on many lines to cut out little-used early morning and late night workings and reduce off peak frequencies in the winter months. In Surrey as elsewhere , commercial pressures were applied with increasing rigour

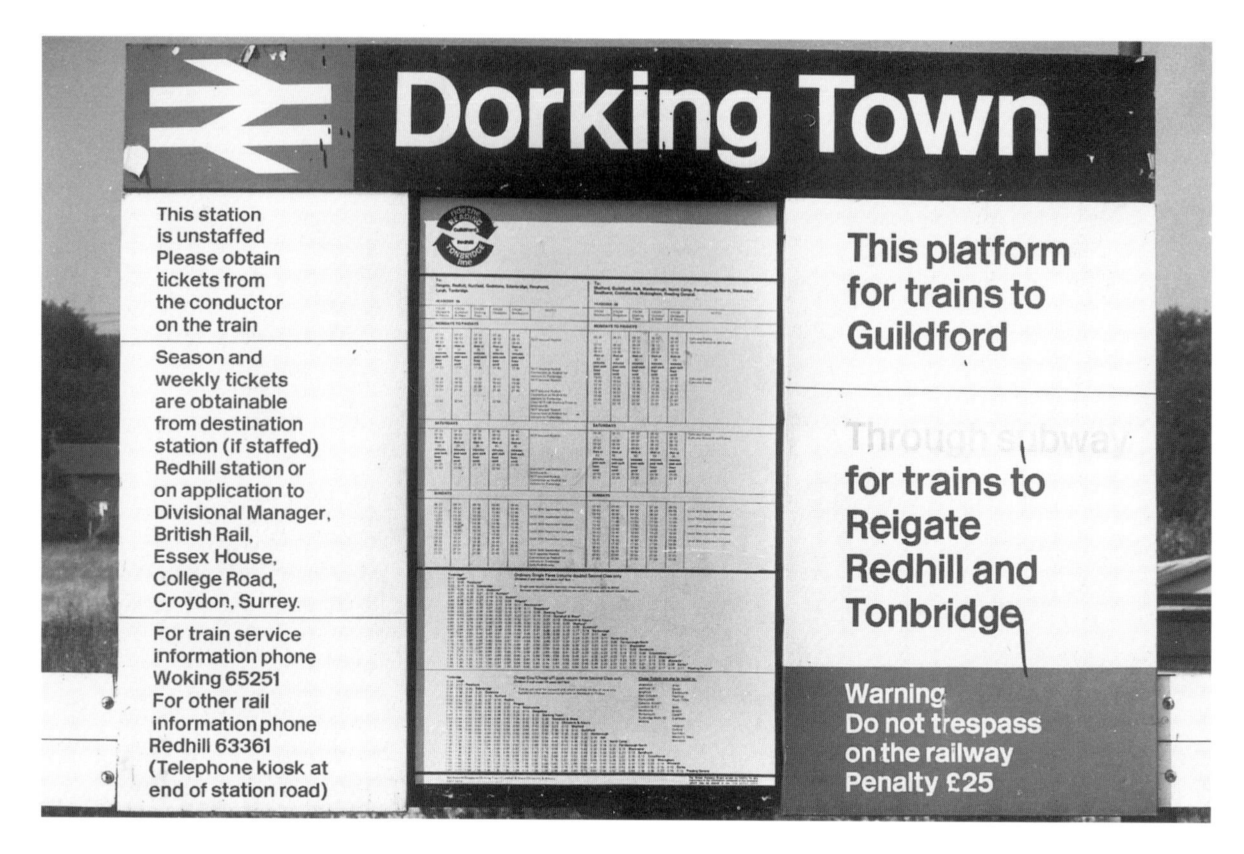

Above *The basic station comes to Surrey (1): an elaborate notice, including details of fares and train times, erected to assist bewildered passengers at the unstaffed Dorking Town (now more accurately titled Dorking West), 29 July 1973* Alan A Jackson.

from the 1970s, as with Government support, any residual concept of operating the railway as a public service was driven into oblivion.

Economies were also effected by introducing conductor-guards on some lines, enabling stations to be left unstaffed. This policy, by no means popular with the public, especially with women travelling alone, was first introduced on the Tattenham Corner branch on 6 September 1965, from which date all off-peak workings were confined to Purley-Tattenham Corner. Conductor guards also appeared on the Staines-Windsor branch on 18 April 1966 and on the Reading-Tonbridge services from 5 November 1967. From the early 1990s the process was carried further by reducing revenue protection to occasional spot checks on trains and at London terminal barriers, where any deliberate evasion detected was punished by imposition of heavy penalty fares. More stations then lost their staff or if there were manned ticket offices, these opened later and closed earlier. many were reduced to simple unmanned 'train stops' where passengers were left to struggle with impersonal ticket machines.

Berthing sidings at outer stations were closed, as at Dorking in 1992 , a move which caused last trains at night to leave London earlier as time had to be allowed for running them back to inner London depots before the night track maintenance period. This also had its effect on traffic, since those wanting to leave town late found alternatives to rail travel.

Another economy measure, damaging to operational flexibility, was the conversion of double track lines to single and removal of crossovers on double track lines. Singling was applied to the Epsom Downs branch beyond a point midway between Sutton and Belmont from 4 July 1982 and to the section between Farnham and Alton from 20 June 1985 (full single line signalling was not in place until 21 July).

Above *The basic station comes to Surrey (2): Dorking Deepdene, looking to Guildford, with a Gatwick train formed by Networker Turbo unit 166207, 8 February 1994. This station, which once had a stationmaster, manned signal box and at least two porters on duty at any one time, now probably sees as much traffic as it ever did* Alan A Jackson.

Infrastructure was also scaled down or eliminated in the struggle to cut costs. Stations, lavishly arranged and spaciously laid out in the late Victorian and Edwardian eras became increasingly burdensome to staff and maintain in good order. Footbridges lost canopies and glazing designed to protect passengers from the worst of the weather; platform canopies were severely reduced in length and depth or removed altogether, to be replaced by tiny bus-stop type shelters; waiting rooms were demolished or boarded up. With the decline in freight business and pressures to reduce staffing costs, stationmasters, once important personalities in their local communities, became an extinct species in the 1960s. Domestic accommodation for them and their families 'over the job' was no longer needed. Reductions in station staff, in hours of attendance or complete removal of staff, closure of signal boxes after signalling modernisation and cuts in funds available for building maintenance all had their repercussions on the appearance and upkeep of lavatories, footbridges, canopies, waiting rooms and other structures. Buildings became neglected, left open to the weather and vandalism until demolition was often the only feasible course. Operational and other changes such as the removal of steam working, electrification, signalling modernisation and the abandonment of the policy of retaining passenger carriages against summer peak use all caused track layouts at stations to be drastically simplified.

Reduction of the spacious layout at Epsom Downs began in the early 1950s when electrified platform tracks were reduced to five. From 1 May 1972 there were but two platforms in use (1 & 2, the former 4 & 5) With the singling of the branch in 1982 all trains used the Down platform at Banstead and at rail level the structures and canopies were dismantled, leaving passengers the minimal protection of a small bus stop type shelter.

At Ash, the long disused Down Bay for the Aldershot steam shuttle service was taken out of use in 1962 along with the Military Sidings on this side; the Up Bay went three years later. Removal of staff from most stations on the Reading-Guildford-Redhill-Tonbridge line in 1967 was followed two years later by destruction of the pretty but sadly-dilapidated 1849 *cottage orné* building at what is now Dorking West, of the Italianate station house on the Up platform at Gomshall, the staff house at Chilworth in the same style and the shabby wooden SER structures at Dorking Deepdene. The two Dorking stations then presented featureless platforms with nothing but small bus-stop type shelters. From around the same time, such shelters, flat-topped and ugly, otherwise became the only adornment to bare platforms at Nutfield and Godstone after the long-neglected buildings at these two stations had been demolished.

At Lingfield, the Down side structures were removed in 1973. Although the very handsome 1905 building on the west side at Earlswood and its generous platform canopies were spared destruction, all other buildings there were demolished in 1983-84, the platforms on the Through lines closed and fenced off. Holmwood's Up side electrified siding was taken out of use late in 1976 and the station building on the road bridge here was demolished in April 1986. Beginning in that year Ash was slowly rebuilt. A small ticket office in Neo-Vernacular style was erected on the Down side and the old canopies on both platforms were taken down. By the early 1990s, the gaunt Italianate station house on the Up side had gone. At around the same time, a substantial shelter in Post-Modern style replaced the old SER wooden structure on the Up side at North Camp and a new road bridge was erected close to the level crossing. Oxted's Up side bay was out of commission by 1992 but its counterpart opposite remained to accommodate the Uckfield shuttle service. As already mentioned, the carriage sidings at Dorking were deemed redundant in 1992. In the following year the car sheds at Effingham Junction fell into disuse.

Whilst many of the changes just mentioned were unwelcome to regular rail users, Surrey was almost totally protected from the severe spate of line closures which affected most of Britain in the 1960s, losing only the two lines mentioned earlier. There were however some minor casualties. At Virginia Water, the West Curve was closed from 27 July 1964 ; the curves to the main line at Frimley (Frimley Junction-Sturt Lane Junctions East and West) were not used after 7 September 1964, and the Staines West Curve was finally abandoned from 22 March 1965. Much of the embankment of the latter was cut away during redevelopment of the town centre in the 1970s.

Notes

(1) For a full account of the electrification of Surrey's railways, see Moody, G T, *Southern Electric: The History of the World's Largest Suburban Electrified System*, 5th edition, 1979.

(2) This term was first used officially in 1925 in the publicity output motivated by (Sir) John Elliot.

(3) Reports on Inspections of New Works etc, SR, 31 December 1936.

(4) Letter from Jocelyn Nangle, *The Times,* 13 March 1957.

(5) Harrod, John, T, 'Up the Dorking', *Southern Notebook*, 88 (1986)

(6) Minutes of the Law, Medical, Traffic and Continental Committee, SR, 8 October 1925 and 26 November 1925.

(7) Special 'Electrification Gala Day' services were worked on 26 and 27 September 1987 to introduce the public to the new facility. For an evaluation of the options and decision to electrify, see Phillipson, George, 'The Oxted Line', *Railways South East*, Summer issue 1988.

(8) The survivor, at Rectory Lane, Buckland, east of Betchworth station (TQ 25 SW 1896) was listed Grade II in 1996.

(9) The letters stood for Consortium [of] Local Authorities Special Programme. These buildings were originally designed and widely used for schools, which subsequently suffered similar adverse effects on theoretical life cost as the buildings aged and sustained rough usage.

(10) Wikeley, Nigel, 'New Stations for the Southern', *Modern Railways,* December 1967.

(11) *Modern Railways,* January 1990.

(12) At the 1991 Census, only just under 18 per cent of households in Surrey lacked a car; almost 41 per cent had two or more cars.

CHAPTER FIVE

Railway Residential and Commuting

The millionaires of Surrey
They dwell in vast Estates,
With little white cottages
That cluster at the gates;
And when the time hangs heavy
However great their store
They motor up to London
And make a little more.

A P Herbert' s verse paints an amusing if distorted picture. Certainly Surrey, with its areas of splendid natural beauty so conveniently close to London, has for two centuries or more not only been the capital's pleasure ground but a place of residence for those who make their living in the metropolis. First to arrive were the very wealthy, enjoying the idea of a country house in which they might live for at least part of the year, where they could entertain guests and indulge in country pursuits. Their great mansions, such as Denbies, The Deepdene , Claremont, and Clandon Park, bear witness to that. They were followed from around the mid 19th century by men who had made their wealth in trade or the professions, whose families lived on only a slightly less grand scale. Whilst today's multi-millionaires might still be found in somewhat reduced pomp at St George's Hill, Wentworth, and in isolated large houses near Leith Hill and elsewhere, and these will certainly 'motor up to London' as did their early 20th century predecessors, it was the railway, not the motor car which so greatly accelerated and widened out the process of residential settlement which had started in the 18th century. In so doing, it aided and abetted something which fundamentally altered the appearance of the county's landscape. As an acquaintance of the author's once remarked with acceptable hyperbole, 'In Surrey there is a house behind every tree'. And with the railways making access to London's workplaces so convenient and so easy, from the end of the 19th century, it was the middle classes in their many thousands rather than the plutocrats in their few hundreds who came to live in Surrey whilst earning their living in London.

As early as the late 1840s, attempts were made by railway managers to encourage commuter settlement by offering season tickets at discounted rates, the L&SWR initially limiting such concessions to First Class passengers. However by 1852, as Williams records, the company was setting its sights lower. 'In order to encourage the erection of houses at moderate rates...adapted to the wants of clerks and similar classes of society', it proposed to issue for the use of the occupiers or their families long period 'Residential Tickets' to builders of 20 or more lower middle class houses. Williams also notes that in 1864 there was an offer of a ten per cent discount in season ticket rates over a period of seven years to the main occupiers of any new houses at Sunningdale rented out at £60 or more a year.

The Early Settlers

At first residential rail travel in Surrey was almost entirely confined to the 'gentry' and the wealthier sections of the middle class. By no means all of these people were obliged to make a daily journey to work in London, since many had sufficient investment or other unearned income to sustain a suitable standard of living. Others were writers and artists like Meredith and Watts who found peace and inspiration in the Surrey countryside. These early settlers lived mostly in newly-built detached houses around the edges of the old towns and villages or, if very wealthy, amidst open country in mansions on plots of several acres, but almost always, since this was Surrey, there would be a railway station accessible after a short drive in their horse-drawn carriage, no matter how deep the rural seclusion of their residence. A glimpse of this privileged 'railway residential' lifestyle at its apogee is given in the recollections of W. G. Tharby, who in 1910 was a trainee booking clerk at Dorking and Westhumble stations . His account also reveals its impact on railway staff at a time when low railway pay was often boosted by 'fluff':

> *Suburban trains had no heating then and during cold weather metal footwarmers filled with hot water were supplied on demand to First Class passengers with any spares going to the Seconds. Dorking was one of the points where the warmers were kept and the porters made a good thing out of it. There was a procession of horse drawn carriages to the station during the morning rush hour. The more important of their top-hatted occupants were deferentially received by the Station master and seen by him into their First Class compartments, which were upholstered in dark blue material*[1].

Writing of Box Hill (now Box Hill & Westhumble), Tharby mentions that at Christmas time the station was 'swamped with turkeys, geese and chickens from the wealthy residents', while head gardeners sent sacks of potatoes, fruit and vegetables for the railwaymen and their families. At all times the Box Hill Stationmaster was obsequious in the presence of the wealthier passengers and once, when on the platform with two daughters of Lord Ryder, who lived at High Ashurst, he had coughed a little, causing the ladies to enquire anxiously after his asthma. That same afternoon six bottles of Wincarnis arrived by train from the Army & Navy Stores, addressed to him. Other gentry patronising this little station in the 1910s included the Hon. Henry Cubitt of Denbies, Leopold Salomons of Norbury Park (later to donate Box Hill to the nation) and Sir Trevor Lawrence of Burford House.[2]

Suburban and Stockbroker Surrey

It was not until the 1890s and 1900s that the less prosperous section of the middle class began in any significant numbers to live in Surrey, travelling to central London workplaces by rail. Their budgets obliged them to choose those locations closest in like New Malden, Surbiton and Purley and before 1920 very few had crossed the present boundary. But this was merely the start of the of a mass exodus into the county, encouraged from the early 1920s onwards by electrification of much of the comprehensive railway network which had been in place since the end of the 19th century and was as yet by no means used to anywhere near its potential capacity.[3] Between the wars this type of resident population grew rapidly as cheap terrace blocks, semis and small detached villas were built in quantity for owner-occupation, causing the edge of continuously built-up London to flow over the LCC boundary into north east Surrey . Thus the population of Epsom & Ewell increased from 22,953 in 1921 to 35,228 in 1931 and 62,960 in mid 1939; Leatherhead expanded from 11,233 in 1921 to 21,170 in mid 1938 and Caterham & Warlingham from 17,108 to 27,100 in the same period[4]. In general this early 20th century suburban type development spread out to a distance of about 15-20 miles from central London, resulting in a maximum home to office journey of around an hour.

Through the 1920s, 1930s and 1940s, the ever-expanding commuter army, mostly the dark-suited salariat, with a sprinkling of soberly-frocked, gloved and hatted unmarried women clerks and typists, were great users of rail transport, not occasionally, to 'make a little more', but daily to make a steady salary, which in most cases, formed their entire income. They tended always to take the same trains, even standing on the platform in the same place every day, leaving their home station between 07.30 and 08.30 and returning from London termini between 17.15 and 18.15. Few, very few, of the married men had cars since their mortgage payments absorbed most of their marginal income, so they and their families also used the railway outside the peak hours. And when they finally retired, many remained in the same house, although some might move out into a more rural setting, deserting the metropolitan edges which had afforded them commuter convenience.

During the between-wars years, mostly across those parts of Surrey beyond the 15-20 mile zone just mentioned, in what became known as 'the stockbroker belt', large and medium size detached houses on plots varying from a quarter acre to three or more acres were still being built for the more prosperous middle class commuters, whilst others of this group occupied the homes of their Victorian and Edwardian predecessors, struggling to make do with far fewer servants. They too had their own private transport, now one or more motor cars, which made distance from a railway station even less crucial, so much so that it became possible for this top layer to use their First Class season tickets from the station that offered the fastest and most frequent train service.

Railways and Developers cooperate

As we have seen in the previous chapter, all through London's great between-wars building boom the Southern Railway, following the pattern set by its predecessor, the L&SWR, established a highly-successful network of efficient electric train services serving existing and new stations not only in the suburban zone but deep into Surrey's countryside, making it easy for those earning a living in central London to establish a home, according to their means, in almost any part of the county. Invariably electrification brought a far more intensive service outside the rush hours and the new journeys this generated amongst the commuters' families were a major factor in rendering the operation profitable.

Southern Electric Surrey was strongly promoted by advertising and other publicity, notably in an annual series of handbooks published from 1926 onwards which detailed, under each station served, the rail journey times from London, fares and season ticket rates, local council charges, subsoil, water, electricity and gas charges and above all, current building developments. On coated paper with a colour cover, these well-produced guides were copiously illustrated, many of the photographs specially taken to show the new housing rising up around the stations. *Live on the Live Line, Southern Electric-The Quickest Way Home* and *Live in Surrey, Free From Worry!* were among the somewhat naive slogans adopted by the railway's enthusiastic but still immature publicity machine. And, as if to cater for every need, some of the maps in these Southern Electric residential guides even included the branch built to carry funeral trains into Brookwood Cemetery although, appropriately enough, this was always worked, not by electric trains but by engines using red hot coals.

Those providing new houses in quantity for mortgager owner-occupiers also played their part in good measure. Their brochures and newspaper and periodical advertisements featured pictures of electric trains, proclaiming proudly that the estate was 'on the Southern Electric' or 'Southern Electric station on the Estate'. This undoubted bonus for commuter purchasers was sometimes made possi-

Right *Railway propaganda for the emerging Owner-Occupier-Commuter market. Pat Keely's cover for the Southern Railway Company's first residential guide, issued free in 1926, 194 pages of coated paper with many photographs and a large folding map. Surrey featured prominently, and by 1937 was sharing with its neighbour the 297-page* Southern Homes in Surrey and Hampshire (Electrified), *also issued free of charge.*

RESIDENTIAL GUIDE.
The COUNTRY at LONDON'S DOOR
Pat Keely

ble because the original developers or landowners had contributed to the cost of providing a new station, or had given land.

Changes since 1950

From the late 1950s there was a significant shift in commuting patterns.[5] Apart from infilling which used the very large plots of the better types of earlier developments, or completion of estates left unfinished in 1939-40, new housing now had to be located beyond the edge of the London Green Belt. This restriction on outward expansion, established under the Town & Country Planning Act of 1947 was fully in place by 1959. Most new private housing erected in quantity in Surrey from the 1950s onwards for commuters was therefore to be found further out, at places like Hurst Green, Horley, and Cranleigh and around the outskirts of Woking and Guildford. Rail commuting to London from these outer areas continued to increase into the 1970s. When the local authorities sought to establish large new housing estates these had to be sited within existing built-up areas or go beyond the Green Belt, like the LCC developments at Merstham and Woking. Since many more women were now in regular employment, such estates produced a noticeable increase in short distance rail commuting to workplaces in nearby towns.

By the mid and late 1960s there was some evidence of a further change in commuter settlement patterns. With the increased mobility given by possession of a car, those seeking family homes were prepared to live further from railway stations, even if they were radial rail commuters. A house in rural or semi-rural surroundings became the desirable first choice, especially as the possession of a car made it possible to minimise the perceived tedium of long distance rail commuting by driving to a station offering a fast and frequent train service. Locations in the between-wars suburban belt or in large post-war estate developments just beyond the outer edge of the London Green Belt were much less favoured by radial commuters even though they might offer houses within easy walking or bussing distance of a station. A steady decline in the quality of bus services since the 1960s, aggravated by deregulation, may also have worked to render these higher density housing areas less acceptable.

These trends, combined with the general decline in central London job opportunities mentioned below, worked to reduce the weight of commuter traffic in Surrey-near-London, from such stations as Epsom, Esher, Hinchley Wood and Weybridge. In contrast, from the late 1950s, at places like Farncombe, Godalming, Haslemere, Guildford, Woking, Farnham and Oxted, the number of season ticket holders at first increased, or at least remained stable[6].

Rail commuting into central London reached a postwar peak around 1961-2, then entered a slow decline, punctuated by a brief recovery in the late 1980s; the resumed decline was accelerated by economic recession. By 1990 it appeared that the traditional pattern of daily commuter flows into central London along radial rail routes was unlikely to assume anything like its former strength.

The 1991 census showed that over the whole of Surrey only ten per cent of commuters were by then travelling by rail, though this figure was exceeded in some areas: in Elmbridge (Walton-Weybridge-Esher) and in Epsom & Ewell it was 15 per cent; in Woking 13 per cent; and in Mole Valley (Dorking and Leatherhead) and in Reigate & Banstead 12 per cent.

Much of the fall in rail commuting arose from a major dispersal of workplaces to new locations all round the metropolitan region which were more conveniently reached by car since the journeys to work cut across the main radial rail traffic flows. This trend, evident since the 1960s, was greatly encouraged by the 1986 completion of the orbital M25 motor way. The M25 also stimulated a growing tendency to locate new office and industrial developments at sites on or near the primary road network, completely without regard to access by public transport. Another factor reducing the level of journeys to central London workplaces was the 1960s boom in office construction in the larger Surrey towns.

As early as the 1970s, around 60 per cent of Woking's working population were employed locally, only 18 per cent commuting to London, with the balance travelling to other Surrey locations. Of these categories, the workplace journeys of the first and last would mostly be by car or bus. Guildford also saw more people arriving daily to work in the town than were commuting to London or elsewhere but in this case a significant proportion were probably coming in by rail.

Other factors have contributed towards dilution of rail commuting from Surrey homes to City and West End workplaces. Advances in computer technology from the late 1970s not only led to a reduction in central London job opportunities but made it possible for more people to work from home. The enduring 'company car' tax privilege, combined with free-at-point-of-use road improvements since the 1960s did much to nurture car commuting on congested roads, even those into central London, this last also reducing rail season ticket travel. By the 1990s, car commuting all round London was the cause of much road congest ion and environmental pollution. In Surrey, where there was only minimal scope for further road construction and improvements, the unacceptable prospect of a continuing upward trend in car use for journeys to work[7] began to stimulate consideration of transport policies and strategies. The extent to which public transport improvements, including conventional rail and also light rail, might be brought to bear on this problem will be examined in chapter 10.

Whatever changes the future brings, the thousands of houses originally provided for railway commuters and other regular rail users, the basis of much of Surrey's modern settlement pattern, will long remain a distinctive feature of the county's landscape. We now turn to examine this in detail.

Notes

(1) Tharby, W G, *Leatherhead Advertiser,* 28 February 1969. The *Appendix to the LB&SCR Service Time Book*, 1910, notes that 64 footwarmers were available between mid-October and end- April at Dorking, 30 at Oxted, and an unstated quantity at Redhill. This facility was also available at Dorking, SE&CR station.

(2) id, 7 March 1969.

(3) Residential expansion in Surrey in the latter half of the 19th century and the first half of the 20th, as in other areas around London, was a product of several factors. Whilst the presence of railway facilities and their improvement could be important, the availability of suitable building land at acceptable prices, the strength of demand for housing and the coincidence of economic conditions favouring both purchaser and supplier were also relevant and need to be considered. These matters are examined in detail in the author's books *Semi-Detached London,* 2nd edition, 1991, and *The Middle Classes,* 1900-1950, 1991.

(4) Population figures from *London Statistics,* vol.41 (LCC), 1939, *Statistical Abstract for London 1937-46* (LCC), and *Greater London Plan, 1944*, Appendix 2.

(5) Some parts of this and the following two paragraphs are based on Harris, Michael, 'Pushing at an Open Door?', *Modern Railways,* November 1986, which analyses changes in commuting patterns in the metropolitan region south of the Thames between 1961 and the mid 1980s.

(6) In August 1962, on a tube train, the author overheard a Guildford commuter relating how when he first moved to that town in 1954 he could easily secure a corner seat on the train every day but by 1962, standing always in the same place as before on the platform, for the same train, he could find no seat at all for his journey to London. Harris (note (5)) mentions that there was an 18 per cent increase in commuters at Godalming and Haslemere between 1961 and 1976 and at Woking the daily figure for passengers joining trains for London increased from 5,340 in 1961 to 6,620 in 1976.

(7) The Surrey County Traffic Model shows 2,000 car-trips daily between Horsham and London [SCC *Study Into Rail Line Improvements In Surrey, Network South Central Operating Area*, 1996]. Most of these are commuter journeys. Between Horsham and Dorking, this flow, much inflated by traffic joining it at intermediate points, parallels a double track electric railway currently used well below its potential capacity.

CHAPTER SIX

Railway Settlement Patterns

In this chapter the patterns of railway-related residential development in Surrey will be considered, using four broad classifications. We begin with the outwards spread of continuously built-up London over the Surrey boundary, the advancing 'Metropolitan Edge'. Truly suburban in character, this was at first mostly occupied by central London office workers and their families, providing much peak and off peak traffic for the railway. The second category, 'Railway Clusters and Railway Spread' not only covers t he development of housing around railway stations and the growth of older communities towards stations but the rail-associated growth of the old Surrey towns. Much of this might be described as remote outposts of suburbia rather than an outer suburban ring. Again there was in the first place a substantial constituency of rail users, though, given the higher fares over the longer distances involved , these commuters needed to have higher incomes. The third group, 'Communities made by the Railway', is of special relevance for the theme of this book. Lastly, we shall look at 'High Quality Residential Scatter', a form of settlement accommodating the most privileged strata of the county's inhabitants, a group which although today relying almost totally on the private motor car, was initially attracted by the availability of railway services to keep them in touch with London.

The Metropolitan Edge

For some 90 years from the middle of the 19th century until a halt was called by the exigencies of World War 2, London's outward spread was relentless and all but continuous. Given the direction of the prevailing wind, a lack of heavy industry and the attractions of its riverside and upland scenery, the south western sector was one of the most favoured areas for this form of settlement, which steadily engulfed the fields, woods and copses of north east Surrey. The outward growth was finally checked, possibly for all time, by the provisions of the Town & Country Planning Act of 1947, legislation which made it possible during the 1950s to establish a statutory Green Belt, broadly at the point where the speculative builders had downed tools in 1939-40. Inspection of a large scale map will show that this Metropolitan edge flows across the 1974 frontier of Surrey, even though it was drawn back to concede territory to Greater London. 'London Surrey', most of it indistinguishable from the contemporary red-roofed semi-detached suburbia around the rest of the metropolitan edge, has long housed a large proportion of lower middle class commuters, living in blocks of four, six or eight units, in small semis, or in small detached houses, mostly erected by private enterprise in the years 1924- 40.

We begin our survey of the 'Metropolitan Edge' at the northern most part of Surrey, proceeding south-eastwards along London's built-up frontier. In the north-eastern corner, Englefield Green, Egham, Glanty, Thorpe Lea and Hythe End had all coalesced by 1940, merging in the east with the old town of Staines. This is by no means pure commuter land; local industry has long been important. At Egham, the Lagonda Motor Works, established in the 1900s, was taken over by Petter Diesel Engines in 1949, an enterprise which stayed in the little town for a further 40 years. But by the 1930s there was also some commuter housing, notably at Englefield

Above *The Victorian and Edwardian settlement at East Molesey alongside Hampton Court station (right), as seen from an aeroplane c.1925* Commercial postcard.

Green, about one mile to the west of the old coaching centre, where detached designs of superior type prevailed. Today the station has almost as many passengers joining daily as there are at Godalming or Stoneleigh.

With its brewery, mustard and papier mâché mills, reservoirs and water pumping plant and above all, its linoleum works, a substantial undertaking which existed from 1864 until 1973 (the associated railway facilities will be mentioned in a later chapter), Staines was able to offer a high degree of self-sufficiency in employment opportunities. These enterprises together contributed rather more to the railway's freight receipts than they did to passenger revenue, since many of the workers lived within walking or cycling distance. However in 1876, Thorne did notice 'a new suburb' by the railway station, mostly of small houses, but with a few more pretentious villas. Outwards expansion at Staines occurred mostly between the wars, generally in the form of small terraced blocks or semis, until by 1940 the area was contiguous with Ashford, which in turn saw so much new low value housing built in the same period that it seemed likely to become part of the London sprawl. In the early 1990s, Staines station was the sixth busiest in Surrey, despatching almost 2,200 passengers daily, about half of them travelling to central London; at Ashford the figures were 846 and 15 per cent (with 62 per cent to outer Greater London).

As the railway to Shepperton had to swing round to the north to avoid crossing the Kempton Park estate, Sunbury's station was located about a mile north of the existing settlement. It developed its own district, partly residential but with a significant industrial element, and in the next 40 years or so the old and new Sunbury joined up , the whole coalescing with Ashford. Today the station lies almost overwhelmed by the brutal concrete sprawl of the adjacent Junction 1 of the M3 motorway.

Shepperton station was built half a mile from Lower Halliford and rather further from the place it was supposed to serve but the 'quiet riverside village' noted by Thorne in 1876 slowly grew towards the

Above *Electric railway-stimulated development at Hinchley Wood, seen from the bridge carrying the Kingston By Pass over the New Guildford line at the station in 1934. A sign at the left directs potential passengers to 'THE SOUTHERN ELECTRIC'. Houses under construction by Messrs. Crouch at the right are advertised on a hoarding at £995 and £800 and there is a notable absence of road traffic to make use of the new 'petrol station'* Commercial postcard.

branch terminus, which for many years dealt with pleasure seekers rather than commuters. Even today Shepperton retains a tenuous separation from London's edge, although by 1940 there was an almost unbroken line of housing northwards along the Upper Halliford Road towards Sunbury. 'Railway Shepperton' saw some outward growth in most directions in the 1920s and 1930s, as did its outlyer, Shepperton Green, where the Film Studios established in Littleton Park in 1928 brought some new traffic to the station . But this remained a remote spot, not by any means classic commuter territory. Although Sunbury has seen more residential building since World War 2, in general the Surrey catchment area of the Shepperton branch, a nondescript, flat, somewhat dreary area of reservoirs, horsey-culture and riverside bungalows, tends to demonstrate how ineffectual even a regular service of electric trains can be in influencing the settlement pattern when other conditions are not favourable.

Moving south east, we come to the area served by the Hampton Court branch. Here at East Molesey, by the 1880s, the railway had already encouraged the building of many new houses, often quite small, those at the western edge near Hurst Road forming a settlement known as Kent Town which lay half-finished for many years. East Molesey steadily grew outwards west and south in the years up to 1914 , the pace quickening in the late 1920s and the 1930s until West and East Molesey were one. Many of those buying houses here between the wars were London commuters, those in the cheaper ones such as Howards' Upper Farm and White Lodge Estates of 1934-35 having lengthy journeys to reach their trains. On the south bank of the Thames, nearer the station, the Hurst Park Race Course provided a fine site for an extensive housing development in the late 1960s. At Thames Ditton, some good quality residential development had appeared near the station before 1914 and either side of the railway (mostly north of the station) there was much building activity in the 1930s, some of it also stimulated by the opening of Hampton Court Way in 1933. As the 1940s began, Thames Ditton station was also benefiting from an inward flow bound for the new Milk Marketing Board headquarters Offices. By that time, built-up London had edged outwards from Surbiton across the railway at Thames Ditton to a point west of Esher station and was joining up with the Thames-side communities of East and West Molesey, served by Hampton Court station. Over 1,500 passengers boarded trains daily at the two branch stations in the early 1990s, around 60 per cent going to central London.

As early as 1911 Scott remarked of the road to the north of Esher station that it 'winds back into suburbia'. Certainly by the end of the 1930s, the Woodlands and Pound Farm Estates of 1931-35, north of the railway at Esher station, with their detached and semi-detached commuter houses, were tenuously joined to London through the hamlet of Weston Green, with its striking 1939 church. This suburban edge was however still separated from the old town by the open spaces of Sandown Park Race Course and Littleworth Common. We shall return to Esher later.

Also part of the London edge hereabouts is Hinchley Wood, a green field development, very much a railway suburb, named after a nearby wood and built around a new electric railway station. An archetypal London settlement of the 1930s, almost entirely the product of three firms of builders (E & L Berg, J Montgomery, and G T Crouch), it had a high proportion of closely-spaced and rather small detached houses. Opened in October 1930 as residential construction was starting, the station was willingly subsidised by a landowner who knew it to be essential if he were to secure the maximum development potential in the shortest possible time. This motivated benefactor also provided the necessary plot, as well as transferring another at a discount for a freight yard which was never built . Amenities were not plentiful, but the place eventually gained a church, a school, small parades of shops in the station approach and a large public house; it never possessed a cinema, an essential feature for the complete suburb of the 1930-60 era. Few of the inhabitants had cars until the 1950s or 1960s but from the start, road access was good, since this new railway-centred suburb also sat squarely astride the 1927 Kingston By Pass, which split it into two just as effectively as the railway divided Stoneleigh - but far more dangerously and unpleasantly. Just before World War 2, further houses were added on the south side of the By pass, east of the station and, to complete pre-war plans, more appeared between Littleworth Common and the railway in 1957-59. Construction of two complexes of single-storey Government offices in the immediate post-war years brought the station some welcome inward commuter traffic for ten years or so until the majority of the workers acquired cars. In the mid 1990s these offices gave way to commuter housing.

To anyone watching the progress of house construction in the late 1930s it would seem that Hinchley Wood and Claygate were about to join up as another extension of London's sprawl but today, although its northern roads are up against Long Ditton, a western outcrop of Surbiton , Hinchley Wood sits at London's edge, any further south and south-western advance arrested by the post-war Metropolitan Green Belt. By the 1990s, the favourable access to the road system had attracted many car commuters to this suburb, causing a drastic decline in rail use. Only some 500 , rather less than half the comparable total at Stoneleigh, were then joining trains here daily, 73 per cent bound for central London.

The 'Metropolitan Edge', or London Surrey, is at its densest along the railway from Raynes Park to Epsom. The present-day county boundary cuts across this area at Stoneleigh but it is convenient to look at it as a whole. Until the 1900s the entire district south of the main line was open countryside interrupted only by small settlements at Malden and Ewell and some Victorian railway-related development west of the line at Worcester Park, described by Thorne in 1876 as, 'a collection of villas and cottages about a station' having some 300 inhabitants. Worcester Park continued to expand up to 1914, with smaller houses, shops and a church built to the east of the railway. H.G. Wells knew the place, using it as the setting for his 1909 feminist novel *Ann Veronica*. A little further north, between 1907 and 1914, new housing was appearing either side of the railway at West Barnes, and at Raynes Park, encouraged by the arrival in the former year of the London United

Above *A new suburban station awaits its suburb. Stoneleigh's deserted island platform soon after opening in 1932, looking towards London* L Catchpole.

electric trams, which offered a convenient and direct link to Raynes Park and Wimbledon stations. But development in the area really took off in the decade or so after the 1925 electrification of the railway, a period which saw housing growth of the most vigorous kind, until by 1940, with the exception of the banks of the Hogsmill stream and the LCC hospital estate, the whole area either side of the tracks as far south as Epsom was thickly covered with small semis and terrace blocks. In appearance, if not in name, this was now London rather than Surrey.

When it was opened with the electrified service on 12 July 1925, the station at Motspur Park stood at the very frontier of south-west London. Quite quickly the island platform was surrounded by small houses, forming a new community, serviced by a parade of Tudorbethan shops and a large public house, both within a stone's throw of the station. Worcester Park's between-wars growth was so rapid that before the 1930s came to an end, the country roadside station of 1859 had to be rebuilt and its goods yard enlarged. New housing, mostly semis, spread out in all directions and more shops and a cinema (1934) lined the main road running east from the station. The result was a railway-centred London suburb, virtually complete by 1939 which was still providing a strong flow of commuter and off peak traffic over fifty years later with nearly 2,000 boarding trains daily.

This was impressive enough but far more dramatic growth was seen at Stoneleigh[1], where two large farms were sold to developers in 1930. Negotiations for a railway station were begun at once, the landowners eventually agreeing to contribute about half the cost as well as two pieces of land. On a site still isolated amid fields and copses, a 520 ft island platform was opened on 17 July 1932 . Concrete roads were very soon laid over the pastureland and building began. Within five years, the station had become the centre of a thriving new commuter suburb, consisting almost entirely of small semi-detached houses and virtually dependent on the railway for its sustenance. Passengers using the cheaply-built station grew from 103,724 in 1933 to 313,647 in 1935, providing a more than three-fold increase in the railway's revenue[2].

By 1940, Stoneleigh had joined up with Worcester Park on the north whilst southwards it had be-

Above *Although this photograph of Stoneleigh was taken in July 1963, all the buildings seen here, with the exception of the flat-roofed range on the left, were erected between 1933 and 1939. The railway station runs across the centre, on the level and by some curious planning quirk, the main central street was built in two separate halves, split by the railway station* Alan A. Jackson

come one with Ewell. Little thought had been given to the street layout which was quite wayward, with the railway line splitting into two parts the central avenue of shopping parades that along with the station, formed Stoneleigh's heart. Access between the two sides of Stoneleigh was only available to pedestrians; road vehicles had to make long diversions. This and the muddled network of residential roads rendered the new suburb almost impenetrable for buses and nowadays difficult territory for motorists. As a result, the railway gained much of the all-day traffic to and from Epsom and towards London, a feature still apparent over 60 years later. In accordance with tradition, a large public house was erected close by the station in 1935, soon becoming something of a social centre, but the new community was completed in the eyes of its 1930s residents when the 1,462- seat Rembrandt Cinema opened its doors in October 1938. Reflecting the priorities of the period, the permanent Anglican church was not ready until the following year. These last two buildings also nestled close to the railway station.

Complaints of overcrowding of rush hour trains at Stoneleigh's new station were voiced as early as 1934. Following much grumbling about restricted access to and from the platform at peak periods over the cheap little foot bridge, the SR constructed a wider bridge which included a larger ticket office. This was completed in 1940/41. Fifty-five years later, commuter flows had subsided, with some 1,300 joining trains daily, though still in original character, three quarters of these were bound for central London.

At Epsom, already the home of some daily commuters to the City (Defoe had noted their presence as early as 1724), the arrival of the railway was soon marked by new housing, ranging from modest terrace homes to detached properties for the comfortable middle class: *Murray's Handbook for Surrey* noted in the 1890s 'a great number of modern villas have been built here'. Residential expansion around the old spa town and the neighbouring village of Ewell accelerated greatly between the wars, surging ahead until the two areas had merged. Some of this new provision was above the average suburban size and quality, but much of the output was aimed at the lower middle class commuter. By the end of the 1930s, as is still the case today, continuously- built up London came to an abrupt end about half a mile southwest and south of Epsom, where the Epsom and Ashtead Commons, Woodcote Park and Epsom Downs tenuously separate the metropolitan sprawl from a series of railway cluster developments we shall examine later. Epsom station, which also has an interchange function, offering as it does three routes to London and two to the south, remained busy in the early 1990s, with around 4,200 passengers joining trains daily, 75 per cent of them travelling to the City and West End.

South of Sutton, London's outward growth had by 1940 reached the present Surrey boundary and was within a few yards of Banstead station. Epsom had expanded south eastwards towards the Downs, sending out a long thin finger of new housing to touch Epsom Downs and Tattenham Corner stations and the northern edge of Tadworth. South of the Epsom Downs branch line, the old landed estates of Great Burgh and Nork Park, over 1,300 acres in all, had been sold for building in 1923 and much of the new housing which then followed here was of the detached variety, although still suburban in character. Immediately south of Banstead station, a few large houses had been erected along the Brighton Road in the 1860s after Charles Garrett, contractor for the branch and Laverick Flower its engineer, had purchased land for this purpose. Then, between 1890 and 1914, some 100 new houses appeared in this area. But this was as nothing to the growth after World War 1: in 1932 the old village of Banstead, which had retained much of its rural character until the 1920s, was by-passed to the north by a new road which was soon to be lined with suburban housing. Both immediately before and after this, new residential development appeared all round the village centre, growing outwards until it almost touched the somewhat isolated railway station. Almost all this between-wars growth was within walking distance of Epsom Downs, Banstead or Tattenham Corner stations, where most of the house buyers met daily to travel to their work in central London. The pace of the commuter settlement is shown by the fact that season ticket sales for stations on the Epsom Downs branch jumped from 3,000 in 1927 to 13,000 in 1933 whilst the journeys made by commuters' wives and children were demonstrated in the totals of ordinary tickets issued: only 329,778 in 1927 but 859,794 in 1935[3].

Further south, the Chipstead Valley line was also reaping a steady residential traffic. Initially there were many First Class ticket holders from up-market housing spaciously set amid attractive scenery around the stations at Chipstead and Kingswood. Large detached houses, many with attic rooms for servants, had been erected in the Edwardian years around these stations and also at Walton on the Hill, the latter under a mile from Tadworth station but separated from the outer edge of the London sprawl by the preservation of Banstead Heath. At Tadworth itself, where the new development was just a little lower down the price scale, a local house builder erected a parade of suburban style shops opposite the station in 1909. Between the wars, led by Costain at Kingswood Warren (from 1923) and at Epsom Lane and Shelvers Lane (1930 and 1934), development of broadly similar quality was continued in the catchment areas of all three stations, though in general the 1930s houses were smaller. Miraculously, a small amount of this beautiful area, at Chipstead Bottom and Banstead Wood, was belatedly saved from the builders' grasp by Surrey County Council and Banstead Urban District Council Green Belt purchases in 1937. Perhaps due to its distance from the railways, the old village of Woodmansterne escaped the suburban swamping experienced by Banstead, although there was some new growth between the two along Woodmansterne Lane in the 1930s.

Such was the quality and price of most of the new housing in the area around the Epsom Downs and Tattenham Corner branches that when these lines were electrified it was necessary for the Southern Railway to provide accommodation for the uniformed employees required to operate the greatly increased train services. At Ashcombe Terrace, just north of Tadworth station, 24 cottages were erected in 1928-9 at a cost of £18,500, including roads. These were followed in 1929-30 by a further 30, built at £695 each on the south side of the line, 750 yd from Epsom Downs station.[4]

From the early 1950s, estate developers and council housing departments were active in this district, filling in the gaps left by the earlier builders in Nork

Above *Southern Railway Company staff cottages at Ashcombe Terrace, Tadworth, photographed on 27 May 1974* Alan A Jackson.

Park and elsewhere and breaking up the many large plots which had been enjoyed by the earlier properties. If the occupants of these more recent developments commute by rail, they do not now make much use of the local stations. Traffic on both branches has declined considerably since the 1960s, and counts at Epsom Downs in the early 1990s showed only just over 100 boarding trains daily, 48 per cent going to central London and a slightly higher number to outer London; at Banstead the figures were just under 200, split 56 and 38 per cent. On the Surrey part of the Tattenham Corner branch, the daily intake ranged from about 110 at Tattenham Corner to around 180 at Kingswood.

Another peninsula of built-up London pushes out over the Surrey boundary in the east, extending into the northern slopes of the Downs south of Caterham. Some of the earliest railway-related residential development in the county appeared here around the Caterham line, thanks to the ready availability of suitable land. Building started in the 1860s along the steep-sided Valley, much of it in the form of very large houses such as Woodside, erected in Stanstead Road in 1861 for Juland Danvers, a Caterham Railway director; Timber Hill Lodge, completed in 1864; and The Priory, next to the station, built in 1868 for the leading Congregationalist, William Garland Soper. Soper, who moved in 1879 to Harestone, an even larger property, was active in community life, becoming the first chairman of the Caterham Urban District Council in 1899. To market houses similar to these and more modest ones, the Surrey Hills Estate Agency was opened near the station in the 1860s. By the end of the 1890s there was a substantial spread of new housing for the London- based comfortable middle class, as represented by the Bond Street jeweller Asprey, who had erected the spacious Beechlands in its own small park immediately north west of the station. Writing in the mid 1870s with a hint of bile, Thorne described the Caterham district as 'perhaps the pleasantest of those near London which have been made the prey of the railway engineer, speculative builder

Above *Railway Caterham or 'Caterham Valley', looking north in about 1912. The station and freight yard are on the left, the back of* The Railway Hotel *of 1902 appears in the left foreground. All this development and much more out of view behind the camera, is principally related to the existence of the railway passenger and freight services*
Commercial postcard

and...building societies'. From a mere 487 when the line opened, the population had grown to 3,594 in 1881 and was approaching 10,000 by 1901.

Doubling of the branch line and rebuilding of Caterham station in 1899-1900 have been mentioned earlier. This work was closely followed by the construction of a new *Railway Hotel* (later the *Valley Hotel*) and shops (The Grand Parade), both opposite the station, in 1902 and 1903 respectively. Nearby, the Urban District Council Offices and Fire Station were opened in January 1912. By the 1910s, largely thanks to its railway, and amid what were still pleasing surroundings, 'Caterham Valley' had become a small town in its own right.

Between the wars, much stimulated by the electrification of the branch in 1928, further building took place, mostly of smaller houses, until in 1940, the district was well and truly joined to London by continuous housing. To the north east, residential development ranged over the Valley sides and uplands through Warlingham, Kenley and Mitchley Wood to join up with Purley. Northwestwards, Caterham was separated from Coulsdon and continuous London only by the interruption of Coulsdon Common. To the south, the 1930s London speculative builders pushed ever further up the slopes of the North Downs in an uncontrolled invasion of some of Surrey's finest countryside. Their activities were enthusiastically portrayed in the 1937 Southern Railway residential guide:

> *The Harestone Valley ends at Dome Hill and rises to a col in the ridge of the North Downs and from this break there is a prospect that embraces all of eastern Surrey and the high points of Kent and Sussex, Here, grouped on the slopes above and below this unsurpassed view are modern houses, constituting one of*

the most beautifully- placed rural settlements in the Home Counties, set almost on the 700 feet line with summits either side approaching 800 feet.... On various estates and road frontages, many houses have been and still are being constructed, and it is a noteworthy feature of Caterham that each of these sections is distinct, being sundered from the others by the ridges separating the various valleys.....houses to suit all tastes can be obtained from £600 upwards.... The Dome Hill Estate is being developed on very careful and exclusive lines, and the houses are mostly in Tudor style with genuine oak beams, tiles, lattice windows etc., prices cover a wide range from £975 to £2,000 according to site and style.

For the active commuter or those prosperous enough to afford a 1930s car, this Tudorbethan arcadia, the Domewood Lake Estate Company's domain, was just over a mile from the station, a journey with houses always in sight. Saaler expresses his admiration for the 50 houses built here in 1934-39 : 'a unified and extremely attractive area of perhaps the finest 1930s Tudor to be seen anywhere'.

Today Caterham and its district remain very much commuter territory and the branch is busier than its western counterpart up the Chipstead Valley. In the early 1990s some 700 passengers were joining the trains at Caterham daily, 53 per cent bound for central London, 36 per cent for outer London. The corresponding figures for Whyteleafe South were 258 and 40 and 46 per cent; for Whyteleafe, 404 and 60 and 31 per cent. By this time, Croydon had developed as a new office centre and an alternative workplace for many living in the area.

Railway Clusters and Railway Spread

Whilst some of this type of residential development dates from the Edwardian and late Victorian eras, most coincides with the extensive inter-wars spread of London. New communities around railway stations sometimes also filled in the areas between the railway and the older settlements the stations were intended to serve. A variation, seen at Esher, was new growth close to the station, combined with expansion of the existing community, both growths owing much to the presence of the railway but separated by open land kept free of building for one reason or another. We shall also include in this category the railway-oriented development of the old Surrey towns, a phenomenon normally seen within reasonable walking distance (half to three quarters of a mile) of the railway stations or in areas accessible by frequent bus services. This again sometimes filled up what had been largely open land between the station and the town centre.

Housing in this type of development varied from roads lined with semis and small to medium- sized detached designs of suburban character to high-quality informal parkland developments of more substantial detached properties with four to six or more bedrooms on plots from one quarter to two or more acres. By their nature, such settlements were further from central London and when first appearing in the late Victorian and Edwardian years, were inhabited by the more affluent middle class commuters, professionals and successful businessmen working locally, the retired, and people such as artists and writers and those subsisting on investments, who had no need to make daily journeys to London. These non-commuters nevertheless chose to live near the railway, for greater convenience, since until the 1950s they and their successors would as a rule rely upon it for almost all journeys of more than a mile or two.

Good examples of railway cluster are to be found at Ashtead, at Bookham and at some stations along the New Guildford Line. As was not uncommon, the railways here had been laid out to follow the easiest reasonably direct route between the two terminal points and this had caused stations to be sited typically half a mile or more from the pre-railway settlements on higher ground whose names they assumed.

At first it was often the case that arrival of the railway made little impact on the size of an existing community. Thus the population of Ashtead[5], grew by only 242 during the first 22 years after the opening of the station. Then, for the reasons given earlier, as the 19th century moved to a close, growth, associated with middle class settlement began to accelerate. Speculative builders moved in to fill the gap between the village and the station. At first the new houses were designed to attract relatively wealthy middle class families whose heads were either exempt from any need to travel to work daily to London or were able to accept the longer journey and higher fares involved in living seventeen miles from the City. Accordingly, the first post-railway houses, in and around the lane between the village and station, were large detached villas, set in spacious garden plots and having accommodation for several servants. In turn, the new residents attracted an influx of supporters - shopkeepers, tradesmen, outdoor servants and gardeners, for whom some cottages and shop premises were also erected. In 1903, as a response to this first wave of new residential construction, the railway goods yard was enlarged and the passenger platforms were lengthened.

Between 1881 and 1921, Ashtead's population grew strongly, from 926, housed in 160 dwellings, to 3,226 in 680. Much of this increase was associated with villa building in the decade or so before 1914 and that which followed in the 1920s was still mainly directed at the prosperous upper half of the middle class able to afford some individuality of style on a chosen plot. Before 1914, when travelling to London, Ashtead's new residents could expect to receive a measure of consideration at the station of the type mentioned in the previous chapter: formal courtesies from the stationmaster, who would be present on the platform for at least the more popular 'business trains', and at all times a porter, who would find them an empty First Class compartment, or arrange for the 'station fly' to meet them on their return.

With the arrival of electric train services in 1925 (and more in 1929), Ashtead's growth not only accelerated but took a different form. Other factors assisted this process. By 1930, sewers had been laid in the area between the village and the station, whilst a town planning scheme approved by the local council in 1932 allowed building almost anywhere, setting out to regulate little more than the number of houses per acre. These events, coinciding as they did with the London suburban building boom, saw the arrival of E&L Berg, a firm of speculative builders with some experience of suburban estate development in south London. Construction of an estate of closely-spaced well-designed medium-sized detached and large semi-detached houses was begun on the low-lying clay pasture land alongside the railway, purchased for the purpose in 1934. Prices started at £1,095 or about twice the amount required for much smaller houses nearer London. Although Bergs' publicity could proclaim with some truth 'Southern Electric station on the Estate', the expenditure required was perceived as high whilst there was a wide choice closer to town and sales were slow. By 1938 Bergs had changed tack and were erecting much smaller and cheaper semis; even so, many plots were unoccupied when work stopped at the end of 1939. Other speculative builders followed Bergs to Ashtead and whilst Hitler was building his power in Germany they covered at 4-6 to the acre all the clay farmland along the south of the railway east of the station. Much of the output was semis with three or four bedrooms. Noting what had happened to Berg, they provided a good choice in the range £750-£1,000 . With a parade of shops and flats erected to serve it about 1938 and roads of houses set close together along a building line, the area close to the station took on a distinctly suburban appearance, indistinguishable from contemporary residential developments all round the edge of London. Further from the railway, on the more elevated chalklands to the south, most houses built in 1925-40 were detached,selling at prices higher than those on the lower clay. Some were in the grounds of the 500-acre Ashtead Park, which had been sold for development in 1924. Summarising the change that occurred, the Rector, at the parish meeting in 1935, ruefully remarked that Ashtead as a village no longer existed, 'the incoming population is more familiar with journeys to London on the Southern Railway than with the place itself, least of all the church'.

Ashtead's population, now containing many London railway commuters and their families, soared from the 3,226 of 1921 to 4,783 in 1931 and an estimated 9,336 in 1939, this last an increase of over 95 per cent. By 1991, thanks to judicious and vigorously-pursued infilling of the spacious plots enjoyed by the Victorian and Edwardian middle class settlers, and the completion of pre-1940 developments, there were 13,363 living in 5,269 households in this much-

Above *In the mid-1930s, semi-detached suburban style housing was erected around the railway station at Ashtead. In this April 1981 view looking towards Epsom 4-car unit 508035 enters on an Effingham Junction service* Alan A Jackson.

expanded and suburbanised 'village', whose further outward spread had been firmly checked since the 1950s by the Metropolitan Green Belt. In 1949 Ashtead had 890 London rail commuters , almost ten per cent of the total population and a far higher proportion of the resident adults under 65; this figure exceeded the rail commuter element (six and seven per cent) of more densely populated Epsom and Surbiton. By the 1960s, Ashtead station had over 1,000 season ticket holders, but they were less comfortably serviced: there was no longer a Stationmaster or a W H Smith bookstall on the platform. In recent years, use of the railway has remained high throughout the day, with off peak passengers seeking the amenities of Epsom or central London. In the early 1980s, the annual total of originating and terminating journeys, about half of which were to and from London, was around 800,000[6] and in the early 1990s some 1,200 were joining trains daily here, 63 per cent bound for central London.

With minor variations, the Ashtead pattern was repeated elsewhere. Effingham, Horsley and the Clandons[7] , more remote from London, saw no significant railway-related growth until the 1920s, when the take-off in residential development was linked as much to the release of building land by the break- up of the Lovelace and other old estates as to the improved railway service which followed electrification in 1925. At East Horsley, most of the new housing was detached, of medium size. Some, with thatched roofs, was set in a twee water park. Individuality in styling was usual, on plots of a quarter acre or more, at the purchaser's choice, with price tags from £1,250 to £3,000 in the years 1926-40. Mostly in secluded private roads or in woodland clearings, these properties were designed to appeal to the upper levels of the salariat able to afford the higher rail season ticket rate.

Much of the activity at Horsley was under the

control of Frank Chown, who enforced design and other restrictions after he had bought much of the former Lovelace estate in the commuter-desirable area between the station and the woodland just south of the Leatherhead - Guildford Road. Chown's publicity prominently featured the railway service and fares. Development in this area was almost entirely lacking in the usual suburban amenities, apart from two Tudorbethan shopping parades. On a smaller scale, a similar pattern of mainly detached houses appeared between the wars around the stations at Clandon and Westhumble . The former had but two shops in 1938, Westhumble none at all. In the early 1990s Horsley and Clandon stations together saw almost 1,000 passengers joining London-bound trains daily.

Effingham parish housed only 605 people in 1921, virtually all of them in the old settlement 1$^{3}/_{4}$ miles from its station. Six years later, houses 'overlooking Effingham Common' were advertised with much stress on the 50 or so new electric trains each way to and from Waterloo daily (45 on Sundays) . Effingham Junction was now within 36 minutes of central London, its service more than double that offered in 1911. Between the late 1920s and 1940 a scattering of new houses appeared along the road from the station to the village, whilst superior detached residences were advertised in 1926-27 on plots south of the old settlement in an area which was to be infilled after World War 2. North west of the station, the 1930s saw some new housing near the little group of cottages the SR had built here for its electric train crews coming on and off duty at the neighbouring car shed. Close to this, by 1940, the residential development hugging the railway between Horsley and Effingham stations was virtually continuous. Commuting remains the major business at Effingham Junction, with almost 500 passengers joining trains daily.

That Bookham saw little or no growth in its first two railway decades may have been in part due to the poor steam train service provided by the L&SWR, which did nothing to alleviate its distance from London. A few houses designed to attract commuters had been erected in Burnhams Road and Maddox Lane in 1905-6 but the 1921 census found the population of this well-scattered area to be but 1,566. Then, with the 1922 sale of almost 1,000 acres of Eastwick Park to a property developer and estate agent and the electrification of the railway three years later, things began to move. Further encouragement was given with the completion of a main drainage scheme for Fetcham and the Bookhams in 1932. Near the Eastwick Park mansion, between the station and the village centre of Great Bookham, 'timbered sites' were reserved for medium to high value houses in the late 1920s and 1930s, but in 1921 south of the main Leatherhead-Guildford Road, either side of Dorking Road, a mile or more from the station, where it was considered commuter interest would be less likely, land was offered very cheaply (£150 an acre) for 'small-holdings or poultry farms'. The result was a rash of unsightly low-cost bungalows set along rutted, unsurfaced roads over the lower slopes of the North Downs. At a Ministry of Health Planning Inquiry at Dorking in September 1934 some strong words were said about this ; one witness described it as the worst blot that had yet been made on the map of Surrey, whilst another referred to, 'that horrible outbreak' of 'bungalow erection' at Bookham. At this distance in time, on the limited evidence available, it is difficult to determine whether the availability of rail services at Bookham station had any significant influence on the emergence of this 'Bungalow Town', now replaced by conventional housing.

The extensive and well-timbered Fetcham Park estate came on the market in 1924, undergoing residential development within three years. Also at Fetcham, the seven-acre Glade Estate, which extended north of the railway up to the edge of Great Bookham Common, offered very small detached houses 'of country cottage type' from 1936. Nearer Leatherhead, between the Cobham Road and the railway, the Cannon Court estate was built over from 1933, mostly with small bungalows sited in long but narrow gardens. Detached houses of a superior kind on large plots were sprinkled along the main Guildford-Leatherhead road to enjoy the extensive views from the rising ground. All this activity brought what was a virtual merging of the Bookhams and Fetcham by 1940, the new residential cluster completely overwhelming the old village cores and extending up to the railway. This new district all but linked up to Leatherhead town where the road from Guildford crossed the Mole, whilst north of Bookham station, only the Common had checked further advance northwards. Although many residents were London railway commuters, this was still not quite suburbia; the layout, with generous garden plots extending to 250 ft or more, many interstices of woodland, the undeveloped surrounds of the old Eastwick Park Mansion, and a strip left for a proposed Outer Orbital Road had a very open, rural feel until the 1950s. But from then onwards , most of the intervening spaces and large garden plots were remorsely built over. Much of this second wave of development took the form of small detached houses with minimal gardens and the increased density imparted a much more suburban appearance.

From the beginning of its residential expansion the Bookhams-Leatherhead cluster brought the railway good custom and with the development of Fetcham, agitation arose for a station to be provided at the north end of Fetcham Street to serve the eastern part of the district. Plans for a station and freight yard were drawn up in 1935 but no work was started. After 1960 increased car ownership made it easier for those living anywhere in this area to get to the better-served Leatherhead or Ashtead stations and the demand for a Fetcham station subsided. Despite the population increase from three decades of infilling after 1960, usage of Bookham station itself also began to decline steeply. Many residents no longer worked in central London and were able to commute all the way by car to workplaces elsewhere, whilst the residual rail commuters transferred their allegiance in the way just described. As a result, the total joining trains daily at Bookham in the early 1990s, just under 400, was one of the lowest amongst Surrey stations at comparable distance from London.

Around the old settlements at Street Cobham, Cobham and Cobham Tilt in 1880-3 a hopeful landowner looked forward to the arrival of the railway, offering 229 acres for sale as 'eligible building land'. Another 155 acres came on to the development market in 1904. New shops appeared in the narrow Cobham High Street about the same time, to serve what was by then already a growing community of middle class rail users.

During the 1920s and 1930s much of the area between the Cobhams and the station was built over, culminating with commuter-oriented estates alongside the railway which were erected in 1937-39. Many of the new houses in this area were detached, their commuter purchasers senior civil servants and other professionals at the upper end of the salary range. Although there was a certain suburban aura to this area , it was well-diluted by the spacious streetscapes and the proximity of open country, saved by the out break of war bringing further activity to a halt in 1939-40. A visitor at that time would have sensed that the Cobhams, Fairmile and Oxshott were nevertheless all but merged into one large upmarket residential area.

Oxshott's 20th century development, well dispersed along what were often private roads, was generally spacious, and residential sites, particularly west of the railway, were given added quality by their closeness to Esher and Fairmile Commons and Oxshott Heath , then still unsullied by the roaring concrete of the Esher By pass. Some of the more substantial detached houses here dated from the 1910s and a Southern Railway guide of 1926 warned prospective purchasers that near the station, all the land was on lease from the Crown Estate and expensive.

Between the wars, houses costing £3,000 or more, around five times the price of the average suburban semi, could be found here. This was commuter land of a very superior sort, neither suburb nor country, but with something of the flavour of both. After World War 2, Cobham and Oxshott saw the completion of pre-1940 schemes as well as judicious infilling but with minimal damage to their semi-rural atmosphere. Both stations were well-used by commuters in the early 1990s, just over 700 joining trains daily at Cobham (85 per cent bound for the City or West End) and almost 800 at Oxshott.

Claygate was an insignificant, little-visited rural parish of just under 800 inhabitants when the New Guildford Line was cut through it in the mid 1880s. Peebles gives a careful account of the subsequent middle class residential growth, which was clearly associated with the railway facilities. One landowner released a large area for building in the year the station opened. On this estate, east of the line and north and south of the station, six new roads were laid out and by 1914 there was a definite suburban feel, with medium-sized and mostly detached villas filling in the area between the old settlement and the station, the latter now approached by a street of shops. Between 1881 and World War 1, when activity was interrupted, almost 500 houses were added to the parish, raising the 1921 population to 2,860.

Building around the outskirts of Claygate continued in the 1920s and 1930s with many of the houses occupied by commuters' families. By 1938 some 700 were travelling by rail daily to London. Isolated from main roads, the place remained a quiet railway-dependent backwater set apart from between wars semi-detached London. Even today it has a special atmosphere that is not entirely suburban despite the usual post-war infilling and some further development at the edges, including four roads over a brickworks site on the east side of the railway just north of the station. The total of 1,320 houses in 1951 had grown twenty years later to over 2,000, accommodating 6,920 but further growth was then halted. Although tenuously linked by housing to Esher since 1938-1940, Claygate's surroundings continued quietly and pleasantly rural until 1976 when, despite a brave fight by residents, its eastern and southern outskirts were belted-in and much degraded environmentally by the Esher By Pass. As at neighbouring Cobham and Oxshott, the station continues to handle substantial numbers of radial commuters . Through the 1960s and early 1970s there were over 820 season ticket holders, some 72 per cent for London termini; in 1991 over 900 passengers joined trains daily 81 per cent bound for inner London.

After the arrival of the railway in Dorking some 20 years passed before there was any significant residential expansion. Between 1851 and 1871, the population of the town increased by under 2,000 to 5,419, much of this arising from the activities of the National Freehold Land Society, which had purchased large areas south and south west of the old centre[8]. These new estates were within a mile of the SER station (now Dorking West), carefully segregated into groups of artisan and workmen's cottages, and large middle class villas. The occupants were mostly the retired or locally-employed. Some villa-building had begun near the LB&SCR station in 1890-1914 and when the Box Hill Estate, strategically sited between the SER Deepdene and LB&SCR stations, was offered for sale in villa plots in 1888 here, as elsewhere, the auctioneers placed

Below *Claygate's Edwardian shopping street, seen from the station footbridge, 20 June 1981* Alan A Jackson.

some emphasis on its 'railway advantages'[9].

The new houses built between the wars were almost all on this eastern side of the town, within ten to fifteen minutes' walk of the former LB&SCR station. Developers at Dorking appear to have concluded that those commuters not deterred by the higher fares involved in living 23 miles from London would be seeking something bigger than the semis and terrace blocks available in quantity further up the line, and accordingly provided a high proportion of medium-sized detached houses within walking distance of the main station. The most expensive, at £1,750 upwards, on plots of a third of an acre or more, occupied the landscaped greensand ridge which became available following the sale of the park of the Deepdene Estate in 1921. Of the three estates of small semis built in the 1930s, only one was close to the main station, which suggests that railway season ticket holders were not expected to predominate amongst the purchasers. Indeed Dorking has never been a major dormitory town for London commuters, although it is interesting to note that following electrification, season ticket sales increased more than fourfold, from 669 in 1924 to almost 3,000 in 1932. Since 1945 only a handful of middle class houses have been erected in the immediate vicinity of the town and the daily total of around 1,200 joining trains here (77 per cent for central London) includes a fair proportion driving in from the rural outskirts; commuters walking to the station are very much in the minority.

South of Dorking, the communities of North, Mid and South Holmwood, and Beare Green, strung along the A 24 road, showed some signs of residential development in the first decades of railway service: the 1876 edition of *Murray's Handbook for Surrey* noted that Holmwood Common was 'being rapidly built on'. Between the wars there was little further growth and a Southern Railway inspection in autumn 1936 reported that traffic at Holmwood station had 'seriously fallen off'. This caused postponement of a plan to erect a covered way on the Up plat form, although the oil lights here and at Ockley were to be replaced by electricity taken from the track[10]. From the 1960s to the end of the 1980s there was some new building, mostly of small houses, at Beare Green and North Holmwood, the latter becoming an extension of Dorking town. At Holmwood station, well sited for the new residential developments at Beare Green, the Bookham pattern was repeated on a smaller scale, the deterioration in train services causing most rail users to drive to Dorking, where ample car parking was available. In the early 1990s, only about 40 passengers joined London trains daily at Holmwood, although this was about ten more than at Ockley.

As it could offer a substantial degree of local employment right through from Victorian times to the present day, Leatherhead has never possessed much railway-related housing. Between the wars, developments on the higher ground south of the old centre mostly took the form of detached houses in the higher price ranges ; some cheaper new property was however available immediately west of the station; both attracted a fair number of rail commuters. At a greater distance from the station were the quality parkland type layouts of detached properties at Pachesham Park, Tyrell's Wood and Givons Grove, the first two with adjoining golf courses. All three had houses of the sort that might attract notice in *Woman's Journal* or *Homes & Gardens* but were in general not grand enough to feature in the advertisement columns of *Country Life*. Givons Grove, soon to be separated from the town by a 1934 By Pass, was laid out from 1927. Here were individually-designed detached houses on large plots, fitted into a well-wooded undulating site served by sinuous private roads. Like the other two quality developments, Givons Grove was at least 1 1/2 miles from the station and devoid of shops or other amenities. A fair proportion of those buying into these three estates, paying up to eight times the cost of an ordinary suburban semi for the privilege, would have been rail commuters, enjoying the quieter late edges of the peak hours but unlike their humbler counterparts, would also be car owners. This made distance from a station of little consequence. Although Green Belt restrictions checked further outward growth of Leatherhead after 1945, here as elsewhere, there was some infilling of the very large plots and spacious layouts provided for earlier middle class settlers. In the early 1990s, around 1,600 joined London trains daily at Leatherhead station, a figure swollen by those motoring in from Bookham, Fetcham and other outlying areas.

Beginning in the second decade after the arrival of the railway in 1845-49, Guildford was slowly transformed from an inward-looking quiet country town into a prosperous centre of trade, industry and residential settlement. An important feature was a substantial ingress of middle class families: businessmen commuted to London, whilst the rentiers and retired soon discovered that the railway service enhanced the town's residential attractions. With its fine scenery, the district also became popular for holidays and as in the Dorking area, houses were taken for the summer by comfortable families from London, a process which could lead to a decision to take up permanent residence. Educational establishments, retail outlets and entertainment facilities all thrived under increasing demand and the process was further accelerated by the completion of the New Guildford line and London Road station in 1885.

Railway-related residential growth began in the late 1860s with some large villas in Woodbridge Road, just east of the station and expansion continued steadily until World War 1. The less pretentious new housing was particularly concentrated around London Road station and at Charlotteville to its south. From the 1890s up to 1914 well-sited custom-built detached properties of substantial proportions were scattered over the high chalk of Guildown and Pewsey Down and at Merrow. This was very much First Class ticket holder territory, housing Chamberlin's, 'influential and predominantly London-based people'. Between the wars, there was further growth around the edges, particularly in the north and north west and at Burpham and Merrow. Onslow 'Village', a pleasing 1920s garden suburb development of some 450 houses between the By Pass and the old Farnham Road, was well-placed for access to the station. Infilling began early in Guildford; in 1924 a large Victorian villa and grounds provided space for no less than 48 small houses.[11]

Here, as elsewhere, there was shortage of low cost housing for railwaymen. In July 1920 the *Transport & Travel Monthly* noted that the Council, which was developing the Old Park Estate immediately north west of the main station, had agreed, in return for an advance from the railway company's pension fund, to allocate a minimum of 20 of the first 124 houses under construction to Guildford-based drivers and firemen.

With its attractive surroundings and excellent train services, particularly after electrification in the 1920s and 1930s, Guildford produced a significant number of rail commuters, despite its location 30 miles from Waterloo. In the post World War 2 decades, outward expansion continued, mainly to the north, north east and north west and the station now serves a very large catchment area. There is a perceived need for more local stations: at Park Barn, on the Reading line; at Bellfields/Stoughton on the main line also serving Jacobswell, a development begun in the 1930s; and most notably at Merrow, to serve that suburb and adjacent Bushy Hill and Burpham. Although growth in car ownership might be said to have diminished the revenue justification for such 'walking catchment area' stations in these new residential communities and none have so far been provided, it had become increasingly obvious by the late 1980s that some or all of these, or possibly a light rail alternative, as mentioned later, would bring a useful environmental improvement to a town centre plagued by fast-moving road traffic and the associated air and noise pollution. Although this factor was rendering pedestrian access to Guildford's main station hazardous and unattractive, it was in the early 1990s one of the busiest in Surrey, with around 7,500 joining trains each weekday. A further 600 were boarding at London Road station.

North of Guildford, the provision of Worplesdon station had little effect on settlement for many years. There was virtually no habitation in the immediate area when it was opened in 1883 and subsequent development was inhibited by extensive tracts of common land. Large scale Ordnance maps show that a mere 20 or so houses were added between 1913 and 1938 to the handful already existing within half a mile of the station at the earlier date. However after 1945 there was some modest growth on each side of the line and at a southern outpost of Woking, which spread southwards towards the station. By the 1970s this activity was producing a sharp increase in usage though the actual numbers remained low; about 200 passengers were boarding trains here each weekday in the early 1990s.

Like Guildford, Godalming also saw residential expansion after the opening of the railway, much of it to the north, where middle class villas sprung up on Frith Hill and along Peper Harow Road . Within a few years the town became linked to Farncombe, where a station was opened in 1897. Farncombe provided sites for low cost new houses between the wars but generally around Godalming, at Crownpits to the south east and elsewhere, housing of this period was in the higher price range of £750- £2500. More building followed at Frith Hill and on Holloway Hill after World War 2, with many of the larger houses built earlier yielding their sites to higher density development. Although much of the housing mentioned was associated with local employment (including Charterhouse School), the quality of the train services at both stations, particularly after electrification, undoubtedly encouraged long distance rail commuters to live in this district and their numbers were swollen by evacuees from London's bombs in World War 2. Along with Haslemere and Petersfield to the south, passenger business at Farncombe and Godalming grew steadily after the 1950s; this section of the Portsmouth line saw an increase of 18 per cent in 1961-76. In the early 1990s, around 2,200 were joining London trains daily at Farncombe and Godalming.

In contrast, Milford station remains isolated from the place it serves, a much expanded village with some modern housing around a complex junction of main roads that has now all but become a suburb of Godalming; there is no railway cluster here, or at Witley, where the station also remains isolated on a rural site. The train service at both is not such as to attract those London commuters who live in their catchment areas, which include the communities of Witley, Hambledon and Chiddingfold. Low figures for those boarding London trains daily in the early 1990s (around 260 at Milford and 320 at Witley) suggest many may prefer to drive to the better-served stations of Godalming or Haslemere.

Reigate, an ancient town, exhibits much visual evidence of post-railway residential development, predominantly of high value houses; indeed a whole new district appeared north of the line either side of the station in the 1860s and 1870s. In the middle of the latter decade, Thorne noted that the place had attracted 'men of means' into villas built since the opening of the station. Before 1914 Reigate's housing had joined up with that of its parvenu eastern neighbour and in the Edwardian era, Underhill Park and Wray Park estates extended the new residential areas north of the railway up the lower slopes of Colley Hill and Reigate Hill, still within a reasonable distance from the station. Between the wars, more new housing, much of it middle range detached properties on ample plots, appeared around Wray Common and at the southern edges of the town. Although some of Reigate's largest residences were occupied by the retired middle class and the more prosperous locally-employed, there were many commuters. Since the 1950s, the spread of car ownership allowed their successors (and others in smaller houses or apartment developments replacing the pre-1914 villas) to reach the superior train services at Redhill station. At Reigate in the early 1990s only 47 per cent of the 700 passengers boarding trains daily were bound for central London.

For some years before 1914 the quality of the train service encouraged significant residential growth around each station on the Surrey part of the L&SWR main line from Esher as far out as Brookwood, so much so that Scott, writing in 1910, felt able to classify this area as 'outer suburbia'. Well-separated from its station by the many acres of Sandown Park Racecourse, the old settlement of Esher was another place much enlarged by railway-related housing. In general, scope for residential development here was restricted until the old landed estates were broken up in the social and financial upheaval which followed World War 1. The district thus remained relatively rural until the late 1920s, then, with distance from the station making it desirable to own a car, and close supervision by the local authority, almost all the new housing tended to be designed for the wealthier echelons of the middle class. Echoing this, the 1937 SR residential guide noted:

> *Esher has always been, and still is, of an exclusive residential character, and it is this very exclusiveness that appeals to many people who, having to work in London, want a country home within an easy journey.... there is no mass production of identical houses on huge estates, or roads lined with small villas- only a few beautiful sites, on which attractive houses are being erected.* [12]

These 'beautiful sites' were west and south of the old centre, notably the 370-acre Esher Place Estate, begun in 1930 in the park of the 1898 mansion. This became an area of large detached houses, some architect-designed, a few of them lavishly detailed, exhibiting art deco at its most exuberant. In 1930 Richings Park Estates (1926) Ltd offered to subsidise a new station, 'Weylands for Esher Place'. Sited at More Lane, between Hersham and Esher, this would also have provided more convenient access to Sandown Park Racecourse than existing facilities but the SR dropped the idea after the firm went into receivership late in 1932. Also between the wars, over Esher Moor, to the south and the south west of the High Street, along private roads, some of these laid in the early 1930s in the former royal estate of Claremont, on plots of a half to one acre, there appeared large detached houses of some quality. Surveying the prospect, the SR guide noted: '...perhaps the Tudor and Sussex Farmhouse type are in the majority, but there are many others, including even a Canadian design...'[13]. This development extended to touch the western edge of Claygate and here, as in the northern parts towards Littleworth Common, a walk to the railway was more feasible. However it would seem likely that even in the 1930s, the bulk of Esher's commuters, many holding First Class seasons, were using their cars to reach either Esher or Claygate stations. With no large scale new building in its catchment area since World War 2, Esher in the early 1990s was in the middle range of Surrey stations for traffic handled, showing daily totals of boarding passengers around the 900 mark, 81 per cent bound for the City or West End.

To the west of Esher, across the Mole, the village of Hersham 'had become encompassed with a belt of good villa residences' by the time Thorne explored it in 1876. Further activity took place in the 1930s, when builders subsidised a new station, opened in 1936 after construction of many houses 'of moderate size and cost' had begun between the centre of the old settlement and the railway and north of the line on the north-eastern outskirts of Walton. This made up for the SR's loss of Weylands, mentioned earlier, and has almost certainly proved more lucrative in the longer run than the other site would have been; by 1940 that part of Walton on Thames north of the railway had grown eastwards to merge with the catchment area of the new station and house building continued here after World War 2 right up to the barrier presented by the 1962 Queen Elizabeth II Reservoir. By the early 1990s, over 1,200 passengers were boarding trains daily at Hersham , 73 per cent bound for central London.

Between Walton and Woking the railway had at first passed through an almost continuous belt of pine woods but as early as the 1890s, *Murray's Handbook for Surrey* mentioned 'numerous villas' built about the railway station at Walton. Between 1890 and 1915 more appeared along Oatlands Avenue, Oatlands Chase and in and around Ashley Rise. Between the wars the old settlement of Walton spread south to the railway and by 1939 was virtually one with its western neighbour, Weybridge. Much of this development consisted of good quality detached houses, as at Ashley Park, where, from 1924, 200 acres were covered with high cost, individually-designed properties, all within walking distance of Walton station.

West of all this lay Oatlands Park, formerly the landed estate of the Earl of Ellesmere, the southern section of which had been split up into villa plots for sale by auction as early as 1846, the first Surrey example of land speculation for middle class settlement riding on the back of new railway services. By 1862, shops, working class cottages (housing those who were to support the way of life of the villa residents) and a church were all present. In more recent years, the larger Oatlands properties have given way to smaller houses. Although Walton had a dental instruments factory from around 1885 until 1981 which built up to require a labour force of some 700, and film studios and workshops from 1899 until the early 1960s, the modern growth of this community exhibits a strong association with railway commuting.

Walton was the home of a number of prominent personalities, all of whom would have been regular First Class rail travellers. Among these were Herbert Ingram, founder of the *Illustrated London News*; Sir Edward Watkin, chairman of three railway companies, who married Ingram's widow; Sir Arthur Sullivan, the composer; Thomas Mason Cook, son of the founder of the travel firm; Robert Gill, another railway magnate; and the 8th Earl of Egmont.

At Walton, as elsewhere, the railway had no immediate effect on growth, having to await the release of land suitable for the comfortable properties which would attract the London-based middle class: the 1831 population of 2,035 had grown only to 2,881 by 1851. After that, progress was rapid, the figure reaching 10,329 in 1901.

South of the railway between Walton and Weybridge lies a large area of well-timbered estates where the greenery conceals low density high-value residential development, much of it dating from the 1920s and 1930s. Here are Burwood Park and St George's Hill, the latter one of Surrey's most 'exclusive' estates. Occupying almost 1,000 acres and rising in the south to a lavishly-planted hill of 520ft, the estate, purchased in 1911 by the master-builder Walter G Tarrant, was planned around an 18-hole golf course. Site work and construction of the golf course began in 1912 but only 27 houses had been completed by the end of 1914; the First World War then checked further progress. Residential building resumed in the early 1920s, continuing through to 1939, although slow sales brought the developer severe financial problems in 1930. A second 18-hole golf course was completed in 1929. As well as possessing a bent for placing his houses in the optimum position in relation to their beautiful surroundings, Tarrant was noted for workmanship of a very high order. The result was one of the finest collections of 'country homes' for prosperous City men in the vicinity of London. Within 30 minutes of Waterloo, those with sufficient wealth could enjoy the enviable privacy and protection afforded by this secluded parkland setting, free of the vulgarities of retail trade but with ready access to their own exclusive golf, tennis and croquet facilities, each of these provided on a lavish scale. All 400 or so St George's Hill houses stand on plots of at least an acre (a minimum still enforced), hidden among mature rhododendrons, oaks and pines. Some of them are very large indeed, in the category present day estate agents like to describe as 'ambassadorial'. From the start, most provided homes eminently suitable for A P Herbert's 'millionaires of Surrey' and for its first two or three decades, this upper middle class preserve attracted a fair number of First Class season ticket holders who, together with their families and servants, generated much lucrative business for the Southern Railway at Weybridge station. After the war, the nature of the population changed. First came the entertainers, to be followed in the 1980s and 1990s by an influx of wealthy foreign businessmen. These latter-day residents were of course more accustomed to travel wearing tinted glasses in the seclusion of dark-windowed limousines than by First Class rail and even their domestics often had the use of motor cars.

The residential growth of Weybridge proper, much influenced by its favourable rail service to London, was impressive, the population rislng from 1,225 in 1851 to 5,300 in 1901, By the latter year, the heathlands around the railway station exhibited a goodly crop of large houses inhabited by City men and professionals commuting daily. To the north, the Portmore Estate received a scattering of villas in the 1890s, this and other contemporary expansion prompting the start of a double-deck horse bus service from the north end of Thames Street to the station from around 1900. Building activity resumed in the 1920s: Weybridge Park, between the town centre and the station, was covered with high value houses from 1929 onwards. In contrast, much of the usable land north of the old settlement was developed in the twenties and thirties with bungalows and other high density housing. South of the station, close to the entrance to exclusive St George's Hill, quality detached houses were erected in the grounds of Field Place from 1932. The High Pine Estate, another area of detached houses on spacious plots, had appeared just north of the railway from 1924. East of this, the growth joining up with Walton has already been mentioned.

Both Walton and Weybridge remained substantially residential in character and in the early 1990s were two of busiest non-junction stations in Surrey, together loading around 5,000 passengers daily. Walton in particular was notable for its high proportion of central London commuters.

What is now Byfleet and New Haw station was opened in 1927 to serve new housing developments north of the railway, but it was also more conveniently sited for the old village of Byfleet, 3/4 mile to the south, than the original 1887 station further west, now called West Byfleet. However although Byfleet village saw a little growth in World War 1 and between the wars, this was mostly high density housing for those employed locally rather than rail commuters. More new housing appeared on the north side of the old village centre in the 1960s.

From the early 1990s an important mix of retail, warehousing, industrial and residential buildings began to appear on the former British Aerospace site at Brooklands, south of the station. Although still at an early stage at the time of writing, it clearly had implications for passenger traffic at Byfleet & New Haw and perhaps also at Weybridge.

In contrast, neighbouring West Byfleet was largely a dormitory area which had grown up on either side of the line in the late Victorian and Edwardian years; indeed building development was already under way before the station opened in 1887 and interested parties had provided both land and financial assistance for the new facility. With frequent and fast train services increasing property values, much of the suitable land had been covered at a comparatively early stage and by 1914 most of the area around the station was built over. Shops and other commercial premises were well-established, some of them on the sites of large villas which had been demolished whilst still fairly new. Dartnell Park, a large area of conifered woodland immediately south of the railway just east of the station, was sold off as building plots up to 3½ acres in extent between 1884 and 1898. Marketing of these plots was attended with some enterprise: prospective purchasers were enticed by the offer of free travel in special trains from Waterloo and given lunch in a marquee overlooking the Wey Navigation, which formed the eastern boundary of the development. Inevitably this very spaciously laid out estate has been subjected to much infilling in recent years.

Between the wars, West Byfleet showed vigorous growth, mostly towards the south west; substantial detached houses were built at Pyrford about a mile south of the station and others appeared around the West Byfleet golf course. In the same period, the district spread north-eastwards over low-lying land through the settlement of New Haw to link up with Addlestone on the Weybridge-Virginia Water railway, most of this small houses of suburban character. At Addlestone itself, the station of 1848 was well sited to serve what was a long-established settlement, described by Scott in 1911 as a 'straggling residential place which, though too big for a village, has not yet become a town'. Expansion here between the wars was mainly to the west and south, mostly with quite small houses. Local industry, including the Linoleum Works (later the Sunbury Leather Company), Coxe's Lock Flour Mills until 1983, and the Weymann Bus Body Works from 1925 to 1965, much reduced the level of commuting by rail but kept the freight yard busy for many years.

After 1945 there was further growth around Woking and West Byfleet, until by the early 1980s the two had merged. A major factor in this process was the 230-acre LCC estate at Sheerwater, opened in 1951, which eventually accommodated a population of over 5,000. Surprisingly, despite its location alongside the railway, no station was provided, probably because most residents reached local employment by cycle or bus. At the beginning of the 1990s, the busiest station was West Byfleet, with nearly 1,700 passengers boarding daily but Byfleet produced only around 600 and Addlestone just 500. West Byfleet showed the highest proportion of central London commuters (69 per cent); in contrast, Byfleet's figure was only 48 per cent and Addlestone's 42 per cent.

Between Egham and Sunningdale, the arrival of a railway service in a scenically attractive district characterised by poor soils encouraged a slow spread of high class residential growth from the 1870s. A distinct railway cluster, mainly west of the line, appeared at Virginia Water, a place given distinction by its lake, and its proximity to Windsor Great Park. A notable residential feature in this district is opulent Wentworth, a 2,000-acre parkland estate developed by W G Tarrant, he of St George's Hill, from the 1920s to attract the wealthiest type of rail commuter. With its informal, kerbless road layout set amidst pines and rhododendrons , Went worth was well-served by Sunningdale and Virginia Water stations, two golf courses laid out from 1923 onwards, and a country club. Its impressive houses were carefully-sited and individually-designed, several by leading architects of the day. As at St George's Hill, in recent years some on the very largest plots have been demolished and replaced by two or more modern ones but minimum plot sizes remain generous. In the 1930s Wentworth house prices reached ten or even twenty times the cost of the average London suburban semi . A private act of parliament in 1964 regularised and formalised the administration and maintenance of the considerable mileage of private roads, giving powers to a Road Commit tee to levy rates on the 800 or so house owners. Here, as at St George's Hill, recent years have seen some changes in the type of resident: wealthy City men commuting by train to London have mostly given way to limousine-borne entertainers and foreign tycoons. In the early 1990s enumerators found only some 500 passengers boarding trains at Virginia Water daily, three quarters of them bound for central London.

Sunningdale saw residential development well before the end of the 19th century. As early as 1871 the census compilers were attributing a decadal increase in population to 'building operations in the neighbourhood of Sunningdale station'. In the Edwardian period, some very high class residences were erected on extensive plots on the Ridgemount Estate, immediately south of the railway, where roads and main services had been laid out preparatory to building. These properties were virtually miniature estates in their own right, with lodges and cottages for gardeners. Golf facilities were available nearby and shops were built in the London Road. It is clear that the early settlers at Ridgemount would have been regular patrons of First Class travel on the railway. The area grew further between the wars, maintaining much of its established tone.

A relatively poor and indirect train service and the existence of several local employment opportunities left the old town of Chertsey without any significant railway-related residential growth. Even the housing boom years between the wars, which generated some expansion to the east and north west, mostly in the form of low cost bungalows and houses, yielded few railway commuters. By the early 1990s, just over 800 residents were joining trains here daily, a mere sixteen per cent bound for central London.

With their circuitous rail access to a somewhat distant London, the adjacent stations of Frimley, Camberley and Bagshot never earned themselves entries in the SR residential guides, although the vigorous post-1951 growth of this district doubtless produced an increase in local rail journeys. After the completion of the Army Staff College in 1862, Camberley started to develop as a separate community, the growth gently accelerated by the arrival of the railway in 1878. Here, and at York Town to the west, the new settlement owed much to the Army presence, and even today this influence still lingers, notably in the character of the old shopping area between the railway and London Road. By 1914 it was clear that the railway was something of a social barrier. To the north was the commercial centre around the High Street, and most of the houses up to the London Road and the Army estates were small. To the south, as far as the Portsmouth Road and even beyond, lay a beautiful area of high value housing in lush parkland settings, hidden away amid masses of rhododendrons, heather and conifers and served by grass-verged roads. Many of these properties were very large indeed, set in plots of several acres. From around 1880 this area attracted senior officers of the Army and Navy, retired Indian Army officers and other servants of the Empire as well as wealthy professionals and business men, many of these having made their money overseas. To some extent the railway played a part, for whilst the train service hardly favoured regular commuting to London, it facilitated a weekly or twice-weekly trip to the club, the theatre or the shops; no doubt the substantial upper and middle-middle class population of south Camberley provided much First Class business in the first half of the 20th century.

After World War 2 the old south Camberley way of life faded fast. By around 1965 the last of the widows and elderly unmarried daughters had vacated the big houses. Within the next 20 years most of the very large properties were demolished, the rest converted to residential apartments, schools and nursing homes. Private developers intent on profiting from a new type of resident attracted by the accessibility offered by the arrival of the M3 motorway in 1972 filled up the many-acred garden plots with smaller houses, some of them quite impressive in their own way. Surprisingly, despite all this, something of the old Betjemanesque aura survives here and there. And some at least of the houses built since 1960 were taken up by rail commuters, but as we shall see later in this book, rail services at Camberley and Frimley are not convenient for travel to workplaces in the busy Reading-Heathrow-Farnborough triangle, needing drastic reshaping if they are to attract commuters from the district's congested road system.

A statement about Frimley in the 1897 *Murray's Handbook For Surrey* that 'building is going on in all directions' seems an exaggeration since the growth between 1878 and 1938 was by no means dramatic. Even in the latter year, this was still a small, straggling place surrounded by countryside. After 1951, Murray's comment would have been much more relevant. So intense was development in the subsequent 40 years that out of the nuclei of Farnborough, Frimley, Frimley Green and Camberley there emerged a small conurbation. This enormous growth - an increase in the population of the old Frimley & Camberley Urban District from

20,400 in 1951 to around 45,000 in 1971 and an estimated 55,000 in 1986 - was related to its situation just outside the London Green Belt. First came the absorption into public housing of some 5,000 'overspill' population from south west London in the 1960s. This was followed by development of industrial and trading estates and business parks in the Blackwater Valley and a very substantial boom in private building stimulated by the prosperity of the Reading-Heathrow-Farnborough triangle and the construction of the M3 motorway through Camberley and Frimley in 1965-72.

Adjacent Bagshot, Bevan's 'dreary town', had seriously declined after the opening of the London & Southampton Railway had removed the 40 a day each way road coach traffic on which it depended for its prosperity. Less than two years after the opening of Bagshot station, Murray was remarking that the railway had brought fresh residents, attracted 'by the extreme salubrity of the district' but again the comment misleads; the railway growth here was unremarkable, even between the wars, despite substantial improvements in train services. Much of the post 1950 development was at nearby Lightwater, which benefited by its proximity to Junction 3 of the 1972 M3 motorway. Even today, despite the through traffic speeding along the busy roads that form its western and eastern edges, and some new housing around the outer fringes, Bagshot retains a sleepy, almost rural air on a summer afternoon - this is no commuterville.

In the early 1990s, Camberley was the busiest of the three stations, with around 750 joining trains daily (58 per cent for central London); the corresponding figures for Bagshot and Frimley were 200 (44 per cent) and 350 (29 per cent).

Farnham's transformation from a sleepy little country town to a place of some bustle and activity arose from its proximity to the Army base established at Aldershot in 1854-59. Many officers, military families and other military hangers-on lived in the town, finding its civilised atmosphere preferable to the crudities of the hastily and often shoddily built civilian settlement at Aldershot. Farnham station undoubtedly benefited from the military presence, even after the opening of Aldershot L&SWR station in 1870. Around that time, the old Surrey town was beginning to expand; villa building to the south was particularly vigorous between 1890 and 1914 in a growth which flowed across the valley slopes of the Bourne up to two miles beyond the historic town centre, a brash new and frequently genteel suburban sprawl which eventually reached Rowledge in the south west and Lower Bourne in the south east . Between 1891 and 1911 the population of this district leapt from around 500 to over 2,000 and 'on all hands, glimpses of new building and raw new roads defy you to persuade yourself you are in a country place' [14]. Farnham's residential expansion continued between the wars, especially to the south east of the historic centre, around the Tilford Road and Waverley Lane. The electrification of 1937 gave the process a boost and towards the end of the 1930s, large plots of up to two acres became available further out, on the Moor Park and Crooksbury Common estates.

Although some cheaper properties were built around Farnham, a very large proportion of the housing erected after 1890 was of a type that for many years provided a fair sprinkling of First Class commuters, some of them Army officers in desk jobs around Whitehall. It also accommodated the more successful shopkeepers and tradesmen of the old town. Amongst the latter, moving into the Edwardian villadom of the Bourne, was the railway engineer Thomas Patterson, who had arrived at Farnham in 1898 as agent for the contractors engaged in doubling the line to Alton; he stayed on to become a gravel merchant, supplying ballast to the SER and play his part in local government [15]. In general the main body of rail commuters lived in the post-1890 housing south of the line. Recording a 1932 threat to reduce the frequency of the Rowledge-Farnham bus service, Ewbank-Smith notes the concern of London season ticket holders, who relied on it to get to and from the station. In the early 1990s, Farnham remained busy , with over 1,500 passengers joining trains daily, a high proportion for central London.

Turning now to East Surrey, we come to the Brighton main line. Here, Merstham, Earlswood, Salfords and Horley all show post 1860 growth clustering about their stations whilst Redhill, to be mentioned later, owes its very existence to the railway.

At Merstham, a new community of small houses appeared south east of the station, supplemented west of the railway by substantial residences for the middle class commuters and retired. This growth

Above *Edwardian Villa development over the Bourne, south of Farnham station, c 1908* Commercial postcard.

was reflected in the population figures: 1,130 in 1841 and 3,597 in 1921. Lord Monson's Gatton mansion was bought in 1888 by the mustard king Sir Jeremiah Colman Bart, who remained in occupation until 1942. For many years, just before 9 am, Colman rode to the station for the London train in a mustard yellow carriage driven by a coachman in livery of similar hue. Low-density development continued into the 1930s in what was still at that time the first, 'real country' due south of London. This was another predominantly middle class area in which the SR had to provide cheap accommodation for its employees. Similar in design to those at Tadworth, and also named Ashcombe, the 20 cottages were erected in 1930 in a hillside cul de sac high above the railway. Soon after World War 2, a major change in the social mix occurred when the London County Council erected its South Merstham Estate on over 308 acres east of the Quarry Line. Opened in 1951, this miniature town housed a population of about 6, 000 in flats and cottages served by 24 shops. It brought a considerable additional traffic to the adjacent station, where in the early 1990s, close to the roar of the M25 motorway, almost 1, 000 were boarding trains daily, 82 per cent bound for central London.

Earlswood emerged in the mid-Victorian era as a southern suburb of the new town of Redhill. At first the development catered very much for the middle class and an early arrival was Robert Jacomb Hood, Resident Engineer of the London Brighton & South Coast Railway, who lived in Woodlands Road from 1854 to 1858[16]. Many of the new villas were occupied by successful Redhill tradesmen seeking residential seclusion from their workplaces. The railway here formed something of a social divide, with the larger properties to the west. The place had grown enough by 1868 to justify a station of its own.

Suburban semis appeared in the 1930s along the Brighton Road to the south of the earlier settlement but railway commuters considering whether to live here would have been deterred by the 15-20 minute walk to the station. Patronage of Earlswood had declined by early 1990 by which time the station had lost some of its platforms and most of its staff; commuters, never very numerous here, were by then tending to drive to join fast trains at Redhill . Only around 150 joined trains daily, 64 per cent for central London.

The Monotype Works, specialising in the manufacture of printing machinery and accessories, was opened at Salfords in 1899, its buildings set in open countryside immediately east of the Brighton line just over a mile south of Earlswood station. So remote was the location that the firm had to provide employee housing in the approach to the main entrance to the works. Other workers rented new cottages nearby. During World War 1, the factory was turned over to the production of machine guns, drawing an expanded work force from a wider area. To meet the transport need, two wooden platforms were built on the Local lines and linked to the works by lattice girder footbridge and field path. When this unstaffed halt was opened in October 1915 it was served only by special trains which brought the factory workers from Croydon and Three Bridges. With a return to normal activities at Monotype in 1919, the halt's private status continued, its use restricted to a single service to and from Redhill on weekday mornings and evenings for factory staff . In 1932, it was opened to the public, served all day by the newly-introduced electric trains, becoming a fully-manned station in 1935. Around this time, an approach road, appropriately named Southern Avenue, was constructed on the west side of the railway. During the 1930s, small semi-detached and detached houses, mostly of a suburban character, were erected in the Salfords catchment area on various sites along the Brighton Road and around Petridgewood Common. East of the railway, towards Outwood, the countryside received a spattering of houses, mostly of the more expensive type. Until the 1960s London commuters from these developments probably used Salfords, but as car ownership grew, most transferred their patronage to Redhill station . By the beginning of the 1990s, less than a hundred passengers were boarding trains daily at Salfords, 69 per cent going to central London.

Up to the 1950s, Horley's continuing growth from a small village of about a thousand people to a medium sized town owed much to the railway. Apart from those engaged in trade and agriculture, until the Albert Brewery opened alongside the railway in 1869 the LB&SCR was the only significant local employer. A market was established near the station and a considerable rail traffic developed in cattle for the London slaughter houses. The surplus railway accommodation was also used around 1900 for scrapping old locomotives. A new community grew up on the Common around the railway and by 1914, middle class residential development to the north of this, on the west side of the line, was well apparent; 'Railway Horley' was then merging with the old settlement of Horley Street, 1/2 mile to the west. Despite this activity, the district was still predominantly rural: Choulder, quoting the memories of an old resident, relates that Sunday mornings in spring and summer around 1900 would see the arrival by train of birdcatchers, encumbered by cages, nets and snares, ready to move off into the surrounding countryside to capture larks, greenfinches and linnets for sale in London.

When resiting and reproviding the station in 1905, the LB&SCR built on a rather lavish scale, correctly anticipating further residential growth. By 1921, the population had reached 6,100 compared with the 2,385 of 1881. The 1930s saw a faster pace, with expansion south west and north west of the station and to a lesser extent to the east along the Balcombe Road. A Southern Railway residential guide of 1937[17] listed 15 new estates in progress in the station's catchment area, offering a wide range of choice from the smallest semis to large detached properties on extensive plots. Most of the usual small town amenities were by then available, not least the 1935 Regent Cinema.

After World War 2, Horley expanded at an accelerated rate: to the north west to embrace Meath Green; south west to the Gatwick Stream over what had been started in the 1930s as the Horley Gardens Estate; north east over Langshott Farm; and less intensively in the south east. For many years Horley was primarily a dormitory town with little local employment other than the between-wars factories along the Brighton Road to the north. Large scale development of Gatwick Airport triggered a 50 per cent increase in local land values. At the 1961 census, the population had reached 16, 052 compared with the 1939 estimate of 10, 325 and the total grew to 18, 320 in the following ten years. In the early post war period, the railway commuter element was substantial: between 1945 and 1959 season ticket issues quadrupled. Although this trend was severely checked by the growth of Gatwick and other local employment opportunities, in the early 1990s around 1,700 joined trains daily, 72 per cent for central London.

Remote from the villages they purported to serve, Godstone and Nutfield stations each slowly generated nodes of development which became known as South Godstone and South Nutfield, the latter larger than its older namesake. Research has so far not fully established the extent of any collusion and insider-dealing related to the opening of South Nutfield station in 1884 and local property development by the MP (Sir) Henry Edwards, but there was evidently what today's journalists would call 'a story'. It is known that Edwards , who purchased large tracts of land each side of the line at South Nutfield between 1867 and 1884, laying out roads, water mains and sewers in 1883-4, had received a free pass over the SER for unstated reasons as early as 1880; and that Sir Edward William Watkin, the SER chairman, bought two of his 3-acre residential plots (although these were sold back later to Edwards without development). It is also significant that (Sir) Myles Fenton, the SER general manager from 1880, moved into Ridge Green House, another Edwards' property.[18]. Once again we have an example of the railway operating as a social barrier. Edwards ensured that the low value housing, the terraces and artisans' semis, were on the north side, leaving the south for 'Nutfield Park', with its villa plots of up to three or more acres. In more recent times this area has however suffered from the environmental effects of the M23 and Redhill Aerodrome and Heliport. From the 1920s, despite what was for many years a sparse and erratic train service, Nutfield and Godstone stations also attracted a steady trickle of car, bicycle and bus-borne commuter traffic from their large semi-rural catchment areas.

Further north, at Warlingham and Woldingham, developers were active on the higher ground east of the railway by the mid 1880s. William Gifford bought a great deal of land at Woldingham as well as the Westall Estate at Warlingham, investing it with the not very original sobriquet *The English Switzerland.* Exclusivity was cultivated by offering plots of a minimum of around half an acre, many much larger. As early as 1886 the SER minutes recorded a complaint that villa sales were being affected by the absence of a convenient train reaching London before 09. 00 but eventually the area received a better train service than the potential revenue deserved. Between the wars, building around these old settlements continued apace, much of it what the SR residential guides deferentially described as 'houses of some importance and character with gardens running to a good size and of a value about £2,000 to £4,000'. Lesser mortals could find new semis nearer Warlingham station or, consider what might be done on the adapted World War 1 camp site which had been renamed 'Woldingham Garden Village'. In 1991 Upper Warlingham loaded about 800 passengers daily, 70 per cent for central London, 22 per cent for the rest of the Greater London area; at Woldingham, the corresponding figures were around 250 and 76 and 11 per cent.

Oxted station was opened in 1884 in open country, almost three quarters of a mile north east of the old village on the Reigate-Sevenoaks road. What became known at first as 'Railway' or 'New' Oxted soon grew up around the station, on both sides of the line, a development enthusiastically promoted by the Leveson Gowers and other landowners. By 1914 there were shops in Station Road to meet the needs of the substantial and well-servanted villas nearby. Vigorous expansion followed in the 1920s and 1930s, supported by Tudorbethan shopping parades in Station Approach . The latter also included the 1930 New Kinema, heavily disguised in similar style. More shops appeared in Snatts Hill on the east side of the station and the whole district around the railway took on a distinctly suburban appearance. By 1940 old and New Oxted had become one continuous built- up area, well-populated with London commuters. Beyond, to the east and south-west, there was now a scattering of larger houses in spacious grounds spread across the countryside either side of the Sevenoaks-Redhill road.

As mentioned earlier, the tiny community of Hurst Green, south of Oxted, which had received a railmotor halt in 1907, expanded vigorously after World War 2. Most of the new arrivals were London commuters, living on both sides of the railway, providing a modern example of railway cluster development. This expansion justified provision of a full-scale station in 1961. By the early 1990s, Old and

New Oxted, Limpsfield, Hurst Green and Holland had coalesced into one continuous residential settlement. About 1,800 passengers were then boarding trains daily at Oxted and almost 800 at Hurst Green, the central London percentages in each case 78 and 59 per cent. Interestingly almost a quarter of Hurst Green' s originating passengers were by this time travelling to places out side Greater London.

Further south, some evidence of railway-influenced residential development is apparent at and around Lingfield, where a threat to build over the fields between the station and the church was defeated in the 1930s. Apart from the race course , there was little local employment here and in 1991 the railway was still receiving almost 500 passengers a day, of which 59 per cent were travelling to central London, 16 per cent to destinations elsewhere in Greater London and the remainder to places outside London.

Between Lingfield and the Sussex border lies the interesting middle class residential area of Dormans Park. Here, south west of Dormans station, are well-dispersed (and often well hidden) detached properties on large plots in a woodland setting, set along private roads in an informal, kerbless layout. Structured residential provision of the most exclusive kind, Dormans Park was started in 1887, three years after the arrival of the railway, as a colony of weekend bungalows called Bellagio. By 1891 there were about 40 'bungalow residences' with a custodian housed in a lodge to keep out intruders, an electric light plant and a clubhouse with a steward who provided meals to order by telephone. Attractions included an hotel, cricket and polo grounds, golf course and trout-filled lakes[19]. Before 1914 some quite substantial houses had been added and most of the original bungalows were eventually to be rebuilt as houses. A 1905 guide hinted intriguingly at the louche beginnings of this development, which had led to the change of name:-

Dormans is the station for Dormans Park....a land-company's building estate. This is a sweet spot, commanding lovely views and beautifully diversified with broken woodland.....dotted about the copse-clad slopes are 'bungalows' large and small....The spot, formerly called 'Bellagio', started about 1890 but too quickly acquired a Bohemian reputation. Propriety, the better paymaster in the long run, has now its turn.[20]

Those who lived here, or stayed at the clubhouse (later the Dormans Park Hotel), would have depended entirely on the railway for some twenty years or so and many for a long time after that. No doubt the station staff watched the comings and goings in the 1880s and 1890s with some quiet interest and amusement. Dormans also serves the separate community of Dormansland, to the east of the line, where some middle class settlement occurred in the first three decades after the arrival of the railway in 1884. Further development took place between the wars and since World War 2 the place has grown as large as Lingfield in area. Few of today's Dormans Park or Dormansland residents make much use of Dormans station, where only around 190 passengers joined trains daily in 1991, 83 per cent for London but only 57 per cent for the central zone. Most of the London commuters drive to Lingfield or East Grinstead stations.

Finally, mention must be made of an example of rail-related spread on a line that has now disappeared. Despite infrequent and inconveniently-timed trains, but no doubt because of the excellence of the London services at Guildford, some residential development occurred at Cranleigh, where the population increased from 1,363 in 1861 to 2,752 in 1901 and 3,231 in 1911. Between 1900 and 1913, a whole new area of housing appeared between the Horsham and Ewhurst Roads, south east of the centre, beginning the transition from large village to small town. Few if any of those taking these new houses would have owned cars and most would have been totally dependent on the railway for their links with workplaces and the outside world. Cranleigh's railway was also undoubtedly a factor in the siting of the Surrey County School, a private establishment at first setting out to educate farmers' sons, which opened in 1865 on the northern outskirts. After a few years the school expanded to accommodate over 300 pupils, mostly boarders. The station, with its W H Smith bookstall, was centrally-located and by the 1950s, along with neighbouring Bramley and Wonersh (which had also seen a very modest amount of rail-related development) had over a hundred season ticket holders, many of them First Class passengers. This traffic justified some short

Above *Edwardian commuter housing at New Park Road, Cranleigh, 12 May 1988. Residents here would have made regular use of the railway until the 1950s, by which time all or most of them had acquired motor cars* Alan A Jackson.

workings between Cranleigh and Guildford . Some also travelled by train daily to work in Horsham. In the 1970s and 1980s, after the closure of the line, further and vigorous residential growth took place at Cranleigh until it became much larger than many Surrey communities which retained railway services.

Communities made by the Railway

We have already noted how the emergence of modern Caterham owed much to the railway. There are however three places in Surrey whose origins can be directly attributed to their railway facilities.

When the London & Brighton and South Eastern first arrived at what is now Redhill in the 1840s, there was nothing but what Bevan describes as 'the most microscopic of hamlets', situated around the junction of Hooley Lane and the main Brighton Road. Before the end of the decade what were propagated as the 'railway advantages' and 'the healthy air' of the surrounding red sand hills had enabled developers to trigger a building boom. Whilst the low lying marshy ground around the 1844 station was left to commercial premises and to workers' cottages, the well-timbered hillside sites were to prove fertile territory for middle class villa-building. At the former, the SER erected 48 houses for its employees along with the station approach, later named Station Road, retaining ownership until 1872. Along with the main London to Brighton road, this thoroughfare, soon extended westwards, formed a new urban commercial centre. House building around it was greatly assisted by the activities of the National Freehold Land Society, the British Land Company, the United Land Company and the Redhill & Reigate Cottage Improvement Society. The purchases of the first-named included surplus railway land on which three new roads were laid out. Warwick Town, north of

Station Road, named after the then Countess of Warwick of Gatton Park, was one of the earliest of these developments, from which, as principal landowners, milords Monson and Somers reaped large profits.

With some 8,000 living in the new community in 1861, changes in local government became urgent and in 1863 the first borough council was formed. Since it included Reigate the new and the old were soon quarrelling furiously. This was a period of great activity: a town gas works, sited strategically between the railway and the Brighton Road, was opened in 1860, mains water arrived in 1867 and a main drainage scheme was completed two years later.

By 1871 the population had reached 9,300. Five years on, Thorne found a 'populous railway town of hideous brick shops and habitations and around it a belt of ostentatious villas, comfortable-looking mansions and tasteful and ornate dwellings of many varieties, with a superabundance of builders' detached and semi-detached malformations'. Perhaps feeling he had been rather too critical, he added that the beauty of the neighbourhood had been little impaired. Convenience of access by rail to London and other centres had certainly attracted a substantial middle class population whose new villas and little mansions required the support of an army of domestics, shopkeepers, builders and other tradesmen. With railway access to Kent , to Reading and beyond, as well as to London and Brighton , Redhill was also attractive as a business location, stimulating for example timber and builder's merchants to set up depots near the goods yard. Writing towards the end of the 1880s, Bevan saw the place, 'a good illustration of the rapid growth of population induced by the facilities of railway travelling' and when the 1891 census was taken, it was found the population had swollen to almost 13,800, far outstripping that of adjacent Reigate. In 1914 , when there had been a further increment of some 2,000, FE Green emphasised the residential attractions of the outskirts:

The southerly side of this line of hills, which suddenly dips down to where the mushroom town of Redhill fills the gap, is occupied almost entirely by the country houses of rich city men who settled here before the advent of the motor car. The comfortable carriage drive to Redhill station, where there is an excellent service of trains to town, seems to have suited the leisurely lives of opulent city gentlemen. The site chosen is certainly an excellent one, for they had found a rustic altitude without being too remote from an excellent railway service.[21]

With its busy station, several signal boxes, freight yards, sidings and locomotive depot, the railway was for many years a major employer of local labour and even in the 1990s there remained enough (with the retired) to justify the continuation of the railway staff club in Hooley Lane. Railway officers and employees working elsewhere also found the town a convenient home base. Large institutions such as The Philanthropic Society's 300-acre farm 'for the reformation of criminal boys' (1849), the Royal Earlswood Hospital (for mental deficients) (1855) and the Schools of the Royal Asylum of St Anne's Society (1884) all added to the railways' traffic and to the supporting population of tradesmen and domestic workers. By the 1890s a brewery, a tannery, fullers earth works and silver sand pits were active in and near the town, all providing much business for the railway.

After 1920 the pace of growth eased considerably although there was some further residential expansion northwards and also east of the railway. Much of this took the form of suburban type roads of semis and small detached houses, as on the 1930s Redstone Manor and Redstone Hill estates, which were favoured by commuters for their proximity to the station. Small houses erected on the former St Anne's Schools lands in the early 1990s were also conveniently sited for rail commuters. In the 1980s large areas east of the railway at Holmethorpe and south of the station along the Brighton Road were redeveloped as industrial and retail warehouse estates, providing substantial local employment opportunities but little or no business for the railway. In the 1990s the station remained busy all day. As a junction with a catchment area which extended well beyond its immediate urban surroundings, it saw over 3,200 passengers boarding trains daily in the early part of the decade, 85 per cent travelling into Greater London (73 per cent to the central zone).

Surrey's largest town owes much to the railway. In the words of its historian, Alan Crosby, 'It is impossible to underestimate the impact of the railway

on the Woking area....(it) provided the essential means whereby urban development took place; it was not its direct cause, but without it the growth of the town would have been impossible'. C S Ward's 1905 *Thorough Guide: Surrey and Sussex* noted that Woking was 'now a large town chiefly of small houses, where as late as 1867 there was little more than an inn'. Indeed, when the station was opened in 1838 it had been correctly named Woking Common, for there was nothing else; Woking proper, now known as Old Woking, was a tiny village 1 1/2 miles to the south. For some 20 years the railway had no effect on the area; what happened then, Crosby's 'direct cause', followed the actions of a cemetery company.

Between 1852 and 1854 almost 2,300 acres of enclosed common and other heathland around the isolated 1838 station and either side of the railway a little further west, were purchased by the London Necropolis Company, ostensibly for use as mega-burial grounds to accommodate most of London's dead for many years ahead. At the time, this scheme would have seemed to seal the future for the station's immediate surroundings, but it was not to be. Despite initial statutory restrictions (later removed), it seems doubtful that the company ever

Above *Redhill clusters around the railway station, depots and yards that caused it to burgeon into a medium sized town. The tunnel entrance to the Quarry Line is seen at the centre; the station is at the left. Looking north east from Redhill Common about 1906* Commercial postcard.

had any serious intention of devoting the whole of its lands to human remains. Very soon after 450 acres had been opened at Brookwood as a cemetery in 1854, the Company set about disposing of its other lands. About 64 acres were purchased by the government in 1858 for the Knaphill Invalid Convict Prison. This establishment, which opened in 1859, became an Army barracks in 1889 and was demolished for a council housing scheme in the late 1960s. Ten acres alongside the railway were taken for The Royal Dramatic College, a home for spent thespians, opened in 1862, and a further 150 acres accommodated the Surrey County Pauper Lunatic Asylum from 1867 . In 1909 7 1/2 acres were occupied by the L&SWR Orphanage, designed to accommodate 200 railway children.

Apart from these several institutions, the main bulk of the Necropolis Company's land was to become the new town of Woking, centred around the railway station, in an unhappy layout shaped by the Company's somewhat short-sighted policies in which any good intentions were swamped by the rush for quick profits. The boggy ground north of the station between the railway and canal, designated for the commercial, industrial and administrative centre of the new community and associated low-cost housing, was developed in an unimaginative and dreary manner from around 1870. To the south of the line, where the soil and views were superior, a middle class residential area was planned. This began to emerge in the early 1880s and Crosby quotes a sale catalogue of 1883 which pointedly referred to the 'exceptionally good' railway communication as a feature in the estate's attraction 'to city men and gentlemen whose daily occupations require their presence in the metropolis'. A good class of railway commuter household was very much in mind, and was soon to materialise. Other farm sales followed and activity here was at its zenith between 1895 and 1914, a period when the Necropolis Company was also undertaking direct development of its lands in the area. On the Company's Hook Heath Estate a golf course was laid out for use of residents and each house plot was at least one acre in extent. This exclusive late Victorian and Edwardian southern district of New Woking attracted residents of high standing such as Gerald Balfour, Conservative minister and brother of the more famous Arthur James, in 1898 and Dame Ethel Mary Smyth, composer and militant suffragette in 1908. H G Wells lived less grandly in Maybury Road for a few years from 1895, here planning and writing his *War of the Worlds* and *The Invisible Man* in a semi overlooking the railway and subject to the clanging and clatter of shunting. Woking also seems to have been known to Conan Doyle, who featured it in his 1893 short story *The Naval Treaty*, where he shows how the railway carried Holmes and Watson to this Surrey elysium;

We were fortunate enough to catch an early train at Waterloo, and in a little under an hour we found ourselves among the fir-woods and the heather of Woking. Briarbrae proved to be a large, detached house standing in extensive grounds within a few minutes' walk of the station....through the open window came....the rich scent of the garden and the balmy summer air.

Rail services were even better in 1911, when the population was just over 28,000 and beginning to overtake that of Guildford. At that time, Scott preferred to describe Woking in cold factual terms as:

Wholly suburban in character, but already one of the larger Surrey towns. Pretty country and healthy air have doubtless helped the growth, but most of it must be owing to the really wonderful train service which brings it as near to Waterloo as, for example, Ealing is to Mansion House.

The years between the wars saw a general outward expansion, particularly towards the favoured south-western quarter, with the outlying villages tending to coalesce with the urban nucleus, where the commercial, administrative and industrial activities remained largely confined to the railway-canal strip. The improvements in train services which followed the 1937 Portsmouth and Alton electrification hastened the pace of commuter settlement in the remaining years of peace and in the postwar years the town was yet further expanded, the population rising steeply until it exceeded 81,000 at the beginning of the 1980s. After 1945 there was much high density housing and commercial development, most of it north of the railway, where the retail, business and entertainment centre was twice rebuilt: in the 1960s and 1970s, and again in the 1990s. More intensive residential development replaced much of the Victorian and Edwardian low density housing. All this continuing vitality owed a great deal to the town's excellent rail communications. Commuting by rail boomed, reaching a peak in the mid-1970s after which the proportion of the workforce commuting by rail out of the town declined, although the mumbers remained high. Over the years the type of commuter changed; the prosperous City men and well-paid professionals who had formed the main element in the late 19th and early 20th century gradually gave way to lower middle class office workers, a change already apparent in the 1930s. Although many of the post-1945 new housing areas were distant from the centre, commuter settlement was encouraged by good bus links to the station. About 34,000 season tickets were issued for travel from Woking in 1980 and ten years later, it was the busiest station in Surrey, with around 7,500 passengers joining trains daily. There was also a significant inwards flow by rail to workplaces in Woking.

For over a hundred years , the station has obstinately turned its back to the town centre. On that side , High Street and Broadway run parallel to the railway, brushing shoulders with it so closely that access to the platforms is gained straight off the pavement through what is little more than a hole in the station's back wall. Why this should still be the case, despite two rebuildings of the station and the continuing development of the commercial and shopping centre immediately north of the railway may seem perverse and certainly demands some explanation. When the railway first arrived in 1838, the station had a large catchment area covering much of west Surrey, but most of its passengers and freight were drawn from the area to the south, the railway to Guildford and beyond not being yet in place. The London-Portsmouth coaches were almost immediately diverted to allow passengers to transfer to the railway here. All this made it sensible to locate the main entrance and offices on the south or Down side. When the station was rebuilt in the 1880s the railway company quite reasonably sought to acquire land on the north side to allow construction of a worthy entrance to serve the developing commercial centre but the local authority frustrated this proposal. In the face of this discouragement, the provision made in the 1880s to meet the townspeople's demands for a ticket office on the north side was restricted to the barest minimum. An ambitious scheme for an open square in front of a new northern entrance to the station was proposed by local worthies in 1897 but again the over-cautious and unimaginative attitude prevailed in the council chamber. After that, with the street layouts firmly entrenched and property values steadily rising in real terms, a major rearrangement demanded a high measure of purposeful boldness which failed to appear. Minor improvements were made in the 1930s station reconstruction but once again the local authority was not ready for large scale change. Nor did any such plan form part of the major post-war rearrangements of the town centre.

Although not an integral part of Woking since it still retains a tenuous physical separation, Brookwood may be conveniently mentioned here. Some new roads had appeared between the railway and the canal before 1914, but with large areas occupied by the military to the north and the extensive cemetery to the south, there was little room for residential or other development. Two housing schemes, one in the north and the other on the Woking side, which had been started in the late 1930s, were completed soon after World War 2 although there has been little growth since. Railway usage here remained buoyant in the early 1990s: with those driving in from the surrounding area, the total number of passengers joining trains daily was just over 900, more than any station on the New Guildford Line and some others nearer London.

Our third case of railway- fostered green field development is quite different from the two so far mentioned. Two miles north of Haslemere the high and wild moorlands of Hindhead, rise to 895ft above sea level. Here, in what had been a bleak and isolated spot, a transformation occurred within a few years from the late 1880s. Since the motor age had not yet begun, the railway at adjacent Haslemere must be seen as crucial to this change. The district was 'discovered' by the eminent physicist and Alpine mountaineer Professor John Tyndall FRS (1820-93), who settled here in 1883, a year later moving into his new Hind Head House at the highest point on the Common. To his annoyance, his widely publicised declaration that the Hindhead air was as health-giving as that of the Swiss Alps was soon arousing interest in the area's development as a minor inland health and holiday resort. By 1891 Tyndall was so incensed at the pace of new building development for which he was in part at least responsible that he not only bought more land to secure his privacy but erected a 40ft high screen of wattle, larch poles and heather thatch to shut off the view of new houses from his attic study.

At this point it has to be said that were Tyndall to return today, the continuous noise and atmospheric pollution produced by heavy motor traffic through Hindhead would certainly cause him to reconsider his assessment of the quality of the air. But in the 1890s and 1900s, when the atmosphere on these breezy uplands was still clear and quiet, a residential and recreational arcadia was shaped for the comfort and pleasure of the more privileged echelons of the Edwardian middle class. At the central crossroads,

Above *Villas spread over Beacon Hill, Hindhead in 1909, a development made possible by buses providing convenient access to the railway services at the nearby Haslemere station* Commercial postcard.

which from around 1900 had been linked to Haslemere station by a two-horse double deck bus, two smart parades of shops in a debased version of the style of Norman Shaw appeared either side of the main Portsmouth Road. A Post Office was opened here in 1901. Just below, Sir Arthur Conan Doyle was living in Undershaw, a house (now an hotel) which he had built in 1897-8 in the hope that the remedial qualities of the air would benefit his ailing wife. By the eve of the First World War, Hindhead and its satellite of Beacon Hill possessed five hotels, a fine 18-hole golf course (opened in 1904), a big church by J D Coleridge (1910), several roads of opulent villas and a colony of smaller houses for servants and gardeners. Beacon Hill's Sandheath Estate was being advertised as offering houses and bungalows of seven or more rooms, designed by Herbert Kenchington, all overlooking the golf course; other new building was proceeding on the Wood Road Estate and the 35-acre Linkside Estate. Advertisements in the 1913 edition of the *Homeland Handbook* offered furnished and unfurnished houses to let, boarding houses and apartments and a nursing home. In the same publication, we read that 'new red- brick villas have sprung up everywhere to the west and south of the Huts Hotel and the once lonely Portsmouth Road is an afternoon promenade for nursery maids and perambulators'. A little further west, across the Hampshire border, Grayshott, another satellite development, was described in a 1912 guide as 'an entirely modern village....in a rather more sheltered position, nearly 700 feet above the sea'.

Contemporary publications stressed the attractions for both the healthy and the sick. In his guide to the area published in 1911, H.J.R. Oliver of Haslemere delicately hinted at the possibilities for the outdoor pleasures of middle class lovers, declaring Hindhead, 'just the place to spend a honeymoon, for among the hills we can soon be free from crowds, and there are no loafers or tramps to worry' - comforting news indeed for sensitive youngers,

Above *The L&SWR Farnham-Haslemere motor bus at Hindhead in 1912. Providing a convenient link to Haslemere railway station, this service sustained the development of Hindhead as a residential and health resort before the age of universal car ownership* Commercial postcard.

whether or not they had good rooms at the Thirlestane or the Beacon. But health remained the main theme for a few more years: a doctor's 1919 book about Britain's health resorts recommended Hindhead for a 'rest cure', and also for sufferers from neurasthenia, neuritis and asthma, adding cautiously that pulmonary tuberculosis patients were arriving yearly in increasing numbers 'and while the hotels refuse such cases, as is quite proper, apartments or houses are always to be had'[22].

In 1899 the L&SWR completed the conversion of the Up platform at Haslemere to an island, work perhaps not unrelated to the traffic engendered by the growing popularity of Hindhead amongst the middle classes. The nature of the new railway business produced by this area was certainly apparent from a note in *The Railway Magazine* for December 1906 which advised that the 00.25 departure from Waterloo to Godalming would be extended on Wednesdays as far as Haslemere (arrive 01.54) in order to give the inhabitants of what the writer described as a popular residential resort 'the opportunity of having a long evening in London'. Conveniently, for the prudent of purse, the cheap L&SWR 'Matinée Excursion Tickets' were available for return by this train.

A motor bus service between Farnham and Haslemere stations via Beacon Hill and Hindhead, connecting with the trains, started on an experimental basis in 1904, was taken over by the L&SWR in September 1905. Profitable at least in the summer months, this no doubt did much to cement the new growth just described at a time when motor cars were still very much an amusement for the wealthy rather than a general utility for almost everyone. In June 1913, after the railway company had failed to obtain parliamentary powers to operate buses, the route was taken over by the Aldershot & District Traction Company[23]. Another operator worked a Haslemere- Haslemere station-

Hindhead-Grayshott service from a similarly early date and by the early 1910s the Royal Huts Hotel was also advertising its own motor bus to and from Haslemere station six times daily. With such good communications assured , the railway at Haslemere profited from a steadily increasing holiday and residential traffic, much of it First Class,

Bus services through Hindhead were further developed by Aldershot & District between the wars, working from a new garage next to the Edwardian shops. By 1934 the character of the area was changing again; although a dozen or so hotels and boarding houses were still advertised in a guide of that year, it was now described as 'a growing residential district' and the electrification of the line through Haslemere three years later would further reinforce that aspect. By this time those visiting the area for recreational purposes were mostly coming all the way by road.

Haslemere had seen some railway-related middle class housing from the 1890s on the Marley Heights above Shottermill, Marley Common, Heath Ball and the Half Moon Estates (the last only 1/2 mile from the station) and other well-dispersed high value housing was built in the splendid countryside all around in the years up to 1914. This process continued after 1920: as G R Rolston records in his *Haslemere in History*, 'The postwar Haslemere began slowly to stretch building tentacles into the surrounding lanes and fields between a number of larger estates which still maintained their integrity'. This activity was accelerated, and the ranks of the commuters much swollen by the improvement in speed and frequency which followed the 1937 Portsmouth Direct electrification. Along with Godalming, Haslemere was favoured as a place of residence by a number of senior railway officers and this did no harm to the train service. In the war years from 1939, the station was kept busy: the population was inflated by evacuees from London and Portsmouth and an Admiralty research station provided steady traffic to both places. After 1945, building began again and by the late 1970s, Haslemere station had become one of the best revenue earners in the south-east, yielding more First Class passengers than almost any other in that area.[24] In 1995, even on Saturday mornings, two men were kept busy issuing tickets to a steady stream of passengers.

Over 1,900 were boarding trains at Haslemere daily in the early 1990s and it would seem that commuters had little reason to complain of the cost of their tickets since property prices in the area benefited substantially from the quality of the train service. This was well demonstrated in a 1994 comparison of house prices around Haslemere and those in the area of Pulborough in Sussex, where rail commuting was said to be in decline because the train service, though electrified, was inferior to Haslemere's 45 minutes to London and its four to five trains an hour. Estate agents noted that for similar properties in good locations, the Haslemere price would always be significantly higher and also that smaller houses could be quickly sold at Haslemere for sums similar to those secured for rather larger properties in Pulborough[25].

High Quality Residential Scatter

To a greater or lesser degree, this final pattern of rail-related settlement appeared in all Surrey districts possessing what the planners call 'outstanding natural beauty'. Its impressive residential properties were usually architect-designed, in the 19th century and early 20th by such leading practitioners as Basil Champneys, Oliver Hill, Edwin Lutyens, Richard Norman Shaw, Charles F A Voysey, and Philip Webb. Elevated situations with extensive views were eagerly sought, and the houses were sited at the end of long curving drives , well hidden in plots of several acres In accordance with Gertrude Jekyll's doctrine that the garden should fade imperceptibly into woodland, the areas beyond the formal lawns and flower beds, the tennis courts and the swimming pool, were often left in their natural state though there would be judicious planting of shrubs and bulbs amongst the conifers flourishing in the sandy soil. Outbuildings would be provided for servants, stables and carriage houses, the last two in more recent times adapted for cars and horses kept for pleasure-riding. Each house would be well apart from any others and out of sight of them. Visits to neighbours would usually involve a ride in a horse-drawn carriage, or after around 1905, in the motorcar.

It will be obvious that this secluded way of life,

Above *An early motor coach (charabanc) and horse-drawn carriages await railway travellers at Haslemere station in about 1910. Many of the passengers emerging from the station would be seeking transport to the well-dispersed hotels, boarding houses, villas and larger houses in the attractive hill country within the Haslemere-Hindhead-Grayshott triangle* Commercial postcard.

which had its origins in the 18th century gentrification of Surrey, has always been totally dependent on the ownership of private transport. It proliferated in Surrey from the middle of the 19th century, when horse-drawn carriages could be used without undue tedium or inconvenience to deliver and collect passengers from a station with a direct train service to London, which might be up to five miles from the house. When motor cars became available to the more prosperous in the 1900s, this style of living was rendered even more attractive and by the early 1910s, the ubiquitous motor van delivery services of the large West End stores were adding further to its enjoyment and civilised comfort.

Here would certainly be found the millionaires of Herbert's jingle, but outnumbering them, upper middle class families who needed to be, or preferred to be in touch with London for business or pleasure, even if that did not involve daily travel to town. This group also contained a fair sprinkling of the wealthy retired or rentier class, successful professional people, leading artists and scientists, politicians, stockbrokers, manufacturers, very senior civil servants, tycoons and the 'shopocracy'. With the widening spread of car ownership after 1920, distance from such well-served main line railway stations as Farnham, Haslemere, Guildford, Dorking or Redhill became even less critical. As motoring all the way to and from London, suggested in A.P. Herbert's jingle, would be tedious and tiring even on the less crowded roads of the 1920s and 1930s, this type of Surrey resident and their visitors, often remained loyal to the railway, which would allow completion of the major part of the journey speedily and comfortably in a First Class compartment. Conveniently, guests would often 'come down' by rail, to be ferried from and to the station by horse-drawn carriage or later, by car. It became a way of life, nowadays lovingly reproduced in films and television productions; it formed the background of hundreds of West End plays for fifty years, featuring too in many a romantic or detective novel. Both plays and stories contained many references to 'the station' and 'the next London train'. Below the address, the house-owners' printed notepaper would invariably show the name of the 'Nearest Railway Station' with the railway company's initials helpfully added in brackets. When such houses came on the market, estate agents would note in their leaflets and advertisements 'Main Line station X miles'. So popular did the remoter parts of Surrey become for this privileged way of life that 'How far are you from Guildford? was a cliché opening for polite social chat at appropriate upper middle class social gatherings.

The business these large houses provided for the railway is described by Tharby in his recollections of Westhumble station and Polesden Lacey in about 1910 . He mentions how the guests' servants came down from London:

> *With mountains of luggage, often an extra van had to be attached to the train. Special luggage carts came down from Polesden to convey the baggage, while the maids and valets were collected by horse drawn carriages. When Mrs Greville was residing in her town house, hampers of garden produce, also laundry, were sent by train and the carriage account was rendered at the end of each month. Mr Bromley (the stationmaster) used to cycle up to collect the money.*[26]

But the motor age had opened; Tharby adds that the 'great ones' travelled from town by road.

'High quality residential scatter' was at its strongest south west of a line drawn from Epsom through Reigate and Horley, an area in which Guildford does indeed form the approximate centre. In the closing age of construction of large country houses on any substantial scale, 1860-1914, the greatest concentration across the Home Counties was to be found in this south western sector of Surrey. The pattern was quite dense in the highlands around Hindhead and Haslemere, where residents included Alfred Lord Tennyson, Conan Doyle and later, Lloyd George ; around Witley and Godalming (this was a favourite for writers and artists such as George Eliot, Birket Foster and Kate Greenaway[27]). It was also to be found near the Hog's Back between Farnham and Guildford but most of all, in the conifer-covered, greensand high ground around Leith Hill. There, within easy reach by private transport of Dorking, Gomshall or Guildford stations, were the delightful wooded uplands of Abinger, Peaslake, Holmbury St Mary, Forest Green, Friday Street and Coldharbour, around which a heavy sprinkling of big houses appeared from the early 1860s. At Holmbury St Mary alone, almost a dozen were built in the space of 20 years from 1860, some with well over 20 bedrooms; all had huge gardens often planted with exotic trees and Himalayan rhododendrons[28]. 'Along this range of hills' wrote Green in 1914, 'I can point out to you the residences of people who have amassed wealth out of ships, law, tea, pottery, ink, banking and "contracting"...Round about Botley Hill, Leith Hill, Pitch Hill, Box Hill, Holmbury Hill, we see houses occupied by members of parliament...'[29]. A more recent book fleshes this out with names, listing the presence in the relatively small Abinger area of the homes of Frederick Mirrielees, head of the Castle shipping line, the Doultons, the Wedgwoods, the Guinnesses, the Brookes (of Brooke Bond Tea), the Stephens (of Ink), Edwin Waterhouse (of the accountants Price Waterhouse), Lord Chief Justice James Scarlett, Mr Justice Vaughan Williams, and colonial administrators Lord Lugard and Colonel Lewin[30]. Nearby, around Newland's Corner, in the 1910s, were the homes of Lord Northcliffe and St Loe Strachey.

A reference to 1910 timetables confirms the convenience the railway afforded to those able to choose this way of life. They might for example leave Gomshall station at 08.42, arriving at Cannon Street for their City office at a comfortable 09.52. In the evening, the 17.19 departure from the City would see them at Gomshall at 18.21, giving ample time to reach home and dress for dinner. Ladies bound for West End shops could leave Gomshall at 10.33, spend an afternoon in Regent Street and Bond Street and be back a good hour or so before dinner. Although there was no suitable train back to Gomshall after leaving a West End theatre at around 23.00, the 23.40 from Charing Cross might well be met at Dorking by a sleepy coachman at fifty five minutes past midnight.

A variation of this Victorian and Edwardian railway-assisted residential culture were the 'pleasure farms' on which wealthy men indulged in agricul-

Above *Gomshall & Shere station in its Edwardian heyday saw fresh watercress on its way to London tea-tables and wealthy commuters travelling to and from London and their fine houses on the High Greensand. At the left, by the goods yard crane, two ladies have alighted from their private carriage, which has brought them down from Holmbury St Mary, Peaslake or Abinger and are giving instructions to their coachman before joining the London train. Two porters pose rather uncertainly with empty sack barrows at the level crossing between the staggered platforms, a facility which is also used by passengers* Commercial postcard.

ture as a side-occupation. The clay plain of the Surrey Weald was a favoured location for such properties, which would be embellished with an improved and renovated farmhouse residence or by a large new house. At their peak in the late 19th and early 20th century, these farms generated new rail traffics at stations in the area south of Guildford, Dorking, Redhill and Oxted, not only passenger journeys of the type mentioned above but in transport of fertilisers, animals and farm produce, notably milk to London. During 1884 Leopold Goldberg, a wealthy City solicitor, erected a country residence at Newdigate, its building materials almost all brought to Holmwood station by rail for onward transport by horse and cart. Once settled there, he farmed the estate, but also travelled daily to his City office, using his private carriage over the three or so miles to and from the railway. In 1903 George Crutcher Senior bought New House Farm, Newdigate, soon advertising 'real country milk from country cows'. His men took the milk twice daily in summer and once in winter to Holmwood station for sale from a dairy he owned in Peckham. For the return journey, they loaded up surplus brewers' grains from a railway truck at Holmwood, these to feed Crutcher's dairy cattle.

The railways also brought a new type of resident to the Weald villages. William Farnell Watson, an Isleworth brewer, moved to Henfold, east of Beare Green, around 1868 and by 1872 was the largest landowner in Newdigate parish . At his house, a mile from Holmwood station, many servants were employed and fox and staghounds were kept. In 1887 a wool merchant, George Herron , bought the 1,400 acre Newdigate Place estate and ten years later built a large new house. Two old Newdigate farms were bought in the 1890s by Captain Elliott Palmer, who erected a mansion in the resulting estate, which he named Oaklands Park; in 1908, yet another wealthy arrival converted an old farmhouse into a substantial residence. Much of the building materials for these properties and all their coal came in by rail and these 'new gentry' and their families were frequent users of Holmwood station, travelling by private horse drawn carriages up to 4 miles to reach the railway[31].

As the 20th Century drew to a close, Surrey's large country houses, many of them originating from the privileged ways of life just described, were the most expensive, size for size, of any in Britain.

Notes

(1) For a fuller treatment of the emergence and growth of Stoneleigh up to 1940, see Jackson, Alan A, *Semi-Detached London: Suburban Development, Life and Transport 1900-39*, 2nd edition 1991.

(2) SR, Reports of Inspections of New Works etc, 22 December 1936.

(3) White, H P, *A Regional History of the Railways of Great Britain: 3 Greater London*, 3rd edition, 1987.

(4) SR, Minutes of Engineering & Estates Committee, 28 June 1928 and 10 October 1929.

(5) The paragraphs about Ashtead are mainly derived from Jackson, Alan A (editor), *Ashtead: A Village Transformed*, 1979.

(6) Surrey County Council0 Public Transport Plans 1983-4, 1984-5

(7) For a detailed account of the modern growth of Horsley and the Clandons, see Connel, John, *The End of Tradition: Country Life in Central Surrey*, 1978.

(8). Some account of the first post-railway residential growth in Dorking is given in Brigham, Allan, *Urban Growth in a Surrey Market Town: A Study of the Expansion of Dorking in the mid-Nineteenth Century*, an unpublished dissertation, 1988. The relationship between the railways and the town is also briefly considered in Jackson, Alan A, *Dorking's Railways*, 1988.

(9) The estate was offered in 35 house plots 'most desirably situated....from its proximity to the Town, and its exceptional Railway Advantages by which the Metropolis is reached in 45 minutes'. (Sale brochure, Dorking Museum, S 300/837).

(10) SR, Reports of Inspections of New Works etc, 23 September 1936. Moody states that the system of lighting stations from the conductor rails was originally installed at Ashtead, Banstead, Effingham Junction and Epsom Downs in the 1920s as it was considered 'out of place' for electric trains to serve oil- lit stations.

(11) Chamberlin, E R, *Guildford*, 1982.

(12) Anon, *Southern Homes in Surrey and Hampshire (Electrified) served by the Southern Railway*, 1937.

(13) Idem.

(14) Bourne, George (George Sturt), *Change in the Village*, 1912.

(15) Smith, Ewbank, *Edwardian Farnham: The Story of a Surrey Town 1900-1914*, 1979.

(16) Jacomb Hood, Robert, *Memoranda for Biography*, 1894, unpublished ms in private hands.

(17) Anon (see note 12).

(18) For the early development of South Nutfield and speculation as to the business relationships, see Finch, Peter, 'H Edwards MP and South Nutfield', *Surrey History*, III, 4, pp 184- 192.

(19) *Murray's Handbook for Surrey*, 1897; King, Anthony D, *The Bungalow: The Production of a Global Culture*, 1984.

(20) Ward, C S, *Thorough Guides: Surrey (South of Epsom) and Sussex*, 1905.

(21) Green, F E, *The Surrey Hills*, 1915

(22) Luke, T D, *Spas and Health Resorts of the British Isles*, 1919.

(23) Cummings, John, *Railway Motor Buses and Bus Services 1902-1933*, vol 2, 1980 and Faulkner, J N & Williams, R A, *The London & South Western Railway in the Twentieth Century*, 1988.

(24) Bowers, Arthur, 'Forty Miles Out', *Daily Telegraph*, 14 November 1979.

(25) Field, Roger, 'What A Difference A Train Makes', *Evening Standard*, 15 June 1994.

(26). Tharby, W G , in *The Leatherhead Advertiser* , 7 March 1969

(27) With somewhat breathtaking exaggeration, the 1871 Census attributed population growth in the Witley area to 'the attractions of the scenery, many artists having taken up residence in the district'.

(28) Bird, Margaret, *Holmbury St Mary: One Hundred Years*, 1979.

(29) Green, op cit (see note 21).

(30) O'Kelly, Terence, *The Villages of Abinger Common and Wotton, Surrey*, 1988.

(31) Details of the Newdigate incomers in this and the preceding paragraph are from Harding, Joan, and Banks, Joyce, *Newdigate: Its History and Houses* 1993 and the *Newdigate Society Magazine*, passim.

CHAPTER SEVEN

Defending the Realm, Racing, Holidays and Burials

Whilst there is no easily discernible connection between these activities, they are brought together here because for many years all of them provided welcome supplementary income for Surrey's railways.

Soldiers across the Border

In the early 1850s, much encouraged by Albert, Prince Consort, military and political pressures built up for the establishment of a permanent Army base in south east England. In view of its proximity to the North Downs, a primary feature in the defence of London, and its excellent railway communications with the coast and the capital, the Reigate area was the first choice but Lord Hardinge, the Commander in Chief, established that it would be impossible to acquire sufficient land in a district where there were also problems about obtaining an adequate water supply. He recommended the infertile heathlands between Farnham and the L&SWR main line, which could be bought cheaply and where, in view of the nature of the land, there would be no requirement to pay compensation for damage to farmland caused by army training. This area, Aldershot and Cove Commons, was also 'admirably adapted for the assembly of a large military force from the interior moving to and from London by two railways in direct communication with Portsmouth, Chatham and Dover....'[1]

Government approval followed and construction of the new permanent camp was started in February 1854, the first phase lasting some four years. Building materials for the southern section were brought in via Tongham station on the L&SWR Guildford-Alton branch but the road transhipment for the final section proved irksome and time-consuming, causing the contractor, George Myers to negotiate with the L&SWR for the construction of a temporary single line to the work sites at what was to become South Camp. This light railway ran north west from a point about half a mile on the Guildford side of Tongham station, passing just east of the

Top Right *The capacious refreshment room and station building on the Down side at North Camp, familiar to many generations of British soldiery moving to and from barracks and officers quarters at Aldershot* Alan A Jackson.

Right *Camberley, another station well-trodden by the military, since it serves both the Staff College and the Royal Military Academy, seen in a summertime view of around 1910, looking to Aldershot. This is also a residential area for the prosperous middle class and a large and well-dressed crowd awaits a Down train; at least two barrows of heavy luggage are ready for loading when it arrives. By the goods yard (top right) an Up service for Ascot enters to pick up the much smaller group on the other platform* Commercial postcard.

COURAGE
North Camp

centre of Ash village. Approaching the new army base, it turned west to run along what were later the Wellington Lines, just north of the present Wellington Avenue, terminating a few yards east of the present Aldershot-Farnborough Road (A 325), opposite the Royal Garrison Church. Completed in 1855, the railway remained in use at least until the middle of 1859, latterly also carrying coal[2]. It is shown on the one inch Ordnance Survey map of Surrey published in 1869 and some large scale maps of the Aldershot area published in 1855-56 which indicate, unsurprisingly, that all crossings of public roads were made on the level, and show only one siding, near the Aldershot terminus.

As Myers' line was deemed unsuitable for royal travel, when Queen Victoria came to open the first section of new Army base in July 1855, she arrived at Ash SER station. The SER did not ignore its new commercial opportunity and that August arranged for three daily deliveries and collections of telegrams between North Camp Post Office and its telegraph office at Ash station[3].

At first, all public and military passenger access to the new camp was via Ash Green or Farnham stations but from October 1856 passenger trains were specially stopped at Tongham public goods station. From here private cabs and other horse drawn transport competed for the Aldershot trade. With an increasing flow of traffic, the L&SWR soon provided the usual passenger facilities at Tongham.

The SER did not stand idly by and in 1858 that company opened a station on its Redhill-Reading line to serve the new North Camp, to which it was connected by a straight military road. Freight facilities were provided here in 1859-60, eased by a subsidy from the War Office. With the object of increasing the efficiency of handling the military traffic, substantial improvements were made in 1863, when North Camp New Sidings were added either side of the line, north of the station. The Up platform of the passenger station was subsequently converted to an island, its outer face dedicated to military use. In the early 1960s, this eastern side of the station became an oil distribution depot fed by trainload workings of tankers from Thames Haven. Another special feature of North Camp station was the refreshment room on the Down platform, managed by the adjoining hotel and mainly concerned with the comfort of travelling soldiery.

There is no doubt that the military value of the Reading-Redhill-Tonbridge railway route, providing direct access to the main Channel Ports, gave it a special strategic importance which lasted until well after the end of World War 2. However a considerable military traffic was also handled at the L&SWR Farnborough station, which provided direct access to the major embarkation port of Southampton, and of course to London.

Yet even these facilities were not enough for the growing needs of the British Army in the last half of the 19th century, not mention the civilian influx, largely engaged in supporting and supplying the requirements of the military. With the 1861 census recording a population of 16,720 (including almost 9,000 soldiers at South Camp) it is hardly surprising that a powerful demand arose for more railway accommodation. This was finally satisfied in May 1870 with the opening of a link between Farnham and the L&SWR main line just west of Brookwood, giving the new town direct access to London. Twenty years later, a small part of the northern end of Myers' 1855 light railway alignment was adapted as a spur from the new line, serving the military stores and a military passenger station.

Military Surrey

The establishment of the Aldershot base was closely related to Army activities in nearby Surrey. For the 1853 Army training programme, Chobham Heath had been chosen as the site of an experimental concentration of up to 10,000 soldiers operating from a temporary camp. This momentous gathering lasted from April to August, attracting public interest, notably on 21 June when Queen Victoria and Prince Albert reviewed the troops, travelling down from Nine Elms by rail as far as Staines. On that day, the spectators were estimated at 100,000, most of them arriving by rail at Chertsey , whence the local jobmasters and fly proprietors made a killing by overcharging for the remainder of the journey. Several hundred of those attending, including a contingent of fashionable ladies in smart riding habits, had arranged for

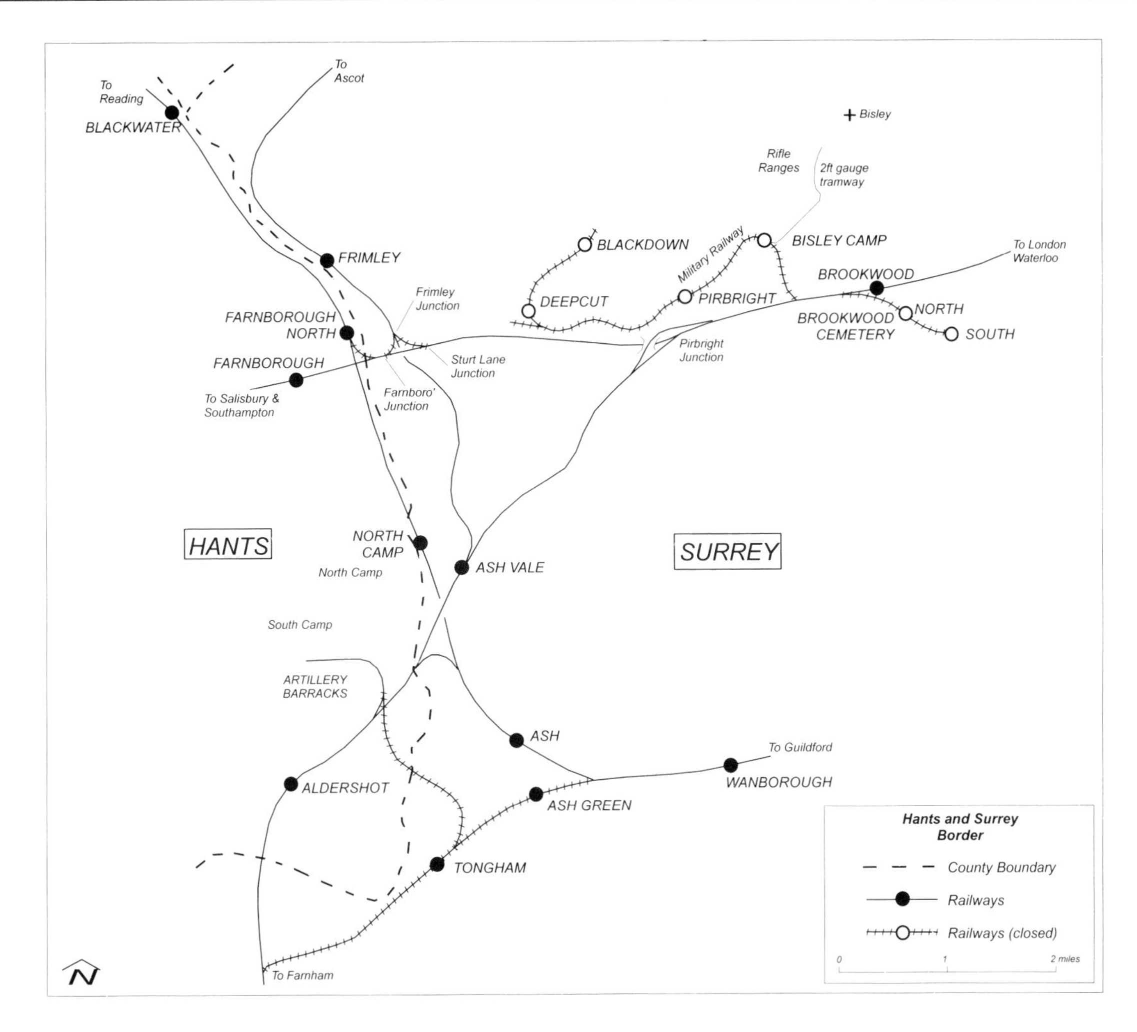

Above *Hants & Surrey border and Military Surrey*

their own mounts to travel down by train. Although rail's ability to handle large crowds was well demonstrated, the local officials' lack of experience was probably the reason why the returning throng, drenched by rain, were not cleared from Chertsey station until late evening[4].

The importance of the Chobham exercise was that it confirmed the case for establishing a permanent army base at Aldershot. And it was not long before all the activity there was having its repercussions in Surrey. In 1860-62 a Staff College was opened on a site very close to the Royal Military College at Sandhurst, which had been set up just over the Berkshire border fifty years earlier. This new development was soon serviced by a new community of shops, hotel, and workers' cottages , at first named Cambridge Town after the Commander in Chief Army, but from 1877 redesignated Camberley to avoid postal and other confusion. As we have seen in chapter 3, this military occupation of the infertile heathlands of north west Surrey stimulated the construction of a new railway.

After its opening in 1878, Camberley became the acknowledged station for both the Army colleges and for many years until the 1920s, the young and active 'gentlemen-cadets' of Sandhurst enlivened the scene at the beginning of each term. A substantial proportion would arrive by the same train, rushing out into the yard, where they would fight for possession of one of the horse-drawn cabs standing ready in line, bribing the drivers to race in noisy competition through the town in an endeavour to be the first to arrive at the old College building.

Above *The National Rifle Association steam tram engine and trailer at the Bisley ranges, about 1912. Heads and necks are in general well protected against the summer sun* Commercial postcard.

In the early 1860s, the War Department began making use of Chobham Ranges and Bisley Common, another large area of poor soils judged ideal for military exercises and accommodation. The first of a long series of annual autumn manoeuvres involving both regular and reserve troops was held on Chobham Ranges in 1871, the railways playing an essential role in massing over 30,000 men in the Aldershot area[5].

By 1914, extensive barracks had been built at Blackdown and Deepcut and a permanent camp erected at Pirbright, of which more in a moment. Firing ranges and training areas were also set up on Pirbright Common, south of the Southampton main line and east of Ash Vale station. These developments brought considerable passenger and freight traffic to the L&SWR at Camberley, Frimley, Brookwood and Ash Vale stations. In 1901 Frimley received an additional siding, crossover and shunting neck, expressly for military traffic. The SER also benefited at what is now Farnborough North, where a long siding was laid in 1902 for Army traffic, and at Ash, where two sidings were provided for Army use, these remaining in place until 1962. Further facilities were added at Farnborough SE&CR in 1909.

This military area yielded another small prize for the railway in 1890. When pressures built up in the late 1880s over the alleged dangers of its continuing annual shooting jamborees on Wimbledon Common, the National Rifle Association (NRA) eventually found a suitable new home for its firing ranges and butts at Bisley on the army-occupied West Surrey heathlands. The L&SWR, anxious to retain the traffic, played its part, promising in 1888 that if Bisley were selected, it would convey Volunteers in uniform from London to Brookwood at the much reduced 3rd Class return fare of 1s6d; competitors in mufti duly vouched for by the NRA could go for 3s return First. The railway company also agreed to help the Royal Engineers construct a 1¼ mile single line branch to serve the new ranges and offered to work the line with its own locos and

Above *The postcard artist Ernest Ibbetson creates an amusing impression of the overcrowded last tram of the day from Bisley ranges down to the Bisley Camp railway station* Commercial postcard.

carriages for half the gross receipts[6].

During the period of construction of the railway and ranges in late 1889 and early 1890, daily working parties of soldiers from Aldershot arrived by train at Brookwood sidings. The new single track branch descended from the Up side of Brookwood station to cross the Basingstoke Canal on a girder bridge before climbing at up to 1 in 50 on to Bisley Common. With its steep gradients and lightly-laid track, it was officially a 'Tramway' and a 10 mph speed limit was in force.

A royal special, carrying Edward and Alexandra, the Prince and Princess of Wales and hauled by Adams 02 0-4-4T no. 185, temporarily named *Alexandra*, opened the new branch on 12 July 1890 but public service by what was later to become known as the 'Bisley Bullet' did not begin until two days later. At the terminus, there was an engine release road and a single brick- faced platform. Some time afterwards, the NRA added a row of trees and a wooden building which externally showed rather more affinity to a cricket pavilion than a railway station.

Passengers arriving at Bisley were able to change on to a 2ft gauge tramway which carried them to the more distant 'Siberia' ranges near Bisley village. This line incorporated material which had been used at Wimbledon, including open cars hauled by the 1877 Merryweather steam tramway engine, *Wharncliffe*, in charge of a L&SWR driver, with a Royal Marine from the Camp Working Party designated to act as guard and collector of fares . Later the NRA's blacksmith took over the task of driving *Wharncliffe*. This engine had received an overhaul at the L&SWR works around the time it began a fresh life at Bisley and in 1900 a new boiler was fitted by Merryweathers. Two open crossbench 'toastrack' cars, longer than the Wimbledon ones, were obtained new by the NRA in 1900. This steam tramway remained in operation until at least the beginning of World War 2.

From an early date the Bisley Ranges were also served by 2ft gauge tramways at the Century and

Siberia butts which were used for moving the targets. That at the former survives. Both tramways were manually-worked until 1961, when the Century Butts line received a 4-wheel Lister 2-cylinder diesel locomotive which was still in use at the time of writing.

For the 1894 July Meeting, three through trains were worked each way between Waterloo and Bisley Camp, carrying members of the NRA and 'Volunteers in Uniform or bearing arms' at 2s return Third Class, 3s6d First, including the journey over the Camp Tramway. As well as passenger traffic to the NRA's annual meeting, the branch from Brookwood transported wagon loads of coal, parcels and other freight as required, including goods for the traders in the Bazaar Lines , ammunition, and empty ammunition boxes. The railway companies and later, BR, maintained a Goods & Parcels Office at the Bisley terminus . Outside the shooting season, trains were also occasionally worked for parties of Volunteers and Territorials attending camps in the area. Over the years, the NRA extracted further fare concessions , free First Class passes for its chairman and secretary and substantial annual donations for the Prize Fund.

There can be no doubt that from the late 1850s, Surrey's railway system greatly facilitated the training and deployment of the British Army at an important period of its development. The annual 'autumn' manoeuvres of regular and reserve forces mentioned above soon spread beyond the immediate area of Aldershot; thus in the 1876 exercise, troops were also based in the Guildford, Petersfield, Horsham and Dorking areas[7]. That year some 3,000 men, with their horses and equipment, constituting the Second Army Corps, were brought to-

Below *On a damp day early in August 1914 a troop train arrives at Dorking SER Up platform. Following the German invasion of Belgium, Territorials, who had been in summer camp in the area, have been summarily ordered to report for duty elsewhere . The Town Band is in attendance to give them a rousing send-off and a large crowd of local people has assembled to watch their departure.*

gether on The Holmwood south of Dorking, where they encamped from 7 to 18 July and were reviewed by the Duke of Cambridge. Most, if not all arrived by train at Holmwood station, some from Portsmouth, and they were afterwards moved to Aldershot via Dorking SER station[8]. Rail also aided rapid deployment of the Volunteers, an important element in the defence of London against an invader. In August 1865, The *County Chronicle* reported over 1,000 Volunteer riflemen massing at Byfleet for a 'sham fight', many of them delivered to Weybridge station in a special train.

Not all the military activity was in west Surrey. The Guards Recruiting Depot at Caterham, replacing one at Warley, Essex, was opened in 1877. Spence mentions that during its construction, the contractor laid a light railway from the main line at Coulsdon, along the floor of the Happy Valley east of Farthing Downs. Enlarged 20 years later to accommodate 1,200 officers and men, the Guards barracks provided a steady business for the Caterham branch line for many years. Early in World War 1 as many as 600 volunteers were arriving in the little town daily by train, bringing the garrison in 1915 to some 15,000, a figure higher than the civilian population. Troop trains at Caterham station were a regular feature, right through to the late 1960s when the main role was transferred to Pirbright. The Depot was finally closed in 1995.

Surrey's railways were also very much involved in elaborate plans for the defence of London drawn up by the War Office in the 1890s. This strategy included a chain of so-called 'forts', officially described as mobilisation centres and lightly-fortified equipment stores, all of which were duly erected along the top of the North Downs around 1896. Guildford station was to serve as an advanced depot for Volunteers manning the 'Guildford Position', Leatherhead for those allocated to the 'Dorking Position', Purley for the 'Redhill Position', Caterham for the 'Godstone Position' and Upper Warlingham (along with Orpington) for the 'Westerham Position'. This scheme, which anticipated a French (and later a German) invasion of south east England, remained in place until 1903-04, after which increased confidence in the growing strength of the Royal Navy caused it to lapse.

Below the North Downs fortifications, the Tonbridge-Redhill-Reading railway provided a favoured route for troop trains. One such, consisting of but four coaches and two brake vans and carrying 150 men of the 2nd Northumberland Fusiliers on their way from Gravesend to Southampton to embark for Mauritius, came to grief at Gomshall station on 20 February 1904. After the long climb up from Dorking, the driver took the 1 in 96 descent into the station too enthusiastically, given that the track was fairly typical of the poor quality then to be found on the SER. In the resulting derailment of the locomotive there were no deaths but serious injuries were sustained by the footplate men and four soldiers. The Inspecting Officer commented that the points and crossings were not strong enough to take the estimated speed of 50 mph, some 20 mph above that normally prevailing on this line.

Surrey Railways in World War 1

When Mrs C S Peel took a furnished house at Hook Heath, Woking, for three weeks in the summer of 1914 she was hoping for a relaxing holiday but in the fateful days of early August her sleep was much disturbed by the 'ceaseless noise of trains running throughout the night, conveying troops to Southampton'[9]. This was the L&SWR demonstrating its preparedness and efficiency by achieving a prompt despatch of the British Expeditionary Force to France in accordance with a pre-arranged plan, and the first indication that Surrey's railways were destined to play a crucial part in four years of armed conflict in Europe. Pratt states that the whole operation was carried through smoothly, without fuss, as was the reinforcement, which followed on quickly. During the weeks concerned, London commuters continued to receive their full train service but there were some cancellations over the affected routes at other times of the day.

Much of the traffic to and from Aldershot at the beginning of the war was worked via Ash Vale and Frimley, causing public services between these stations to be entirely suspended from August 1914 until November 1916. According to Ewbank-Smith, the local historian, the line between Aldershot, Farnham and Bordon was also 'commandeered' in early August 1914 by the military, with sentries placed at strategic points; he adds that during this time, a man writing a letter whilst sitting on a platform seat at Farnham station was arrested as a spy and locked in the waiting room. This incident suggests that some public trains were being operated despite the Army presence. In the following month, many trains carrying recruits arrived at Farnham, whence the men were marched to new camps on Frensham Common.

Another aspect of mobilisation was the mustering of the large numbers of horses needed for military purposes. Bowley mentions that many animals were brought by train into Horsley station, to be put out into adjacent fields for assessment and selection by the Army authorities and notes that a similar process occurred here at the beginning of the South African War of 1899-1902.

Throughout the war period, the cross-country line from Tonbridge to Reading via Redhill was in heavy use: countless troop and ambulance trains passed over it; military stores and huge quantities of ammunition were moved in special freight trains from war factories in the Woolwich Munitions Area and the explosives and gunpowder complex at Davington, near Faversham to replenish military and naval bases west of Reading, also to Southampton and Newhaven, for the war fronts. In the opposite direction, coal for the army in France was brought from South Wales and petrol from Avonmouth. Details of some of these workings are given by Gould. A particularly hazardous traffic mentioned by Pratt was the regular transport of cordite paste in special GWR dustproof vans from Pembrey, South Wales to the Admiralty Cordite Works at Chilworth and the Davington factories. As a result of all this additional activity, congestion often built up at Redhill, requiring new works in 1918. Two sidings, of 800 and 850ft ,were added on the Down side at Reigate whilst a connection was made between the Up Siding Dock Line and Up Siding to allow freights to be held clear of the running lines when Redhill was saturated with traffic.

Military use of the LCC Hospitals at Epsom and large camps established at Woodcote Park and on Epsom Downs brought much activity to the two stations in the town and also to the Epsom Downs and Tattenham Corner branches. At Tattenham Corner, for four years from September 1914 the station buildings were given over to war purposes . Then in 1919-20, the spacious layout here provided a temporary home for around 100 surplus War Department steam locomotives awaiting disposal. Other new camps for British and Empire troops were opened at Esher (two), Hampton Court (two), Sunbury, Woking, Walton, Staines, and Milford (two, served via Godalming station). All provided extra traffic at the stations concerned, where middle class women volunteers were often to be seen refreshing the weary men with great quantities of tea and buns before they marched on to their temporary accommodation.

At Bookham, the 1885 Merrylands Hotel opposite the station was acquired in 1917 by Waring & Gillow. A war factory was built in the grounds, the hotel itself becoming offices, but a projected siding into this new industrial site had not been built by the time the war ended. Afterwards the premises were converted to manufacture light car and motor cycle engines, providing a new traffic for the railway[10].

An Aircraft Acceptance Park with a grass aerodrome, established for the Royal Flying Corps on Kenley Common in 1917 brought heavy traffic to Whyteleafe and Upper Warlingham stations, firstly in construction materials and very soon in the steady delivery of complete aircraft and aircraft components, which were carried or towed up the hill to the new facility by heavy Leyland lorries . Away to the north west of the county, many German prisoners of war passed through Frimley station on their way up to a large compound at Frith Hill, an event carefully recorded for posterity by local picture post card publishers.

Kempton Park Race Course became a motor vehicle store, whilst Woking freight yard handled aircraft manufactured at Messrs Martynside's works in the town. Staines L&SWR yard dealt with shell cases produced in the Linoleum Factory whilst at Guildford, Dennis Brothers' private siding was busy with the wartime output of that works. Weybridge station received traffic arising from the . Vickers aircraft assembly factory set up at the Brooklands Motor Racing Circuit in 1915. On the New Guildford line, Benton's Little Heath Brickworks, just south of Oxshott, with its own siding, became a rail-served munitions depot.

Air raid damage to Surrey's railways was not serious but a high explosive bomb, one of 12 dropped in

Above *A large dump of locomotives built at the order of the Ministry of Munitions for duty with the military Railway Operating Department overseas but not required for that purpose following the armistice, await disposal in the ample siding space available at Tattenham Comer station in 1919. The building in the background is the stables provided by the SE&CR for the convenience of racehorse owners using the railway horse box service*
Alfieri Agency.

the Guildford area, carefully aimed from German Zeppelin L13 at 22.10 on 13 October 1915, exploded between the two tunnels south of the station. Fortunately, the damage caused was not sufficient to seriously disrupt rail services. Ambulance trains, conveying wounded and sick servicemen, mainly disembarked at Dover and Southampton, were received at Brookwood, Clandon, Egham, Epsom, Guildford, Holmwood, Walton on Thames and Witley stations. Their progress along the railway was often watched from vantage points by civilians barely aware of the heavy suffering experienced by their passengers.

Pratt comments on the fact that throughout the war years, huge quantities of explosive materials and finished ammunition were carried by rail with virtually no personal injuries or deaths. There were however some hair-raising narrow escapes, one in Surrey. On 18 April 1918 an Up freight train divided, the rear section coming to a stand inside Redhill Tunnel on the Quarry line. This was run into by a following up freight, the locomotive and first three trucks of that train derailing. A third freight, on the Down line, then ran into the wreckage, becoming almost wholly derailed. All three trains were loaded with ammunition including high explosive shells; cordite was scattered all around. Incredibly, teams of men using acetylene lamps worked for two days without incident until the line was cleared.

The Bisley branch was taken over by the War Department in a move which brought it much additional traffic, including camp construction materials, military equipment and supplies of all kinds. Wartime demands required an extension of some three miles through Pirbright and Deepcut Camps to Blackdown Camp. At each of these places, stations with concrete-faced platforms were erected by the military in 1916-17. Contemporary photographs show a particularly striking building at Deepcut in handsome Rocky Mountains log cabin style executed by Canadian Army Engineers. This structure housed a large ticket hall, ticket office, a W H Smith bookstall and offices for the stationmaster and Railway Transport Officer in rooms separated by asbestos partitions. Surviving until well after World War 2, it served latterly as the Royal Army Ordnance Corps Museum but has now been demolished. Also at Deepcut, a spur at the Bisley end of the station led to sidings and a small engine shed. A 60cm gauge railway, used for earth moving between Bisley and Blackdown and perhaps originally provided in connection with construction of the standard gauge extension, appears to have remained active until 1921, carrying earth to make recreation grounds[11].

Below *The impressive and handsome station constructed at Deepcut by Canadian Army Engineers in 1917. Although this building survived World War 2 to become a military museum, it was later demolished* Commercial postcard.

Standard gauge services to Deepcut began on 1 August 1917, to Blackdown in the following December. On 8 August 1918 the L&SWR took over working of the entire line and all the stations, under the supervision of the Brookwood stationmaster, who also assumed control of Blackdown in the following December. Passenger and freight traffic, the former mainly weekend leave trains, continued until the end of 1921, after which the Bisley-Blackdown section was dismantled.

The Last Years of the Bisley Branch

Between the wars, the Bisley branch reverted to its peacetime role of serving the NRA ranges in the three weeks of the summer shooting season. When normal working was resumed , the L&SWR no longer paid over to the NRA half the fare receipts, explaining that revenue from the branch barely covered its working expenses and maintenance. For the Annual July Meeting in 1920, a service of around 30 trains daily each way was provided on the branch, almost all with reasonable London connections at

Above *BR 30027 at Bisley Camp station, 12 July 1952; note the level crossing gates for the abandoned extension to Deepcut and Blackdown, still in place at this time* Pamlin Prints.

Brookwood. This must have been seen as over generous, since by 1924 the number had fallen to 12 each way and in subsequent years never exceeded 15-16. On the busiest day and also on the closing day of the Meeting when a large number of competitors were returning encumbered with quantities of luggage, two or three through trains were worked from Bisley to Waterloo. From around 1930 the normal provision was a vestibuled push-pull unit drawn by a Dl 0-4-2T or an M7 0-4-4T, with the guard issuing or examining tickets en route. Although in the 1930s the service started at 07.48 from Brookwood, there were few if any passengers until 10.00 or later. In 1931, the arrangements included a special freight train over the branch, connecting with the scheduled overnight Down service at Brookwood and arriving at Bisley Camp at 07.00; there was also a 07.10 Up freight from Bisley Camp. This seems to have been the routine throughout the between-war years, with the branch trips worked by the loco off the pick-up freight shunting Brookwood Yard.

World War 2 saw another expansion of military activity in West Surrey. Much of the Bisley NRA Camp was requisitioned and in the summer of 1940 the military railway was relaid by Royal Engineers for about a mile, to terminate just short of the 1917 platforms at Pirbright. Here an engine run round loop and two new platforms were constructed. At Bisley Camp station a shunting siding and crossover were added. Shortly after the end of the war, the extension, mostly on spiked flat-bottomed track, was again removed and about 1950 the terminus at Bisley Camp was reduced to a single track alongside the platform.

Although the Bisley NRA operation was totally uneconomic, the SR and its nationalised successor loyally continued working it until the summer of 1952. With the end of the shooting season that year, the line was closed completely, not without ceremony (including a firing party) and some genuine sadness on the part of old NRA hands. With indecent haste, BR withdrew discounted weekend tickets between Waterloo, Brookwood and intervening stations from 1 September 1952. Today, at Bisley Camp, the platform and station building survive; on the site of the old run round loop stands a former BR sleeping car on a short length of track, fulfilling a new role as the headquarters of the Lloyd's Bank Rifle Club.

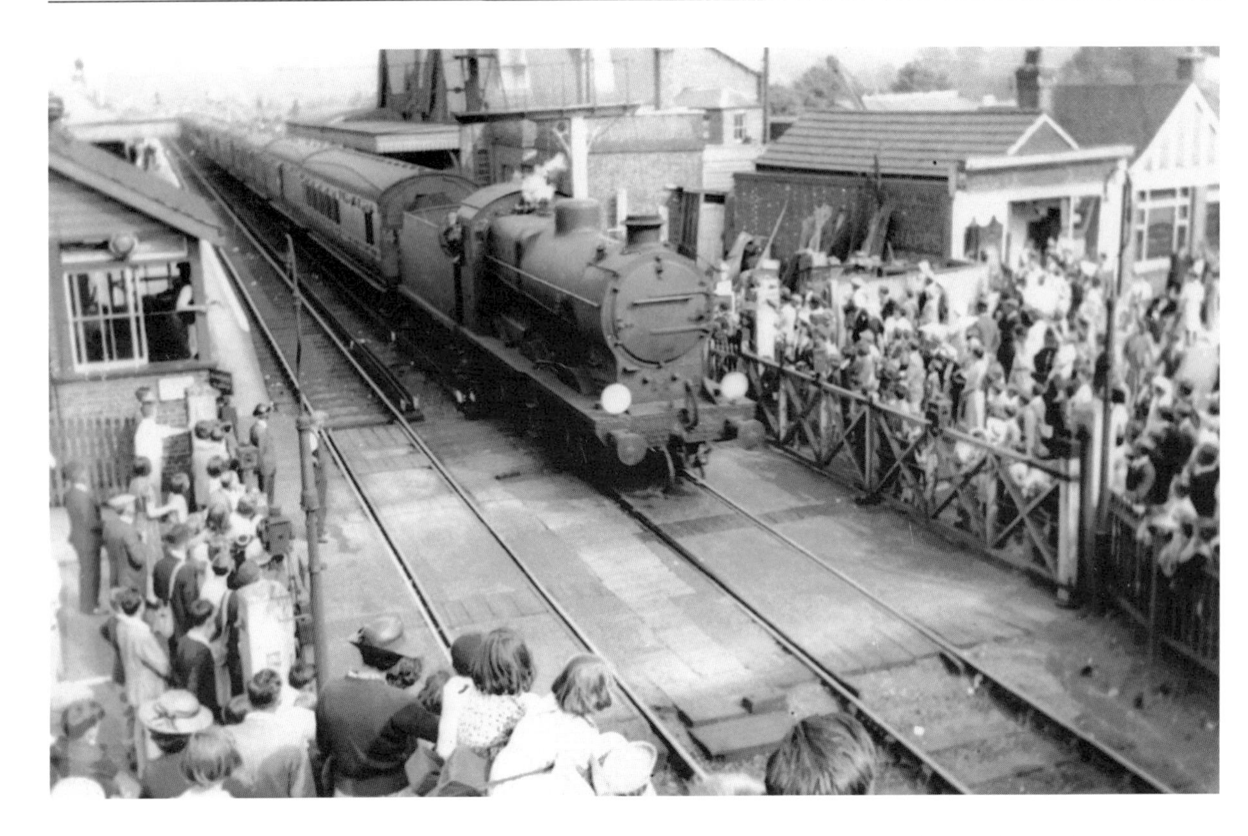

Above *A casualty evacuation Ambulance Train of L&NWR stock carrying wounded from the Dunkerque withdrawal passes through Reigate station westbound on Sunday 2 June 1940. The sympathetic public interest is very evident* G.L.Gundry.

Surrey Railways in World War 2

Without doubt the hours of greatest glory for the county's railways in World War 2 were in the summer of 1940, when the Tonbridge-Redhill-Reading line played a major role in the evacuation of British and Allied troops from Dunkerque. All normal traffic around Redhill was suspended between 27 May and 4 June to allow the railways to give total round-the-clock attention to troop trains moving westwards from the Channel Ports. As fast as it could be cleared, the empty stock was worked back east to pick up further troops arriving from France. In these few hectic days, 565 heavily-laden trains reached Redhill, 293 of them continuing westwards through Dorking. All were worked without timetables and although the SR managed to muster enough suitable locomotives, its carriage stock had to be supplemented from that of other companies. Engine changes at Redhill averaged only four minutes and in one case the operation was achieved in 2 1/2 min. Since Redhill depot could not cope with servicing all the locomotives, many were sent down to Three Bridges. A canteen was hastily organised on the platform at Redhill to provide refreshments whilst the trains briefly halted there. Local people stood at the lineside and at the stations, watching with interest and compassion as successive trainloads of exhausted men, many wounded and with uniforms in tatters, some with only a blanket to cover them, passed through. Arms stretched out through open windows offering slips of paper with names and addresses to inform loved ones of a safe return to England. These were posted by railway staff and others, often with an explanatory cover note.

In anticipation of the expected German invasion in 1940, the earthworks along the Reading-Redhill-Tonbridge line and the Epsom Downs branch west of Belmont were fortified with tank traps and pillboxes to form part of defensive lines designed to

check any advance towards London. Other wartime works included a connection between the GWR and SR branches at Staines, one of a series designed to provide alternative routes between the main lines north of the Thames and the SR, principally against the contingency of bomb damage to the City Widened Lines and the central London Thames crossings. Ready on 23 June 1940, the Staines curve was first used on 15 September for relief rather than emergency traffic. Working through trains via Staines Moor did however entail some operational problems, notably main line occupation for locomotive changes at Northolt Junction and delays associated with the flat crossing of the SR main line at Woking. When the new connections at Oxford and Reading were completed (8 June 1941) these offered a more convenient emergency alternative and the Staines Curve was last used for a through working on 17 May 1941. It did nevertheless play an important part in the war effort, carrying the 18-inch howitzer 'Boche Buster' on its way from Catterick to Bishopsbourne (2-3 February 1941) and possibly other heavy artillery around the same time. Although the connection was formally taken out of use in December 1947, it featured in reconstructed form in an abortive 1959-60 plan associated with new road works. This proposed diversion of trains to and from West Drayton into a new bay at Staines Central.[12]

Above *One of the many trains carrying British and Allied troops rescued from Dunkerque passing westbound through Westcott, near Dorking, on Sunday 2 June 1940, watched by children evacuated from London* Courtesy Dorking Museum.

At Dorking, the curve linking the former LB&SCR and SER lines, which had been severed about 1900 and entirely removed about 1926 was reinstated for emergency purposes from 3 September 1941. Little used, it was again removed in September 1950 and in 1976 part of the alignment was used for new housing. Kenley, established as a permanent airfield in 1920, provided a steady flow of traffic at Whyteleafe station both before , during and after the war, and this continued until the RAF personnel were withdrawn in 1974.

Apart from the Dunkerque evacuation already mentioned, the strategic importance of the Tonbridge-Redhill-Reading line again brought it a very substantial increase in train movements. In October 1941 a Down loop was installed at Gomshall, controlled from a new signal box of the standard wartime blast-proof pattern with flat concrete roof, situated on the Up platform. At the same time (19 October) a nine-road marshalling yard with sidings extending up to 415yd. was brought into operation east of Shalford station on the Up side. With the ending of the war, the Shalford yard was adapted for various railway purposes, eventually becoming a permanent way depot but all tracks were subsequently removed. Further east, the Buckland Tile Works west of Redhill (chapter 8) was given additional sidings on the north side of the line when the site was converted to an ammunition and petrol storage depot. Unsuccessful air raids were made on this installation in 1940 but one bomb distorted the running lines east of Betchworth station, briefly interrupting the train service[13]. An Up loop was also inserted at Buckland and the layout was controlled from a new signal box of standard wartime pattern . After the war the Buckland military site was used for a time for storing theatrical scenery and as a Charrington solid fuels depot.

On the Portsmouth main line, between Guildford and Farncombe on the Up side, a siding was laid in about 1942 to serve a new government depot, the Artington Cold Store, one of many similar rail-served installations then appearing all over Britain. Emergency Food Stores were also set up on railway property: large quantities of flour and biscuits were hoarded at Redhill and stacks of corned beef found their way into goods sheds at Caterham and Ewell East.

As in 1914-18, Redhill was the focus of a great deal of wartime activity, becoming very congested at times . In an attempt to relieve matters, five reversing sidings were laid on the Down side at Merstham in 1940. This facility allowed freight trains to be held until they could be cleared through the junction.

On the Guildford to Christ's Hospital line, US troops were encamped in Baynards Park and a station which in peacetime saw no more than a score or so passengers daily received a considerable weight of passenger traffic as well as armoured fighting vehicles and ammunition. Since this line had considerable strategic value in affording an alternative through route between the Midlands, Thames Valley and the south coast, the authorities arranged for 24-hour manning of its signal boxes to ensure that any bomb damage was observed and promptly reported.

An interesting operation located immediately south west of Horley station and described by Buss and Davis appears on the 1945 edition of Sheet 170 of the One-Inch Ordnance Survey. Here, on a partially-completed 1930s housing estate, a site which had been used as a rail-served ammunition dump in World War 1, the Royal Canadian Engineers established and maintained a large stores complex from 1940-41 until about 1946. Rail access was via a lengthy loop siding which made a junction with the Up side of the main line just north of Gatwick Race Course station. Within the depot, material was moved around over a narrow gauge layout.

Two stations owe their existence to wartime needs. A halt opened in 1940 at Longcross, between Virginia Water and Sunningdale was at first restricted to personnel at the adjacent military establishment on Chobham Common but was made available to the public from 21 September 1942. It had no road access and amenities were rudimentary, consisting of no more than open-fronted shelters of breeze blocks and corrugated iron and an unroofed concrete footbridge. Nearby, on the Down side, a siding and headshunt served the Army establishment from 8 November 1942, remaining in place until 1958. A few miles to the east, on the Shepperton branch, the British Thermostats Factory, converted to production of aircraft components, required transport provision for its much expanded workforce. A single platform halt on the Down side between Sunbury and Shepperton was opened on 1 May 1944; at first called Halliford, it was known as Upper Halliford from 22 May. Passenger facilities here were very similar to those at Longcross but since the branch beyond Sunbury was at this time worked as a single track with the other line used to store crippled wagons, the new halt had to wait until 6 May 1946 for its second platform and footbridge.

With the threat of war increasing, the Southern Railway secured the Deepdene Hotel at Dorking in June 1939, the cost partly met by the government as air raid precautions expenditure. A hurried conversion to offices followed, the intention being that this 1830s mansion should serve as the railway's wartime headquarters. When hostilities began in September, the offices of the General and Traffic Managers, Chief Engineer, Accountant & Cashier, Superannuation Fund and Savings Bank were moved to Deepdene, whilst the Audit Accountant and staff were housed in hutments at nearby Dorking North station. During the 'phoney war' period between September 1939 and the summer of 1940, some staff returned to Waterloo, remaining there when bombing started. However the General Manager took up residence in Dorking and the Chief Engineer and the Traffic Manager likewise, their staff working at Deepdene, where an underground telephone exchange, radio link and operations room were set up to establish contact with all parts of the SR system. The post-Dunkerque movements mentioned above were controlled from Deepdene as were the rail and port aspects of the 1944 landings in France. After the end of the war, some railway staff remained at this country outpost until March 1966, when the hutments at Dorking station were also vacated. During the Deepdene era, a daily special train was operated between London Bridge station and Dorking for the use of railway staff, with a bus connection up to the offices. Dorking station also provided wartime refuge for Prime Minister Winston Churchill's special train, which was for a time accommodated on the back road of the freight yard.

Another control centre in protected accommodation was established at Redhill for the Divisional Superintendent London Central and his staff. His opposite number for London West Division was similarly housed at Woking, at the London end of the station, on the Down side. As at Deepdene, the bunkers here were equipped with radio as well as telephones, ready to keep Surrey's railways moving in the event of German invasion. Along with London East at Orpington, Kent, they were linked to Deepdene and all four points were assisted by an Emergency Road Service of motor cycle despatch riders and chauffeured cars available to carry messages and ferry officers and railway workers to any location where they were needed. Redhill Control remained in place until 1969 when the facility was moved to East Croydon.

Although many wounded during the invasion of France in 1944 were transported by air, ambulance trains were seen again in Surrey, at Tattenham Corner station or the former LB&SCR station at Epsom. From these railheads they were moved to hospitals at Epsom Race Course and Horton in converted Green Line coaches[14].

Since it would be tedious to relate all the bombing incidents we shall confine this account to the more interesting and serious occurrences affecting the county's railways. In general, as elsewhere in theatres of war, damage to railway lines from aerial bombardment was always repaired with remarkable speed. On 22 August 1940 a 47-wagon ammunition train moving between Tongham and Farnham was set alight but railwaymen succeeded in isolating the damage by separating the bombed section of the train from the rest. An electric substation at Weybridge was destroyed on 28 September and on the following day, a landmine caused some damage at Merrow siding. On 29 October a train was set on fire at Tattenham Corner station but there was no serious damage to structures. Buildings on the Up side at Sunbury station were however destroyed on 29 November and bombs on sidings at Hampton Court station on the night of 8/9 December burnt out seven coaches, damaging six others. Subsequent years were less eventful in this regard but a high explosive bomb landed on the track between Banstead and Epsom Downs on 28 May 1941, sending a 20ft section of rail into a bedroom of a house in Warren Road. On the afternoon of 16 December 1942 a Dornier 217 aircraft bombed and machine-gunned a Guildford-Horsham train near Bramley station with tragic effect on what was essentially a civilian target: the driver and guard and eight of the 20 passengers were killed, and most of the rest injured. Normal services were resumed the next day. Finally September 1944 saw a V1 missile landing on the Quarry Line skew bridge over Nutfield Road at Merstham and on 2 November following, a V2 missile demolished the Down side viaduct and signal box at Hampton Court Junction, destroying all running lines at this point. After the first incident the line was reopened within 24 hours and at Hampton Court Junction all tracks were restored within two days.

The Railway Downfall of Colonel Baker

Whilst on the military theme we must not overlook the bizarre tale of an Army officer, passenger on a Portsmouth-London train brought to an unscheduled stop in Surrey in June 1875. Colonel Valentine B R W Baker, 48, married, a friend of the Prince of Wales (later Edward VII), and Commanding Officer of the 10th Hussars (Prince of Wales' s Own), joined an afternoon train at Liphook on his way to dine in London with the Duke of Cambridge, Commander in Chief of the Army.

On entering a First Class compartment in an unvestibuled carriage, the colonel found it in sole occupation by a Miss Rebecca Dickinson, aged 22, passenger from Petersfield and daughter of a respectable middle class family. The two soon engaged in animated conversation about the weather, the theatre, the exhibition at the Royal Academy and foreign travel, this light discourse continuing happily enough until the train was just beyond Woking, whence it was scheduled fast to Clapham Junction. The colonel then moved to sit alongside the lady and began to kiss and caress her. After some five minutes, perhaps more (given the timing of the train), she started to resist these attentions and tried to summon the guard but as the apparatus was faulty she opened the carriage door and stood on the footboard. Baker, no doubt fearing for her safety, tried to bring her back into the compartment.

This dangerous behaviour was observed by railwaymen at Walton on Thames, who caused the train to be halted at Esher, where the colonel was locked into another compartment with three men. A clergyman needed little persuasion to mount guard over the insulted lady for the remainder of the journey. Police met the train at Waterloo where, somewhat curiously, Miss Dickinson refused to lay any charge, merely stating that Baker had been 'over-bold' in his behaviour. Her forgiving mood was overcome on the following day, when her brother persuaded her to swear out a warrant. Baker was very soon found and arrested on a charge of 'indecent assault'. At the Guildford Assizes, the judge indulged in a scholarly lecture on the ethics of kissing, with special reference to kissing on trains. He averred that if a woman were kissed against her will, with 'criminal passion and intent', this was in his view 'indecent assault' adding, 'A kiss, remember, which gratifies or excites passion, is undoubtedly indecent'. Acting the part of the perfect English gentleman, the colonel refused to testify or even to allow his counsel to embarrass the lady by cross questioning. Guided by the judge' s remarks, the jury quickly found Baker guilty of the charge. The punishment was harsh indeed, even for the period; he was sentenced to a year's imprisonment with hard labour, heavily fined, and made to pay all the enormous costs of the action. Queen Victoria had to be informed of the matter and, unable to accept that a lady of Miss Dickinson's background could have indulged in any provocation which might have prompted the colonel's behaviour, required his dismissal from the Army. Despite much pleading by senior Army officers, she subsequently refused to allow his reinstatement, either as a commissioned officer or in an Army civilian post, even for pension purposes.

Miss Dickinson was said to have been visibly moved by the severity of the sentence. It has sometimes been suggested she was not as innocent as she appeared and, in the privacy afforded by the unvestibuled railway compartment, may well have played the somewhat transparent colonel along[15]. Baker's subsequent career in the armies and police forces of Turkey and Egypt was both impressive and heroic, showing that but for his encounter with Miss Dickinson and the attitude of the Queen, he might well have gone on to become a valued General or even a Field Marshal in the British Army.

Surrey Races

Given its proximity to London, it is not surprising that Surrey possessed an abundance of popular race courses. Others, to be found just across the county boundary at Ascot, Windsor and Gatwick also contributed to the bustle and revenue of Surrey's railways on race days. Epsom's Summer Meeting was always the greatest crowd-puller; as many as 36,143 tickets were issued at Victoria and London Bridge to Epsom and Epsom Downsby one company alone (the LB&SCR) on 29 May 1883.[16] Although a decline in attendances set in as the Victorian age ended, for a further three decades or so those courses nearest to London would continue to attract as many as 14,000 on their most popular race days, virtually all using rail.[17] A major headache for the railway operator was that although racegoers were delivered to the courses over a period of several hours, they all wanted to return home immediately the last race was over, often at a time when normal commuter traffic was also passing over the same lines.

With their Pullman cars, card sharpers, bookies and spendthrift winners, the race trains, no place for the naive tyro, had a character and atmosphere of their very own. On the special trains, where class distinction was expected, few complained at the often substandard nature of the 'First Class' accommodation[18] which segregated the wealthy patrons and members of the grandstand associations from the common herd. In conditions of a virtual captive market, premium fares were the order of the day. On Derby Day 1922 for example, the LB&SCR charged racegoers from London to Epsom Downs a 'special fare' of 42½p (8s6d) return, with no particular class of carriage guaranteed, against the normal day return fare of 9p (ls9d). Beside the special trains for racegoers' exclusive use, the logistics of horse racing required the running of numerous horsebox specials before and after the race days to carry the animals to and from their home stables at Newmarket, Lambourn and elsewhere. Over the years, and often but by no means always with some financial help from the course authorities, the railways installed a good deal of special infrastructure , including dedicated stations and platforms, sidings for empty trains awaiting the returning throng, docks for unloading and loading horses, and additional signalboxes to expedite the working of extra trains. In two cases, race traffic was a major factor in the promotion of Surrey branch lines .

Efforts to raise revenue from race traffic began early. For 30 May 1838 (Derby Day), the London & Southampton Railway had advertised eight special trains to Kingston , their station in what is now Surbiton, the fare of one guinea including a road coach to the Epsom race course, over six miles to the south. Such was the response that the London station at Nine Elms was besieged and the police had to be called to clear a mob far in excess of the train capacity available. Later that year special trains were organised from Nine Elms to Woking for the Ascot races.

These early race trains were operated under the time interval signalling system, an extremely risky procedure for anything like an intensive service. Its perils were amply demonstrated on 7 June 1864, when two race specials, returning punters from Ascot, were involved in the worst train accident ever to occur in Surrey. The first train had been stopped at Egham for ticket inspection, a delay made worse by a complaint about card sharpers at work in one coach. Another special, with a locomotive running tender first and not booked to stop, was following five minutes behind at a good speed. It ran into the first train just as that was moving away from Egham station. On impact, the last two flimsy wooden coaches were completely destroyed and another coach was badly damaged. Having appreciated the inevitable, the guard of the first train jumped for his life, severing his long coat tails in the process. Five passengers were killed immediately, two more died later and 23 were injured.

By Rail to Epsom Races

One of Britain' s premier racecourses, the home of the Derby, lies across the summit of Epsom Downs. In regular use since about 1730, it was remote from railways until a station in the nearby town became available in 1847, and a second was opened in 1859. Although both were rather more than 1½ miles below the racecourse, they did afford racegoers much easier access than the previous scramble for transport (or walk) over the six or so miles of road to and from the London & Southampton' s station at what is now Surbiton. Not all those presenting themselves as passengers at these Epsom stations on race days were welcomed: Acworth[19] relates how at the LB&SCR premises in the early years,

> *Porters were placed all round the yard....armed with thick sticks with which to rap the knuckles of the roughs who, in spite of wet tar and tenter-hooks, endeavoured to clamber over the palings and get into the trains without the preliminary ceremony of taking tickets.*

With an optimism that today seems astounding, a 4 ¼ mile branch line was promoted in 1861 to bring the crowds nearer to the course. From its terminus, opened in May, 1865, the 70,000 racegoers conveyed in the line's first week found they still had to trudge uphill for almost 3/4 mile to reach the object of their desire. There was no proper road between the two points until 1892.

At Epsom Downs station, if horse box facilities and engine roads are included, there were eventually eleven tracks. Beyond the outer ends of the platforms were five carriage sidings and a 42ft locomotive turntable, coal stage and tank house . Passenger trains unloaded and loaded at nine platform faces, all without protection from the weather on what was a bleak windswept site at the 350 ft contour. The only shelter was a small concourse within the station building and a narrow awning across the end of the tracks which was removed in the late 1940s. In 1892 the site of the terminus was described as 'an absolute wilderness and the most god-forsaken place in the world' through which it was alleged only 20-30 passengers passed on a normal day.[20] As the building was at a lower level than adjacent tracks across the Downs, the railway company installed a flagstaff to fly the legend RAILWAY STATION for the guidance of bemused or sozzled pleasure seekers returning to London.

Below *Race Special at Epsom Downs station, c. 1908/09 with class 13 4-4-2T, 21 (built 1907). The flag marked 'Railway Station' mentioned in the text can be seen above the second coach.*

Very soon the LB&SCR must have had doubts about the wisdom of its investment in this branch, which had done little more, even on the most popular race days, than abstract some traffic from its own Epsom station. Many racegoers continued to favour the traditional approach from Epsom town, where there was overnight accommodation and a plenitude of licensed premises, whilst the road approach from London, which could take on the character of an extended pub crawl, also remained very popular. To make matters worse, attendances at the Summer Meeting were falling as the 19th century drew to a close. In the 1890s, when the motor car was still a rare sight, the surplus over working expenses on the branch taken over the year as a whole, including race days, barely exceeded £200.[21]

This disappointing revenue does not seem to have deterred the management from further investment in the line. Signalling was improved to provide greater capacity on race days: a new signal box was opened at Epsom Downs in May 1879 and intermediate boxes (designated A, B and C) for use on race days only were provided between Sutton and Belmont, Belmont and Banstead and between Banstead and the terminus in 1901-1902. Enthusiastic pa-

Above *Race Day staff at Epsom Downs, LB&SCR, 1919. This splendid group of smartly - attired staff was probably posed for the camera during the brief respite before the race crowds poured homewards. It includes guards, ticket collectors, inspectors and porters, and in the centre, the station master (top hat) and assistant stationmaster (bowler hat). The two passenger guards in the centre of the back row wearing full dress uniform with shoulder bands are presumably senior men allocated to the Royal Train.*

tronage by Edward, Prince of Wales, later King Edward VII, added a degree of colour and pizazz to the scene at Summer Meetings in the 1890s and 1900s, when at the terminus special trains of Pullman cars for private parties, were drawn up alongside the beautifully-groomed royal train, its highly-polished locomotive decorated with the royal coat of Arms, whitewashed coal and a gilded crown. Those arriving were greeted by floral displays which lightened the drab shoddiness of the unpretentious station buildings.

The 1890s saw the promotion of a second branch line up to Epsom Downs, in part to seek a share of the race traffic but also in the hope of promoting residential development of the Chipstead Valley. For the first time the railway station delivered the racegoer almost on the course, at Tattenham Corner. Successful efforts were made to have the line completed for opening on Derby Day, 1900. At the terminus the layout was generous indeed, with gravelled 20ft wide platforms varying in length from 550 to 750ft, enough room to allow half a dozen long trains to load or unload at any one time. Operation in steam days was facilitated by provision of an engine release road placed between each pair of platform lines. On the west side, a dock line was available for handling horseboxes and alongside this were brick built stables for the convenience of the horse owners and their staff. A nest of four sidings, later increased to seven, accommodated horse boxes or empty stock marshalled for the returning racegoers. There was also a siding and a 54ft locomotive turntable on the east side. At its maximum extent in the late 1920s, the layout here could hold in its platforms and sidings a total of 24 normal length trains. As mentioned in chapter 4, with the decline in both race and horsebox traffic and the abandonment of freight working in 1962, much of the layout described was removed, until from November 1970 there were but three platform faces and one electrified siding.

A wide concourse was placed across the ends of platforms 3 to 6, its canopy offering weather protection entirely absent on the long platforms. Behind this was a wood- framed slate-roofed ticket hall and entrance building with hipped roof, in typical SER rural weather boarded style but given an architectural feature in the form of a central gable on the road frontage. Designated temporary, this structure was to remain unaltered for almost a century before a driver over the legal drink limit crashed his empty train into it in December 1993. Other smaller buildings contained refreshment rooms, staff messroom and a large urinal. Off the approach road was 'The Mound', a raised lawn made from soil excavated when levelling the site for the station. This feature offered railway company directors, senior officers and their guests a fine view of the finishing straight.

The rebuilding that followed the 1993 over-run took the form of a small single-storey red brick pavilion with a ridge roof of asbestos slates, accommodating a ticket office and waiting area. This was sited on the north west corner of the site near the head of platform 3. A small glazed shelter was placed in the centre of the now uncovered concourse. This work was completed in spring 1994. Two relics of the old station remained at the north east corner: a large lavatory block and a small square wooden building nearby. Railway land to the west of the remaining platforms was developed as a housing estate around 1979/80 but the exit near the head of platform 3 for royal cars meeting the Derby Day royal train was carefully retained.

Epsom race traffic remained heavy between the wars and for a few years after World War 2. Over this period, around 100,000 racegoers would appear on Derby Day, some 60 per cent travelling each way by train. After the formation of the Southern Railway in 1923, a wise decision was taken to concentrate the main flows on the more convenient and spacious facilities at Tattenham Corner. Derby Day 1925 saw 115 special trains worked to that station from Charing Cross and London Bridge up to midday, all these returning between 15.45 and 18.30 in the teeth of the evening rush hour exodus. About 50, 000 punters were carried each way by these workings, all of which ran to time[22]. Until electrification in 1928, the Down line as far as Kingswood would be taken over for storing trains, marshalled with their locomotives at the London end, ready for the exodus after the last race. Tattenham Corner station had no less than three signalboxes to facilitate efficient working of the race traffic, and along the branch, extra cabins, used only on race days, were available in daylight hours: Tunnel Intermediate (between Hoppity and Kingswood Tunnels); and Chipstead Intermediate (between Chipstead and Kingswood). Since not all the Tattenham Corner sidings were electrified, steam locomotives fitted with the Westinghouse brake would be imported on race days from 1928 to shunt electric stock. Another feature of race days was the diversion of all the London to Caterham trains to Tattenham Corner, effectively doubling the service and leaving Caterham passengers to a shuttle to and from Purley. Derby Day 1937 saw 68 trains arriving at Tattenham Corner between 07.30 and 15.00, including steam-hauled specials from Gillingham, Sittingbourne, Canterbury, Ramsgate, Sandwich, Hastings and Rye. In the four days of that Derby week, 39, 405 tickets were collected at Tattenham Corner.

Despite the concentration on Tattenham Corner in the between-wars period and for some years after racing resumed in 1946, Epsom and Epsom Downs stations continued to be used by racegoers either from habit or convenience. At the latter two stations in the four Derby Week days of 1937 , tickets collected were 26,180 and 19,058. That Derby Day 54 trains , arrived at Epsom Downs station between 08. 00 and 14.00 and up to 19. 00 the total number of arrivals (matched by a similar Up service) was 85. Average lateness at all three stations was at most 2.1 min over the four day, period.[23] Until 1939, the Epsom Downs line carried special steam-hauled race trains, including some with First Class and Pullman accommodation but as we shall see in a moment, there were no royal trains on any of the routes to the course from 1925 until 1939.

From summer 1927, after the opening of Morden tube station in the previous year, the Southern Railway began to face strengthened competition for the

Top Right *Tattenham Comer, platforms 2 and 3, looking to Tadworth on Derby Day just after World War 1 with two Pullman car special trains in the foreground awaiting returning racegoers. The sidings in the distance (right) are chock-a-block with trains of horse boxes.*

Right *The extensive and elaborately - s ignalled lay out at Tattenham Corner, ready for Derby Day, 1901, looking to the buffers. Not all the accommodation has been completed at this date.*

BUFF TICKETS.
CARS
K L M N O P R S
BLUE TICKETS.
CARS
A B C D E F G H

Above *Down all-Pullman Race Special no.71, hauled by SR Mogul 1863, passes through the pleasant countryside between Chipstead and Kingswood stations just after World War 2*

Epsom race traffic. For almost 20 years there had been motor buses bringing racegoers from London and elsewhere but the London General Omnibus Company now began to work bus services between the tube terminus and the racecourse, eventually concentrating around 180 vehicles culled from garages all over London at the Derby day peak. In the first year of the Morden service these carried 22,000, 53,000 in 1928 (when a bus was leaving Morden station every 45 seconds), and 61,400 in 1931 [24]. Open-topped vehicles (which usefully doubled as a grandstand) were employed until 1934. This bus/tube facility on Epsom race days was resumed in 1946 and still runs today in very much reduced form.

From the 1920s until 1939 and again from 1946 for another 20 years or so, up to 22,000 racegoers would be handled on Derby Day at Epsom station, most of them travelling to and from the course by buses waiting in the approach road. Although no special race trains were worked from London to Epsom after 1923 (the special intermediate Cuddington Cutting signal box south of Worcester Park, used only on race days was closed in 1924), the subsequent years up to 1939 did see some race specials to Epsom from centres to the south. Coastal services via Dorking also called at Epsom on race days.

When racing resumed in 1946 the Epsom Downs branch continued to play its part for a few more seasons. That year there were 26 trains from Victoria on Derby Day between 09.00 and midday but 34 ran to Tattenham Corner. Steam-hauled race specials with First Class and Pullman car accommodation very soon disappeared from the Epsom Downs line; thus on Derby Day 1952, when 202 trains were worked to and from Epsom Downs, over half of them between 11.00 and 19.00, all were composed of electric multiple-unit sets, apart from a police special hauled by an electric locomotive. This intensive traffic, as on the other routes, was still controlled by semaphore signals worked from mechanical signal boxes.

By the later 1960s the share of public transport in

moving racegoers had much diminished; total attendance figures were also falling as a result of wider ownership of television sets and the legalisation of off-course betting from 1960. Railborne race traffic to Epsom, Epsom Downs and Tattenham Corner stations had declined significantly, no longer justifying the operation of special trains and dedicated signalling arrangements. The intermediate block posts on the Epsom Downs branch were last used in 1955 and those on the Tattenham Corner line in 1970, the year in which the terminal layout was drastically simplified. As mentioned elsewhere, five of the platforms at Epsom Downs station were taken out of use in 1972 and the branch was singled and shortened in 1989 in a manner which completely removed any ability to handle extra traffic. Whilst a few racegoers continued to filter through Epsom station after the 1960s, it was the Tattenham Corner branch that now carried the main weight. Thus on Derby Day 1995 (a Saturday) the arrangements involved the time-honoured practice of diverting all the through London-Caterham trains on to the Tattenham Corner line, along with extension of the Victoria- Smitham trains to run non-stop

Above *Racegoers arriving at Tattenham Corner on Derby Day, 2 June 1976. Their tickets were to be carefully checked by a trio of burly senior inspectors* Alan A Jackson.

from Smitham to Tattenham Corner and non- stop working of the regular Victoria-Tattenham Corner trains beyond Purley. The Caterham branch and intermediate stations on the Tattenham Corner line had to make do with shuttles to and from Purley.

One special working does survive. Although no royal trains had been run in Derby week between 1925 and 1939 (royalty had taken to going to the races by motor car) this feature reappeared after the war, initially because petrol was still rationed. In 1946, for the first post-war Derby, the SR's new West Country Pacific locomotive 21C 129 proudly hauled a royal train of four Pullman cars from Victoria to Tattenham Corner. After that, royal trains again became a tradition on Derby Days (and sometimes Oaks Days), but with the exception of one year (when the return was made from Chessington South), were required only in the outward direction.

In time, with increasingly-congested roads, it became apparent that rail to Tattenham Corner provided a less stressful and faster journey (nowadays 30-35 minutes non-stop) so the practice continued. But steam-haulage, which with all its associated trimmings, added a certain degree of glamour to the occasion, ceased after 1964.

Other Surrey Race Traffic

We now turn to Surrey' s other race courses and the part played by rail in sustaining them. A 190-acre course was opened at Sandown Park, between Esher station and the town, in 1875. It was the first 'Park', or enclosed course in Britain, an improvement which made racegoing an acceptable and safe pursuit for the respectable middle class and their ladies. The formula proved popular, one London guide describing Sandown in the 1890s as 'pretty and very fashionably attended'.[25] From 1882, to handle the heavy additional traffic on race days, the L&SWR provided two special platforms with three faces, sited on the Up side just west of the main station. Further west, sidings were constructed to accommodate trains awaiting the returning racegoers. Empty race trains were later also temporarily parked on the Up Local line between Walton and Esher, but since this practice greatly inconvenienced users of the new Hersham station by preventing the normal Up services from calling there, it ceased around the end of 1936. In 1883 the race platforms were directly connected to the race course by a subway under the railway which had been financed by the Racing Club. A second signal box (Esher East) was also provided especially for race traffic. After World War 2, for the reasons given above, attendances declined and more of the remaining racegoers travelled by road. By the mid 1960s there was no longer any justification for working additional trains since the traffic offering could be accommodated by lengthening the regular timetabled workings and stopping the Waterloo-Basingstoke semi- fast services additionally at Esher on race days. Taken out of use in 1965, the Sandown Park race platforms were demolished in 1972.

The Kempton Manor Estate was purchased in 1869 for conversion to a race course and nine years

Below *H.M. Queen Elizabeth II alighting from the Royal train at Tattenham Corner on Derby Day, 1976. Six royal limousines were lined up on the platform to transport the royal party to the adjacent race course* Alan A Jackson.

Above *Kempton Park Racecourse station in the 1950s. The bay line (left) was taken out of use in 1962 but the other platforms are still served by the Shepperton branch trains on Race Days.*

later, when racing was about to start, the prospect of additional traffic caused the L&SWR to double the Shepperton branch using land wisely purchased at the outset. With insufficient siding space at Shepperton to accommodate the special trains as they waited for the returning crowds, the custom developed of stabling the empty stock nose to tail along the Up line between Sunbury and Shepperton, a distance of some 2¼ miles. At these times, the public train service to and from Shepperton reverted to single track, using the Down line only, a practice resumed for some years after World War 2. In the 1900s and 1910s some 50 special trains would be operated to Kempton Park race meetings and to facilitate working on race days, three temporary block posts were required along the branch.[26]

When racing began on 18 July 1878, a private station, financed by the Kempton Park Racing Club, was ready for use by Club members, who had access to the best seats in the grandstand. There was just one canopied platform, sited on the Down side, lacking facilities but long enough to accommodate two Members' First Class special trains simultaneously. Some importance was attached to keeping the Members' heads dry, since there was also a canopy over the full length of the path from the station to the grandstand. An Up platform, connected by a covered footbridge, was added in 1879; this platform also had an extensive canopy, supported on cast iron columns and was served by a second track on the outside until around 1970. The private station, which has never had any access to the public road system, was further improved in 1890, when it became available to the general racegoing public for the first time. Signal levers used only on race days were housed in a wooden hut on the Down platform. After the branch had been electrified, the special race day trains for Kempton Park Club Members, with all seats at First Class fares, continued to be steam-worked until 1939. Nowadays the residual race traffic can be accommodated on the normal electric services, which are specially stopped at Kempton Park station.

Hurst Park Race Course, 121 acres on the Surrey bank of the Thames, was opened in 1889, with a grandstand and paddock just over a mile west of

Hampton Court station. It was closer to London than all the other Surrey courses, which made it a popular resort for punters. Within a few years, the traffic generated and that to Hampton Court Palace was such as to justify enlargement and resignalling of the branch terminus, works completed in 1899. A little earlier a branch line into the race course from a point just south of Hampton Court station had been considered by the L&SWR but the idea was dropped when it was realised the necessary property demolition and construction costs would raise the outlay above an acceptable level. In 1908 two more sidings to hold race trains awaiting returning passengers were put in alongside the station. At this time and indeed for another thirty years or so, around 50 special race trains would be worked over the branch for the Whitsun Meeting. Whit Monday, which also brought many additional visitors to the Palace, was the busiest day of the year for the branch with trains running every five to ten minutes before and after the races. This lasted until the beginning of the 1960s, latterly without the assistance of the intermediate signal box on the Up platform at Thames Ditton, which had been provided solely for race day working. By that time, the course had become superfluous to the needs of the declining interest in racegoing. It was closed in October 1962, after which a large part of the site was redeveloped by Messrs. Wates, who covered it with some 800 houses and flats.

Ascot, which also had special railway facilities, was a major earner for the L&SWR; some 35-40 special race trains ran out of Waterloo through Surrey on Gold Cup Days in the Edwardian era and between the wars. When racing resumed in 1919, the L&SWR carried almost 38,000 to the course in Ascot week. But erosion of the once heavy and lucrative First Class race traffic caused by growing use of motor cars was noticed by the management as early as 1906. West Surrey railways were also traversed by Ascot race trains coming from other parts of the system. From June 1939 all race workings to Ascot were handled by electric trains.

At Lingfield Park, the 140-acre race course, set in an estate of 337 acres, was opened under National Hunt Rules in 1890 and enlarged for flat racing four years later. It was over 1/4 mile south of the LB&SCR station, which was somewhat rebuilt to handle the new traffic. In May 1894 a Down Loop was provided, converting the eastern platform to an island; an additional siding was also installed parallel to the new loop and the platforms were extended. The loading dock behind the signal box was lengthened to allow it to be used as a departure platform for Up race specials as well as for unloading and loading horses, whilst the sidings each side of the dock were signalled as passenger lines. Other work in 1894 included an additional covered footbridge at the country end leading to a new covered way for Racing Club Members between the Up platform and the course. Four years after these improvements, in 1898, the LB&SCR obtained powers, which were never exercised, to build a line into the racecourse.

On Lingfield race days, as late as the 1950s, empty stock which could not be accommodated in the station area was moved forward to East Grinstead for berthing until the time came to carry the crowds home. Locomotives hauling Lingfield race specials were also turned at East Grinstead. In the 1950s, race specials were still worked through from Brighton as well as from Victoria and Cannon Street. Although the rail journey from London to Lingfield took less than an hour, these trains often included a Pullman car and remained a race days feature until the East Grinstead service was dieselised in 1964, although latterly only one or two ran. Between the wars, horse traffic at Lingfield was not associated solely with the racecourse; two hunting stables nearby provided a steady flow of foals and brood mares through the year on their journeys to and from Newmarket.[27]

Motor car racing failed to promote a similar outbreak of infrastructure expenditure by the railway authorities, perhaps because there was a belated realisation that too much had been spent without suitable return on facilities for horse racing. When the 2 3/4m, 100ft wide Brooklands Motor Circuit, surveyed and laid out by the railway engineer Alexander W Donaldson, was being built in 1907, a request for a passenger station was refused by the L&SWR. Early that year a temporary siding was however laid from the Down side at Weybridge to bring in 50,000 tons of chalk and 200, 000 cu yd of concrete and take out 300, 000 tons of excavated soil. Three small steam tank locomotives were imported to haul work trains of side and end-tip wagons over the temporary tracks.[28] Very soon after the opening in June 1907 the race track began to disintegrate (only six inches of concrete had been used) and the subsequent reconstruction brought further traffic to the railway siding. Motor racing and aviation enthusiasts arriving by rail used Weybridge station whence Brooklands paddock could be reached by a footpath alongside the railway and a footbridge or subway across the racing circuit. Combined rail and admission tickets were issued for many years from Waterloo and certain other stations. After the station now known as Byfleet & New Haw opened in 1927 this was convenient for the Aero Club and the factories at the south end of the site but not for access to the racing circuit.

Surrey for Holidays and Recreation

In his evidence to the parliamentary committee on the Reading, Guildford & Reigate Railway Bill in May 1846, Richard Wix Phelps, proprietor of the Dorking Waterworks, perceptively suggested that the railway would be of benefit to the tourist trade. Writing of the line's potential in August 1847, the *Illustrated London News* made a similar point. And so it was to be. The railways along and through the North Downs and those serving other scenic parts of Surrey were soon much used by tourists and day trippers, this patronage persisting for the rest of the 19th century and the first 50 or so years of the 20th. Guide books of the period before 1930 lay great stress on the convenient accessibility the railways provided to the most beautiful parts of the county and although summer visitors, tourists and invalids were making use of such centres as Dorking in the 18th century, they came in far greater numbers once the railways were in place.

With the reduction in journey time the railways brought, businessmen and professional people were able to take a house or apartments amid the Surrey countryside during the summer, commuting daily to London. This practice extended to the larger properties such as Betchworth House and nearby Wonham Manor, which were often let out by their owners to extended families desiring a few months in the country. With their mountains of luggage and retinues of domestic servants, these temporary occupants often needed to reserve one or more coaches and a special luggage van when in transit[29].

By the last decade of the 19th century, Coldharbour, at the foot of Leith Hill had assumed some popularity as a holiday village, with most of the cottagers letting rooms in season. Visitors normally arrived at Holmwood station, about two miles to the east over a winding and narrow road but the railway also served this holiday trade in other ways; should a visitor wish to send a telegram (or if one were sent to someone staying in the village) this was transmitted or received at the railway station and was then subject to a porterage charge of one shilling. The Holmwood stationmaster was also willing to arrange the supply of daily newspapers to Coldharbour visitors from the regular supply brought in by train.[30]

Cranleigh also enjoyed some popularity as a holiday centre in the late 19th century. *Murray's Handbook For Surrey* for 1876 noted that it was 'considered to be one of the healthiest places in the county....a good deal resorted to in summer and autumn by families seeking seeking change of air and quiet.' Such middle class visitors would of course almost invariably arrive by rail.

The railway made day excursion traffic into the hilly central parts of the county cheaply and easily accomplished from London. Much of this was concentrated on popular locations such as Box Hill and Leith Hill, both readily accessible from railway stations after a little mildly strenuous footwork. Shared with the motor bus from the 1910s, these day trips remained a major traffic for the Surrey railways until the early 1960s and were enjoyed by even the lowest paid groups, for whom they were often the only holiday. There is evidence they had begun as early as 1851, for we read in the *Sussex Express* of 2 August that year of 'three drapers' assistants from London' given into custody the previous Sunday evening after disorderly conduct at Box Hill station (now Dorking Deepdene) and:

> *....obstructing the stationmaster in the execution of his duty when the train was about starting....It appeared in evidence that the young men came to Dorking by an early train on Sunday morning for the purpose of rusticating on our airy hills and so gratified were they with the beautiful scenery about Dorking that it produced - of course it could be nothing else- a peculiar tone of conduct which was decidedly objected to by the station*

Above *Bank Holiday crowds on Box Hill, Dorking in 1906. Almost all these people would have arrived by train at Box Hill LB&SCR station* Commercial postcard.

master and hence the unpleasant dilemma in which they found themselves. They were fined 5s each which, with the expenses amounted to £1 9s 6d

Forty years later, in August 1891, the annual outing of the United Society of Boiler Makers and Iron Shipbuilders, nearly 5,000 men, women and children, marched with bands and banners from the East India Dock to London Bridge station, whence they were carried to Box Hill and Dorking in five special trains. Although there was much drunkenness, singing and dancing before nightfall brought a somewhat confused return to London, no arrests were made, possibly because the local police were simply overwhelmed by the sheer weight of numbers[31]. When the Boilermakers returned the following year, this time 3,000 strong, there was a heavier police presence and the demeanour of the invaders was reported as somewhat less rowdy, although 'the women accompanying the excursion were worse behaved than the men' and the trains returned to London at 8 pm, 'to the relief of everyone'.[32]

During the 1890s, the Easter, Whitsun and August bank holidays would see between 4, 000 and 5,000 day trippers arriving at Box Hill and Dorking stations. Numbers grew steadily: on August Monday 1938 there were 10,746 arrivals and departures at Box Hill station, 9,514 at Dorking North; at the height of the rush, trains were run every 10 minutes to keep the platforms clear. A peak was reached in the immediate post war years: Whit Monday 1947 saw 14,000 passing through Box Hill & Westhumble station and over 12,000 through Dorking North.[33] Then, as car ownership increased in the 1950s, railborne bank holiday crowds in the Mole Valley and smaller numbers of day trippers brought by the trains at fine weekends declined to a trickle. By the mid-1960s this traffic had all but vanished.

Caterham, a good starting point for hill walking and countryside pursuits, was another destination popular with day trippers, although on a much

Above *Children's 'Treat' and amusements on Epsom Downs, c. 1905, Epsom Downs station at right* Commercial postcard.

smaller scale. The local newspaper proudly reported arrivals at the station on Easter Sunday and Monday 1901 as exceeding 1, 400 on each of these days, when teas were served in quantity to the thirsty pleasure seekers in the gardens behind the Railway Hotel. This little railway-made town was for a few years also a very minor health and holiday resort. The Surrey Hills Hydropathic Establishment, on its 22-acre site, opened for business in 1898, offering Turkish, sulphur, electric and mustard baths and 21 bedrooms. From 1903 until the 1920s it functioned as a 'sanitarium', advertising a restorative regimen based on a simple diet, fresh air and unrestricted clothing. When this ceased, the building operated as an ordinary hotel until a disastrous fire in 1941.

With the railway providing easy and convenient access, walking in Surrey, particularly over the hills, became popular in the last half of the 19th century. A pioneer was the poet and novelist George Meredith, whose published letters reveal that as early as the 1860s he was organising walking excursions based on Surrey railway stations for his London associates and friends. In 1867 he took up residence at Flint Cottage, below Box Hill, close by the station opened that year. The train brought him many visitors, including Robert Louis Stevenson, and the walks continued. Louis J Jennings, another early Surrey rambler, was well aware of the way the railway facilitated this recreation, recording in 1876 the possibilities and pleasures of walking some seven miles from Holmwood station to Gomshall station:

> *By properly timing his trains, any man may accomplish this delightful excursion in the course of a summer's afternoon, and how could he spend his time to greater advantage?*[34]

But it was in the 1930s under the new name of 'hiking' that country walking in Surrey and elsewhere reached its peak of popularity, again with the railway playing an essential role. A London Bridge booking clerk, impressed by the quantities of tickets he was selling to walking parties at weekends, summer and winter, suggested to management that this business might be maximised if special trains were organised. This met with a positive response and the first 'Ramblers' Special' was advertised for Whit Sunday, 15 May 1932. These trains ran regularly until September 1939 when World War 2 forced suspension until April 1949. They were advertised as 'open to all who want to see nature in nature's way' and ran regularly for many years thereafter; some are still run today. They certainly provided good business for the Southern Railway, as in 1936, when 54 trains carried 27,609 walkers.[35] Publicised by handbills and posters at stations, they offered cheap fares and convivial company. Apart from the provision of the train and the ticket arrangements, everything else was left to volunteers, mostly members of the Ramblers' Association. Each train would load up to around 500 in summer, 300 or so in winter, and once it was on its way out of London, the organisers moved along the corridors, distributing details of six or more different conducted walks from the destination station, graded as to length and the physical effort involved. Surrey stations were among the most popular objectives. A typical ten shilling trip in early January in the 1950s left Victoria at 09.35 bound for Gomshall. After alighting there, those who had selected the 11-mile walk were led through Abinger Hatch and Pasture Wood to the King's Head at Holmbury St Mary. where the party paused for lunch. Afterwards. the ramblers continued over Holmbury and Longhurst Hills, with a descent to Peaslake for tea before a roaring fire at the Hurtwood Inn. Thus refreshed. they moved through the dusk towards Gomshall station. where their train was waiting to leave at a quarter to seven [36].

Hiking was further encouraged by the SR's 'Go as you please' day return tickets which, on payment of any difference in fare. allowed ramblers to return from a station different from the one from which they had begun their walk, even if it were on another line.

Touring cyclists also used the railway in substantial numbers from around 1895 until the 1940s, often travelling down from London with their machines on a Saturday afternoon to stay overnight at the local inns in Clandon, Horsley, Bookham, Effingham, Westhumble or Holmwood.

Another aspect of recreation in Surrey facilitated by the railway, from the last quarter of the 19th century through to September 1939, was the Day or Sunday School Treat. Every week in summer, large parties of children from inner south London, travelling in regular or specially-chartered trains, would invade Epsom Downs, Ashtead and Bookham, intent on enjoying themselves in the fresh air of the Downs, the woods and the open common land. At Ashtead, where sidings were provided in 1883/1885 for this traffic, three tea places were erected near the station and alongside the common, all with ample space for large numbers, one of them equipped with swings, pony-powered roundabouts, helter-skelters and other amusements. Similar facilities were conveniently located outside Epsom Downs station,[37] where again berthing a special train or even two offered no problems. At Bookham, the 1885 Merrylands Hotel built opposite to attract the railway trade, was soon supplementing its income in the same way: tea houses accommodating up to 1,000 children and 300 supervising adults were available in its gardens. When not refreshing such noisy hordes, this temperance establishment continued as an ordinary hotel, advertising a dining room for 200 and 21 bedrooms, these last sharing a grand total of two bathrooms.[38] As we have noted in chapter 7, Merrylands assumed a sterner role in 1917. Never resuming its original functions, it was demolished in the 1980s, the site remaining in industrial use.

In the eastern part of the county, Marden Park, Woldingham was a favourite destination for childrens' treats from Croydon and adjacent areas. Special trains working this traffic had to go forward to Oxted to reverse until October 1887, when the SER considered the trade justified investment in a set of crossovers at the station.

Bodies by rail to Brookwood

The manner in which Surrey's largest town was brought into being by the combined efforts of the railway and a cemetery company has been described in chapter 6. It remains to explain how the company used the railway for the purpose of giving 'rest' to London's dead in its great cemetery at Brookwood.[39]

By the middle of the 19th century the churchyards

Above *North station, Brookwood Necropolis, c .1905, looking towards the terminus of the cemetery branch line. This station was dedicated to all except Anglicans, whose mortal remains were rewarded with a sightly longer railway ride, to the South station* Commercial postcard.

of London were becoming outrageously overcrowded and the 14,601 deaths in the cholera epidemic of 1848-49 only served to draw attention to the problem created by the refusal of the churches to allow burials on alternative sites. The reforming Victorian mind produced a solution and in 1852 parliament sanctioned the establishment of The London Necropolis & National Mausoleum, a vast cemetery to be sited near Woking, a location deemed well beyond any possible future extension of the metropolitan built-up area. This legislation enabled the new company to secure huge tracts of land at Woking on relatively favourable terms and it is now reasonable to assume it never had any intention of using more than a small amount for the ostensible purpose of the undertaking[40]. But here we shall confine ourselves to the way in which the burials side of their activities was aided by the railway and indeed would not have been feasible without it. The idea was that this distant and hygienic repository for human remains would be served by funeral trains worked down from London by the L&SWR, which would supply train crews, motive power and the passenger carriages for the mourners. The Necropolis Co. owned the special hearse vans capable of carrying up to 12, and in a later version, 24 coffins.

During 1854 a dedicated Necropolis Terminus was built for these trains close to the eastern side of Waterloo station and the first of the funeral specials ran from London to the newly-completed and consecrated Brookwood cemetery on 13 November 1854. This unusual railway facility continued on a regular basis until April 1941 when it was brought to a sudden end by a German bomb which destroyed the company's private departure station in Westminster Bridge Road. Alternative facilities in Waterloo station itself were offered by the SR but there is no evidence that the special trains ever ran again.

At Woking, about 450 acres south of the main line at what is now Brookwood station had been laid out for the company's cemetery, whose facilities included a single line 3/4 mile branch, which left the

Down side of the L&SWR at a point just beyond the country end of what was to become Brookwood station, curving away south east. Two single platforms were erected in the Necropolis grounds, the 'North Station', for Roman Catholics, Nonconformists, Jews and other sects and denominations , and the 'South Station', for burials under Anglican rites. Designed by Sydney Smirke, the neat wooden buildings at each housed waiting and refreshment rooms and lavatories for the funeral parties and living accommodation for a caretaker. A siding to serve the Necropolis Company's masonry works was added near the outer end of the branch about 1905. As noted in chapter 2, Brookwood station, built partly at the Necropolis Company's expense and on their land, was opened in 1864.

At first what the irreverent Aldershot soldiery called the 'cold meat trains' were hauled over the branch by four black horses adorned with black ostrich feathers and attended by outriders in full funeral garb. Later the little L&SWR tank engines which normally brought the funeral trains down from Waterloo ran over the private railway track to the appropriate cemetery station. The trains, consisting of one or more hearse vans and First and Third Class coaches for the funeral party, were for most part worked non stop from London in about 50-60 minutes (40 minutes after World War 1), returning to Waterloo with the mourners after the funeral. For many years there was one return run daily (including Sundays) but with the availability of large new cemeteries near London and the increasing use of cremation, business fell away and towards the end, trains ran only twice or three times a week.

All trackwork in the cemetery grounds was taken up around 1946 but the two private stations, designated 'temporary' in 1854, remained in use as refreshment pavilions for mourners. North station, a victim of dry rot, was eventually demolished in the 1960s, whilst South, closed as a refreshment bar in 1967, suffered extensive fire damage at the hands of vandals and was demolished in 1972. Reminders of this curious Victorian enterprise remain in the cemetery, where it is still possible to discern the platforms. Another point of interest about the Brookwood Cemetery is that it was the official burial place for L&SWR staff, for whom special areas were set aside.

Notes

(1) Cole, Lt Col Howard N, *The Story of Aldershot: A History of the Civil and Military Towns*, 2nd edition, 1980.

(2) idem, quoting *All The Year Round*, July 1859.

(3) idem.

(4) Janaway, John, *Surrey: A County History*, 1994.

(5) Verner, Col Willoughby, *The Military Life of HRH George, Duke of Cambridge*, vol 2, 1905.

(6) L&SWR Board Minute 7 June 1888; letters from L&SWR General Manager, 8 November 1888 and 15 February 1889; National Rifle Association (Bisley Common) Tramway Confirmation Order, 4 August 1890; Agreements NRA/L&SWR, 9 June 1890 and 14 August 1895. For a full account of the Bisley NRA branch and the associated military railways, see Harding, Peter A, and Clarke, John M, *The Bisley Camp Line*, 1986.

(7) *Army List*, July 1876.

(8) Cole, Maureen, , 'The Army at Holmwood, 1876', *Dorking History*, 13 (1995).

(9) Peel, Mrs C S , *Life's Enchanted Cup. An Autobiography 1872-1933*, 1933.

(10) Fortescue, Stephen, *People & Places: Great and Little Bookham*, 1978.

(11) Ronald, D W, and Carter, R J, *The Longmoor Military Railway*, 1974.

(12) Davey, Richard, *My Life on the Footplate*, 1974.

(13) Christensen, M, and Balfour, G, *World War 2 Railway Study Group Bulletin*, First Series, 9, 8; 11, 10.

(14) Graves, Charles, *London Transport Carried On*, 1947 and verbal recollections of Miss Pamela Payne to the author.

(15) Notably in a BBC radio dramatisation *The Young Lady From Midhurst* by Frederick Bradnum, broadcast on 15 October 1979.

(16) Wade, G R, 'What Race Meetings mean to Railways', *The Railway Magazine*, December 1900.

(17) Faulkner, J N & Williams, R A, *The London & South Western Railway in the Twentieth Century*, 1988; the figure relates to the Hurst Park, Kempton Park or Sandown Park race courses.

(18) One example of this was the conversion of Third Class seats to First Class by the simple expedient of adding antimacassars.

(19) Acworth, W M, *The Railways of England*, 5th edition 1900.

(20) Evidence of William Quartermain East, 20 years resident at Woodcote Grove, Epsom, before the House of Commons Committee on the Epsom Downs Extension Railway Bill, 1892.

(21) Evidence of Allen Sarle, secretary and general manager LB&SCR, and resident of Banstead, to the Commons and Lords Committees on the Chipstead Valley Railway Bill, March and June 1893.

(22) Information on 1925 Derby Day from Bennett, E P L, *Tales of the Trains* (Southern Railway, 1925). For a detailed survey of the working of Derby Day traffic between the wars see Kirby, Dick, 'Derby Day', *Railways South East*, summer 1993.

(23) Statistics from *Southern Railway Magazine* , July 1937.

(24) Traffic figures from *TOT Magazine*, July 1927 and July 1931 and Thomas, J P, *Handling London's Underground Traffic*, 1928.

(25) Dickens's *Dictionary of London*, 1896.

(26) For a detailed account of race day working on the Shepperton branch see Faulkner, J N, 'Easter Monday at Kempton Park', *The Railway Magazine*, April 1955.

(27) *Southern Railway Magazine*, July, 1938.

(28) Faulkner & Williams , op cit and Fletcher, John, 'Brooklands Motor Circuit Construction', *Surrey Industrial History Group Newsletter*, 62.

(29) Ryan, Meg, *Within Living Memory: The Big Houses of Betchworth*, 1986.

(30) Anon (Roffrey, R *A Guide to Coldharbour with Some Account of its History*, 1891.

(31) *Surrey Advertiser*, 29 August 1891.

(32) *Surrey Advertiser*, 27 August 1892.

(33) *Dorking Advertiser*, 30 May 1947.

(34) Jennings, Louis J, *Field Paths and Green Lanes*, 1877.

(35) Faulkner, J N, 'South for Sunshine', *Railways South East*, Winter 1992-93.

(36) Corringham, Mary, 'The Ramblers Special', *British Tourist Authority Magazine*, March 1969.

(37) Depicted on picture postcards published in the 1900s; references in Acworth, op cit and Jackson, Alan A, (ed), *Ashtead: a Village Transformed* 1979; also evidence of the Rev. H J Greenhill to Commons Committee on the Epsom Downs Extension Railway Bill, 1892.

(38) Fortescue, S E D, *The Story of Two Villages: Great and Little Bookham*, 1975.

(39) This section is largely based on Clarke, John M, *The Brookwood Necropolis Railway*, 1988.

(40) This matter is considered by Crosby, Alan, in *A History of Woking*, pp 60-3.

CHAPTER EIGHT

Industry and Freight

For over 100 years from the mid-19th century, the railway was the principal carrier of solid fuels for heating Surrey's houses, its hospitals and other large institutions; it brought in the fuel needed for many of the county's public utility undertakings and the fuel and raw materials required for the factories, whose considerable variety of products were in the main distributed by train. And it also carried the seeds, fertilisers and animal feed needed for the farms, taking away their produce for distribution.

A major inward and intra-county traffic, which continued until the early 1960s , by which time it was fading fast, was the transport of building materials for the many thousands of new houses erected in Surrey in the preceding hundred years, particularly between the wars. All over Britain, railway transport facilitated development of large scale brick-making and the marketing of what was often superior building stone at prices competitive with local stone. As Sowan has pointed out,[1] the completion of the main Surrey railnet around 1860 resulted in a decline in other than very local use of the firestone quarried underground in the Upper Greensand between Reigate and Godstone, although the popularity of hearthstone as a whitening material was to secure the survival of this Surrey industry for another hundred years. Railway sidings into extractive workings along the southern scarp of the North Downs gave those industries ready access to the large London markets for their output. But, bearing in mind what has just been said about local stone, we must also remember that the railways did not always bring prosperity to the communities they served; they sometimes diverted it elsewhere.

The ability of rail to move thousands of tons of freight each year into, within and out of the county was an essential element in Surrey's economic prosperity for almost a hundred years from the completion of the trunk network around 1860. In that period it faced little or no effective competition. Navigable waterways were hardly significant, indeed non-existent over much of the area. Until freight-carrying motor vehicles came on to the scene around 1910-14, road transport was largely confined to meeting purely local needs. Even then its development was held back until road surfaces were improved, a process not completed until the mid-1920s. From that time, the eclipse of rail as the major freight-carrying mode in Surrey was inevitable but hardly rapid. Interrupted by World War 2, road transport's advance to dominance in the carriage of freight was not completed until well into the 1950s. Ironically, motor transport at first provided some new business for the railway. In the late 1910s and early 1920s petrol (and also paraffin) was sold in one gallon cans, moved from a central filling plant to be distributed by road vehicles from strategic railheads. One such was the B P depot opened at Dorking Town station in 1922.

To give some indication of the freight activity on Surrey's railways, we might look at Redhill in 1964. At that time, just before the Beeching revolution, the pace of traffic and pattern of operations here, where lines converged from all four points of the compass, were much as they had been for many years. There were four yards, all very busy, dealing with around 40 trains of mixed freight arriving daily. Alongside and south of the main passenger platforms was the Up Yard and nearby, south of the locomotive depot, the Down Yard. Other trains were directed to South Yard at Earlswood, or to the Merstham Sidings to the north of Redhill. Every day some 1,000 wagons were received in these yards, checked, allocated to an appropriate outgoing train and then marshalled into it. All these complicated operations, supervised by the Redhill stationmaster, were carried through each 24 hour period, seven days a week, by three Yard Inspectors and teams of shunters working eight hour shifts[2]. Similar activity would be taking place simultaneously at the other major Surrey freight centres at Woking and Guildford.

By the middle of the 20th century, rail freight movement in Surrey, as elsewhere, had developed broadly to provide fast direct services, running on a daily or more frequent basis between major national centres (including the three just mentioned). These fed traffic into and out of the classic pick-up freight trains which at least once daily served all the public goods yards along their route, dropping off wagons and taking up others. Small yards, as Appendix II shows, existed at almost every Surrey station until the 1960s. Calls would also be made as required at the various private sidings of which more will be said later.

A 1955 BR booklet on Southern Region freight train services shows that full truck loads destined for most English towns would arrive on the second day after loading at Redhill or Guildford, on the third day if going to Aberdeen. Guildford to Oxford loads would however reach their destination on the first day after loading. Loads despatched by the freight train due to leave Nine Elms Yard in London at 00.25 daily would reach Guildford at 01.33, Godalming at 06.50, and Haslemere at 07.18, the last two destinations involving a shunt into a second train at Guildford. Freight loaded into the 17.10 at Dover would reach Redhill at 02.10 that night and goods leaving Southampton Docks in the 22.30 train would reach Woking at 01.40 and, after shunting, Redhill at 05.32. These speeds are hardly striking, but were probably reasonably competitive with road transport in those pre-motorway days.

From the same 1955 source we learn that there were daily wagons despatched for carriage of small consignments from London (Bricklayers Arms) to Banstead, Caterham, Cranleigh, Dorking North, Epsom, Leatherhead, Oxted, Redhill, Tadworth, and Upper Warlingham. A similar facility existed from London (Nine Elms) to Addlestone, Camberley, Chertsey, Egham, Farnham, Godalming, Guildford, Haslemere, Shepperton, Staines, Sunbury, Walton on Thames, Weybridge, and Woking.

Private Sidings and Private Industrial Rail Systems

Most freight traffic moved through the public goods yards but as Appendix III shows, there was still enough specialised business in the 1930s to sustain over 70 private sidings . A major element here was the very heavy tonnage of coal for the public utilities, notably gasworks, some of which possessed private-owner wagons for this traffic. The railway's greatest single loss of freight business in Surrey probably took place when gas manufacture was at first centralised and then displaced by the changeover to natural gas in the 1960s.

As well as solid fuels, minerals, bricks and lime, Surrey's private sidings handled a great variety of loads: commercial and military vehicles , ambulances and fire engines and the materials required for their manufacture at Dennis, Guildford; invalid carriages at Egham; timber at Ashford and Dorking; millboard and wall coverings at Sunbury; linoleum at Staines; bones, hides and tannery products at Redhill; chemicals at Nutfield; dog biscuits at Tongham; grain and flour at Addlestone and Ewell; gunpowder at Chilworth and Holmwood; and ferro- concrete products at Shepperton. There were at least three dedicated facilities for agricultural traffic : the North Looe Farm (Gadesden's) siding, opened in 1886 a quarter mile east of Epsom Downs station; Chiphouse Farm, on the Down side east of Kingswood station, which received a private siding in 1907 , and for some 40 years from about 1856, Halliloo platform, south of Whyteleafe on the Caterham branch. This last served a farm of that name about a mile to the east, as well as doubling as a passenger platform for children attending school treats in the area. As we have seen in chapter 3, at Dorking, on the north side of the SER, Thomas Cubitt paid for a private siding to service the establishment and later the maintenance of his extensive Denbies mansion and estate.

Sidings serving industry were necessarily of standard gauge but in addition a number of industrial establishments and works possessed their own internal rail systems, usually of narrow gauge and sometimes forming an important element in the industrial process. Many of these had transhipment facilities alongside standard gauge sidings bringing in raw materials and taking away the final products. In the era when rail was the normal choice to meet other than short distance transport needs, it was the scale of operations which tended to dictate whether a private siding would be laid to connect with the national rail system, but sometimes, with labour cheaply available, if the distance between the two was not great, horse drawn cartage could be seen as a reasonable alternative to heavy outlay on a private siding, even for a sizeable operation. An example of this was the old-established lime works just north of Dorking SER station which will be mentioned later. But, before the days of the JCB and the motor dumper truck, all but the smallest of extractive sites would usually require an internal light rail layout over which tip wagons were moved by men or small locomotives. Yet here again there were exceptions as at Apted's pit, Redhill, where certainly by the late 1920s, sand was being loaded directly into main line wagons standing on a private siding.

The last private industrial rail installations to operate in Surrey were those at Holmethorpe, Redhill (referred to below) and the Redland Brickworks, Beare Green, near Dorking. Both were closed in the early 1990s . Although the examination of private rail facilities which follows is not comprehensive (*) it will serve to demonstrate the variety which once existed. We begin with the public utilities, large institutional complexes, and manufacturing industries, going on to survey the extractive industries and brickworks, enterprises so long heavily dependent on rail, and concluding with mention of some miscellaneous and perhaps unexpected Surrey users.

(*) With the exception of the gas and electricity undertakings, this has proved a difficult area to research since written accounts are scarce and Ordnance Survey maps did not always record this category of railway on the sometimes erroneous premise that certain layouts (such as those within sewage farms) were of a temporary nature.

Public Utility Undertakings

Between the years 1897 and 1940 when solid fuel was used in its pumping station off London Road, Staines, the Metropolitan Water Board (MWB) relied on the railway for supplies. Coal was moved from the Staines-Windsor branch over a three-quarter mile private siding.

On its extensive Hampton and Kempton Park estates some distance south east of Staines, the MWB installed and operated a 2ft gauge rail system of some 3 1/2 route miles. Completed in 1915, this connected the Thames-side coal wharf at Hampton with the pumping stations there and at Kempton Park, replacing horse-drawn carts formerly used for haulage of the coal and pipes off-loaded from Thames barges at Hampton. Laid with 35lb per yard flat bottom rails, this interesting and substantially-built line had gradients up to 1 in 40 with a short length of 1 in 20 and the minimum curve radius on the main part of the line was 40ft. Traffic was handled by three neat little Kerr, Stuart outside cylinder 0-4-2T, *Hampton*, *Kempton*, and *Sunbury*, later joined by *Hurst*. All four were built to the design of the Board's engineer, Sir James Restler. At its peak of activity, the line possessed 138 tipping, hopper and other wagons. There was less work for it to do after 1936 when coal conveyors were installed between the riverside wharf at Hampton and the engine houses there. With the conversion to oil firing in all the pumping stations in the 1940s, its main task was over. The line closed in 1946 and the handsome little locos were scrapped soon after.

This was not however the last of MWB rail operation. At the Kempton Park end were two pumping stations ; although only the easternmost was served by the narrow gauge line, both were reached by standard gauge tracks connected to the MWB private siding off the Shepperton branch. These lines were used for moving coal brought over the narrow gauge from the Hampton barge wharf into the fuel drops and also provided a back-up facility for rail delivery of oil and water pipes to the Kempton Park site. From 1928 the layout was worked by a 4-wheel petrol loco and later there were two 4-wheel diesels. This part of the MWB rail operations survived until August 1956.

Above *A train on the Metropolitan Water Board Railway, viewed in 1920 from Upper Sunbury Road, just across the London border* G.L. Gundry.

At Ash Road, Aldershot, just over the Hampshire border, the gas works had become sufficiently large and important by the mid-1890s to require rail access to the main system. A branch line almost a mile long, authorised by the Aldershot Gas & Water Act, 1896, built northwards from a junction just west of Tongham station, was opened for traffic about 1901. By the 1930s this line was bringing around 36,000 tons of coal a year into the works and large quantities of tar and ammoniacal liquor were moved out over it in tank wagons. At the works end, where several sidings were provided for wagon handling, there was a shed for the gas company's four standard gauge 0-4-0T locomotives. Beyond here, one track ascended on a steel incline and bridges over Ash Road into the coal store, whilst others crossed the road on the level, at one time also serving a Council depot and works. Rail activity here continued until June 1960 when gas production ceased at Aldershot, Ash Road.

A number of Surrey gas works had private sidings to allow coal to be imported by rail and by-products to be sent away. Indeed, by the latter part of the 19th century, when the railnet was almost complete, in Surrey as elsewhere, railways had become a major factor in the siting of new gasworks and electricity generating stations. Rail-served gas works existed*

(*) The dates given here relate to the period of gas production on each site, not to the life of the private sidings. Though it was often the case that the two sets of dates more or less coincided, there were exceptions, as at Leatherhead where the rail siding (shared with Faldo Asphalte) was not installed until 1906.

at Cranleigh, (1877-1933); Chertsey (1861-1936); Godstone (1892-1925); Horley (1886-1955); Leatherhead (1850-1938); Lingfield (1892-1934); Oxted (1885-1933); and Redhill (1860-1955). Yorktown (Camberley) or Blackwater gas works was served by a 1907 siding which left the SER Reading line between Blackwater and Farnborough North stations . This was at first worked by a series of outside cylinder 0-4-0ST, then from 1958 by an 0-4-0 John Fowler diesel. There was also a small internal 3ft9in gauge system in the works operated by a 1953 Planet 4-wheel diesel loco. Rail operations on this site ceased with the end of gas production in 1965. By 1867 a carter named Atkins had secured a private siding at Whyteleafe from which he carted coal into the nearby gas works in Old Barn Lane but Skuse notes that by 1891 this works was receiving fuel carted down from Upper Warlingham yard. Four years later the original siding was extended right into the gas works. Gas production on this site ceased soon after the Caterham & District Gas, Light & Coke Co. was taken over by the Croydon Gas Co. in 1905.

Many small gas works were of course active long before rail access was available. At Cobham, the coal needed for the 1869 works had to be carted over six miles of road until the L&SWR station opened in 1885. Road cartage until closure in 1912 was then reduced to just over a mile. Dorking's gasworks had been opened on the north western edge of the town in 1834 on a site which was to be very close to the SER station and goods yard when these were built 15 years later. Despite the proximity no rail connection was ever made at Dorking, where gas production continued until 1956. No doubt the expense of obtaining the necessary parliamentary powers and the cost of construction provided sufficient disincentive at time when human and animal labour were readily available at low cost, especially as this method was flexible in distributing the coal to various stacks around the site.

Some town gasworks had small internal narrow gauge layouts. usually for removing hot coke from the retort houses. The Godalming Gas & Coke Co. (later the South Eastern Gas Board and in production 1836-1957) in modern times operated two four-wheeled electric trolley wire locomotives over 2ft 9 1/2in gauge tracks. At Woking works (opened in 1892) there was never any connection to the main line; coal was delivered in barges of 200- ton capacity to a wharf at Monument Bridge, Horsell Common. From there, between 1909 and about 1935 the fuel was moved manually in 10-cwt skip wagons to the Boundary Road works coal store over a short narrow-gauge tramway . Subsequently, until closure in 1958, coal was imported by road from Wandsworth.

No example has been found of a Surrey electricity works with an internal rail system but some generating stations did receive their coal supplies (and transformers) over private sidings. Thus Reigate Corporation Electricity Department had a rail connection (off an existing sand pit siding) from the opening of the works in 1901 until its closure at the end of 1935. This access would have been a major factor in the siting decision. In 1932, at the request of the Central Electricity Authority, a private siding was installed at the country end of Byfleet (now West Byfleet) station, on the Up side. This was used to bring in the heavy equipment of a new substation and switching station and for later replacements.

Another public utility using rail was the Thames Conservancy Board, which acquired a collection of 2 f t gauge Motor Rail and Planet petrol locos and a few diesels which were used for temporary lines laid for river bank works such as the River Wey Improvement Scheme of 1931-35. The Board's plant depot was situated at Halliford, near Shepperton where at least two of the locos remained in store until the mid 1980s.

Whilst it was not unusual for the larger sewage disposal works to have light narrow gauge layouts over which tip wagons were manoeuvred manually only one such as been traced in Surrey. This was operated by Reigate Corporation at its Earlswood works.

Serving major institutions

Major institutions such as the Royal Earlswood Hospital, the Royal Holloway Sanatorium at Virginia Water and the Kensington & Chelsea District Schools at Banstead all had the benefit of private sidings to receive deliveries of solid fuel and other bulk supplies.

Something more was needed by the London County Council's vast mental hospitals complex at Epsom, which grew into what was almost a small town in its own right, with a peak population of around 7,200 patients and staff between the wars. When construction of these hospitals was first started, the contractors brought building materials in by road from the goods yard at Epsom Town (LB&SCR), using horses and steam traction engines. In 1902 the LCC opened Horton, the first of several large hospitals for mental patients and completed conversion of the existing Horton Manor for the same purpose. St Ebba's, a colony for epileptics,was ready in the following year. By this time the local authorities , becoming concerned about the damage being inflicted on their soft-topped roads by the contractor's steam traction engines, produced a bylaw restricting the hours in which the road locomotives could be used. Faced with the possibility of large claims for compensation, and delays in completing the contract, Foster & Dicksee, contractors for the superstructure of the third hospital, Long Grove, decided to obtain a Light Railway Order, purchasing land for exchange sidings alongside the L&SWR Up line immediately south of what is now Ewell West station. The resulting standard gauge single track railway, which ran west from the exchange sidings and then south to the Long Grove site came into use on 20 April 1905, worked by the Manning Wardle 0-6-0ST *Hollymoor.*

Below *Horton Light Railway* Hendon *with a coal train for the Hospital Power Station in January 1938* Greater London Council.

At the Long Grove Hospital, completed in 1907, up to 11,000 men were employed on construction, about 900 of them brought in daily from London in special trains running to and from Ewell L&SWR. Impressed by the contractor's line, the LCC decided to build a permanent railway to serve the whole estate. As authorised by the London County Council (General Powers) Act of 16 August 1909, this was to comprise a main 'siding' of 3 miles 5 chains from just south of the Chessington Road bridge at Ewell L&SWR station to West Park, with branch 'sidings' to St Ebba's Colony (2 furlongs 4 chains, not built), Long Grove (4 furlongs 4 chains) and the Central Pumping Station and Electric Light Works (3 furlongs 3 chains, terminating at a point less than a quarter of a mile from the Horton and Manor Hospitals but on the opposite side of Horton Lane). The legislation allowed the LCC to work the system itself, providing all necessary plant and rolling stock.

Between Ewell station and Long Grove, the course of the LCC railway ran north of the contractor's line, much closer to the Chessington Road. Its single track with passing loops was formed of lightweight flat-bottom rails spiked to wooden sleepers set in ash ballast. At some locations, the line was enclosed between high fences to hide the trains from patients who might otherwise be provoked into attempting suicide. A footbridge was similarly screened.

When LCC operation of the railway began in May 1913 an early task was delivery of materials for the construction of West Park Hospital. Although work started in 1915, progress was delayed by wartime and immediate post war constraints and the hospital was not ready until June 1924.

The first locomotive under the LCC regime was an Andrew Barclay 0-4-0ST named *Crossness* which had been purchased by the Council's Works Department in 1904 for the Southern Outfall Sewer improvement scheme completed in 1908. This engine was kept in a shed at the end of the Central Electric Light and Pumping Station branch. Five dumb-buffered three-plank timber-framed wagons were also bought but there was no passenger stock, the line being used solely to bring in stores, building materials and solid fuels in main line wagons and to take out boiler ash and clinker. Even under the pressures of wartime, with Horton and The Manor in use as military hospitals in 1915-19, the wounded and sick troops were carried from a special platform at Epsom L&SWR station in motor ambulances. When Horton became a military hospital again in World War 2, the patients were ferried from local stations by road ambulance, although use of railway ambulance coaches was apparently considered.

Between the wars, increasing amounts of hospital supplies were diverted to road transport, leaving the railway to carry around 15,000 tons of fuel to the power house and estate glasshouses alongside the Power Station spur. A second locomotive, a 1926 Manning Wardle 0-6-0ST, *Hendon*, was acquired from the St Helier LCC Housing Estate contractors C J Wills & Son in 1935. In 1947 this was sold and replaced by a new Robert Stephenson & Hawthorns outside cylinder 0-4-0T which bore no nameplate. When the LCC hospitals were transferred to the National Health Service in 1949, the new management decided to close the railway, by then requiring some costly renewals. Early in 1950, the three-year old locomotive, the track and some of the wagons were sold for further use elsewhere but the exchange sidings at Ewell remained in place until the late 1950s. It is still possible to trace the alignment of much of the railway in the Horton Country Park, where it forms a footpath.[3]

Small internal layouts on Commercial Premises

Before describing the internal rail layouts associated with the extractive industries and brickworks, mention should be made of the very small number of other such installations on commercial premises.

Coxe's Lock Mill at Addlestone, a watermill on the Wey Navigation dating from 1777, was converted to a turbine roller mill in 1900 and equipped with a large grain silo. Although the wheat continued to be imported by barge from the London docks, the enlarged mill was then connected to the main rail system by a private siding, mainly to move out the increased production of finished flour and other products. A small internal narrow gauge layout was also installed to connect the private siding with the

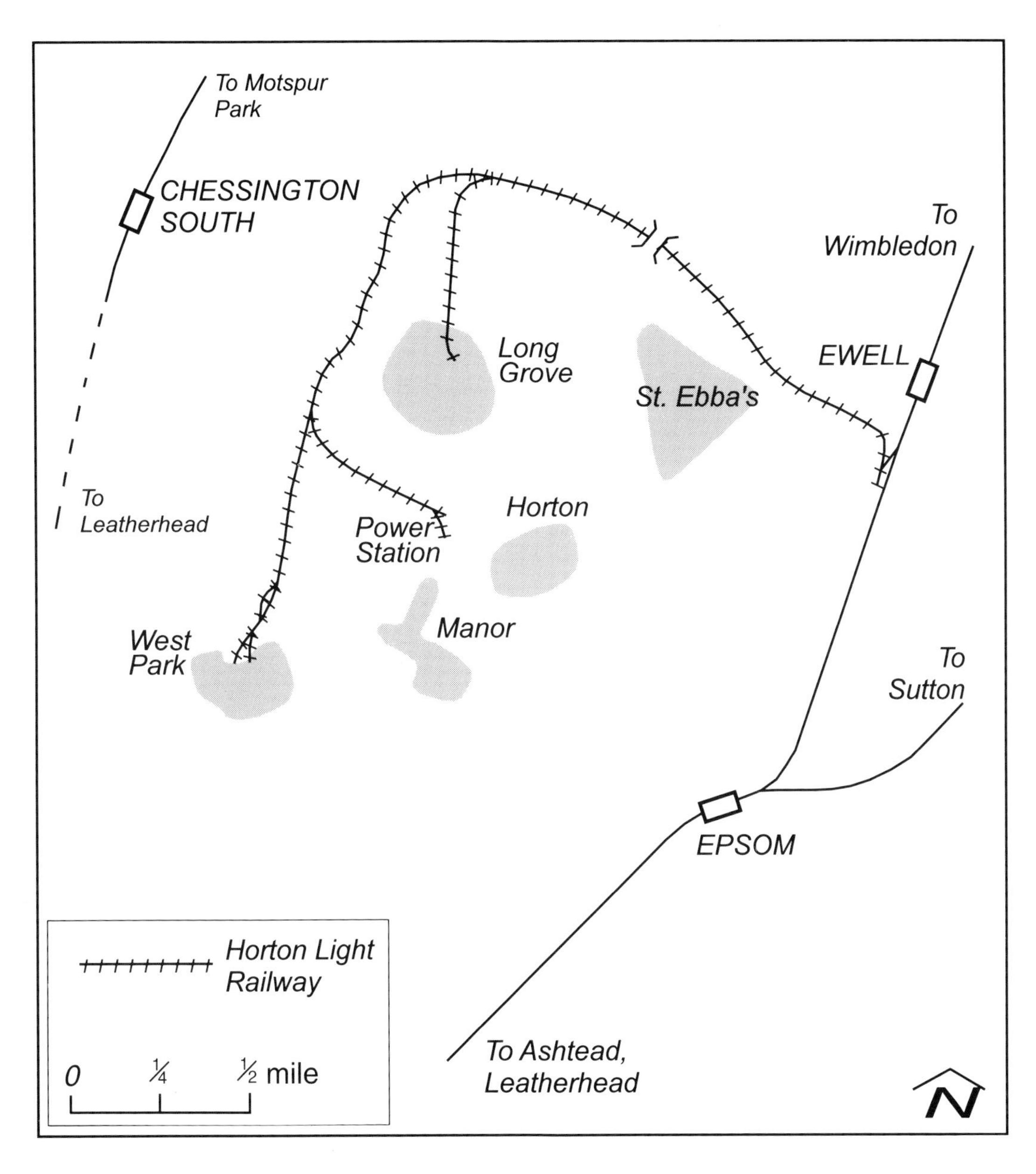

Above *The Horton Light Railway.*

western side of the site. Within the boundary, rail wagons were winched over the tracks, using a Ransomes & Rapier electric capstan, supplied in 1905. From around 1964, imported wheat mostly came in by rail but the mill ceased production in 1983.

At Dorking from around the middle of the 19th century, Brooker's Timber Works (also known as Taylor & Brooker and the British Timber Works) made, amongst other items, railway fencing, compressed oak railway keys, treenails and navvy barrows (navvies usually had to buy their own, at around 10s6d). About 1900, when this establishment was at its peak of development with over 100 employees and several acres of stacking yards, a narrow gauge system was installed for internal transport purposes. Trucks were manhandled and curiously, the layout did not enter the adjacent SER goods yard, despite the advantages this would have given in easing transhipment. This firm had ceased business here by 1936 and the site was acquired in January 1938 for expansion of the adjacent gasworks. Another timber works with its own narrow gauge system existed at Pitfold Mill, Haslemere, a site formerly devoted to paper bleaching and later, leather manufacture.

A variation on this theme, mentioned by Davis, was the provision towards the end of the 19th century of a 400yd single track with passing loop to connect Egham goods yard with the storehouse of a seed and corn merchant at the corner of the High Street and Station Road, and apparently worked by horses. The existence of this installation is confirmed by its appearance on large scale Ordnance Survey maps.

The Linoleum Works at Staines. served from May 1887 by a siding from the GWR (and later by another from the L&SWR) eventually possessed both narrow and standard gauge internal lines in a layout of some complexity over which wagons were moved by horses. Latterly concrete was laid to facilitate the use of industrial road tractors for the shunting of rail vehicles, but the whole system went out of use in 1965.

In 1927 the Vulcanised Fibre Co was established at Broadford Mills, Shalford, on the southern outskirts of Guildford. With the approach of World War 2, the activity here expanded until around 600 were employed. A 4-wheel Lister petrol locomotive was acquired in 1939 to work about 200yd of 2ft gauge track linking Stonebridge Wharf (where coal was delivered from London by barge over the River Wey) to the works boiler house. With conversion to oil firing in March 1947 this little operation fell out of use, but the factory survived for another 20 years.

Though not an internal layout in the usual sense, the 31-acre Dennis Brothers motor vehicle works, opened in 1905 at Woodbridge Hill, Guildford, boasted a fairly elaborate group of private sidings which entered the factory area and were connected at the other end to the Up side of the Reading line. Shunting here was at first undertaken by a 4-wheel petrol loco built by Dennis in about 1913 using some of the firm's contemporary road lorry parts. In 1942, when the works was very busy with military orders, this loco was replaced by a new Ruston & Hornsby 4-wheel diesel named *William*. After the sidings here were closed in 1963, *William* was sold for further service elsewhere.

Chalk Extraction and Lime Works

Under this heading, pride of place must go to the complex of chalk pits and lime works just north of Betchworth station, which provided perhaps the largest and most spectacular industrial railway layout in Surrey. From 1865 the site was owned by the Dorking Greystone Lime Co., incorporated in that year by local and Kentish interests to take over workings begun many years earlier on a small scale[4]. Extraction of chalk was pursued with vigour here for many years until the workings reached a width of over a quarter of a mile and a height of 300ft, producing a scar on the North Downs which remains visible today over long distances. This expansion of what had previously been a very minor enterprise was much assisted by the close proximity of the SER Redhill and Reading line. From 1866 the works were served by a siding which climbed steeply from behind the Up (north) passenger platform of Betchworth station to reach the lime kilns. There was an internal standard gauge layout to transport hydrated or lump lime from the kilns and, after 1924, from the hydrator plant.

The siding was for many years in heavy use to carry the finished lime products (and later also white chalk) down to the main line and bring in trucks loaded with coal to feed the kilns. The SER extended its approach to the siding in 1875. Initially worked by horses, the Betchworth standard gauge lines received their first steam locomotive in 1871, a geared, vertical-boilered and cylindered machine built by Thomas Howard Head of Stockton on Tees. Inevitably nicknamed Coffeepot by the

Top Right *Standard gauge* Coffeepot *hauling a transporter wagon loaded with 2ft gauge skips at Dorking Greystone Lime Works, near Betchworth station, c 1938.*

Right *Ruston & Hornsby 4-wheel diesel* William *(built 1942) shunting coal wagons on Messrs. Dennis' private siding, Guildford, probably in the 1950s* Courtesy Dennis Specialist Vehicles Ltd.

WILLIAM

workmen, it served the company continuously for 81 years. Two further standard gauge locos of more conventional appearance, an 0-4-0ST and an 0-4-0T, were acquired in 1875 and 1877 respectively. The instability of the saddle tank led to its disposal after three years but the 1877 engine, a product of Fletcher Jennings & Co. of Whitehaven, worked at Betchworth until 1960.

A second system, with the unusual gauge of 3ft 2 1/4in, was installed at a higher level to link the chalk pits with the tops of the kilns. This was initially worked by horses but two 0-4-0T steam locomotives (nos. 4 & 5) were supplied by Fletcher Jennings in 1880. As the terrace-worked extraction process moved to new high level workings, the 1 in 2 'Great Incline' was built to carry loaded wagons down. Since this gradient was far too steep for locomotive working, the empty trucks were moved up by wire ropes which passed over rollers and were attached at the other end to a steam locomotive descending a second, much gentler gradient set at an angle at a lower level. The reverse procedure applied when loaded trucks came downhill. This Heath Robinson arrangement was the scene of a spectacular accident in January 1937 when the cable broke and loco no.4 was thrown off the ledge of its incline track by the impact of the runaway wagons, landing on its side after an 8ft drop, Fortunately the driver jumped to safety and there was no major damage.

At the higher levels of the Upper Western Pit, 3ft2 1/4in gauge trucks were moved manually until 1945, when a second-hand Montania diesel locomotive (built by Orenstein & Koppel in 1936) was obtained and converted by the importers from 2ft to 3ft 2 1/4in gauge. The Eastern Greystone Pit, opened in 1930, was served by a new 300yd 3ft2 1/4 gauge line, which ran due south to the tops of the kilns and was steam- worked until 1952. In that year a second Montania diesel (Orenstein & Koppel, 1937) arrived. Since this was 2ft gauge, the top line in the Upper Eastern pit was relaid to allow it to be used there. The 'Great Incline' was then abandoned and replaced by a conveyor belt which linked the new top level 2ft gauge line to the 1930 3ft2 1/4in gauge connection between the Eastern Greystone Pit and the kilns, this line then being worked by the earlier Montania diesel. Before chalk extraction finally ceased, much of the 'Great Incline' had been quarried away.

A second 2ft gauge layout, manually-operated, connected the kilns to the 1924 hydrator plant, passing over the standard gauge line. This became the last rail operation on the site, surviving until a new hydrator plant was built next to the kilns in 1963. There was also a 2ft gauge line serving the associated hearthstone mines, to be mentioned later.

This complicated mix of rail operations was serviced by an internal engineering workshop which carried out locomotive repairs, also taking in similar work for other Surrey industrial railways, including those at Merstham and Oxted.

Chalk and hearthstone extraction and lime production at Betchworth continued through World War 2, aided by German prisoners of war brought in daily from the Aldershot area by special trains. With the return of peace, road transport gradually assumed the larger share of the movements into and out of the works and by the end of the 1950s, the traffic accepted by BR at Betchworth station was reduced to one or two wagons of lime a week, still brought down from the kilns by a steam locomotive.

The glorious assortment of rail transport on this site and the extended use of steam locomotives well into the era of the internal combustion engine and road trucks was not unconnected with the fact that E W Taylerson, the managing director from 1926-1960, was a mechanical and locomotive engineer with a strong affection for railways. It was he who named the locomotives and ensured that even when the older ones were retired in the 1950s they were kept under cover on the site. When the business was re-formed as the Dorking Lime Co. Ltd. in 1959, the new management decided to transfer all internal and external transport to road vehicles and with the exception of the manhandled trucks of the hydrator line, which lasted another three years, rail operation on the site ceased in 1960.

Another rail-served site between the Redhill-Reading line and the North Downs existed at Brockham, between Dorking and Betchworth. Chalk extraction and lime making began here well before the railway arrived and a brickworks had been established alongside by the late 1860s. A private siding off the SER about 3/4m west of Betchworth station, provided in 1866 or 1867, was extended on the SER side of the gate in 1875. Brick making here was taken over by the Brockham Brick, Stone & Coal Co. in 1873 and from the following year by the Brockham

Brick Co. (BBC) which soon also began to exploit the under lying hearthstone and sand to the south of the main line. We shall return to these activities later, but here we are concerned with the lime making and chalk extraction, which passed into the control of the BBC from 1881. In the lime kilns yard, horses were used to move standard gauge wagons but the steeply-graded siding up from the SER, unsuitable for locomotives, was worked partly by horses and partly by cable moved by a stationary steam engine.

The chalk pits at a higher level were served by an isolated 2ft gauge layout linked to the tops of the limekilns worked throughout its life by horses. Ordnance Survey maps reveal that this narrow gauge system was considerably expanded between 1882 and 1914, suggesting a significant growth in the extraction activity. Following the bankruptcy of the BBC in 1910, only the chalk pits and lime making remained under a new firm, the Brockham Lime & Hearthstone Co. This company fell on hard times in the 1920s and final closure came in the summer of 1936.

The site then remained largely undisturbed until 1962, when efforts began to establish a narrow gauge railway museum. Various locomotives and other industrial railway equipment were assembled, but when Surrey County Council took over the freehold in 1977, it ruled that the very narrow and restricted approach, a lane with a level crossing over the Redhill-Reading line, was unsuitable for public access . Following the formation of the Chalk Pits Museum at Amberley, Sussex, in 1979, a decision was made to transfer all activities and most of the exhibits to that location.

Dorking town' s chalkpits and lime kilns below Ranmore, well-established long before the arrival of the railway in 1849, produced a high-quality lime valued for its property of hardening under water. Latterly this site possessed a small internal 2ft gauge light railway system using manhandled V-tip wagons; physical connection to the nearby SER was never achieved, probably because of the difficulties created by the difference in levels and the necessity of crossing a public road. Work here ceased at the start of World War 2.

Still further west, but in a similar situation to the three sites just mentioned, were the coke-fired kilns of the Mid-Surrey Lime Works. Rail access was provided by Evelyn's Siding and ground frame, opened in October 1926 on the Up (north) side of the main line, at White Down Lane east of Gomshall station. Chalk was brought down to the kilns from pits higher up the scarp of the North Downs in wagons moved over a wire cable-worked incline of 2ft gauge. A combination of national financial depression and poor quality lime caused the enterprise to fail and the plant was offered for sale in 1932. As was not unusual, the railway company, hopeful of alternative use, left the private siding connection in place for some time afterwards. It was eventually removed in 1940.[5]

East of Reigate were two other rail-connected North Downs lime works, at Merstham and at Oxted. Merstham was served by the 1805 Croydon, Merstham and Godstone Iron Railway mentioned in chapter 1 and when that disappeared, was connected to the London & Brighton Railway around the time that opened in 1841. This lengthy approach, variously known as Peters', Ashcombe, or the Grey-stone Lime Works siding, left the main line at milepost 20 1/2, north of Merstham station , then running north east and throwing off an east ward branch to serve the stone workings. When the Redhill cut-off (the Quarry Line) was built in 1899, the siding was carried over the new line by a bridge but the hearthstone branch disappeared.

In the railway era the Merstham site was worked until 1864 by G V Hall and his three sons, using horses. Subsequently the pit was operated by the Peters family, who introduced steam locos, eventually possessing four outside cylinder 0-4-0ST, one of which was rebuilt by Sentinel in 1928 with that firm's vertical boiler and geared engine unit. Latterly there was also a 4-wheel geared Sentinel steam loco incorporating the power unit of the 1927 Jersey Eastern Railway passenger railcar *Brittany*. With the closure of the Merstham Grey-stone Lime Co.[6] operations about 1946, the 1927 Sentinel saw further service hauling sand at the Holmethorpe site, to be noticed later. At the time of writing, a short section of the siding track remains in situ in the woods between the old Brighton line and the Quarry line; the parapets and top of the southern face of the arch of the bridge carrying Limeworks Road over the siding can also be seen.

The other major chalkpits and lime works site below the southern scarp of the Surrey North

Downs was situated about 700yd south of Oxted tunnel on the east side of the line. Activities here, which had begun before the arrival of the railway, were greatly expanded after the 1885 formation of the Oxted Greystone Lime Company Ltd. Eventually there was an impressive array of 12 kilns, all in line. This locally-based firm installed an internal rail system and connected their works to the 1884 LB&SCR/SER Joint Line by a 3/4 mile standard gauge branch equipped at the south end with a loco shed. By 1898 the traffic handled here justified replacement of the ground frame with Oxted Lime Sidings Box, which was staffed throughout traffic hours. Two exchange sidings were added on the Lime Co. land about 1901. The latter year also saw repositioning of the signal box to the Up side, where it remained until March 1933, after which entry to the siding was via a ground frame controlled from Woldingham box. On its standard gauge lines, the Lime Co. moved wagons with its own steam locos, owning a total of four, though not all were in stock at the same time. As at Betchworth, the more flexible 2ft gauge was chosen to move the chalk to the tops of the lime kilns and this layout was worked latterly with a 4-wheel petrol loco and four Orenstein & Keppel diesel locos . There were two levels, connected by a chain-operated incline. The standard gauge lines at Oxted fell out of use around 1947-48 but not all were lifted until the early 1960s. Most of the narrow gauge was replaced by road trucks in 1953 but about 50 metres was retained for accurate feeding of the kiln mouths until early in 1970.

Brickworks

Since brickworks were normally sited at or near deposits of brick earth or clay, they were not necessarily easily or economically connected to the main rail system. If of sizeable extent, it was usual for there to be some form of internal tramway at the pits and perhaps between the pits and the kilns. In addition what were sometimes separate lines might be found at the production site. Brickworks which could be connected to the main railway network enjoyed an economic advantage since the manufacturing process demanded a considerable quantity of coal - about one ton was needed to fire 16,500-17,000 bricks.

An example of a typical rail-served brickworks was that sited between Oxted and Lingfield stations on the Up (west) side. a mile south of the bridge carrying the Redhill-Tonbridge line. Here the two private sidings of the Lingfield Works of the Sussex Brick Co. (latterly Redland) saw a regular inward movement of coal for the brick kilns and outward transit of the finished bricks. Coal traffic ceased with the 1950s conversion to oil firing but inward movement of domestic refuse for tipping into the old clay pits and outward conveyance of bricks continued until the 1960s. Operations here were controlled from the adjacent Lingfield Intermediate Box until 10 August 1958, when this was replaced by a ground frame remotely released from Lingfield Station Box. Loaded wagons were worked into Lingfield station by the daily pick-up freight train and on the Up journey, its locomotive would shunt them into the Brick Works siding, moving out any empty wagons and others loaded with bricks. Until the early 1950s there was also a 2ft gauge layout in the clay pit, worked by two 4-wheel petrol locos and a 4-wheel battery electric mounted on a wagon chassis.

A small brick and tile works was opened just west of South Nutfield station in the 1880s to supply the needs of the Henry Edwards residential developments mentioned in chapter 6. In 1925 the site was acquired by the Nutfield Manufacturing Co. for production of hydrofluoric acid and other chemicals. This later activity, served by a long private siding from the Up line, had ceased by 1984, when the plant was demolished and replaced by a housing estate.

Also on this section of line, a private siding was opened in 1896 for a brickworks just south of the railway about 3/4 mile west of Godstone station. This operated under various names (Trollope's, Williams', the South Eastern Brick & Terracotta Works and Lambe's). Under the Lambe regime, there was an 18in gauge cable-worked system down an incline into the claypit and some standard gauge lines including the connection to the main line. This site was requisitioned to serve as an ammunition dump in World War 1, reverted to a brickworks af-

Above *This view of c.1910, shows a Down train which has just left the south end of Oxted Tunnel passing the Exchange Sidings with Oxted Greystone Lime Co. One of that undertaking's standard gauge locomotives is approaching the engine shed with a loaded train brought down from the kilns.*

terwards, and then became a Canadian armoured fighting vehicle depot in World War 2. Brick making was once more resumed , still continuing at the time of writing. A short standard gauge line between a clay stockpile and the works survived into the 1970s but the narrow gauge had fallen out of use some time earlier. Standard gauge tracks remain in use at the time of writing to allow dumping of old railway ballast in the claypits.

Further east on the same line, at Crowhurst Lane End, near the Kent border and opposite the public siding mentioned earlier, was the Tandridge Brick & Tile Works. This had no connection of its own to the main line but did possess a 2ft gauge tramway worked latterly by two petrol locos, which brought clay from pits situated rather more than a quarter mile to the south east.

Two brickworks, both with private sidings, existed between Worcester Park and Epsom. Cunliffe's Siding was installed for the Worcester Park Brick Co. (later the Wanborough Brick & Tile Co), south of Worcester Park station, on the Up side between the present Inveresk Gardens and Cunliffe Road. Brick production here started in 1898. The works was reached by a siding parallel to the L&SWR but rising above it , with wagons moved up by rope haulage beyond the gate. This facility seems to have been used mainly to bring coal in to the kilns, most of the brick output apparently being distributed by road for local housing construction. The 1909 working timetable shows a daily train into the siding, but no loaded working outwards. A little further south, Messrs. Stone & Company's establishment on the Down side between Ewell West and Epsom, dating from about 1922, had not only a standard gauge siding but an internal narrow gauge horse-worked system. The layout here was changed in 1926. This company had previously operated a works on the LB&SCR close to Epsom station. Both Cunliffe's and Stone's sidings were worked by ground frames released from Ewell West signal box and both had fallen out of use by the 1950s following cessation of brick production.

A large brickfield established by John Earley Cook at Little Heath, on the Up (west) side between Oxshott and Cobham stations, possessed a private siding which dated from the railway's arrival here in 1885. London rubbish brought in by rail was burned on the site to produce ash which was used to make a cheap type of brick. After Cook's death, the yard was taken over by W E Benton whose name was then attached to the siding. This facility remained active until brickmaking ceased in 1959. A housing estate was subsequently erected around the waterlogged claypit[7].

After some 30 years of operation to meet purely local requirements, the tiny Lee-Steere brickworks, using adjacent deposits of sand and weald clay, found itself close to Ockley & Capel station when this opened in 1867. A weekly traffic of about three trucks of bricks developed, with railborne coal coming in to feed the kilns. A start was made in 1913 on construction of a private siding into the site but this was never completed because production was brought to an end in 1914 following the discovery that the supply of clay was at the point of exhaustion.[8]

Buckland Tile Works, which operated until the 1930s north of the Guildford-Redhill line at Clifton Lane had a private siding off the Up road. Military use of this site has been mentioned in chapter 7.

Brickmaking at Brockham, in the Crabtree brickfield just south east of the lime works mentioned earlier, had begun by the 1860s. A large pit was dug in the Gault Clay and by the 1890s the site was served by a standard gauge spur connecting the kilns to the lime works private siding. Brickmaking ceased around 1910 and the 1914 Ordnance Survey 25in plan shows that most of the rail tracks had been removed by then.

Several Surrey brickworks isolated from the main rail system acquired internal railways. One such was opened about 1870 at North Holmwood on the Weald clay south of Dorking. Producing the very hard dark red high quality Dorking bricks, this operation was to become the Dorking Brick Co., then the Sussex & Dorking United Brick Co., and finally Redland Bricks. A 2ft gauge layout, bringing clay through a subway from a pit on the opposite side of Inholms Lane, initially worked with horse traction , was later in part powered by stationary engines and ropes. Three diesel locomotives were acquired in the 1950s and from 1952 this site boasted a crude system of automatic driverless working using three 4- wheel battery-electric locomotives. Operations at North Holmwood ceased in May 1981, allowing much of the area to be covered with small houses.

Phorpres Clock House brick and tile works, opened in 1932 on a site 1 1/4 miles south east of Ockley station, at one time employed a workforce of 250. Although the works were less than a quarter mile east of the Dorking- Horsham line, no private siding was ever built, the bricks and coal moving by road lorry to and from Ockley station until rail freight facilities were withdrawn in 1962[9]. Until 1963 this works was served by an internal 2ft gauge line with four 4-wheel diesel locos which moved clay from the pits to the production area in V-skips. In the kilns area there were also 2ft 11in and 3ft 11in gauge electric lines with a mixture of third rail and overhead trolley wire traction supply operated by five 4-wheel locos. The 3ft 11in gauge was closed about 1965, the other in 1978.[10]

In addition to those brickworks already mentioned, Surrey had a few others with small internal rail layouts, all of 2ft gauge. These are listed in Chapter Note 11.

Fullers Earth

Fullers earth was extracted and processed at three Surrey locations possessing internal rail lines, two at sites some distance from ordinary railways. These last, owned by Fullers Earth Union Ltd, were the Park Works (Cockley Quarry), north west of Nutfield village and the Fullers Earth Works, Copyhold Quarry, Redhill, east of Redstone Hill. Both had 3ft gauge lines worked by 4-wheel Planet petrol and 4 wheel diesel locos until the 1950s.

The third site was that of the Baynards Estate Fullers Earth Co. (later F W Berk). Baynards Estate took over a brickworks with standard gauge tracks connected to the Guildford-Horsham line near Baynards station. It acquired from the brick company a vertical boilered 0-4-0T and this was rebuilt as a petrol loco which worked until 1949, when a standard gauge Motor Rail 4-wheel diesel was purchased . There was also a 2ft gauge line in the pit a short distance away, this worked by a 4-wheel petrol loco until the late 1940s. The site received its final train load of sulphur a week before the complete closure of the Guildford-Horsham line in June 1965.

Sand and Gravel Extraction

Good quality industrial sand deposits north of Redhill in the area known as Holmethorpe were worked successively by the Standard Brick Co., the Standard Brick & Sand Co. , British Industrial Sands and Hepworth Mineral & Chemical Co. The pits, east of the old main line, together with the adjacent Ormside Silica Works, were from 1867 linked to the railway system by the Holmethorpe siding, controlled until 1983 by a dedicated signal box on the Up or west side of the line between Redhill and Merstham stations. The Sand Co. employed two vertical boiler geared 4-wheel steam locos acquired from J S Peters, Merstham Lime Works and also possessed a 4-wheel Motor Rail petrol loco. Later other 4-wheel diesels arrived. As was not unusual when sand or gravel was extracted on a sizeable scale, there was an ancillary narrow gauge system serving the standard gauge outlet. This was 2 ft gauge and was worked originally by two 0-6-0WT, later by a sizeable fleet of 4-wheel diesels, acquired new and secondhand and a sole 4-wheel battery loco. The internal narrow gauge lines were replaced by conveyor belts in 1963/4. Sand traffic out of Holmethorpe, latterly for glass making at Warrington, was still reaching up to 300 tons daily in the late 1980s but use of rail ceased soon after, bringing closure of the private siding around 1990.

Apted' s Pit, a much smaller operation nearby, between Redhill and Reigate stations, on the Up or north side of the line south of Wray Common, exploited the medium to coarse-grained white or silver sands of the Folkestone Beds, which were principally used for scouring purposes. From the last quarter of the 19th century until around the 1940s, this Pit was entered by a private siding from the SER, which, as already noted, also provided rail access to the adjacent Reigate Corporation electricity works of 1901. Hall & Company's sandpit at Redhill was exporting about 70 tons daily via the LBSCR in 1902.

Another sand pit in the area, located in Broome Park, on the north side of the old Reigate-Dorking road, was reached by a standard gauge line constructed by the Brockham Brick Company (BBC) from its brickworks private siding mentioned earlier. This passed under the SER and appears to have come into use by the l890s, its wagons hauled by horses. When the BBC ceased trading in 1910, it became derelict and the tracks had mostly been removed at the time of the survey for the 1914 edition of the 25 in. Ordnance Map.

Nearby was the 2f t gauge system, almost a mile in extent, of the Buckland Sand & Silica Co, passing under the Reigate-Dorking line to connect the Buckland Tile Works mentioned above to two sand pits north of the Dorking-Reigate road. Operation began about 1928. An ex-Air Ministry Hudswell Clarke 0-4-0WT of 1918 was supplemented by five 4-wheel petrol and diesel locos, all purchased new from 1928-40, these surviving until the line was closed in 1952.

Buckland' s 1918 loco serves as a reminder that following the end of World War 1, the availability of very cheap military light railway equipment from the War Surplus Disposals Board caused some industrial light railway users to use 60 cm gauge equipment which in practice, given the rough and ready nature of the operations, could be mixed with 2f t gauge with little difficulty. One example of this appeared at Weydon Lane, Farnham, where the private siding to the sand and gravel pits of Thomas Patterson & Son (later Ballast Producers Ltd) was fed until around 1950 by a 60cm/2ft layout employing three petrol locos, including two ex-War Department 20 hp Motor Rail machines. Other lines at Farnham for working sand and gravel existed at Ballast Producers Lt d/Hyde-Crete Ltd, Alton Road, Upper Hale and at Farnham Flint, Gravel & Sand Co, Coxbridge, both using petrol or diesel locos on 2ft gauge. All the Farnham sand systems mentioned had ceased operation by the early 1950s.

Lines of 2ft/60cm gauge built to handle sand, gravel and grit with locomotives and tip wagons were also to be found at several other Surrey locations, as listed in Chapter Note 12.

Building Stone, Hearthstone and Concrete

The very first examples of private industrial railways in the county were the plateways associated with the underground extraction of building stone from the Upper Greensand of east Surrey at Merstham, where the firestone quarries were served by the CM&GIR (chapter 1); at nearby Godstone Hill (a mile north of Godstone village); and at Winders Hill and Marden (both near the South Lodge of Marden Park). That these plateways came into use as early as the first decades of the 19th century is evident from discoveries made in recent years of rails similar to those used by the CM&GIR and indeed in some cases marked with these initials, so presumably second hand from that source.[13] The plates were attached directly to the floor of the mine workings. It has also been found that the walls in the mine exhibit marks made by the whippletree which held the harness of the towing horses. Further evidence of the early date of these lines is the appearance of the Merstham plateway in a watercolour by John Hassell dated 1823. At Godstone Hill, where the workings remained active until the 1940s, photographs taken around 1901 indicate that in the main gallery more modern. lightweight narrow gauge track had by that time been laid over the original plateway. The later hearthstone mine at Marden also had lightweight narrow gauge track which appears to have been laid on the floor and moved around as required.

A light railway layout was also in use from the late 19th century at the Colley Hill hearthstone mine near Reigate. The main length ran some 900ft into the adit, terminating some 400ft below the hill. Workings here continued until the 1960s, latterly with manhandling of the wagons instead of the horse traction formerly used. Colley Hill's output was carted by road downhill to the SER (later SR) at Taylor's Siding. This, with its dedicated signal box, was sited on the west side of Colley Lane about 3/4m west of Reigate station. It went out of use after mining operations under Colley Hill ceased.

From 1908 until the 1950s, at the Surrey Hearthstone Mines, beneath the Betchworth lime works, a 1 ft7in gauge line was operated by a stationary winding engine, (latterly an electric motor), which hauled the skips filled with stone up the main drive to the surface transfer shed where the contents were loaded into standard gauge main line wagons.

Hearthstone mining at the Brockham lime works started around 1873 continuing, with some periods of inactivity, until 1925. The underground gauge workings here were served by narrow gauge tracks (probably 2 ft gauge), with horses hauling the wagons.

Bargate stone was quarried around Godalming. The largest site, at Ockford Hill, on the south western edge of the town, was served by a 1/4-mile private siding off the Down Portsmouth Line about 3/4 mile south of Godalming station. There was also a small internal narrow gauge layout. By the 1930s this type of stone had fallen out of use for building purposes, and after experiment, had also proved itself unsuitable for metalling modern motor roads. The siding closed in 1935, quarrying on this site ceasing soon after.

Although not an extractive industry, mention may be made here of the Norcon Ltd (Redland Pipes from 1962) concrete works at Ripley, which possessed a 2ft gauge system worked with three 4-wheel diesel locos until 1975. This was used to move the completed pipe sections (the main product) around the site.

Given the absence of canals and navigable rivers in central and east Surrey and the difficulty of moving heavy freight in bulk by horse-drawn vehicles over totally inadequate and soft topped roads, it is clear that but for the railway, in the hundred years or so after 1840, most of the industries mentioned above would have found it virtually impossible to expand their activities beyond the very small quantities required to satisfy the demands of the immediate locality. Use of railways on the site itself also made the extraction of chalk, sand, gravel, building stone, hearthstone and fullers earth easier and cheaper by reducing the demands on manpower.

Gunpowder at Chilworth at and Holmwood

North of Chilworth station on the Guildford-Redhill line there existed until 1920 a rail-served industrial installation unique in Surrey. As far back as the early 17th century this site on the Tillingbourne river had been devoted to gunpowder production, initially by the East India Company.[14] The arrival of the SER in 1849 seems not to have affected in any way the long-standing use of road carts for moving materials into and out of the site or the internal use of wheel barrows and punts. However the year 1885 marked the beginning of a new era, as the factory was then taken over by a German firm which installed an internal tramway system of 800mm gauge, using German equipment. At first about 1 1/2 miles (2.6km) in length, the tramway was extended south in 1889, crossing the Dorking-Guildford road on the level, to reach transhipment facilities at a new private siding just west of Chilworth & Albury SER station. With expansion of the works increasing, the consumption of coal required for charcoal burning and for the steam-powered gunpowder mills, rail transport of incoming supplies offered the most favourable solution.

Within the works, the wooden trams were moved by two men, as were the empties up to the SER siding. It was fortunate that the lie of the land provided gravitational assistance for loaded trams, each of which carried about a ton of coal. Gunpowder was moved around the site in trams with wooden bodies bound with brass instead of steel, and where close to buildings sensitive to explosion, the track was built of wood. War and preparations for war caused the works to be further enlarged and with it the tramway, which by 1914 had reached a maximum route length of over three miles (5.2km). Located in an otherwise rural area, the labour force of around 300 formed a close-knit community, organising social events, including an annual outing to the seaside in special trains from Chilworth station.

In 1915 the Chilworth site was further enlarged by the construction of an Admiralty Cordite Works. This addition, to the north east of the older buildings, added further to the already considerable strategic importance of the Redhill-Reading line during World War 1. An internal tramway system of unknown gauge served all production buildings but no attempt appears to have been made to provide connection with the 800mm layout in the Gunpowder Works or the railway sidings at Chilworth station. A steep drop in demand for cordite and gunpowder after the end of World War 1 and keen competition from Belgian suppliers led to closure of the whole site in 1920. Nature then took over , but there remained enough relics, including narrow gauge sleepers and a tramway swing bridge over the Mill Stream to attract and intrigue the enthusiastic devotees of industrial archaeology .

Gunpowder was also handled at Holmwood station, where it arrived in the special vans which the main line railways provided for this purpose. It was destined for the Schermuly Pistol Rocket Apparatus Works at Newdigate, which also manufactured marine flares and Verey Lights. Schermuly had come to this rural location in 1933 and for some 30 years their products were despatched by rail through Holmwood yard. This traffic reached a peak in World War 2 and continued until the closure of the Holmwood freight yard in 1964.

Nurserymen and Market Gardeners benefit from the Railway

Although not favourable to agriculture, the peaty, sandy soils around Bagshot were found to produce vigorous growth in azaleas and rhododendrons. This characteristic was exploited from around 1795 in nursery grounds set up by Messrs. Waterer and others specialising in all types of hardy trees and ornamental shrubs, and nurserymen were among the traders and farmers supporting the Staines, Wokingham and Woking Junction Bill of 1853. That the prosperity of this industry was much advanced by the arrival of the railway through Sunningdale station in 1856 was apparent from evidence given by Frederick Waterer to the parliamentary committee on the Sunningdale & Cambridge Town Railway Bill in 1864. He estimated his daily business at Sunningdale station as between two and ten tons of trees and shrubs at busy times of the year, adding that he was also making use of Blackwater and Farnborough stations.

The opening of Bagshot station in 1878 gave a further boost to the nursery industry, which reached a peak in the 1880s, when it was occupying almost 280 acres of land in the district[15], It seems unlikely it would have developed on this scale without the convenience afforded by the area's railway facilities. But from around 1890, the railway's influence on land use and social development showed itself in another form; nursery activities in some parts of this district began to contract as the owners discovered the land would realise a higher return if offered as plots for middle class villas.

In the same area, in 1964, Daydawn Nurseries of Chobham installed a 2 ft gauge tramway over which they operated a 4-wheel Planet diesel loco bought secondhand from gravel pits at Waltham Cross. This layout was abandoned about 1972 after some years of very infrequent use.

Further east , the fertile soils along the banks of the Thames west of Kingston for many years sustained market gardens growing produce for London's millions. This was a particularly successful operation as the capital's huge horse population provided a cheap, regular and convenient source of fertiliser. These steaming deposits arrived in truckloads at Shepperton freight yard and after transhipment into 2ft gauge tipping wagons were towed along a tramway by a somewhat muzzy dobbin and driver to nearby fruit and vegetable gardens at Upper Halliford.

Watercress at Gomshall and Bananas at Lingfield

Another small Surrey industry nurtured by the railway was watercress cultivation in artificial ponds along the Tillingbourne river between Abinger Hammer and Chilworth. A strong flow of pure water from springs on Leith Hill descended over sandy subsoil to provide ideal growing conditions, but it was the proximity of the railway which was crucial to marketing success and it is perhaps no coincidence that the establishment of this industry dates from soon after the opening of the Guildford-Redhill line. Since they could be consigned as parcels traffic travelling in the guard's vans of passenger trains, the baskets of cress were on sale in London markets within an hour or two of their being left on the Up platform at Gomshall station. By the late 1880s, when the brothers Richard and John Coe were cultivating about 25 acres with an annual output of some 400 tons and employing around 30 workers, the railway was not only taking the produce to London, but to major provincial centres.[16] As late as 1934 the average annual consignment by rail amounted to 20,000 baskets or 450 tons. Although light to handle, it was a bulky, labour-intensive business which produced little or no net return for the railway company, yet one which, as a common carrier, it could not refuse. Goods managers would have had few regrets when soon after World War 2, it was transferred to road transport.

Following a decision almost certainly connected as much with the low rentals obtainable for surplus railway property in the area as anything else, a Surrey country station became the scene of an unexpected bulk freight traffic in the late 1950s. A banana ripening shed was erected in Lingfield goods yard for Geest Industries, to be kept busy by a regular service of block trains of banana vans originating at Avonmouth Docks, near Bristol. This traffic outlived the withdrawal of public freight facilities at Lingfield in 1968, not ceasing until September 1971, when the imminent completion of the M4 motorway was no doubt a major factor in Geest's decision to change over to road transport containers.

A freight failure at Worplesdon

An even shorter burst of specialised freight activity occurred at the somewhat unsuccessful station which the L&SWR had opened at Worplesdon in 1883. In this case the eclipse of the traffic was unrelated to transport economics. A site on the Up side, south of the passenger platforms, was selected for the erection of a factory serviced by a private siding where, from 1897, the Owen Stone Co. began to manufacture an artificial building stone, using the railway to distribute its output. Alas, there was something fundamentally wrong with the recipe. The patented product was soon found to be impermanent. With sales rapidly vanishing towards nil, the works were quietly closed in 1905.

Temporary Railways

As we have noted when considering the Horton Hospitals at Epsom and Caterham Barracks, in the days before heavy duty motor trucks and JCBs were perfected, it was common practice to lay light temporary railways to assist the rapid progress of major construction projects. Between the wars, other examples of this were seen in Surrey on both public and private works such as the building of trunk roads and large factories or housing estates. The Surrey County Council' s Highways Department possessed a stock of lft 11 1/2in/2ft gauge Jubilee track and a number of steam and internal combustion locomotives which were employed in this way, equipment much in evidence in the 1920s and 1930s, when By Pass roads were being carved out around the outskirts of Guildford, Dorking, Leatherhead and elsewhere. Similar temporary systems, usually of standard gauge, with steam locomotives, were a feature of new railway construction in Surrey, up to and including the completion of the line from Motspur Park to Chessington in 1936-38.

Temporary railways were also laid for special projects related to World War 1. To meet an exceptionally heavy demand for timber for hutments, trench construction and ammunition boxes, a great deal of tree felling was carried out around Leith Hill and elsewhere in the county. German prisoners of war employed on this work in the Leith Hill area in 1916 built a light railway along the Broadmoor to link areas where trees were being felled to two specially-built saw mills near the Broadmoor cottages. Horse or mule haulage was almost certainly used but no photographs of these operations appear to have survived. Much of the timber was taken to Holmwood station for onward despatch by rail.[17] Similar light railways were operating in the same period at Holmbury St. Mary and at the edge of Windsor Great Park, near Egham.

Feeding the Mouth that Bites

We have noted earlier how the railway assisted the growth of its major rival by distributing petrol in the 1920s. In more recent years, rail transport also played an important part in the construction of Surrey's first (and probably last) motorways, infrastructure provided from the public purse free at point of use which would accelerate transfer to road of a significant proportion of the railway's remaining freight business as well as much of its passenger traffic. Use of rail for motor road construction materials no doubt avoided the severe environmental problems which would otherwise have occurred on Surrey's congested road network .

Longcross or Farr's Sidings, complete with a seven-lever ground frame, were opened on 18 July 1971 between Virginia Water and Sunningdale to receive Mendip roadstone for the building of the M3 motorway. At the peak of activity, two trains were arriving daily from Merehead Quarry near Westbury. Travelling via Reading, these constantly refilled the voracious hoppers which had been installed here. On 12 May 1974, the dire deed done, this rail facility was taken out of commission.

To form the foundations of the land-hungry M23/M25 interchange some ten to twelve trains of roadstone were moved daily in 1972-75 from Merehead via Salisbury, Woking and Dorking to Merstham and Gatwick. Gravel for these works was also brought in by rail from Lydd, as was sand from St Ives, Cambridgeshire.

Surrey' s railways have also sustained air transport , moving aviation fuel to airports and reference has been made in chapter 3 to the use of a depot at Colnbrook for this purpose. Rail deliverles to Gatwick Airport from Thames Haven began in 1969 and from 1971 the tanker trains were worked into new sidings at Salfords where the fuel was discharged into storage reservoirs before being pumped to the airport through an underground pipeline. Up to 400, 000 gallons a year were carried from Thames Haven, Stanlow (Merseyside) and Fawley (Hants) until a pipeline built to connect the Fawley Refinery to Salfords brought this traffic to an end in 1982. Rail transport was briefly resumed in 1984-5 when the new pipeline was giving problems. Around the same time, Salfords (along with Purley) also received twice weekly trainloads of sea-dredged sand and gravel landed at a rail terminal at Cliffe, north Kent . At the time of writing, roadstone railed to the stone terminals south of Woking represents virtually the only remaining freight business consigned into or out of Surrey yards.

Whilst most of the activity discussed above is now history, freight transport on railways across Surrey may soon return in some strength following the full opening of the Channel Tunnel in 1995 and the transfer of freight operations to private enterprise. However any restoration of freight movements using private sidings in Surrey appears unlikely, despite the environmental benefits (one thinks for example of the daily procession of large trucks carrying pallets of bricks along the congested A 24 road whilst the parallel and under-used Horsham-Dorking line could move many lorry loads in a single-manned train) Although this does not apply to the example just quoted, a major inhibition is that the existing government subsidies for such sidings are inadequate to cover the heavy cost of linking them into the sophisticated centralised signalling systems now installed over much of the rail network.

Notes

(1) Sowan, Paul W, *Firestone and hearthstone mines in the Upper Greensand of East Surrey*, Proc. Geologists' Assoc. , 86 (4), 571-591 (1976).

(2) *Leatherhead Advertiser*, 17 April, 1964.

(3) For fuller accounts of the railways on the Horton Hospital Estate see Jackson, Alan A, 'The Horton Light Railway', *Railway Magazine*, October 1981, and Essen, R I, *Epsom's Hospital Railway*, 1991.

(4) Although in Betchworth parish, not Dorking, the town's name was adopted because its long-established works had a reputation for a high quality lime. For a fuller account of the Betchworth railways, see Townsend, J L, *Townsend Hook and The Railways of the Dorking Greystone Lime Co. Ltd*, 1980.

(5) Sowan, Paul W, 'The Mid-Surrey Lime Works at Abinger', *Newsletter Surrey Industrial History Group*, October 1988.

(6) The Merstham Grey-stone Lime Co. was formed in 1934.

(7) Taylor, David C, *The Book of Cobham*, 1982.

(8) Harrod, John T, 'Up The Dorking', *Southern Notebook*, 88, (1986).

(9) Id, 89, 1986.

(10) Tonks, Eric S (editor), *Industrial Locomotives of South East England*, 1958 and later ammendments.

(11) Hammer Brickworks, Shottermill, **Haslemere**, Down side: no rail connection: no locos.

A Hone & Sons, **Ewhurst**: petrol, diesel and battery locos, closed 1971.

Newdigate Brick Co, **Newdigate**: two diesel locos, closed 1963.

Ockley Brick, Tile & Pottery (SmokeJacks Works), Wallis Wood, **Ockley**: diesel locos and a battery loco, Replaced by conveyor c 1969.

Manfield's & Smithbrook Brickworks, **Cranleigh**: diesel and petrol locos. System worked manually and by cable 1955-1965.

Brookhurst Brick & Tile Works/Swallows Tiles, **Cranleigh**: diesel loco out of use c 1955. Works closed 1963.

Guildford Park Brickworks, **Guildford**: no locos; private siding into freight yard.

Gatwick Brick Co, **Hookwood**: petrol and diesel locos. Ceased operations c1968.

Hazelwood Brick Co, **Baynards**, standard gauge vertical boiler 0-4-0T, closed c1930. Premises and loco transferred to Baynards Fullers Earth Co.

Catling's Brickworks, **Shepperton**: no locos but private siding to Down side.

Sussex & Dorking United Brick Co, Old Park Brickworks, **Farnham**: petrol, diesel and battery locos. Works closed c 1955.

Sussex & Dorking United Brick Co, (later Redland), Nutbourne Brickworks, **Hambledon**, diesel and battery locos, closed mid 1987.

(12) W J Lavender Sand Pits, **Reigate**: diesel loco, closed 19??

Hall & Co, Woodlands Sand Pits, **Reigate**: petrol loco (replaced by rubber tyred dumper trucks 1936).

Titsey Estate Pits, on the Kent border near **Moorhouse Bank**: petrol loco (?) closed 19??
Longside Sand & Gravel Co, Thorpe, **Chertsey**: diesel locos, replaced by conveyor belts in 1950s.

Surrey Sand & Gravel, Thorpe, **Chertsey**: petrol and diesel locos. Closed in 1950s.

Ham River Pits, **Chertsey**: steam, petrol and diesel locos. Closed c 1950.

Ham River Grit Co, Town Farm Sand Pits, **Bletchingley**: steam, petrol and diesel locos, replaced by conveyor belt, c 1965.

Hall & Co, Papercourt Farm Gravel Pits, **Ripley**: diesel locos (rep1aced by conveyor belt in 1950s).

War Department, Caesar' s Camp Sand Pits, Upper Hale, **Farnham**: diesel locos 1940-c1960.

Bennett' s Sand & Gravel, **Sunbury on Thames**: petrol loco. Closed c 1950.

Charlton Sand & Ballast Co. , Littleton, **Shepperton**: steam and diesel locos, closed c 1950.

(13) See Osborne, Bruce E, 'Early Plateways & Firestone Mining in Surrey: An Interim Report', *Proceedings Croydon Natural History & Scientific Society*, vol 17 (3) (February 1982), and Burgess, Peter, 'The Use of Plate Rails in the Godstone Firestone Quarries: Some Recent Discoveries', id, vol 18 (4) (March 1994). The author is also indebted to Paul W Sowan for elucidating this subject .

(14) For the history of the Chilworth site, see Crocker, Glenys, *Chilworth Gunpowder*, 1984, and Crocker, Alan, 'The Tramway at Chilworth Gunpowder Works', *Surrey Archaeological Collections* (Surrey Archaeological Society), vol 82, 181- 195, 1994, on which these paragraphs are based.

(15) Eedle, Marie de G, *A History of Bagshot and Windlesham*, 1977.

(16) Corke, Shirley, *Abinger Hammer, Surrey: A Short History and Guide to the Village*, 1993.

(17) Memories of J Fane (born 1900) in conversation with Charles Thompson of the Newdigate Society, published in *The Dorking Advertiser*, 11 August , 1994; also O' Kelly, Terence, *The Villages of Abinger Common and Wotton, Surrey*, 1988.

CHAPTER NINE

Dreams Frustrated, Dreams Fulfilled

Surrey had its share of frustrated proposals for railways and tramways of various kinds, too numerous to be mentioned here in what would be little more than a tedious rehearsal of place names and dates. Study of maps soon shows up the most obvious gaps in the network, exploited from the 1910s with varying degrees of success by motor buses, and from the early 1930s by Green Line coaches. Thus, imagining ourselves to be 19th century railway promoters as we gaze at the map, we may note the lack of a cross country line linking the Farnham area with Godalming, Cranleigh and Horley and of another to join up Bagshot, Woking and Leatherhead as well as a seeming failure to extend south of Caterham. But perhaps the most obvious 'railway desert', given its proximity to London and its potential attractions for house buyers, seems to be the area around the Surrey-Kent border across the North Downs between Croydon and Westerham. It is no surprise to find that all these voids were the subject of railway or tramway proposals, mostly after 1880, and in one case as late as 1926.

No Narrow Gauge to Cobham

Before the construction of the New Guildford line between Surbiton, Effingham Junction and Guildford, there were several attempts to fill the void between the London & Southampton main line and the North Downs. A Kingston solicitor, one Bell, concerned himself greatly with this deficiency, obtaining some support from Cobham interests wanting to reduce the cost of road cartage from the Thames Ditton barge wharf and facilitate the movement of agricultural produce to the London markets. In 1869 Bell piloted the promotion of a 3ft gauge light railway which would run more or less due north east from the centre of the village to Esher station. However the bill was thrown out by the Lords Committee; it had been opposed on behalf of Queen Victoria on the grounds the track passed too close to her Claremont Estate, which lay near the direct route. This was rather a pity, since Surrey never had a narrow gauge line providing a regular public passenger and freight service, but it does provide a delightful exercise for the imagination as we picture in our mind's eye what it might have looked like, both before and after the opening of the New Guildford line. No doubt it was a great disappointment for Cobham's 2,133 inhabitants; for a few more years the wealthier among them had to make do with the shilling horse bus from Ripley to Esher station, whilst everyone else walked or cadged a ride on cart

The Southern Heights Light Railway

As this interesting scheme to fill the aforementioned 'desert' was considered at some length in an earlier book [1], we shall confine ourselves here to a summary. An 1898 scheme for a line from Orpington to Tatsfield (all except the terminal section would have been in Kent) rested its hopes on residential development in the Tatsfield and Biggin Hill area, where a large estate was about to be broken up into tiny £10 plots. Although a Light Railway Order was obtained in 1902, the scheme, unable to attract the interest of the SER, failed to raise its capital. Yet, in this pleasant upland scenery, which rises to over 800ft towards the south, a good deal of self-build plotland development did appear from the 1900s, resuming in the 1920s , as war-weary ex-servicemen were tempted to chance their demobilisation gratuities to start what seemed like an idyllic and peaceful life. From the latter part of 1913, the London General Omnibus Company had begun to open up this district by linking it directly to Bromley. This was a partial attack on the main problem of the area - its sheer inaccessibility ; few of the plotlanders possessed even a motorcycle, and the London trains were way over the hills to the north east or well to the west in the valleys around Caterham. Once reached, the services were good, even more so after the SR electrified to Orpington in July 1925.

At this point the Light Railway King, Holman Fred Stephens stepped on to the scene, proposing a 16-mile standard gauge single line, not only from Orpington to Tatsfield as suggested earlier, but curving back into Surrey, through Warlingham and Chelsham, to join the Oxted line at Sanderstead, thus feeding the Southern Railway at two points instead of one. Stephens also hit upon an appealing name - *The Southern Heights Light Railway*. Securing conditional approval from the Ministry of Transport in 1926, he got a Light Railway Order two years later. More importantly, he was successful in interesting the commercially-minded SR management in his low cost scheme; seeing the potential for housing developments and a new source of traffic, the main line company agreed to work the line with electric trains for 75 per cent of gross receipts, guaranteeing up to 5 per cent on the SHLR debentures. Stephens' company would however have to pay for the electrification to SR requirements, in cash, or in paid-up SHLR preference shares.

Although some preliminary work was authorised at Orpington and the SR publicity people added the line to their maps, nothing of any significance was undertaken; the early optimism was soon to be evaporated by the financial depression that followed the 1929 Wall Street crash. Stephens was quite unable to raise the required capital and it also became more difficult for the Southern to offer financial help. The impending formation of a single body to operate London's passenger transport was another unhelpful factor. When Stephens died in 1931, the SHLR expired with him and public transport across the railwayless uplands at Surrey's eastern border was left to London Transport Country Services and Green Line coaches.

South of Caterham

In the same area, an extension of the Caterham Railway to Godstone village was first proposed in 1873, the new line to have no less than four tunnels. Two years later, a Metropolitan & Brighton Railway was projected from Penge LC&DR and Beckenham SER through Warlingham to Caterham and Godstone and on to the south coast resort via East Grinstead. Finally, in 1876 came the Caterham & Godstone Valley, which, unlike its two predecessors, did manage to secure parliamentary sanction. But this line, which was to have run south from Caterham SER station to Godstone village, on to Oxted and then east to make end-on junction with the SER Westerham branch, also came to nothing since its catchment area was largely covered by the railway opened from South Croydon to Oxted in 1884.

Seeking First Class Passengers across the Surrey Weald

Lobbying for a cross-country line from the LB&SCR in the Dorking area to Cranleigh and Midhurst and beyond began in the early 1880s[2]. In time this resolved itself into the more limited objective of improving railway facilities at Cranleigh, whose existing LB&SCR services made very poor connection with the L&SWR London trains at Guildford, a matter of little interest to the LB&SCR.

Eventually the LB&SCR sought to quieten the agitation by including in its 1897-98 bill an eight-mile single line from a point just north of its Dorking station to Cranleigh via Ewhurst. This required a fourth station in Dorking, at the west end of the town, lavish provision indeed for a place with a population of only some 7,500. But the Dorking people were ungrateful; envying Leatherhead, already benefiting from fare reductions as two companies fought for the London traffic, they wanted more competition, not more of the LB&SCR. They saw as too cosy the relationship between the LB&SCR and the SER in their own town. Although there was some support for a Holmwood-Cranleigh line, Dorking did not relish the disturbance of a new railway across the town, on a route which they rightly perceived as an attempt to block a L&SWR extension into their area. At this, the LB&SCR caved in, withdrawing the proposal from its bill.

In the following year (1899), the LB&SCR tried again, this time for a line from Holmwood station to Cranleigh, but now opposition came from landowners and the Surrey County Council, which objected to some aspects of the alignment. The Commons Committee threw out the Bill. A final attempt was made in 1905 in the form of a Holmwood, Cranleigh, Midhurst and Havant Railway. This was cleverly proposed as a shorter (78m 78ch instead of 89m35ch) route for LB&SCR trains from London to Portsmouth which would also stimulate high quality residential development through a poorly-served area. The engineering survey was the work of Holman Fred Stephens, then starting to make his name in the railway world[3]. But unable to persuade the military that the improved access to Portsmouth would be an advantage to national defence or to secure any backing from the by now much disillusioned LB&SCR, the promoters could make no progress.

Electric Light Railways for West Surrey

The 1900s saw a number of schemes coming forward for light railways worked by electric traction, normally taking the form of street tramway type operations which would use a segregated private right of way or tracks at the roadside when traversing rural areas. One such, the Woking & Bagshot Light Railway, sponsored by the West Surrey Light Railway Co Ltd, was approved by the Light Railway Commissioners in 1906. With a length of 7m 38ch, this would have run from Bagshot station via Lightwater, Windlesham, Chobham and Horsell to Woking, where it was intended to operate over the tracks of a proposed street tramway system serving the town, the station and the suburbs of St Johns, Knaphill and Maybury. Following an objection to the operation of the Bagshot service between Horsell and Woking station, a diversion between these points, passing slightly further to the west, was incorporated in the Light Railway Order of 18 May 1906.

When the promoters had addressed the parish councils in 1903 , promising sidings for the several nurseries in the Bagshot and Windlesham area and explaining they had in mind 'booming the country passed through', there was a general welcome for the proposal. However although a start was promised in autumn 1906, financing proved an insuperable barrier. The two main promoters, had in 1903 also proposed (and later withdrawn) a scheme for an electric light railway from Woking to Send, Ripley and Effingham and two years later had obtained a Light Railway Order for street tramways in Guildford extending out to Stoughton, Merrow, Stoke and Shalford. By 1906 they had become bankrupt and nothing more was heard of any of these schemes. Another proposal for an electric light railway between Addlestone, Weybridge and Walton on Thames station, with a branch to Weybridge station, was announced in the autumn of 1900 but this even failed to obtain statutory approval.[4]

In 1899 Surrey County Council had sought the views of the Farnham Urban District Council on possible routes for light railways, receiving suggestions for one (largely in Hampshire) from Farnham to Basingstoke via Crondall and Odiham, and another from Farnham to Hindhead via Frensham and Churt. This last emerged as a firm proposal in 1901. over a route which would also serve Grayshott and Headley, going on to Haslemere via Hindhead. Boldly optimistic. even for a time when the motorbus was still in the future, it is no surprise that it fell flat on its face.[5] The Farnham-Basingstoke line was revived briefly in 1919 as a possible unemployment relief project but no progress was made.

As it had a few yards of track inside the county boundary, constituting one of only two short lengths of street tramway so far completed within the present limits of Surrey,[6] brief mention should be made of the 2m 55ch horse-worked Aldershot & Farnborough Tramway[7]. Mostly in Hampshire, this operated over a single standard gauge track laid in Lynchford Road and Farnborough Road, connecting North Camp station and Farnborough station . Operations began in 1883 with two tramcars and about a dozen horses but seem to have petered out around 1897. Little business was attracted, perhaps because the trams were not used by the impoverished soldiery who formed the main population hereabouts. The unfulfilled dream in this case was to convert the line to electric traction over 3ft6in gauge tracks and extend it to serve Aldershot town and Ash Vale . A new company was formed for this purpose and some 3ft 6in gauge track was laid in 1905 but financial problems emerged. There was also some opposition from the military who fussily suggested that the overhead trolley wires would offer a hazard to their artillery observation balloons. By this time the motor bus was on the scene and the services of the ambiguously-named Aldershot & District Traction company (formed in 1912) were soon effectively meeting this area's local transport needs.

Cut Down By a Green Belt

Aiming to attract Government financial assistance under the Development (Loan Guarantees and Grants) Act of 1929, the SR that year deposited a bill for a railway through an area seen as likely to have considerable potential for residential development. It had the advantage of being sufficiently far from central London to be free of competition from road services.

The proposed line was to form a loop from Motspur Park through Chessington to Leatherhead, an alignment likely to afford some relief to the existing railway via Epsom at a time when house building was proceeding at a rapid pace around the edge of London. Since an account of this line has been given in some detail in another book,[8] we merely note here that the northern section as far as Tolworth was opened on 29 May 1938 and as far as Chessington South station (4 1/2 miles) on 28 May 1939. By the latter date, land for the remainder of this railway, through open country south into Surrey, had been purchased and fenced. It is interesting that in laying out this southern section, the SR allowed a building depth between the A 243 road and the railway to accommodate what was obviously expected to be a three-mile stretch of houses and back gardens. Indeed, but for the outbreak of war, the scheme would probably have been completed in 1940 or 1941, carrying along with it the ceaseless sprawl of semi-detached London in this direction.

During 1938 and 1939 the contractors had dumped spoil from the cuttings north of Chessington South to form an embankment southwards almost as far as Chalky Lane. Although work ceased with the outbreak of war, in 1942 army engineers, in training for wartime tasks, erected the bridge over Chalky Lane and carried the embankment to within less than half a mile of the proposed station at Malden Rushett. This somewhat unexpected burst of activity was a consequence of the construction of wartime sidings at Andover and Basingstoke which produced a quantity of chalk for which this was considered a suitable home.[9] Although nothing more was done, the statutory powers were kept alive until 1961 and the strip for the railway remained protected in the Surrey Development Plan for a decade after that. By the 1970s it seemed clear that with most of the area now part of the Metropolitan Green Belt, and thus preserved from building development, it was highly improbable the Surrey section of the line, with its proposed station at Leatherhead North and intended junction with the Dorking line near the site of the original Leatherhead station, would ever be completed.

Dreams Fulfilled

Other dreams of laying rails in Surrey were sometimes fulfilled. In 1937, the steam enthusiast

Above *Four of the Surrey Border & Camberley Railway's live steam locomotives pose in the throat of the railway's impressive Farnborough Green (Frimley) terminus for one of the set of official post-cards issued in 1938.*

Alexander Davenport Kinloch, son of a Brigadier-General, who had already built the Foxhill and Farnborough Miniature Railways just across the Hampshire border, acquired a large area of low-lying land in the Blackwater Valley on which he laid down just over two miles of 10 1/4in gauge line, most of it double track. In practice this Surrey Border & Camberley Railway linked Frimley and Camberley York Town, wending its way through the intervening woodland and scrub[10]. An ambitious scheme involving an investment of well over £2m at 1996 prices, with Kinloch as chairman and managing director, it was partly opened on 30 April 1938 and in full use from the following 23 July. A daily timetabled service of nineteen steam-hauled trains each way was worked between 10.30 and 22.05, the one way journey taking 10-15 minutes. Additional trains were put on at weekends, when passenger totals could rise as high as 2,000 a day. With the exception of the last two evening trains each way, this timetable was maintained throughout the winter of 1938-39 but on winter Sundays trains ran only in fine weather. Everyone worked very hard on this labour of love; special occasions, such as the Aldershot Tattoo saw trains running well into the small hours. This was a far more ambitious spread of train service than is offered by most pleasure and tourist lines in Britain today and it is not surprising that a few people are reputed to have used the SB&CR as public transport rather than for amusement.

The Frimley terminus, named Farnborough Green, was situated between the Redhill-Reading line and the Blackwater, just off the A 325 road, on a site now occupied by the Frimley Business Park. Elaborate in its layout and buildings, it had three island platforms with five faces, two carriage sidings and a locomotive run-round road. Much of all this was protected by a twin-gabled all-over glass roof. The associated buildings were carefully-designed, the facilities including a ticket office, waiting room, stationmaster's office and a large cafe in the car park. There was a public address system and train

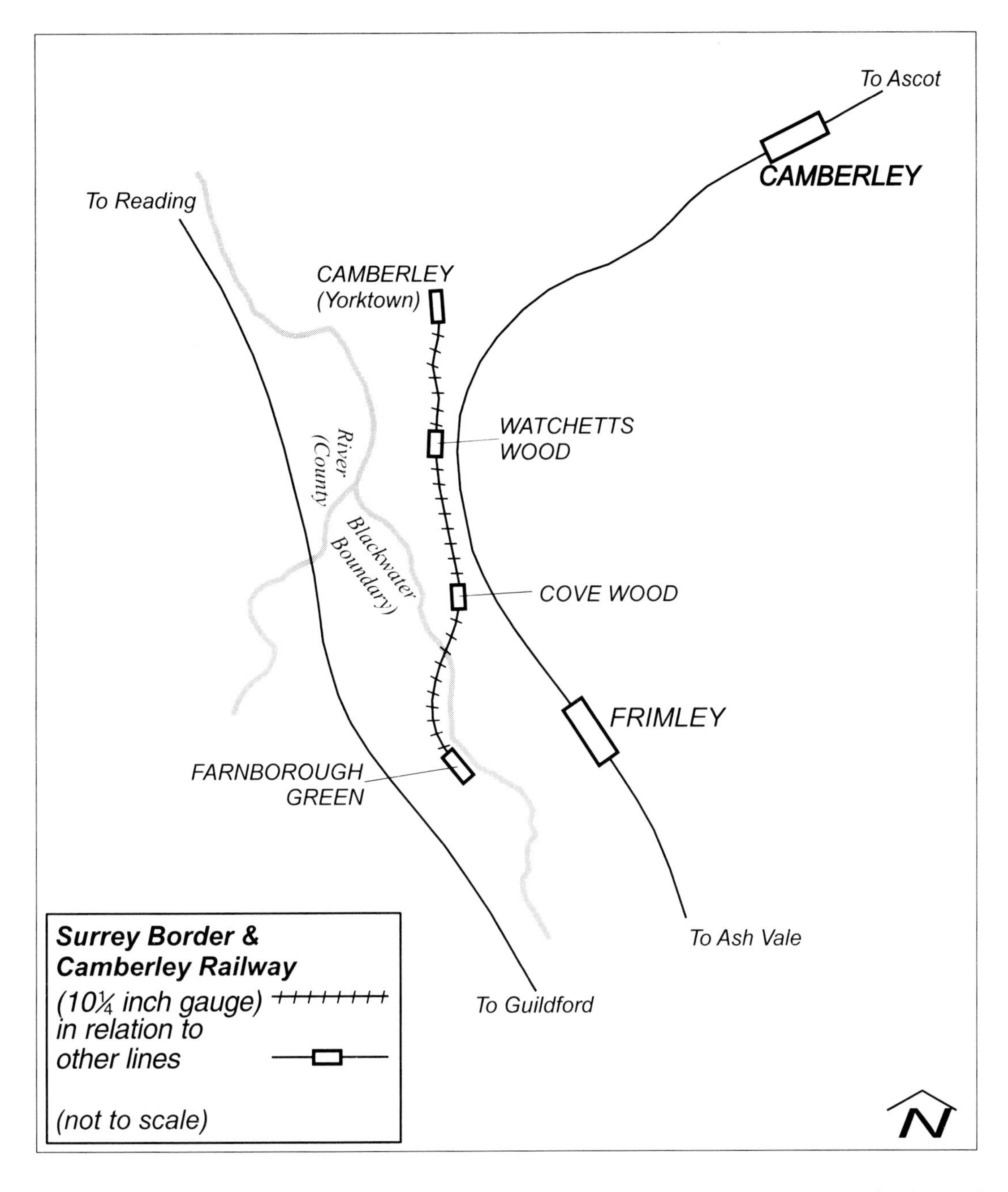

departure indicator. A three-road wooden locomotive shed was located near the turntable at the entrance to the station yard. At Camberley, the arrangements were simpler, just one long platform with a wooden building containing a booking office, locomotive shed and workshops. Signalling throughout was based on main line practice with miniature semaphores controlled from scaled down signal boxes.

At the outbreak of war, Kinloch was recalled to Army Reserve service in the Grenadier Guards, the line closing quite suddenly as a consequence. In fact financial problems were already looming. This splendidly extravagant enterprise had soaked up vast sums, with much more likely to be needed to continue operations had war not come. As it was, the operating company went into receivership

Above *The Surrey Border & Camberley Railway*

within two months of closure, causing most of the assets to be offered for sale. War conditions made this operation slow and difficult. So much left the site that resumption of service after World War 2 was out of the question. Kinloch, who had severed all connections with line soon after its closure, died in 1982. His dream fulfilled has left few traces; much of the site is now splattered with ugly new roads, including the M3.

Another extensive miniature line, possessing both steam and internal combustion locomotives, is the Great Cockrow Railway, to be found on a woodland site close to the roar of the M25, near Chertsey. In comparison with the line just described, its train service is very limited - relying entirely on volunteers with busy lives, the management is obliged to restrict public access to Sunday afternoons, closing just after tea time. Dating from 1968-69, but using locos and other items from an earlier private garden railway, it has the even smaller gauge of 7 1/4in (one eighth full size). This can produce a somewhat uncomfortable ride for adult passengers, compelling drivers to adopt an awkward astride crouch with their feet only inches above the ballast. Unlike the Surrey Border & Camberley, the Great Cockrow goes from nowhere to nowhere, through an area of woodland and stream over a highly convoluted layout of the type more commonly seen on indoor model railways trying to make the maximum use of limited space. Its operators revel in the complication and potential of its signalling[11], which exactly follows traditional main line practice and indeed uses full size block instruments and miniature lever power frames obtained as redundant items from BR. This makes it possible to run trains at close headways. The semaphore and colour light signals themselves are miniatures built to slightly over true scale size to make them easily visible.

As one might expect from its title, the miniature line operated by the Malden & District Society of Model Engineers Ltd is somewhat lacking in the romantic charms and complications of the two lines just mentioned, the emphasis being very much on the motive power and its performance. It is to be found at Claygate Lane, Thames Ditton, where it was established in 1946, ten years after the Society was founded and it features raised tracks of 3 1/2in, 5in and 7 1/4 in gauge as well as a 7 1/4 in gauge line at ground level, all following more or less straightforward circuits. Glimpses of it may be had from trains on the main lines above and there are public open days.

Finally we should mention that Surrey now has a few narrow gauge railways operating as visitor attractions in pleasure parks, museums and garden centres, such as the 2ft gauge operation at Thorpe Pleasure Park, Chertsey, and the 2ft gauge light railway at the Old Kiln Museum, Tilford, near Farnham. This last, operated by volunteers with preserved steam and diesel locos, is closer to the serious and mostly private pleasure which is obtained from even more modest narrow gauge installations, some ten in all, in the gardens and grounds of private houses, some of them using locomotives and other equipment from abandoned industrial installations.

Notes

(1) Jackson, Alan A, *London's Local Railways*, 1978, pp 374-376.

(2) This paragraph is partly based on Hart, H W, 'The Holmwood, Cranleigh & Midhurst Railway 1884-1905', *Journal of the Railway & Canal Historical Society*, vol VIII, 5 & 6 and vol IX, 1; also on reports in *The Dorking Advertiser*, 20 November 1897 and 8 January 1898.

(3). Printed circular in a private collection: *Proposed Holmwood, Cranleigh, Midhurst & Havant Railway*, 1905, published by J C Buckwell & Co, solicitors, North Gate House, Pavilion, Brighton.

(4). Gillham, J C, 'The Woking & Bagshot Light Railway', *Railway World*, May 1960; *The Railway Times*, 1900-06 passim; Eedle, Marie de G, *A History of Bagshot and Windlesham*, 1977.

(5) Smith, Ewbank, *Victorian Farnham: The Story of a Surrey Town 1837-1901*, 1971; Gillham, John, and Bett, Wingate H, *Great British Tramway Networks* 1957.

(6) The other was the outermost section of the London United Tramways' Long Ditton (Winter's/Window's Bridge) line, opened in 1906 and closed in 1931. This had been authorised to extend further into Surrey, through Thames Ditton and back to Hampton Court but the final section was never constructed.

(7) For a full account see Gillham, J C, 'The Aldershot & Farnborough Tramways', *The Tramway Review*, vol 5, 36 and 37.

(8) Jackson, op cit (note 1), second edition, 1999, pp 152-160.

(9) SR Board Minutes, 26 March 1942.

(10) For a full account of the railway and its predecessors, see Mitchell, Peter, Townsend, Simon, and Shelmerdine, Malcolm, *The Surrey Border and Camberley Railway*, 1993, on which this account is mainly based.

(11) For a full description of the signalling, with layout plans, see *Railway World*, August 1971 and July 1974.

CHAPTER TEN

Looking Forward

By the early 1990s there was an increasing awareness that the long-held Department of Transport policy of expanding the capacity and extent of the road system in order to try to meet its own forecasts of growth in road use and car availability was neither tenable nor wise, given the appalling environmental consequences. Serious consideration was turning to means of discouraging car use and diverting traffic on to an improved and more attractive public transport system.

This had particularly urgent relevance in Surrey, where by that time car ownership was 21 per cent above the national average and increasing and car availability was over 40 per cent above the national average, thanks to the proliferation of company cars; almost 50 per cent of Surrey households had two or more cars and 70 per cent of all journeys were made by car (90 per cent of all journeys to work). As a result of this heavy use of cars and of a vast increase in commercial road traffic, pressures of road usage, environmental pollution and the extent of new road construction were already approaching the limits of tolerance. Under the leadership of the County Council (SCC), much more attention was being focused on raising the capacity of the county's rail network and adapting it, so far as that might be possible without unacceptably high expenditure, to meet the needs of new and predicted changes in traffic flows.

An Examination of Possibilities

Some remarks have already been made about possible future changes and additions to Surrey's rail facilities. Other ideas will now be discussed, notably those emerging from two detailed studies, commissioned by the Surrey County Council and published in 1995 and 1996,[1] which examined emerging needs and feasible solutions.

The 1995 Report was by no means negative about rail and it is interesting that it concluded: 'Given forecast traffic growth and increased road congestion, the attractiveness of rail services linking the major urban areas in Surrey will increase'. It is worth examining both documents in some detail since they provide pointers to future rail developments in the county.

Against the objectives of reducing pressure on the road network and of increasing the attractiveness of rail services in those areas where the share of rail in total traffic movement was low, the task of the consultants was to identify worthwhile new railway services and the most cost-effective improvements to rail infrastructure. In view of the fact that there existed a high demand for travel to Heathrow and Gatwick airports from most parts of Surrey, they were also given a specific directive to examine what could be done to improve rail access to meet this, including the feasibility of a rail link across Surrey between the two airports.

New rail links Proposed

Taking infrastructure improvements first, the 1995 SCC Report saw the most significant need to be a rail service from Surrey direct into London Airport (Heathrow). This was subsequently developed further by the London Airports Surface Access Study, whose report published in September 1996 considered a rail route from Guildford via Woking, a new west curve at Staines, the southern section of the former GWR branch to Staines and new construction thence into the airport at Heathrow, An alternative, using the east side of the M25 motorway, although more direct, was thought unlikely to justify the significant extra cost involved in new construction. The proposed service would link Surrey's two busiest stations with the Airport and could form an extension of a proposed Thameslink service into the Airport via West Hampstead and Ealing Broadway.

It was also recommended in the 1995 SCC Report that support should be given to British Rail's 1991 'Thames link 2000' proposals, since if implemented, these would improve access from most important Surrey centres to the proposed Channel Tunnel Rail Link terminal at St Pancras as well as to the proposed CrossRail east-west line and direct journeys to destinations north of London such as St Albans, Luton, Bedford, Welwyn Garden City, Hertford, Stevenage, Peterborough, Cambridge and King's Lynn.

The 1995 Report also suggested that reinstatement of two of the closed Surrey curves might be worthwhile as a means of improving the existing poor rail services to and from burgeoning population centres in north west Surrey. A renewal of the north to east Frimley Junction to Sturt Lane Junction curve would permit an improved through service to London for the currently disadvantaged but populous area around Camberley and although a flat junction with the main line might create operating difficulties, it was considered a more feasible solution than the preferred option of a chord on to the Aldershot-Woking line at Ash Vale.

Reopening of the east to west curve at Virginia Water, said to be achievable at modest cost as there were no serious engineering problems, was also proposed. This would allow introduction of valuable new service flows such as Camberley-Ascot-Chertsey-Waterloo and Waterloo-Chertsey-Reading.

The case for reopening the Cranleigh-Guildford line as a conventional railway was identified by the study as requiring a high level of investment which might offer as little as a three per cent direct return on the capital cost. However it was admitted this assessment was based on worst case traffic estimates, taking no account of reduced road accident costs, vehicle operating cost savings and the other environmental benefits arising from reduced road use, The 1995 Report did not mention the alternative of light rail either here or elsewhere in the county and we shall return to this later.

A southward extension of the Chessington line, in large part over the alignment proposed in the 1930s was mentioned in the 1995 report as a means of serving the proposed development of around 1,500 housing units on the former LCC hospitals estate west of Epsom, Although a feasible project, this new railway, which would remove some traffic from the A 243, a congested M25 feeder, and would also improve access to the Chessington World of Adventure leisure complex, was not thought likely to attract any significant private finance.

Major rail infrastructure works were also tentatively recommended ('there may be a case') by an earlier (1991) study,[2] which had already addressed the need for improving rail access in the Blackwater Valley Area, where existing facilities gave rail a relatively small market share of local traffic and encouraged London commuters to use their cars to reach the nearest main line stations. The works suggested in the 1991 report involved closure of the section between Ash Vale Junction and Camberley via Frimley[3] and the construction of a short link between Camberley and the Reading-Guildford line, which would be given new curves west of Ash Vale to allow through running between Camberley and Aldershot via Ash in both directions. A new station for Frimley would be built north of the existing Farnborough North station which would then be closed. At the point of crossing the main line between London and Southampton, a two-level interchange station, 'Farnborough Interchange' was proposed. We shall return to this in a moment.

Only one new rail link was suggested in the 1996 SCC Report -the construction of a north to east curve at Dorking to improve access to Gatwick Airport from south west London, Epsom and Leatherhead as well as supplying an alternative route to a road system overloaded both environmentally and operationally. It was recognised that this new construction would require electrification from Reigate to Dorking and possibly some rearrangement of the layout and platforms at Redhill. Once open, it was suggested traffic over the new curve would generate an annual fare income of £0.7m against a construction cost of £3m (or £10-12m with electrification). If the environmental benefits are taken into account, the estimated 7.2 per cent first year rate of return on capital cost (disregarding operating costs) seems reasonable. It is interesting that the land for such a connection would be available without property demolition and indeed it had only been sold by BR in the early 1990s having been purchased by the SR for construction of a similar connection which received parliamentary sanction in 1924/27.

Separately from the two SCC studies , the Heathrow Western Connections Feasibility Study proposed the creation of a north-south link from the Great Western main line to Staines, making use of the partially-abandoned West Drayton - Staines railway. This would be given a London Airport (Heathrow) hub station, connected to the airport terminals either by extension of the present Heathrow Express Railway, an extension of the Piccadilly tube line, or a dedicated light transit system. Between the main line and Staines this revived rail link would not necessarily require electrification and with reinstatement of the former north to west curve at Staines could accommodate through services from Oxford and beyond and from the West Country and Wales via London Airport to Woking, Guildford , Gatwick and beyond.

New stations proposed

The 1995 SCC Report rehearsed a number of sites for new stations and station relocations, most of which had already been given detailed consideration in earlier studies. Some have already been mentioned in this book. These were:

1. **Artington/Shalford** (on the Portsmouth main line, a park and ride station for Guildford centre).
2. **Park Barn/University** (on the west side of Guildford on the Reading line, also serving the Royal Surrey County Hospital). This was the subject of a feasibility study by SCC in 1995-96.
3. **Stoughton**, (north Guildford, on the Guildford-Woking line).
4. **Merrow** (east of Guildford, on the Guildford-Surbiton line).
5. **Farnborough Interchange**; a split level interchange between the Guildford- Reading and Waterloo- Southampton/Salisbury lines which would allow closure o f Farnborough North station. A proposal of the 1991 Blackwater Valley Rail Study, this was dismissed in the 1995 SCC report as 'unlikely to take place', a reasonable conclusion given that for the majority of modern British travellers, the need to change from one train to another en route reduces the attraction of a rail journey, especially a comparatively local one. Another problem is that construction of a station on this site would entail a detoriation in the quality of train service at the existing Farnborough station, which is sited close to the town centre.
6. **East Camberley**, (on the Ash Vale to Ascot line, to serve a new development of some 400 houses.
7. **Fetcham**, (between Bookham and Leatherhead stations).

Of these, only 1,2,3 and 4 seem likely starters as viable conventional railway stations. For the reasons given above, 5 seems to be ruled out and the traffic potential of 6 and 7 appears vulnerable to erosion by car users making road journeys from their catchment areas to existing stations with higher quality train service. Should a light rail scheme eventually emerge for the Guildford area as discussed below, 1,2 and 3 (and possibly 4) could be replaced by cheaper and more accessible roadside stops . Since this group of conventional rail stations appears to have emerged principally as a means of reducing road use in Guildford centre, light rail stops, providing direct access to the centre of Guildford as well as to the main station would seem a more logical solution.

Whilst no new stations were specifically recommended in the 1996 SCC Report, a proposed development of 1,800 houses at Horley was identified as possibly requiring provision if planning gain we re to be available for financing construction. Should any new station be built, it may allow closure of Salfords.

Possible new train services.

The 1995 SCC study proposed a number of options for new services over existing lines, again stressing the need for improving access to and from the growth areas served by the Ash Vale to Ascot and Weybridge to Virginia Water lines, where there appeared to be considerable potential for diverting traffic from the road system. These proposals sought to remove the need for rail passengers to and from Bagshot, Camberley, Frimley, Chertsey and Addlestone to change trains at the junctions with the main lines. The relatively poor train service given at present to some stations between Guildford and Haslemere was also noticed and a direct Farnham-Guildford-Haslemere service was proposed as a way of remedying this.

. To provide a link between the Gatwick and Heathrow airports and important Surrey centres, the study considered the inevitably somewhat circuitous 85km (52.8m) route via Redhill, Dorking, Guildford, Working, Chertsey and Staines, noting that this would require electrification of the section between Reigate and Shalford junction and a firm decision to build the new railway mentioned earlier into Heathrow Airport from Bedfont on the Staines- Feltham line. The best overall journey time between the two airports was estimated as 80 minutes (this compares with 65 min by express road coach in favourable traffic conditions). However undue importance should not be attached to the length of journey since much of the traffic would be between one or other of the airports and important intermediate stops, notably Guildford and Woking, where passengers could make easy transfer to and from fast rail services serving other destinations.

For the area in the south east of the county, the 1996 SCC Report made a number of short term proposals of which the most important affected Reigate, the only major centre without a good through service to central London. Although the track between Reigate and Redhill was electrified in 1932 its use by electric trains had been confined to peak hours since 1970. A new hourly service from Reigate to Victoria was proposed, stopping only at Clapham Junction after East Croydon. The low use made of the Dorking to Horsham electrified line was also identified against the background of an astonishing 2,000 motor car trips made daily over congested roads between Horsham and London. It was proposed that rail might become a more attractive option if the late evening service south of Dorking was restored. Horley, an area of proposed further housing growth, was also seen as justifying improved off peak services.

Is there a place for Light Rail in Surrey?

Although SCC officials had considered light rail, it seems they retained some major reservations about its practicability in Surrey. Yet light rail's attractions as offering at least a partial solution to the problem of reducing road use will surely receive increasing attention in the future, especially with the opening in 1999 of the Croydon Tramlink network, just across the county border. Such systems built in the last two decades in the USA, Germany and France and in the United Kingdom at Newcastle, London Docklands, Manchester and Sheffield and Birmingham have demonstrated their value; light rail vehicles are very versatile, able to operate over discarded conventional railway alignments, share tracks with conventional rail services, run over or alongside roads, or on dedicated reservations built especially, or over combinations of all these. Civil engineering costs can be reduced by installing signalling systems to allow sharing of existing structures such as bridges and road crossings with motor traffic.

Two locations suggest themselves as having potential for this mode of rail transport in Surrey, although it must be emphasised that as yet no detailed planning or firm proposals exist for either. We have already mentioned a possible light rail system at Guildford, incorporating the former conventional railway alignment through Bramley to Cranleigh, most of which survives. Reinstatement of the latter, either as a conventional or a light railway which would remove some traffic from very congested roads, was shown as feasible in a 1996 SCC Study.

In the Guildford urban area, a light rail system would offer an alternative to providing the conventional railway stations at 1 to 3 (and possibly 4) above, given that any sensible system would need to serve the town's main rail station as well as pass through the retail and business centre. Light rail would bring the town valuable environmental benefits, reducing the level of pollution caused by buses and cars as well as affording significant relief to its heavily-used, pedestrian-unfriendly inner road system. Whilst a light rail service to Merrow might not be an initial priority, a low cost light rail penetration into the north eastern quarter of the town might permit the closure of London Road station on the New Guildford line, allowing the long-planned conventional rail station at Merrow to be inserted without any reduction in journey times.

Another possible candidate for light rail is the Woking district, where it could be designed to act as a feeder to the main line station as well as reducing demands on the road system in the growth area between Woking and Bagshot and Camberley , where further housing development is likely.

Although only partly in Surrey, it should be mentioned here that the Epsom Downs branch line may be considered as an extension to the proposed Sutton Light Rail (between Morden and Sutton). This latter scheme. which would connect with the Croydon Tramlink, has been identified by London Transport as one having priority for further study.

Channel Tunnel traffic provision

Although a superficial appraisal might suggest that the Tonbridge-Redhill-Guildford-Reading line offers itself as a ready-made route for moving freight traffic to and from the Channel Tunnel, avoiding transits over congested lines through London, this could not be achieved without very heavy capital expenditure. Realignment and reconstruction of the track between Redhill and Shalford Junction south of Guildford, electrification between Reigate and Guildford and between Ash and Wokingham, a flyover across Redhill, new tunnels at Guildford, improved connections at Reading and resignalling might all be necessary at no small cost. Even so, it is possible that the weight of traffic carried through the Channel Tunnel to and from destinations other than London may well grow sufficiently in the longer term - say by 2025 - to levels justifying such infrastructure investment. In the meantime Railtrack's planning envisages refurbishment by 2005 to allow the line to carry 'Piggyback' trains (road transport vehicles on flat wagons). Resignalling between Guildford and Reading is also planned for completion by 2008[4].

This tentative survey of future possibilities has perhaps shown that Surrey remains an area where rail has an important role to play. Given the absence of a major cataclysm, the medium and long term future of the county's largely intact rail network seems assured. Indeed, with a modicum of political will, it is likely that the 21st century will see rail in its various forms developing further and assuming new importance for both passenger and freight traffic.

Notes

(1) *Rail Line Improvements in Surrey (South West Trains Operating Area): Final Report*. Surrey County Council Engineering Consultancy Division. Highways & Transportation Department, in association with Colin Buchanan & Partners, 1995, and *Study into Rail Line Improvements in Surrey: Network South Central Operating Area,* Surrey County Council Engineering Consultancy Division, Highways & Transportation Department, 1996.

(2) *Blackwater Valley Rail Study*, Steer Davis & Gleave, for the Berkshire, Hampshire and Surrey County Councils and British Rail, Network SouthEast, 1991.

(3) Hampshire County Council later suggested a possible alternative alignment south of Camberley for the new link, which would have avoided relocation of Frimley station.

(4) *Railtrack Network Management Statement for Great Britain*, 1998.

Appendices

APPENDIX I: PASSENGER STATIONS - OPENING DATES AND CHANGES

	Opened	Changes
Addlestone	14.2.1848.	
Ash [SER]	20.8.1849	Ash & Aldershot 7.1855: Aldershot (Ash) 9.1858: Ash & Aldershot 1859: Ash Jc 6.1863 : Ash 11.1926
Ashford	22.8.1848	Ashford (Middlesex) 9.7.1923: Ashford (Surrey) 12.5.1980
Ash Green	8.10.1849	Opened as Ash: Ash Green 12.1876; Ash 9.1891: Ash Green 1.10.1895: Ash Green Halt 1.12.1926: CLOSED 2.7.1937
Ashtead	1.2.1859	
Ash Vale	2.5.1870	Opened as North Camp & Ash Vale: Ash Vale for North Camp & South Farnborough 30.3.1924; Ash Vale 13.6.1955
Bagshot	18.3.1878	
Banstead	22.5.1865	Banstead & Burgh Heath 1.6.1898: Banstead 8.1928
Baynards	2.10.1865	CLOSED 12.6.1965
Betchworth	4.7.1849	
Bookham	2.2.1885	
Boxhill & Westhumble	11.3.1867	Opened as West Humble for Box Hill; Box Hill and Burford Bridge 1.11.1870; Box Hill and Westhumble 15.9.1958
Bramley & Wonersh	2.10.1865	Opened as Bramley; Bramley & Wonersh 1.6.1888; CLOSED 12.6.1965
Brookwood	1.6.1864	
Byfleet & New Haw	10.7.1927	Opened as West Weybridge; Byfleet & New Haw 12.6.1961
Camberley	18.3.1878	Opened as Camberley and York Town; Camberley 9.7.1923
Caterham	5.8.1856	Resited and enlarged 1.1.1900
Chertsey	14.2.1848	Resited 1.10.1866
Chilworth	20.8.1849	Opened as Chilworth & Albury; Chilworth 12.5.1980
Chipstead	2.11.1897	Opened as Chipstead & Banstead Downs; Chipstead 9.7.1923
Clandon	2.2.1885	Opened as Clandon & Ripley; Clandon 1910 ('Clandon for Newlands Corner' on some platform boards)
Claygate	2.2.1885	('Claygate for Claremont' on some platform boards and in some timetables)
Cobham & Stoke d'Abernon	2.2.1885	Opened as Cobham; Cobham & Stoke d'Abernon 9.9.1951
Colnbrook	9.8.1884	CLOSED 27.3.1965
Cranleigh	2.10.1865	Opened as Cranley; Cranleigh 6.1867* CLOSED 12.6.1965
Dorking	11.3.1867	Opened as Dorking; Dorking North 9.7.1923; Dorking 6.5.1968
Dorking Deepdene	4.7.1849	Opened as Box Hill & Leatherhead Road; Box Hill 3.1851; Closed 31.12.1916; reopened 1.1.1919; Deepdene 9.7.1923; Dorking Deepdene 11.5.1987
Dorking West	4.7.1849	Opened as Dorking; Dorking Town 9.7.1923; Dorking West 11.5.1987
Dormans	10.3.1884	
Earlswood	8.1868	Rebuilt on same site 1905
Effingham Junction	2.7.1888	
Egham	4.6.1856	
Epsom [L&SWR]	1.2.1859	New station on same site 3.3.1929
Epsom [LB&SCR]	10.5.1847	Epsom Town 7.1923; CLOSED 2.3.1929
Epsom Downs	22.5.1865	Reprovided on new site 13.2.1989
Esher	21.5.1838	Opened as Ditton Marsh; Esher & Hampton Court 1840; Esher & Claremont 7.1844 Esher 1.6.1913; Esher for Sandown Park 8.1934; Esher 13.6.1955
Ewell East	10.5.1847	Opened as Ewell; Ewell East 9.7.1923
Ewell West	4.4.1859	Opened as Ewell; Ewell West 9.7.1923
Farncombe	1.5.1897	
Farnham	8.10.1849	
Frimley	18.3.1878	

(* At the request of the General Post Office, which had experienced confusion with Crawley.)

Station	Date	Notes
Godalming (I)	15.10.1849	CLOSED 30.4.1897
Godalming (II) 1	1.1859	Opened as Godalming New; Godalming 11.5.1897
Godstone	26.5.1842	
Gomshall	20.8.1849	Gomshall & Shere 1850; Gomshall .1980
Guildford	5.5.1845	(name boards read 'Guildford Junction' in the 1860s)
[Guildford London Road - see London Road]		
Hampton Court	1.2.1849	Hampton Court & East Molesey 1.6.1869; Hampton Court 1900
Haslemere	1.1.1859	
Hersham	28.9.1936	
Hinchley Wood	20.10.1930	
Holmwood	1.5.1867	
Horley	12.7.1841	Reprovided on new site 31.12.1905
Horsley	2.2.1885	Opened as Horsley, Ripley & Ockham; Horsley 12.1914
Hurst Green [Halt]	1.6.1907	Closed 11.6.1961 and replaced by;
Hurst Green	12.6.1961	
Kingswood	2.11.1897	Opened as Kingswood & Burgh Heath; Kingswood 9.7.1923
Leat herhead (I)	1.2.1859	CLOSED 3.3.1867
Leatherhead (II)	4.3.1867	(opened by LB&SCR; present station)
Leatherhead [L&SWR]	4.3.1867	CLOSED 9.7.1927
Lingfield	10.3.1884	
London Road Guildford	2.2.1885	Opened as London Road; London Road Guildford 9.7.1923
Longcross	21.9.1942	Restricted to peak hours weekdays 11.5.1992
Merstham (I)	1.12.1841	CLOSED 30.9.1843
Merstham (11)	4.10.1844	
Milford	1.1.1859	
Monks Lane [Halt]	1.6.1907*	(* some sources give 1.7.1907) ; CLOSED 10.9.1939
North Camp	1858	Opened as North Camp Aldershot;Aldershot Camp 6.1883; Aldershot (North Camp)5.1879; Aldershot (North Camp & Sout h Farnborough) 1.5.1909; Aldershot (North) 9.7.1923 North Camp & Ash Vale for South Farnborough 30.3.1924; North Camp 13.6.1955
Nutfield	1883	
Ockley	1.5.1867	Opened as Ockley; Ockley & Capel 1.7.1869; Ockley 1.4.1887. Ockley & Capel 15.9.1952; Ockley 12.5.1980
Oxshott	2.2.1885	Opened as Oxshott & Fairmile; Oxshott 1.6.1913; ('Oxshott for Fairmile' in some later timetables)
Oxted	10.3.1884	
Poyle Estate Halt	4.1.1954	CLOSED 27.3.1965
Poyle Halt	1.6.1927	Opened as Stanwell Moor & Poyle Halt; Poyle for Stanwell Moor 26.9.1927. CLOSED 27.3.1965
Red Hill & Reigate Road	12.7.1841	CLOSED 4.1844 replaced by Redhill (II)
Redhill (I) [SER]	26.5.1842	CLOSED 4.1844 rep1aced by Redhill (II)
Redhill (II)	15.4.1844	Opened by SER as Reigate; Reigate Junction 4.7.1849; Red Hill Junction 1858; Redhill Junction 9.7.1923; Redhill 9.1929
Reigate	4.7.1849	Opened as Reigate Town; Reigate 1.11.1898
Salfords	8.10.1915	Opened as Salford Halt [Private]; opened for public use 17.7.1932; opened as public station named Salfords 1.1.1935
Shalford	20.8.1849	
Shepperton	1.11.1864	
Shere Heath	20.8.1849	Opened on trial basis; CLOSED 1850, replaced by Gomshall & Shere
Staines [GWR]	2.11.1885	Staines West 26.9.1949; CLOSED 27.3.1965
Staines [L&SWR]	22.8.1848	Staines (Old) 1.1885; Staines Junction 9.1889; Staines 1920; Staines Central 26.9.1949; Staines 18.4.1966
Staines High Street	1.7.1884	CLOSED 30.1.1916
Stoneleigh	17.7.1932	
Sunbury	1.11.1864	
Sunningdale	4.6.1856	Sunningdale & Bagshot 1.1.1863; Sunningdale & Windlesham 1.3.1893; Sunningdale 12.1920
Tadworth	1.7.19O0	Opened as Tadworth & Walton on the Hill; Tadworth 1.12.1968
Tattenham Corner	4.6.1901	Opened for race days and summer traffic; closed to public 9.1914; opened race days only from 1919; fully open 25.3.1928
Thames Ditton	11.1851	
Tongham	10.1856	CLOSED 2.7.1937
Upper Halliford	1.5.1944	Opened as Halliford Halt; Upper Halliford 22.5.1944
Upper Warlingham	10.3.1884	Upper Warlingham & Whyteleafe 1.1.1894; Upper Warlingham 1.10.1900
Virginia Water	9.7 1856	
Walton on Thames	21.5.1838	Opened as Walton; Walton for Hersham; 1.1849; Walton on Thames 30.9.1935
Wanborough	1.9.1891	'Wanborough for Normandy' on platform boards and in some timetables
West Byfleet	1.12.1887	Opened as Byfleet & Woodham; Byfleet 4.1913; West Byfleet 5.6.1950

Weybridge	21.5.1838	
Whyteleafe	1.1.1900	
Whyteleafe South	5.8.1856	Opened as Warlingham; Whyteleafe South 11.6.1956
Witley	1.1.1859	Opened as Witley for Chiddingfold; Wit ley 6.10.1947
Wok ing	21.5.1838	Opened as Woking Common; Woking c 1843; Woking Junction 1845; Woking 4.1913
Woldingham	1.7.1885	Opened as Marden Park; Woldingham 1.1.1894
Worplesdon	1.3.1883	
Yeoveney	1.3.1892	Opened as Runemede Range Halt; Runemede 9.7.1934; Yeoveney 4.11.1935; CLOSED 14.5.1962

PRIVATE AND SPECIAL PASSENGER STATIONS

Bisley	Opened 14.7.1890; Rifle Ranges and Army traffic only. CLOSED 19.7.1952
Blackdown	Opened December 1917; Military traffic only; CLOSED December 1921
Brookwood Cemetery North	Opened 13.11.1854; Funeral trains only; CLOSED c 1941
Brookwood Cemetery South	Opened 13.11.1854; Funeral trains only; CLOSED c 1941
Deepcut	Opened August 1917, Military traffic only; CLOSED December 1921
Kempton Park	Opened 18.7.1878 for Racing Club members only; opened for public use (race days only) 1890
Pirbright	Opened August 1917, Military traffic only; CLOSED December 1921; REOPENED on new site 1941 Military traffic only; CLOSED c 1946
Salfords Halt	See main list above
Sandown Park Race Platforms	Opened 1882 for race days only; CLOSED 1965
Westcott Rifle Range Halt	Opened 11.1916 for rifle range parties only; CLOSED c 1925

APPENDIX II: CLOSURE OF PUBLIC FREIGHT YARDS

nb *Exact dates for last public use of freigh t yards are difficult to establish with precision since railway authorities have used differing criteria when publishing 'official, da tes; there are therefore many discrepancies in previously published material. The following list is accordingly confined to month and year, with the proviso that the mon th of last public use may in some cases have been the one previous to that stated here.*

Ash [L&SWR]	11.1926
Epsom [L&SWR]	1.1928
Staines West [GWR]	10.1953
Woldingham	5.1959
Oxshott	9.1959
Merrow Siding	3.1960
Ewell East	4.1960
Virginia Water	5.1960
Shepperton	8.1960
Sunbury	8.1960
Ash Siding [SER]	12.1960
Tongham	12.1960
Milford	3.1961
Brookwood	5.1961
Ewell West	5.1961
Ashtead	12.1961
Kingswood	3.1962
Tattenham Corner	4.1962
Frimley	4.1962
Ockley	4.1962
Chipstead	5.1962
Tadworth	5.1962
Chilworth	5.1962
Wanborough	5.1962
Witley	6.1962
Bramley & Wonersh	9.1962
Baynards	9.1962
Cranleigh	9.1962
Gomshall	9.1962
Esher	12.1962
Clandon	2.1963
[Beeching Report published 3.1963]	
Claygate	5.1963
Dorking Town	5.1963
Worplesdon	9.1963
West Byfleet	9.1963
Upper Warlingham	5.1964
Godstone	5.1964
Horsley	5.1964
Weybridge	8.1964
Banstead	9.1964
Betchworth	9.1964
Caterham	9.1964
Holmwood	9.1964
Horley	9.1964
Whyteleafe	9.1964
Reigate	9.1964
Chertsey	10.1964
Egham	1.1965
Ashford	1.1965
Camberley	4.1965
Epsom [LB&SCR]	5.1965
Hampton Court	5.1965
Bookham	5.1965
Cobham	5.1965
Leatherhead	8.1965
Colnbrook	1.1966
Bagshot	1.1966
Dorking North	11.1966
Nutfield	11.1966
Addlestone	12.1966
Walton on Thames	12.1966

Shalford	5.1967	North Camp	1.1969
Lingfield	8.1968 (except banana traffic)	Salfords	6.1969
Sunningdale	1.1969	Farnham	5.1970
Godalming[Old]	1.1969	Woking	6.1970 (reopened for wine traffic 8.1985, closed 9.1991)
Peasmarsh Siding	1.1969		
Haslemere	1.1969	Staines [L&SWR]	8.1971
London Road Guildford	1.1969	Surbiton	11.1971
Merstham	1.1969	Redhill	1.1982
Oxted	1.1969	Guildford	10.1985

APPENDIX III : RAILWAY FREIGHT FACILITIES (OTHER THAN STATION GOODS YARDS)

Sources: *This list mainly shows sidings existing in 1934 and is based on* Southern Railway General Central-Eastern and Western Appendices to the Working Timetables, *26 March 1934. Some additional information and entries, shown in square brackets [] has been extracted from L&SWR minutes,* Hand-Book of stations...., *Railway Clearing House, 1895 (amended to 1900) and 1904 editions,* LB&SCR Appendix to the Service Time Book *June 1910, and miscellaneous sources.*

Station in charge	**Location**	**Name**
BRIGHTON MAIN LINE		
Merstham	Down Side	Peters' Lime Works [also 1895] [also Merstham Lime in 1895; deleted 1900]
Redhill	Up Side bet ween Merstham & Redhill	Thornton' s [also in 1895; on site of first Merstham station]
Redhill	Down Side " " "	Holmet horpe [Trower' s in 1895; latterly British Industrial Sands]
[Redhill	" " " "	Pope' s (in 1895)]
Redhill	Up Side between Redhill & Earlswood	Shell Mex oil
Redhill	Up Side " " "	Hall & Co. [sand; from about 1860]
Redhill	Up Side " " "	East Surrey Gas Co. [Redhill Gas Co in 1904]
Redhill	Down Side at Earlswood	Royal Earlswood Institution
[Redhill	?	Stenning & Sons (in 1895]
Horley	Down Side	Horley & Dist rict Gas Co.[also in1904]
Horley	Down Side Gatwick	Lamb' s
Horley	Up Side Gatwick	Gatwick Race Course Co.
OXTED & EAST GRINSTEAD LINE		
Upper Warlingham	Down Side	Riddlesdown Lime & Fuel Co. [Nichols' in 1895]
Oxted	Down Side between Woldingham & Oxted [served only from Down line]	Oxted Greystone Lime Co. [also in 1895]
Lingfield	Up Side between Lingfield and Oxted	Sussex Brick Co. [Crowhurst Brick and London & Brighton Brick Co. in 1904]
Dormans	Up side between Dormans and East Grinstead [47ch south of station, Annett's lock (from Dormans) and ground frame; worked via East Grinstead]	Dormans Park Estate. [Closed by 1934]
EWELL EAST-EPSOM		
[Epsom	Up side, east of Epsom Town station.	Hall & Co. c 1899 Stone & Co. [Brickworks by 1904, replaced by siding at Ewell West by 1934]
EPSOM DOWNS-BANSTEAD		
[Epsom Downs	Up side between Epsom Downs & Banstead , Annett's lock (Epsom Downs)	Gadesden's (North Looe Farm) 1886, closed by 1934]
[Banstead	Down Side between Epsom Downs & Banstead , 400yd south of Banstead station. Annett's lock (Banstead)	Crockett' s (Kensington and Chelsea District Schools) 1880, closed by 1934: also shown as Kerr's]
GODSTONE-REDHILL-NORTH CAMP		
Godstone	Up Side between Edenbridge & Godstone	Crowhurst Public Siding
Godstone	Up Side between Godstone & Nutfield	Williams' South Eastern Brick & Terracotta Works [1896-c 1950; now used by rly civil engineers]

Nutfield	Up Side	F. Wilkinson (Kingsmill) [in 1895 Barnes' or Mid Street Siding]
Redhill	Down Side between Redhill & Reigate	Tanyard [Barrow's in 1895 ?]
Redhill	Up Side " " "	Silver Sand [also in 1895]
Redhill	Up Side off above	Reigate Electricity Wks
Redhill	[between Redhill & Reigate	Pym's (in 1904)]
Reigate	Up Side between Reigate & Betchworth	Taylor's Tile & Hearthstone works [1907]
Reigate	Up Side " " "	Buckland Sand & Silica Co.
Betchworth	Up Side	Dorking Lime Co.
Betchworth	Up Side between Betchworth & Deepdene	Brockham Brick Co.
Gomshall	Up Side between Dorking & Gomshall	Evelyn's [sand, 1904]
Shalford	Down Side off goods yard	Premier Cooler Co.
Guildford	Up Side between Wanborough & Guildford	Dennis Bros [closed 1964]
Wanborough	Up Side " " "	Lamb & Son [brick works 1897-1964] Wanborough Brick Co. in 19041
Wanborough	Down Side between Wanborough & Ash Jc	Coussmaker's
North Camp	Down Side	Mid Southern District Utility Co.
TONGHAM BRANCH		
Tongham	Up Side	New Siding (Public)
Tongham	" "	Mid Southern District Utility Co. [opened 1898 by Aldershot Gas & Water Co.]
Tongham	Down Side	Hyde's (out of use in 1934)
FARNHAM AREA		
Farnham	Up Side between Farnham & Aldershot	Patterson's [Badshot Lea 1
Farnham	Down Side between Aldershot & Farnham	Farnham Gravel Co. (Snailslynch)
Farnham	Down Side between Farnham & Bentley	Hookstile Minerals
Farnham	" " " "	Farnham Gravel Co. Weydon Hill
Farnham	" " " "	Patterson's (Weydon)
Farnham	" " " "	Patterson's (Wrecclesham)[by 1904]
GUILDFORD-BAYNARDS		
Bramley	Down Side between Bramley & Cranleigh	Surrey County Council
Bramley	Down Side[Annett's lock (Bramley)]	Birtley (Street's) [by 1904]
Cranleigh	Up Side[off refuge siding 1/2m west of station]	Cranleigh Gas & Coke Co.
Cranleigh	Up Side	Elliott's
Baynar ds	Down Side	F. W. Berk & Co. [Cranleigh Brick & Tile Co. (E. A. Miles) in 1904]
CATERHAM BRANCH		
[between Kenley & Whyteleafe		Atkins' in 1895, closed by 1934]
Whyteleafe	Down Side	Coulsdon & Purley Urban District Council
Whyteleafe	Down Side	Cohen's
TATTENHAM CORNER BRANCH		
[Kingswood Down Side		Chiphouse Farm (1907)]
MAIN LINE, ESHER-FARNBOROUGH		
Byfleet	Up Side	Central Electricity Bd.
Brookwood	Down Side	Necropolis Co.
[between Brookwood & Farnborough		Pirbright; by 1895; closed by 1934]
WOKING-HASLEMERE		
[Worplesdon Up Side south of station		Owen Stone Co. 1897-1905]
Guildford	Up Side, off goods yard	Sussex Brick Co.[Guildford Park Brickworks closed c 1956]
Guildford	Up Side between Farncombe & Gfd	Peasmarsh (Public) [opened 1899;later BP (oil); closed 1969]
Godalming	Down Side between Godalming & Milford	Busbridge [Bargate stone quarry; abolished 1935] Farnham Flint & Gravel Co. [1908-34]
Milford	Up Side	Surrey County Council
ASHFORD-SUNNINGDALE		
Ashford	Down Side	Ashford Builders Co. and Imported Timber Co [Ashby's in 1904]
Virginia Water	Down Side [London end]	Holloway Sanatorium [coal siding]
SUNBURY-SHEPPERTON		
Sunbury	Up Side between Kempton Park & Hampton	Metropolitan Water Board [East London Water Works in 1904; closed 1964]

Sunbury	Up Side between Kempton Park & Sunbury	Metropolitan Water Board [New River Waterworks in 1904; closed 1962]
Sunbury	" " " "	Collins' Patent Impermeable Millboard Co. [Walter's Lincrusta Co. in 1904; later Sundeala Hardboard, closed c 1965]
Sunbury	Down Side between Sunbury & Shepperton	Fear Bros.
Shepperton	" " " "	Lavender's [W J Lavender house builders opened 10. 1931 closed 3. 1938]
Shepperton	Down Side	Ferro-Concrete Roof Plate Co. [closed c1960]
Shepperton	"	Firmston's
[Shepperton	"	Catling's Brickworks in l895, closed by 1934]
WINDSOR BRANCH IN SURREY		
Staines	Down Side between Staines & Wraysbury	Staines Linoleum Co. [closed 9.1965]
Staines	Up Side " " "	Staines Linoleum Co. (coal) [also in 1904; closed 3.1965]
Staines	Up Side between Staines & Wraysbury	Metropolitan Water Board Staines Reservoir [Pumping station; 1897-1940]
Staines	" " " "	Boyer's ballast pit
CHERTSEY BRANCH		
Addlestone	Down Side between Addlestone Jc & Addlestone	Coxes' Lock Milling Co. [cornmill]
Chertsey	Down Side	Chertsey Gas Consumers' Co. [by 1904]
RAYNES PARK-EFFINGHAM JC		
Worcester Park	Up Side between Stoneleigh & Worcester Park	Cunliffe's (Wanborough Brick & Tile Co.) [by 1904]
[Ewell West	Down side between Ewell West & Stoneleigh	Hall & Davidson's Flour Mills, by 1895, closed by 1934]
Ewell West	Down Side	Epsom Rural District Council
Ewell West	Up Side (country end)	London County Council (Horton Light Rly)
Ewell West	Down Side between Ewell West & Epsom	Stone's
NEW GUILDFORD LINE		
Oxshott	Up Side (country end)	Benton's [Little Heath Brickworks, formerly Cook's; also in 1904; brickfield]
Clandon	Down Side between Clandon & London Road	Merrow Siding [Sutton & Co's Brickworks later Surrey County Council depot; closed 1961]

APPENDIX IV: SIGNALLING MODERNISATION : MAJOR SCHEMES

nb *Dates given relate to final completion of the scheme.*

Staines area	24.4.1904	semaphore signals operated by compressed air and controlled by track circuits, two signal boxes replacing five
Woking- Basingstoke	7. 1907	semaphore signals operated by compressed air and controlled by track circuits
Staines area	1. 6. 1930	two signal boxes and 1904 installation replaced by one mechanical box

nb *From this point the list shows the major conversions from the traditional semaphore signalling operated from mechanical lever frames to colour light signals and subsequent further modernisation*

Brighton main line	5. 6. 1932	south of Coulsdon North via Quarry line
Malden-Hampton Court Jc	28. 6. 1936	
Woking-Guildford	27.6.1937	including Woking power box and Junction
Haslemere	18.7. 1937	with intermediate colour-light signals at Grayswood on Up line Haslemere-Witley
Mickleham-Holmwood	15.5.1938	with new cabin at Dorking
Leatherhead—Epsom	26. 4. 1964	
(Woking)-Pirbright Jc/Ash Vale - Farnborough	5.6. 1965	
Raynes Park-Epsom	27.2.1966	Worcester Park and Ewell West boxes closed.

Guildford Area Resignalling	17. 4. 1966	Aldershot South Jc-Ash-Wanborough- Guildford; Guildford-Shalford Jc; Guildford-Horsley; Shalford Jc- Goldalming; (new power boxes at Guildford and Ash Crossing
Brookwood	6.1966	Brookwood box closed, Woking-Pirbright Jc controlled from a panel in Woking box
Effingham Jc-Cobham/ Horsley/Bookham	20.4.1969	worked from Guildford panel
Cheam (excl) -Epsom	11.5.1969	
Epsom Downs (excl) -Sutton (excl)	21.12.1969	
Surbiton Area Resignalling	22.3.1970	Surbiton-Woking; Surbiton-Oxshott; Byfleet Jc/Addlestone Jc -Chertsey; Hampton Court branch; New power box at Surbiton
Ash Vale-Aldershot	23.8. 1970	
Tattenham Corner Branch	29.11. 1970	
Leat herhead- (Dorking)	21.10.1971	
Motspur Park -Chessington South	30.1. 1972	
Oxshott-Cobham	9.9. 1972	(Cook' s Crossing) box closed: lifting barriers and remote control from Surbiton
Camberley-Ash Vale Jc	25.3. 1973	
FarncombeHaslemere	9.12.1973	
Feltham Area Resignalling	8.9. 1974	Staines-Windsor; Virginia Water-Chertsey; Bracknell-Ascot -Whitton; Camberley-Ascot;Newpanel box at Feltham
	3.2. 1975	Chertsey, Camberley and Egham Crossing gate boxes closed and crossings controlled from Feltham
	8. 1975	Sunningdale gate box closed, crossing controlled from Feltham
	10.1.1979	Shepperton branch controlled from Feltham
Ash Crossing- Wokingham	7.5.1980	North Camp box closed; track circuit block and colour light signals
Betchworth-Shalford	6.11.1980	Gomshall box closed, track circuit block and colour light signals
	14.4.1981	Gomshall Lane (Burrows Lane) Crossing box closed, automatic half barriers
Epsom Downs branch and Ewell East;	4.7.1982	Sutton-Epsom Downs singled
	3.10.1982	Waddon/Carshalton-West Sutton/Epsom Downs (controlled from Victoria Signalling Centre)
Earlswood- Horley	7.11.1982	(controlled from Three Bridges)
Reigate-Betchworth	6. 6.1983	track circuit block Reigate-Shalford; Betchworth signal frame closed
Coulsdon North-Merstham -Redhill (excl.)	26.2.1983	
Coulsdon North-Quarry -Three Bridges (excl.)	2.7.1983	new signalling centre Three Bridges
Caterham/Tattenham Corner branches	14.1.1984	controlled from Three Bridges
Redhill	12.5.1985	controlled from Three Bridges
Godstone (excl.)-Reigate	12.5.1985	(see also 31.5.1986 below)
Sanderstead- Oxted (excl)	2.11.1985	controlled from Oxted and Three Bridges
Godstone	31.5.1986	box closed; controlled from Three Bridges
Oxted-East Grinstead	19.7.1987	new signalling centre at Oxted
Hurst Green Jc-Uckfield	8.1. 1990	controlled from Oxted
WATERLOO AREA RESIGNALLING (WARS)		
	22.7.1990	Motspur Park box closed, control from Wimbledon Signalling centre
	25.7.1990	Epsom box closed* area controlled from Wimbledon
	5.8.1990	Leatherhead box closed, area controlled from Wimbledon
WORKING AREA RESIGNALLING		
	14.4.1998	Surbiton and Woking boxes closed; new signalling centre at Woking
GUILDFORD AREA RESIGNALLING		
	4.1.1999	Guildford and Ash boxes closed; Shalford box closed and Guildford area extended to Gomshall; new control centre (GD) at Guildford

* *After some controversy regarding its preservation this rare survivor amongst over-line signal boxes was demolished in March 1992.*

APPENDIX V: THE BUSIEST PASSENGER STATIONS IN SURREY 1991

(500 OR MORE PASSENGERS BOARDING TRAINS DAILY BETWEEN 0600 AND 2100)

Source: Surrey County Council Highways & Transportation Department, 1995

	Number (to nearest 100)	Percentage to London		Other Destinations
		Zone 1	Zones 2-5	
Guildford	7,500	56	7	37
Woking	7,500	not available		
Epsom	4,200	75	15	10
Redhill	3,200	73	12	15
Walton on Thames	2,800	82	8	10
Staines	2,100	48	23	29
Weybridge	2,000	69	8	23
Haslemere	1,900	not available		
Oxted	1,800	78	16	6
Horley	1,700	72	10	18
West Byfleet	1,700	48	13	39
Leatherhead	1,600	77	11	12
Farnham	1,500	not available		
Stoneleigh	1,300	74	19	7
Godalming	1,300	not available		
Dorking	1,200	77	10	13
Ashtead	1,200	63	14	23
Hersham	1,200	73	14	13
Egham	1,200	not available		
Hampton Court	1,100	67	25	8
Merstham	1,000	82	13	5
Brookwood	900	not available		
Farncombe	900	not available		
Ewell East	900	59	34	7
Esher	900	81	6	13
Claygate	900	81	9	10
Upper Warlingham	800	70	22	8
Chertsey	800	16	11	73
Ashford	800	15	62	23
Ewell West	800	67	18	15
Hurst Green	800	59	17	24
Oxshott	800	68	21	11
Ash Vale	800	not available		
Caterham *	700	53	36	11
Sunbury	700	57	36	7
Cobham & Stoke d'Abernon	700	85	10	5
Camberley	700	58	14	28
Reigate	700	47	14	39
Sunningdale	700	60	13	27
Horsley	600	76	7	7
Thames Ditton	600	52	35	13
Guildford (London Road)	600	23	6	71
Byfleet & New Haw	600	69	8	23
Effingham Junction	600	70	11	19
Hinchley Wood	500	73	17	10
Virginia Water	500	75	11	14
Shepperton	500	62	30	8
Lingfield	500	59	16	15
Addlestone	500	42	16	42
Horsley	500	not available		

**likely to increase in short term as new housing is proposed on Barracks site*

APPENDIX VI: TRAIN ACCIDENTS

nb: *This list is not comprehensive - most accidents involving no or only minor injuries are omitted:*
SE = Signalling error SPAD = Signal passed at Danger

Date	Place	Accident	Deaths
14: 1. 1848	WOKING (near)	Train collided with stationary crippled locomotive; indadequate signalling	1
4. 3.1853	MERSTHAM	Collision between freight and ballast trains	-
11.8.1860	WOKING	Derailment -broken rail	-
7.6 1864	EGHAM	Rear end collision; inadequate signalling and brakes	7
17.1.1867	GUILDFORD	Rear end collision in station. SE	-
9.6. 1873	GUILDFORD (Peasmarsh)	Up Portsmouth express ran into a bullock; all coaches derailed. Driver continued with his engine into Guildford station to get help.	3
26. 12. 1872	WOKING	Collision between two freight trains SPAD (loco crew drunk)	-
2.9. 1874	ESHER	Derailment of express at site of work on track	-
11.6.1877	WOKING	Rear end collision between two freight trains	-
18,6 1877	MERSTHAM TUNNEL	Derailment of LB&SCR train on SER track under repair	-
13.6. 1882	STAINES	Collision between passenger train and coal trucks being shunted. Inadequate brakes	-
12.6.1889	STAINES	Collision between goods and passenger trains SE	-
10. 12. 1890	GUILDFORD	Coll ision bet ween passenger train and light engine	-
11.4. 1898	BISLEY	Violent contact between mishandled loco and train in station. 23 serious injuries	-
20.2. 1904	GOMSHALL	Derailment (see Chapter 7)	-
18.4. 1918	REDHILL	Tunnel (Quarry line) Collision between three goods trains (see Chapter 7)	-
1. 4. 1934	CATERHAM	Collision outside station between two electric trains SE	-
28. 1. 1945	ESHER	Rear end collision SE	1
26.6. 1945	CATERHAM	Collision out side station between two electric trains SPAD	2
10. 11. 1945	WOKING	Rear end Collision SPAD	-
27.12.1946	BYFLEET	Derailment of 12-coach express due to poor track drainage	-
15.6. 1947	CHERTSEY	Collision between electric & freight trains in station	-
28. 7. 1949	EPSOM	Collision at Junction SPAD	--
1.2. 1950	EAST SHALFORD	Collision with car at level crossing: crossing keeper' s erro	2*
8. 11 1952	GUILDFORD	Collision between electric train and light engine due to failure of braking system on the electric train	2
18.9. 1953	GUI LDFORD	Buffer stop collision; first car ran into station buildings; mismanagement of brakes by driver	1
23. 12. 1955	WOKING	Rear end collision in station between steam passenger train and stationary electric train SPAD	-
22. 11. 1956	between BROOKWOOD and FARNBOROUGH	Electric train derailed by broken rail; minor collision followed	-
9.8. 1957	STAINES	Collision between electric train and light engine SPAD	-
19.8. 1976	GUILDFORD	Collision between Down passenger train and empty train being shunted. SPAD	
30.3. 1978	WEST BYFLEET	Empty train ran away wrong line from Woking and collided with stationary train in platform	-
22. 12. 1978	MILFORD	Down train over ran onto level crossing when driver mishandled brake	1*
8. 6. 1984	EGHAM (Pooley Green)	Motor van attempted to dodge around lowered level crossing barrier; van struck by oncoming train	2*
29. 1. 1989	MERSTHAM TUNNEL	Collision between a passenger train and displaced load on engineers' train	-

* *occupants of road vehicles.*

APPENDIX VII: RAILWAY COMPANIES/UNDERTAKINGS OPERATING IN SURREY

nb: *Dates are date of company formation or name changes*

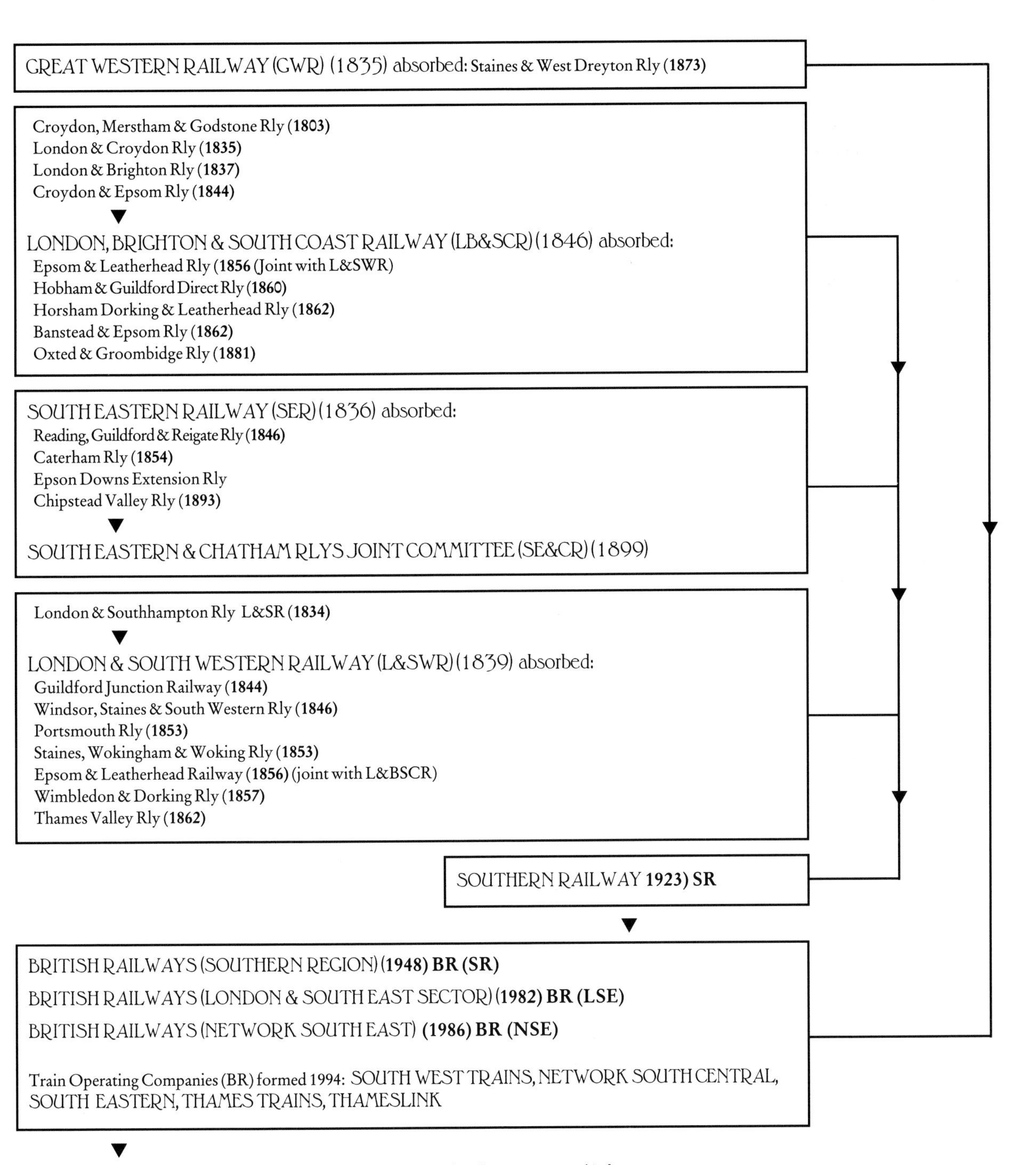

GREAT WESTERN RAILWAY (GWR) (1835) absorbed: Staines & West Dreyton Rly **(1873)**

Croydon, Merstham & Godstone Rly **(1803)**
London & Croydon Rly **(1835)**
London & Brighton Rly **(1837)**
Croydon & Epsom Rly **(1844)**

▼

LONDON, BRIGHTON & SOUTH COAST RAILWAY (LB&SCR) (1846) absorbed:
Epsom & Leatherhead Rly **(1856** (Joint with L&SWR)
Hobham & Guildford Direct Rly **(1860)**
Horsham Dorking & Leatherhead Rly **(1862)**
Banstead & Epsom Rly **(1862)**
Oxted & Groombidge Rly **(1881)**

SOUTH EASTERN RAILWAY (SER) (1836) absorbed:
Reading, Guildford & Reigate Rly **(1846)**
Caterham Rly **(1854)**
Epson Downs Extension Rly
Chipstead Valley Rly **(1893)**

▼

SOUTH EASTERN & CHATHAM RLYS JOINT COMMITTEE (SE&CR) (1899)

London & Southhampton Rly L&SR **(1834)**

▼

LONDON & SOUTH WESTERN RAILWAY (L&SWR) (1839) absorbed:
Guildford Junction Railway **(1844)**
Windsor, Staines & South Western Rly **(1846)**
Portsmouth Rly **(1853)**
Staines, Wokingham & Woking Rly **(1853)**
Epsom & Leatherhead Railway **(1856)** (joint with L&BSCR)
Wimbledon & Dorking Rly **(1857)**
Thames Valley Rly **(1862)**

SOUTHERN RAILWAY **1923) SR**

▼

BRITISH RAILWAYS (SOUTHERN REGION) **(1948) BR (SR)**
BRITISH RAILWAYS (LONDON & SOUTH EAST SECTOR) **(1982) BR (LSE)**
BRITISH RAILWAYS (NETWORK SOUTH EAST) **(1986) BR (NSE)**

Train Operating Companies (BR) formed 1994: SOUTH WEST TRAINS, NETWORK SOUTH CENTRAL, SOUTH EASTERN, THAMES TRAINS, THAMESLINK

▼

From 1996 disintegration into private train operating companies, freight operators and infrastructure owner company (Railtrack)

Sources and Select Bibliography

nb *For articles in periodicals, see the Chapter Notes.*

Railway history, traffic and infrastructure

Parliamentary papers: (House of Lords Record Office)
Board and committee minutes of Southern Railway and constituent companies: (Public Record Office)
Various editions of the Ordnance Survey sheets, one,six and twenty-five inches to one mile.
Southern Railway: General, Central-Eastern and Western Appendices to the Working Time Tables, 1934 and Supplements; public timetables; maps of the Main Line and Suburban Systems (various dates)
British Railways, Southern Region and Network South East : public timetables
Railway Clearing House: *.Junction Diagrams,* 1915 (with amendments)
Railway Clearing House: *Airey's Railway Map of the South of England,* 1892
Correspondence NRA/L&SWR/SR etc 1913-31 (private collection)
Correspondence NRA/War Depart ment 1940 (private collection)

Anon [Supplement to 'The Railway Gazette']: *The First Main Line Electrification in England....,* 1932; *Southern Railway Electrification; Extension: Arundel, Littlehampton, Bognor Regis, Chichester and District,*1938
Anon [Surrey County Council] , *Surrey Movement Monitoring Report,*1992; *Study into Rail Line Improvements in Surrey; South West Trains Operating Area,* 1995; *Study into Rail Line Improvements in Surrey; Network South Central Operating Area,* 1996
Anon [British Railways] *Freight Train Services (Southern Region),* 1955
Acworth, W M, *The Railways of England,*five editions 1889- 1900
Bayliss, Derek A, *Retracing The First Public Railway,* 1981
Biddle, Gordon, *Victorian Stations,* 1973
Buck, Gordon, *A Pictorial Survey of Railway Sta t ions,* 1992
Clark, R H, *Southern Region Chronology and Record 1803-1965,*1964
Clarke, John M, *The Brookwood Necropolis Railway,*1988
Cooke, R A, *Track Layout Diagrams of the GWR and BR WR,* sect ion 24,1975
Course, E A, *The Railways of Southern England: The Main Lines,* 1973. *The Railways of Southern England:Secondary and Branch Lines,* 1974 *The Railways o f Southern England: Independent and Light Railways,* 1976. (ed) *Minutes of the Board of Directors of the Reading, Guildford and Reigate Railway Company,* 1987
Cumm ings, John, *Railway Motor Buses and Bus Services in the British Isles: Vol 2,* 1980
Darwin, Bernard, *War on the Line: The Story of the Southern Railway in Wart ime,* 1946
Davey, Richard, *My Life on the Footplate,* 1974
Davis, Ron, *Railways from Staines to Sunningdale,* 1856-1996. 1996
Dean, Ian, Neal, Andrew, and Smith, David, *Industrial Railways of the South-East,* 1984
Essen, R I, *Epsom's Hospital Railway,* 1991
Gould, David, *The South-Eastern & Chatham Railway in the 1914- 18 War,* 1981
Gray, Adrian, *South Eastern Railway,* 1990, *South Eastern & Chatham Railway,* 1997
Harding, Peter A, and Clarke, John M, *The Bisley Camp Branch Line,*1986
Harding, Peter A, *The Tongham Railway,* 1994
Harrod, John, 'Up the Dorking', *Southern Notebook,* nos 83-90 (1984-86)
Heselton, Kenneth Y, *Sunbury and the Thames Valley Railway,* 1975
Hodd, H R, *The Horsham-Guildford Direct Railway,* 1975
Howard Turner, J T, *The London, Brighton & South Coast Railway: vol 1 Origins and Forma t ion,* 1977; *The London, Brigh ton & South Coast Railway: vol 2 Establishment & Growth,* 1978; *The London, Brighton & South Coast Railway: vol 3 Completion & Maturity,* 1979
Lee, Charles, E, *Early Railways in Surrey: The Surrey Iron Railway and its Continuation, The Croydon, Merstham & Godstone Iron Railway,* Trans. Newcomen Society, 21, 49-79, 1941 [Reprinted separately, 1944]
Mitchell, Peter,Townsend, Simon, and Shelmerdine, Malcolm, *The Surrey Border and Camberley Railway,* 1993
Mitchell, Vic and Smith, Keith, *Epsom to Horsham,* 1986; *Reading to Guildford,* 1988; *Woking to Southampton,* 1988; *Waterloo to Windsor,* 1988; *Guildford to Redhill,* 1989; *East Croydon to Three Bridges.* 1988; *Branch Lines Around Effingham Junction including the Hampton Court Branch,* 1990; *Kingston and Hounslow Loops including the Shepperton Branch,* 1990; *West Croydon t o Epsom,* 1992; *Caterham & Tattenham Corner,* 1994; *Croydon (Woodside) t o East Grinstead,* 1995; *Wimbledon to Epsom,* 1995
Moody, G T, *Southern Electric 1909-79: The History of The World's Largest Suburban Electrified System,.* 1979
Pratt, Edwin A, *British Railways and the Great War (2 vols),*1921
Pryer, G A, *Track Layout Diagrams of the Southern Railway and BR SR,* sect ions S8,S9, 1984 and 1986
Spence, Jeoffry, *The Caterham Railway: The Story of a feud - and Its Aftermath,*1952
Tonks, Eric S (ed), *Industrial Locomotives of South Eastern England,* 1958, and subsequent amendments published by the Industrial Railway Society.
Townsend, Charles E C, *Further Notes on Early Railways in Surrey,* Trans. Newcomen Society, 27, 51-68, 1958

Townsend, J L, *'Townsend Hook' and The Railways of The Dorking Greystone Lime Co. Ltd.*,1980
Wakeford, Ian, *Woking 150: The History of Woking and Its Railway*,1987
White, H P, *A Regional History of the Railways of Grea t Bri tain: Vol 2 Southern England*,1982
Wikeley, Nigel and Middleton, John, *Railway Stations, Southern Region* ,1971
Williams, R A, *The London & South Western Railway, vol I: The Formative Years*, 1968, *vol II: Growth and Consolidation*, 1973
Williams, R A, and Faulkner, J N, *The London & South Western Railway in the Twentieth Century*, 1988

Residential Developement and Social and Industrial history

Various editions of the Ordnance Survey Sheets, one,six and twenty-five inches to one mile
The Authentic Map Directory of London and Suburbs, 3rd edition, 1933
Geographia London Map Directory: A Street Atlas of London and Its Surrounds, 1964
A-Z Surrey street Atlas, 1993

Census Report s

Material on specific residential and commercial developments has been obtained from the Southern Railway and other Resident ial Guides listed below; also from advert isements and feat ures in the *London Evening News*, 1900-39, various other daily newspapers read less thoroughly; and periodicals, notably *The Estates Gazette* and *The Homefinder and Small Property Guide*. Topographical information was also derived from contemporary picture postcards and the large scale maps mentioned above.

Anon [Southern Railway], *The Country At London's Door*, 1926; *Country Homes At London's Door*, 1927; *Country Homes At London's Door* 1928; *Southern Homes*, various editions from 1929; *Southern Homes in Surrey & Hampshire (Electrified)*, 1937
Banstead History Research Group, *Banstead: A History*, 1993
Bevan, G Phillips, *Tourists' Guide to the County of Surrey*, 1887
Bird, Margaret, *Holmbury St Mary: One Hundred Years*, 1979
Blackman, M E, and Pulford, J S L, *A Short History of Weybridge*, 1991
Bourne, George [Sturt, George], *Change in The Village*, 1912
Bowley, Pam, *East Hors1ey: The History of A Surrey Village*, 1995
Buss, Brian and Davis, Bernard, *Horley in Wartime*, 1994
Chamberlin, E R, *Guildford*, 1982
Choulder,W H, *Horley: Pageant of A Wealden Parish*, n.d. but c 1973
Cole, Lt Col Howard N, *The Story of Aldershot : A History of the Civil and Military Towns*, 2nd edition, 1980
Connell John, *The End of Tradition: Country Life in Central Surrey*, 1978
Corke, Shirley, *Abinger Hammer, Surrey, A Short History and Guide to the Village*, 1993
Crocker,Glenys, *Chilworth Gunpowder*, 1984; (ed) *A Guide to t he Industrial Archaeology of Surrey*, 1990
Crosby, Alan, *A History of Woking*,1982
Dobson, C G, *A Century and a Quarter The Story of Our Business [Hall & Co] from 1824 to the Present Day*, 1951
Drew, Gillian, *Wanborough from White Barrow to World War*,1993
Dunne, Nigel, *The Redhill Story*, 1994
Eedle, Marie de G, *A History of Bagshot & Windlesham*, 1977
Flint, Peter, *RAF Kenley: The Story of the Royal Air Force Station 1917-74*, 1985
Fortescue, S E D, *The Story of Two Villages: Great & Little Bookham*, 1975; *People & Places: Great & Little Bookham*, 1978
Green, F E, *The Surrey Hills*, 1915
Harding, Joan, and Banks, Joyce, *Newdigate, Its History and Houses*, 1993
Hooper. Wilfrid. *Reigate: Its Story Through the Ages*, 1945
Jackson, Alan A, *Semi-Detached London: Suburban Development, Life and Transport*, 2nd edition, 1991; *The Middle Classes 1900-1950*, 1991: (ed.) *Ashtead: A Village Transformed*, 1979: (ed.) *Dorking.: A Surrey Market Town Through Twenty Centuries* 1991
Jennings, Louis J, *Field Paths & Green Lanes* (4 editions) 1877- 1884
Luke, T D, *Spas & Health Resorts of the British Isles*, 1919
Mercer, Doris and Jackson, Alan A, *The Deepdene, Dorking* 1996
Morris, J E, *Black's Guide to Surrey* various editions; *Homeland Handbooks No.28: Haslemere & Hindhead* 5th edition 1913
Murray, John, *A Handbook for Travellers in Surrey, Hampshire and the Isle of Wight*, 1858, 1865, 1876, 1888; *Handbook of Surrey including Aldershot* 1897,1898
O'Kelly, Terence, *The Villages of Abinger Common & Wotton, Surrey*, 1988
Peebles, Malcolm W H, *The Claygate Book: A History of a Surrey Village*,1983
Peel, Mrs C S, *Life's Enchanrted Cup:An Autobiography 1872-1933*, 1933
Rolston, G R, *Haslemere 1850-1950*, 1964
Row, Prescott (ed.), *Where to Live Round London (Southern Side)*, various editions 1905- 13
Ryan, Meg, *Betchworth within Living Memory: The Big Houses of Betchworth*, 1986
Saaler, Peter, *The Houses of Caterham Valley 1863-1939*, 1982
Skuse, Peter R, *A History of Whyteleafe*, 1987
Smith, Ewbank W, *Victorian Farnham: The Story of A Surrey Town 1837-1901*, 1971 ; *Edwardian Farnham: The Story of A Surrey Town 1900-1914*, 1979; *Farnham in War & Peace*, 1983
Smith, John Owen, *A Balance of Trust: The Story of 50 Years in the History of Haslemere & Hindhead*, 1995
Stephens Ian D, *The Story ofEsher*, 1966
Stuttard, J C ,(ed.) *A History ofAshtead*, 1995
Taylor, David C, *The Book of Cobham*,1982
Thorne, James, *Handbook to the Environs of London.....*, (two vols.) 1876
Turner, Stephen 'William, Earl of Lovelace 1805-1993', *Surrey Archaeological Collections, LXX*,1974
Ward, C S *Thorough Guides : Surrey (south of Epsom) and Sussex (including Tunbridge Wells)*,1905
Wright, Thomas *Hindhead, or The English Switzerland*, 1898 .

Index

Note: *Stations are indexed under their latest names. Page numbers in bold type refer to illustrations. Please note that there may be more than one reference on the page indicated. A number of locations just beyond the present Surrey border are included in this index; other 'foreign' places are not, unless the textual mention is of special significance.*